Combinatorial Optimization: Networks and Matroids

EUGENE L. LAWLER

University of California at Berkeley

HOLT, RINEHART AND WINSTON

New York   Chicago   San Francisco   Atlanta

Dallas   Montreal   Toronto   London   Sydney

To my parents,
and to my children, Stephen and Susan

Library of Congress Cataloging in Publication Data

Lawler, Eugene L
    Combinatorial optimization.

    Includes bibliographical references.
    1. Mathematical optimization.   2. Matroids.
3. Network analysis (Planning).   4. Computational
complexity.   5. Algorithms.   I. Title.
QA402.5.L39   519.7   76–13516
ISBN   0–03–084866–0

Printed in the United States of America
        8   9   038   9   8   7   6   5   4   3   2

Preface

Combinatorial optimization problems arise everywhere, and certainly in all areas of technology and industrial management. A growing awareness of the importance of these problems has been accompanied by a combinatorial explosion in proposals for their solution.

This book is concerned with combinatorial optimization problems which can be formulated in terms of networks and algebraic structures known as matroids. My objective has been to present a unified and fairly comprehensive survey of solution techniques for these problems, with emphasis on "augmentation" algorithms.

Chapters 3 through 5 comprise the material in one-term courses on network flow theory currently offered in many university departments of operations research and industrial engineering. In most cases, a course in linear programming is designated as a prerequisite. However, this is not essential. Chapter 2 contains necessary background material on linear programming, and graph theory as well.

Chapters 6 through 9 are suitable for a second course, presumably at the graduate level. The instructor may wish to omit certain sections, depending upon the orientation of the students, as indicated below.

The book is also suitable as a text, or as a reference, for courses on combinatorial computing and concrete computational complexity in departments of computer science and mathematics. Any computer scientist intending to do serious research on combinatorial algorithms should have a working knowledge of the material in this book.

The reader should be aware that certain algorithms are easy to explain, to understand, and to implement, even though a proof of their validity may be quite difficult. A good example is the "primal" matroid intersection algorithm presented in Section 10 of Chapter 8. I can well imagine situations in which an instructor might legitimately choose to present this algorithm and its applications, without discussing its theoretical justification in Section 9.

Conversely, there are algorithms whose theoretical justification is not too hard to understand, in principle, but whose detailed implementation is quite complex. An instructor might well choose to discuss the duality theory underlying the weighted nonbipartite matching algorithm, going as far as Section 9 of Chapter 6 and skipping the material in Sections 10 and 11. I might mention, incidentally, that the algorithm in Section 11 is the one instance in which I have had cause to regret using a simple iterative description of the algorithms in this book. In this case, a few simple procedure declarations would have simplified matters substantially.

I began work on this book in the fall of 1968. In my innocence, I contemplated a two-year project. I did not know that, after many interruptions, I would still be laboring on the book more than seven years later.

Needless to say, there was much progress in the technical area during this seven-year period. I managed to make a few contributions myself, including the development of matroid intersection algorithms and an $O(n^3)$ implementation of Edmonds' algorithm for weighted nonbipartite matching. Naturally, these are in the book. There are some results which I did not put into the book, and possibly should have. These include the $O(n^{5/2})$ algorithm for unweighted bipartite matching of Dinic and of Hopcroft and Karp, and its recent generalization to the nonbipartite case by Even and Kariv. These must await a second edition, if there is to be one.

Because the writing of this book extended over such a considerable period, I have had the opportunity to receive advice, assistance, and encouragement from a large number of people. A special word is necessary for some of them.

Ray Fulkerson was very kind in giving me advice in the early stages of writing. I am most fortunate to have received his counsel. His untimely death in January 1976 was a blow to all of us who knew him, as a scholar and as a friend.

The last half of this book exists only because of the pioneering insights of Jack Edmonds. He originated the key ideas for nonbipartite matching, matroid optimization, and much, much more. I am happy to acknowledge my personal debt to his creative and fertile mind.

Victor Klee, as consulting editor, was extremely helpful. His criticisms, based on classroom use of the manuscript, were particularly useful in revising Chapter 4.

Harold Gabow helped me avoid a number of blunders in Chapter 6. (I, of course, retain sole proprietorship over the errors which remain, as elsewhere in the book.)

Stein Krogdahl, whose name is seen in many lemmas in Chapter 8, provided may definitions and proofs where mine were either incorrect or incomprehensible.

Donald Knuth somehow found time to communicate many useful suggestions and provided much appreciated encouragement.

The Air Force Office of Scientific Research provided support which contributed to the writing of this book. I am indebted to that office and to Captain Richard Bush.

I am also indebted to Nicos Christofides, Stuart Dreyfus, Alan Frieze, Dan Gussfield, T.C. Hu, Richard Karp, Sukhamay Kundu, Ben Lageweg, Howard Landeman, Jan Karel Lenstra, Francesco Maffioli, Colin McDiarmid, George Minty, Katta Murty, Alexander Rinnooy Kan, Arnon Rosenthal, Phil Spria, John Suraballe, Robert Tarjan, Roger Tobin, Klaus Truemper, Robert Urquhart, Dominic Welsh, Lee White, and Norman Zadeh.

The manuscript was typed and retyped by Sharon Bauerle, Doris Simpson, Ruth Suzuki, and many others. I thank them all.

Rocquencourt, France   *E. L. L.*
July 1976

Contents

ix

Chapter 8
MATROID INTERSECTIONS 300

Chapter 9
THE MATROID PARITY PROBLEM 356

ONE

Introduction

1
What is Combinatorial Optimization?

Combinatorial analysis is the mathematical study of the arrangement, grouping, ordering, or selection of discrete objects, usually finite in number. Traditionally, combinatorialists have been concerned with questions of existence or of enumeration. That is, does a particular type of arrangement exist? Or, how many such arrangements are there?

Quite recently, a new line of combinatorial investigation has gained increasing importance. The question asked is not "Does the arrangement exist?" or "How many arrangements are there?", but rather, "What is a *best* arrangement?" The existence of a particular type of arrangement is usually not in question, and the number of such possible arrangements is irrelevant. All that matters is finding an optimal arrangement, whether it be one in a hundred or one in an effectively infinite number of possibilities.

The new study of combinatorial optimization owes its existence to the advent of the modern digital computer. Most currently accepted methods of solution to combinatorial optimization problems would hardly have been taken seriously 25 years ago, for the simple reason that no one could have carried out the computations involved. Moreover, the existence of the digital computer has also created a multitude of technical problems of a combinatorial character. A large number of combinatorial optimization problems have been generated by research in computer design, the theory of computation, and by the application of computers to a myriad of numerical and nonnumerical problems which have required new methods, new approaches, and new mathematical insights.

2
Some Representative Optimization Problems

Perhaps the best way to convey the nature of combinatorial optimization problems is to give some specific examples. The first six problems listed below involve graphs. We assume that a connected undirected graph G is given, together with a nonnegative length for each arc (when applicable). If the reader is not already familiar with graphic terminology, he should consult Chapter 2.

ARC-COVERING PROBLEM

An arc (i, j) is said to "cover" nodes i and j. What is the smallest possible subset of arcs that can be chosen, such that each node of G is covered by at least one arc of the subset?

ARC-COLORING PROBLEM

It is desired to paint the arcs of G various colors, subject to the constraint that not all the arcs in any cycle are painted the same color. What is the smallest number of colors that will suffice?

MIN-CUT PROBLEM

It is desired to find a subset of arcs (a "cut") such that when these arcs are removed from G, the graph becomes disconnected. For what subset of arcs is the sum of the arc lengths minimized?

SPANNING-TREE PROBLEM

It is desired to find a subset of arcs such that when these arcs are removed from G, the graph remains connected. For what subset of arcs is the sum of the arc lengths maximized? (The complementary set of arcs is a "minimal spanning tree.")

SHORTEST PATH PROBLEM

What is the shortest path between two specified nodes of G?

CHINESE POSTMAN'S PROBLEM

It is desired to find a tour (a closed path) that passes through each arc in G at least once. What is the shortest such tour?

ASSIGNMENT PROBLEM

An $n \times n$ matrix $W = (w_{ij})$ is given. It is desired to find a subset of the elements in W, with exactly one element in each row and in each column. For what subset is the sum of the elements minimized?

MACHINE SEQUENCING PROBLEM

A number of jobs are to be processed by a machine. For each job a processing time and a deadline are specified. How should the jobs be sequenced, so that the number of late jobs is minimized?

A "TWENTY QUESTIONS" PROBLEM

Consider the following game, not unlike the parlor game of Twenty Questions. One player chooses a "target" object from a known set of n objects. The probability that he chooses object i is p_i. These probabilities are known to the second player, who is to identify the target object by formulating a series of questions of the form, "Is the target contained in subset S of the objects?", for some specified S. Assuming the first player answers these "yes or no" questions truthfully, how can the second player minimize the mean number of questions he must ask?

"RESTRICTED" SATISFIABILITY PROBLEM

A Boolean expression is given, in conjunctive normal form (i.e., "product-of-sums" form), with at most two literals in each term (sum) of the expression. For what assignment of 0, 1 values to the variables does the expression take on a "maximum" value? (The expression is satisfiable if and only if there is an assignment for which the expression takes on the value 1.)

3

When is a Problem Solved?

Of the ten problems listed in the previous section, the first seven can be solved by algorithms described in this book and the last three by well-known algorithms referenced at the end of this chapter.

But what does it mean to "solve" one of these problems? After all, there are only a finite number of feasible solutions to each of these problems. In a graph with m arcs and n nodes there are no more than 2^m possible subsets that might be arc coverings, no more than m^m possible arc colorings, no more than 2^m possible cuts, no more than n^{n-2} possible spanning trees, no more than 2^m possible paths, and no more than $(2m)!$ tours of the type required for the Chinese Postman's Problem. There are no more than $n!$ feasible solutions to the assignment problem, no more than $n!$ feasible sequences for n jobs, no more than $(n!)^2$ solutions to the Twenty Questions problem, no more than 2^n possible assignments of values to n Boolean variables in the satisfiability problem. In order to solve any one of these problems, why do we not just program a computer to make a list of all the possible solutions and pick out the best solution from the list?

As a matter of fact, there may still be a few (very pure) mathematicians who would maintain that the problems we have listed are actually nonproblems, devoid of any real mathematical content. They would say that whenever a problem requires the consideration of only a finite number of possibilities the problem is mathematically trivial.

This line of reasoning is hardly satisfying to one who is actually confronted with the necessity of finding an optimal solution to one of these problems. A naive, brute force approach simply will not work. Suppose that a computer can be programmed to examine feasible solutions at the rate of one each nanosecond, i.e., one billion solutions per second. Then if there are $n!$ feasible solutions, the computer will complete its task, for $n = 20$ in about 800 years, for $n = 21$ in about 16,800 years, and so on. Clearly, the running time of such a computation is effectively infinite. A combinatorial problem is not "solved" if we cannot live long enough to see the answer!

The challenge of combinatorial optimization is to develop algorithms for which the number of elementary computational steps is acceptably small. If this challenge is not of interest to "mathematicians," it most certainly is to computer scientists. Moreover, the challenge will be met only through study of the fundamental nature of combinatorial algorithms, and not by any conceivable advance in computer technology.

4

The Criterion of Polynomial Boundedness

Suppose an algorithm is proposed for a combinatorial optimization problem. How should we evaluate its effectiveness?

There is a very pragmatic (and realistic) point of view that can be taken. When the algorithm is implemented on a commercially available computer, it should require only a "reasonable" expenditure of computer time and data storage for any instance of the combinatorial problem which one might "reasonably" expect to solve. It is in exactly this sense that the simplex method of linear programming has been proved to be effective in solving hundreds of thousands, perhaps millions, of problems over a period of more than 20 years.

The "rule of reason" is an accepted principle of adjudication in the law. But more objective, precise standards should be possible in a mathematical and scientific discipline. One generally accepted standard in the realm of combinatorial optimization is that of "polynomial boundedness." *An algorithm is considered "good" if the required number of elementary computational steps is bounded by a polynomial in the size of the problem.*

The previous statement should raise a number of questions in the reader's mind. What is an elementary computational step? Does not that depend on the type of computer to be used? What is meant by the "size" of a problem? Might not there be more than one way to define size? And, most important, why is a polynomial bound considered to be important?

Consider first the significance of polynomial bounds. A polynomial function grows much less rapidly than an exponential function and an exponential function grows much less rapidly than a factorial function. Suppose one algorithm for solving the arc-covering problem requires $100\,n^3$ steps, and another requires 2^n steps, where n is the number of nodes. The exponential algorithm is more efficient for graphs with no more than 17 nodes. For larger graphs, however, the polynomial algorithm becomes increasingly better, with an exponentially growing ratio in running times. A 50-node problem may be quite feasible for the polynomial algorithm, but it is almost certain to be impossible for the exponential algorithm.

This is not to say that such comparisons may not be misleading. The crossover point may be well beyond the feasible range of either algorithm, in which case the exponential algorithm is certainly better in practice. Moreover, there are algorithms which are theoretically exponential, but behave like polynomial algorithms for all practical purposes. Prime examples are the simplex algorithms, which have empirically been observed to require an amount of computation that grows algebraically with the number of variables and the number of constraints of the linear programming problem. Yet it has been shown that for a properly contrived class of problems the simplex algorithms require an exponentially growing number of operations.

However, polynomial-bounded algorithms are, in fact, almost always "good" algorithms. The criterion of polynomial boundedness has been shown to have both theoretical and practical significance.

The other questions concerning the nature of elementary computational steps and the definition of problem size can be given formal and precise answers. But to do so is unnecessary for our purposes and beyond the scope of this book. We simply mention that theoretical studies of the complexity of computations, e.g., the "machine independent" theory of M. Blum, have indicated that it is relatively unimportant what computer model is considered and what "elementary computational steps" are available in its repetoire. If an algorithm is found to be polynomial bounded when implemented on one type of computer, it will be polynomial bounded (perhaps by a polynomial of a different degree) when implemented on virtually any other computer.

When estimates of algorithmic complexity are made in this book, we have in mind a hypothetical computer of the following type. The computer has unlimited random access memory. Input data reside in this memory at the beginning of the computation and output data are left in it at the end. Thus, there is no need to consider input-output operations. The memory stores logical constants and integers in words of any required size. We assume that the access time for these words is constant, unaffected by the size of the words and the number of words stored.

The hypothetical computer is capable of executing instructions of a conventional and mundane type, e.g., integer arithmetic operations, numerical comparisons, branching operations, and so on. We do not find it necessary to indicate explicitly what these instructions are. Ordinarily, we assume that each executed instruction requires one unit of time, regardless of the size of the operands involved.

Now let us consider the question of problem size. The reader may have already noted two different uses of the word "problem." For example, we speak of "the" arc-covering problem, and "an" arc-covering problem, i.e., an "instance" of the arc-covering problem, represented by a given graph. (The same sort of distinction exists in game theory between a "game," e.g., chess, and a "play" of the game.) The exact manner in which problem instances are to be encoded as input data is considered to be part of the problem definition. Thus, in the case of the arc-covering problem we may decree that graphs are to be represented by adjacency matrices. For the purpose of evaluating algorithmic complexity, *the size of a problem instance is the number of bits (i.e., symbols) required to encode it.*

In the case of a problem involving the specification of various numerical parameters, e.g., arc lengths, the magnitudes of these parameters should, strictly speaking, be taken into account. For example, approximately $\log_2 a_{ij}$ bits are required to specify an arc length a_{ij}. Ordinarily, we do not take explicit notice of this fact and we pretend that the magnitudes of these parameters do not matter. Thus, in the case of the shortest path problem, we take n, the number of nodes in the graph, to be the natural measure of problem size, whereas $n^2\alpha$, where

$$\alpha = \max_{i,j} \log_2 a_{ij}, \qquad (4.1)$$

would be a more accurate measure. (Note that if an algorithm is polynomial bounded in n, it is polynomial bounded in n^2 as well.)

Suppose n is taken to be the measure of problem size and the number of computational steps required by a certain algorithm is found to be

$$a_k n^k + a_{k-1} n^{k-1} + \ldots + a_1 n + a_0, \qquad (4.2)$$

where $a_k > 0$. Then we say that the algorithm is "of order n^k," written $O(n^k)$.

The reader will soon discover that we are not much concerned with the magnitude of the leading coefficient a_k in (4.2). Similarly, he will learn that we greatly prefer an $O(n^k)$ algorithm to any $O(n^{k+1})$ algorithm. Our reasons for doing so are largely the same as those that cause us to prefer any polynomial-bounded algorithm to an exponentially bounded one. Yet it is admittedly hard to claim that an $O(n^3)$ algorithm which requires $10^{10} n^3$ steps is better than on $O(n^4)$ algorithm which requires $10\, n^4 + 20\, n^3$ steps, only because the $O(n^3)$ algorithm requires less running time for very large n. In practice one rarely, if ever, is confronted by such bizarre alternatives. Insights that are sufficient to obtain a solution method of lower degree are almost invariably sufficient to provide an acceptable size for the leading coefficient of the polynomial (4.2).

A cautionary note is in order. We have mentioned that all arithmetic operations are assumed to require unit time, regardless of the size of the operands. And we have admitted that we shall often ignore the magnitudes of numerical parameters in measuring problem size. This sometimes results in an underestimate of the complexity of a computation. For example, in Chapter 3 we shall state that certain shortest path algorithms are $O(n^3)$, whereas $O(n^3\alpha)$ would be a more accurate measure, where α is defined by (4.1). We consider that this is an inconsequential error. In practice, arithmetic operations can be considered to require unit time. One expects to perform either single precision or double precision or triple precision arithmetic. Between these quantum jumps, the complexity of a shortest path algorithm is, in fact, essentially $O(n^3)$.

It is important that our somewhat casual attitude toward the evaluation of algorithmic complexity does not cause us to declare that an algorithm is polynomial bounded when it is not. In Chapter 4 we solve the so-called min-cost network flow problem. The input data include an n-node graph, various arc parameters, and a specified flow value v. The complexity of one algorithm is estimated to be $O(n^2 v)$. This is not a polynomial-bounded algorithm, although in practice it is a fairly good one. The number of bits required to specify v is $\log_2 v$, so the complexity of the algorithm should be polynomial in $\log_2 v$, not v, in order for the algorithm to be considered to be polynomial bounded.

5

Some Apparently Nonpolynomial-Bounded Problems

We must not give the impression that all significant combinatorial optimization problems have been effectively solved, in the sense described in the previous section. The "NP-complete" problems listed below have defied solution in a polynomial-bounded number of computational steps, and we strongly suspect that polynomial-bounded algorithms do not exist.

NODE-COVERING PROBLEM

A node i is said to "cover" all arcs (i, j) incident to it. What is the smallest possible subset of nodes that can be chosen, such that each arc of G is covered by at least one node in the subset?

CHROMATIC NUMBER PROBLEM

It is desired to paint the nodes of G various colors, subject to the constraint that two nodes i and j are not painted the same color if there is an arc (i, j) between them. What is the smallest number of colors that will suffice? (This is the "chromatic number" of G.)

MAX-CUT PROBLEM

It is desired to find a minimal cut such that the sum of the arc lengths is to be maximized.

STEINER NETWORK PROBLEM

This is the same as the spanning tree problem of Section 2, except that a *specified subset* of the nodes of G are to remain connected.

LONGEST PATH PROBLEM

What is the longest path, without repeated nodes, between two specified nodes of G?

TRAVELING SALESMAN PROBLEM

This is the same as the Chinese Postman's Problem, except that the tour is to pass through each node (rather than each arc) of G at least once.

THREE-DIMENSIONAL ASSIGNMENT PROBLEM

This is the same as the assignment problem in Section 2, except that the matrix W is three dimensional, with the obvious generalizations of the problem statement.

MACHINE SEQUENCING PROBLEM

This is the same as the machine sequencing problem in Section 2, except that for each job there is, in addition, a specified penalty cost which is incurred if the job is not completed on time. How should the jobs be sequenced, so that the sum of the incurred penalty costs is minimized? (In the previous problem each penalty cost was, in effect, unity.)

CONSTRAINED TWENTY QUESTIONS PROBLEM

This is the same as the twenty questions problem in Section 2, except that the second player is constrained to choose questions from a specified list of questions.

SATISFIABILITY PROBLEM

This is the same as the corresponding problem in Section 2, except that there is no restriction on the number of literals that may appear in each term of the Boolean expression.

No one has yet been able to prove that the problems listed above cannot be solved in a polynomial number of computational steps. However, it is possible to elicit strong circumstantial evidence to that effect. It is also possible to show that either all of these problems can be solved by a polynominal-bounded algorithm or none of them can be.

These results have been obtained by a set of clever problem reductions, mostly due to R. M. Karp. That is, it has been shown that for any pair of problems *A* and *B* on the list, the existence of a polynomial-bounded algorithm for problem *B* implies the existence of a polynomial-bounded algorithm for problem *A*. The technique of problem reduction is employed repeatedly in this book, generally with respect to the problems listed in Section 2.

6

Methods of Solution

We have indicated something about the types of problems we wish to solve, and something about how we intend to evaluate algorithms for their solution. Let us now consider some of the mathematical techniques which can be employed in these algorithms.

One can classify solution methods into five broad categories: (1) linear programming, (2) recursion and enumeration, (3) heuristics, (4) statistical sampling, (5) special and ad hoc techniques.

Linear programming, as the reader probably already knows, is concerned with extremization of a linear objective function subject to linear inequality constraints. From a geometric point of view, the linear inequality constraints describe a convex polytope. The "simplex" computation of linear programming proceeds from one vertex of this polytope to another, with an accompanying monotone improvement in the value of the objective function.

One way to solve a combinatorial optimization problem by linear programming is to formulate a system of linear inequality constraints which will cause the vertices of the convex polytope to correspond to feasible solutions of the combinatorial problem. Sometimes this results in a relatively small number of constraints which can be listed explicitly in advance of the computation. Problems for which this is the case include the network flow problems, with the shortest path, min-cut, and assignment problems as special cases. For example, $2n$ inequalities, together with nonnegativity constraints on n^2 variables, describe a convex polytope with $n!$ vertices, corresponding to the $n!$ feasible solutions of an $n \times n$ assignment problem.

There are other problems for which there exists a good characterization of the inequality constraints, but the constraints are far too numerous to list. Instead, inequalities are generated as necessary in the course of the computation. Problems which are solved by this approach include certain matroid problems, with the arc-covering, arc-coloring, and spanning-tree problems as special cases. For example, there are 2^n constraints that describe a convex polytope with n^{n-2} vertices, corresponding to the n^{n-2} possible spanning trees in a complete graph on n nodes.

Even though the number of constraints of these linear programming problems are sometimes exceedingly large and the structures of the convex polytopes exceedingly complex, it has been possible in many cases to devise algorithms requiring only a polynomial-bounded number of computational steps. These algorithms are not obtained by simply invoking the simplex method. Special techniques are necessary, and the duality theory of linear programming is of fundamental importance in algorithmic analyses and proofs of convergence.

Combinatorial optimization problems can also be solved by linear programming methods, even in cases where there is no good characterization of the necessary inequality constraints. In the approach of "integer" linear programming, one formulates a set of linear inequalities which describe a convex polyhedron enclosing points (with integer coordinates) corresponding to feasible solutions of the combinatorial problem. A variant of the simplex method is applied and additional inequality constraints are generated as needed in the course of the computation. These additional inequalities or "cutting planes" ordinarily bear little predictable relation to each other or to the original set of constraints.

Integer linear programming algorithms usually do not exploit any special combinatorial structure of the problem at hand. For this reason, they are sufficiently general to "solve" virtually any combinatorial optimization problem. But there is no possibility of establishing good a priori bounds on the length of computations, and practical experience with these algorithms has been very uneven.

Under the heading of recursion and enumeration, we include dynamic programming and branch-and-bound. Dynamic programming, as popularized by Bellman, is a technique for determining optimal policies for a sequential decision process. A surprisingly large number of optimization problems can be cast into this form and some of the most useful applications of this technique are in the combinatorial realm. In some cases, dynamic programming can be applied to solve problems with a factorial number of feasible solutions, e.g., the traveling salesman problem, with an exponentially growing number of computational steps. Other dynamic programming algorithms are polynomial bounded. Interestingly, most of the shortest-path algorithms described in Chapter 3 can be given either linear programming or dynamic programming interpretations.

Branch-and-bound methods have been developed in a variety of contexts, and under a variety of names, such as "backtrack programming" and "implicit enumeration." Essentially, the idea is to repeatedly break the set of feasible solutions into subsets, and to calculate bounds on the costs of the solutions contained within them. The bounds are used to discard entire subsets of solutions from further consideration. This simple but effective technique has scored a number of notable successes in practical computations. However, it is rarely possible to establish good bounds on the length of the computation.

Under the heading of heuristics we include algorithms whose justification is based on arguments of plausibility, rather than mathematical proof. Often, these algorithms permit good computational bounds. However, generally speaking, only solutions which are "close" to optimal or, at best, not demonstrably optimal, are obtained.

By statistical sampling, we mean the random generation of a number of solutions from the population of all feasible solutions for the purpose of making some sort of statistical inference about the closeness of the best solution sampled to the actual optimum. This type of solution method appears to be in its infancy.

The heading of special and ad hoc methods includes those techniques which do not conveniently fall into one of the other categories. Examples are Moore's method for the machine sequencing problem and Huffman's coding method for solving the Twenty Questions problem, referenced at the end of this chapter.

In brief, this book is concerned with linear programming techniques for which good computational bounds exist, and incidentally with recursion and enumeration. We do not discuss integer linear programming nor heuristics nor statistical sampling. Nor is any comprehensive survey of special and ad hoc methods attempted.

COMMENTS AND REFERENCES

SECTION 1
An elementary introduction to classical combinatories is given by

N. Ya. Vilenkin, *Combinatorics,* translated from the Russian edition by A. Schenitzer and S. Shenitger, Academic Press, New York, 1971.

For a somewhat more advanced treatment, see

C. L. Liu, *Introduction to Combinatorial Mathematics,* McGraw-Hill, New York, 1968.
H. J. Ryser, *Combinatorial Mathematics,* Mathematical Association of America and John Wiley, New York, 1963.

An excellent overview of recent research in many areas of combinatorics, including optimization, is given by a conference proceedings

R. Guy et al., editors, *Combinatorial Structures and Their Applications,* Gordon and Breach, New York, 1970.

An extremely useful and well-written introduction to some of the computational aspects of combinatorics is given by

M. B. Wells, *Elements of Combinatorial Computing,* Pergamon Press, Oxford and New York, 1971.

See also

D. E. Knuth, *The Art of Computer Programming*, Vol. 4, to be published by Addison-Wesley, Reading, Mass.

SECTION 2

All, except the last three, of the problems listed in this section are treated in this book. An elegant solution to the machine sequencing problem is given in

J. M. Moore, "An *n* Job, One Machine Sequencing Algorithm for Minimizing the Number of Late Jobs," *Management Science,* **15** (1968) 102–109.

The Twenty Questions problem was solved, in another form, by

D. A. Huffman, "A Method for the Construction of Minimum Redundancy Codes," *Proc. IRE,* **40** (1952) 1098–1101.

The significance of the satisfiability problem is indicated in the papers of Cook and Karp, referenced below.

SECTIONS 3, 4, 5

The criterion of polynomial boundedness was possibly first stated explicitly in the literature by Jack Edmonds, in his papers on matching (see Chapter 6). The problem reductions referred to in this section were inspired by

S. Cook, "The Complexity of Theorem-Proving Procedures," *Conference Record of Third ACM Symposium on Theory of Computing* (1970) 151–158.

and most of the reductions are indicated explicitly in

R. M. Karp, "Reducibility among Combinatorial Problems," in *Complexity of Computer Computations,* Pergamon Press, Oxford and New York, 1972.
R. M. Karp, "On the Computational Complexity of Combinatorial Problems," *Networks,* **5** (1975) 45–68.

On the subject of problem reductions, we should cite a story, which we quote from Vilenkin's book, page 11:

A mathematician asked a physicist: "Suppose you were given an empty teakettle an an unlit gas plate. How would you bring water to boil?" "I'd fill the teakettle with water, light the gas, and set the teakettle on the plate." "Right," said the mathematician, "and now please solve another problem. Suppose the gas were lit and the teakettle were full. How would you bring the water to a boil?" "That's even simpler. I'd set the teakettle on the plate." "Wrong," exclaimed the mathematician. "The thing to do is to put out the flame and empty the teakettle. This would reduce our problem to the previous problem!"

That is why, whenever one reduces a new problem to problems already solved, one says in jest that one is applying the "teakettle principle."

SECTION 6

For methods of solution of combinatorial optimization problems, other than those presented in this book, see

T. C. Hu, *Integer Programming and Network Flows,* Addison-Wesley, Reading, Mass., 1969.

G. Nemhauser and R. Garfinkel, *Integer Programming,* John Wiley, New York, 1972.

T. L. Saaty, *Optimization in Integers and Related Extremal Problems,* McGraw-Hill, New York, 1970.

H. M. Salkin, *Integer Programming,* Addison-Wesley, Reading, Mass., 1975.

TWO

Mathematical Preliminaries

1

Mathematical Prerequisites

Some background in graph theory and in linear programming is essential for reading this book. This chapter provides a review of some of the more important background concepts, as well as a consistent set of definitions and notational conventions.

The most important concepts from graph theory, for our purposes, are those which have to do with connectivity properties. Before attempting the study of network flows, the reader should be familiar with the notions of path, directed path, tree, directed tree, cycle, directed cycle, cocycle, and directed cocycle, and the duality relations between them. The study of matroids is also made much easier if one is able to make graphic interpretations of the matroid generalizations of these same concepts.

The linear programming concepts we draw upon most frequently concern duality relations. The reader should be able to formulate the dual of a linear program and determine the orthogonality conditions which are necessary and sufficient for optimality of primal and dual solutions. Familiarity with the simplex method is not necessary. However, the reader should have some appreciation of convex polytopes and polyhedra, and know that the simplex computation proceeds from one vertex of the feasible region to another. In later chapters some emphasis is placed on the fact that certain convex polyhedra have integer vertices. This is proved by showing that an integer optimal solution is obtained for any possible objective function. The reader should be equipped to follow this line of reasoning.

In addition to strictly mathematical background, the reader should have some familiarity with the principles of computation. He should understand the concept of an algorithm, and how an algorithm is coded in machine language and executed by a computer. He should be able to count the number of levels of nesting of iterative loops in an algorithm and thereby estimate its complexity. No serious attempt is made to explain these matters in this chapter or elsewhere in this book. If the reader is unfamiliar with these concepts, he should consult a text on computer programming.

2

Sets and Relations

We assume that the reader is familiar with basic set operations and conventional set notation: $\in$, $\notin$, $\sim$, $\cup$, $\cap$, $\subseteq$, $\subset$, $\varnothing$, etc. We write $S \subset T$ if S is a *proper subset* of T, i.e., $S \subset T$ but $S \neq T$. We use braces $\{,\}$ to indicate a set, and parentheses $(,)$ to indicate an ordered set or sequence. For notational convenience, we use "$+$" and "$-$" as follows:

$$S + e = S \cup \{e\}$$

and

$$S - e = S - \{e\}.$$

The *symmetric difference* of two sets is indicated by the symbol $\oplus$, i.e., $S \oplus T$ is the set of all elements contained in S or in T, but not both. By an abuse of notation, we occasionally apply set operations to ordered sets, as though they were unordered. For example, if

$$S = (4, 1, 0, 5)$$

and

$$T = (1, 3, 2, 4),$$

then

$$S \oplus T = \{0, 2, 3, 5\}.$$

We let $|S|$ denote the number of elements in S, the *cardinality* of S. For example, if $e \notin S$, then $|S + e| = |S| + 1$. We let $\mathscr{P}(S)$ denote the *power set* of S, the set of all subsets of S. $|\mathscr{P}(S)| = 2^n$, where $n = |S|$. Thus $|\mathscr{P}(\varnothing)| = 1$.

Suppose $\mathscr{T}$ is a family of sets. We say that $S \in \mathscr{T}$ is *minimal* in $\mathscr{T}$ if there is no $T \in \mathscr{T}$ such that $T \subset S$. Similarly S is *maximal* in $\mathscr{T}$ if there is no $T \in \mathscr{T}$ such that $S \subset T$. Obviously, a minimal set is not necessarily unique nor does it necessarily have minimum cardinality. A set may also be both minimal and maximal in $\mathscr{T}$. For example, if $\mathscr{T} = \{\{0, 1\}, \{0, 1, 3\}, \{4\}, \{3\}, \{1, 3\}\}$, then the minimal sets in $\mathscr{T}$ are $\{0, 1\}$, $\{3\}$, and $\{4\}$. The maximal sets are $\{0, 1, 3\}$ and $\{4\}$. Quite often we have occasion to speak of a set S which is *minimal* (maximal) with respect to some property P. Such a set is minimal in the family of all sets conforming to the property in question.

The same concepts of minimality and maximality are applicable to ordered sets. For example, suppose we define a "d-sequence" to be a sequence of integers in which two successive elements of the sequence differ by no more than d. For the given sequence $S = (0, -1, 3, 1, 6, 8, 10, 2, 7, 0)$, both $(0, 3, 6, 8, 10, 7)$ and $(0, -1, 1, 2, 0)$ are maximal three-subsequences of S.

If S is a finite set of numbers, min S (max S) denotes the numerically smallest (largest) element in S. Thus if $S = \{-1, 2, 3, 8\}$, min $S = -1$ and max $S = 8$. By definition, min $\varnothing = +\infty$ and max $\varnothing = -\infty$. Alternative notations for min A, where

$$A = \{a_1, a_2, \ldots, a_n\}$$

are

$$\min \{a_i \mid 1 \leq i \leq n\}$$

or

$$\min_{1 \leq 1 \leq n} \{a_i\}$$

or simply

$$\min_i a_i$$

where the range of i is understood from the context.

As a further example, suppose A is a matrix whose typical element is a_{ij}, written

$$A = (a_{ij}).$$

Then

$$\min_j a_{ij}$$

is the smallest element in row i and

$$\max_{i} a_{ij}$$

is the largest element in column j. In the matrix

$$A = \begin{pmatrix} 0 & 4 & 3 \\ 2 & 1 & 7 \\ 9 & 8 & 6 \end{pmatrix},$$

$$\max_{i} \min_{j} a_{ij} = 6,$$

$$\min_{j} \max_{i} a_{ij} = 7.$$

The reader is assumed to be familiar with the algebraic concepts of relations and functions, and with equivalence relations and partial orderings in particular. He should know that an equivalence relation is reflexive, symmetric, and transitive; also, that an equivalence relation on a set induces a partition of that set and that, conversely, a partition induces an equivalence relation. He should know that a partial ordering is reflexive, antisymmetric, and transitive and that a partial ordering can be represented by a Hasse diagram.

Suppose $\leq$ is a total ordering of A, i.e., a partial ordering such that for each pair of elements a, b, in A either $a \leq b$ or $b \leq a$. Then this total ordering induces a *lexicographic ordering* "$\leqslant$" of A^n, the set of all n-tuples of elements of A. (That is, A^n is the n-fold *cartesian product* of A.) Let

$$a = (a_1, a_2, \ldots, a_n)$$

and

$$b = (b_1, b_2, \ldots, b_n).$$

Then $a \leqslant b$ if either $a = b$ or there is some k, $1 \leq k \leq n$, such that $a_i = b_i$, $i = 1, 2, \ldots, k - 1$, and $a_k < b_k$.

Suppose $\mathscr{A} = A \cup A^2 \cup A^3 \cup \ldots$. We can define a lexicographic ordering on $\mathscr{A}$ as follows. Let

$$a = (a_1, a_2, \ldots, a_m)$$

and

$$b = (b_1, b_2, \ldots, b_n),$$

where $m \leq n$. Then $a \leqslant b$ if $a \leqslant (b_1, b_2, \ldots, b_m)$, as defined above, and $b \leqslant a$ otherwise.

Or, suppose $\mathscr{A} \subseteq \mathscr{P}(A)$. Let

$$a = \{a_1 a_2, \ldots, a_m\},$$
$$b = \{b_1 b_2, \ldots, b_n\},$$

where $m \le n$. Assume, without loss of generality, that

$$a_1 \le a_2 \le \ldots \le a_m,$$

and

$$b_1 \le b_2 \le \ldots \le b_n.$$

Then $a \preccurlyeq b$ if $(a_1, a_2, \ldots, a_m) \preccurlyeq (b_1, b_2, \ldots, b_n)$.

A lexicographic ordering of any one of these three types is a total ordering. This property is handy for "breaking ties." For example, suppose we pose the following optimization problem. Given a positive integer n, for what factorization of n is the sum of the factors a minimum? (Assume only positive factors.) For $n = 8, 2 \times 2 \times 2$ and 2×4 are both optimal. However, if we wish there to be a unique optimum, $2 \times 2 \times 2$ can be declared the smaller of the two by lexicography.

Lexicographic ordering of n-tuples ("vectors") should not of course be confused with the more common partial ordering: i.e., if $a = (a_1, a_2, \ldots, a_n)$ and $b = (b_1, b_2, \ldots, b_n)$, then $a \le b$ if $a_i \le b_i$, for $i = 1, 2, \ldots, n$. We commonly make use of this type of relation when we write

$$Ax \le b,$$

where $A = (a_{ij})$ is an $m \times n$ matrix and A and b are, respectively, an n-vector and an m-vector. The vector inequality above means that

$$\sum_{j=1}^{n} a_{ij}x_j \le b_i, \qquad \text{for } i = 1, 2, \ldots, m.$$

PROBLEMS

2.1 Verify each of the following:
  (a) $\min S \cup T = \min (\min S, \min T)$,
  (b) $\min S \cap T \ge \max (\min S, \min T)$.
  (c) If $S \subseteq T$, then $\min S \ge \min T$.
  (d) $\min \{s, t\} = - \max \{- s, - t\}$.
2.2 Formulate a duality principle whereby "min" and "max" can be interchanged in relations like those stated in Problem 2.1. Rewrite each relation according to this principle.

3
Graphs and Digraphs

A *graph* $G = (N, A)$ is a structure consisting of a finite set N of elements called *nodes* and a set A of unordered pairs of nodes called *arcs*. A *directed graph* or *digraph* is defined similarly, except that each arc is an ordered pair, giving it direction from one node to another. In the literature of graph theory (where terminology is quite unstandardized), nodes are also referred to as vertices or points and arcs as edges or lines.

Any system or structure which may be considered abstractly as a set of elements, certain pairs of which are related in a specified way, has a representation as a graph or digraph. Thus graph theory is really of a theory of relations, with graphs representing symmetric relations and digraphs asymmetric relations.

In many applications in the physical, biological, social, and engineering sciences, graphs or digraphs are not sufficient to adequately specify the system or structure under study. Numerical values may be attached to the nodes or arcs of a graph to represent construction costs, flow capacities, probabilities of destruction, and so on. In general, any graph to which such additional structure has been added is called a "network."

For both undirected and directed graphs, an arc from node i to node j is denoted by (i, j), even though $\{i, j\}$ would be more appropriate for undirected graphs. An arc (i, i) is called a *loop*. Ordinarily we deal with undirected graphs with no loops and at most one arc between a given pair of nodes i, j. Thus, if $|N| = n$ and $|A| = m$, it follows that $m \leq n(n - 1)/2$. In the case of directed graphs, we permit both (i, j) and (j, i), so $m \leq n(n - 1)$.

We commonly represent a graph by a drawing in which nodes are points (drawn as circles) and arcs are lines connecting pairs of points. If the graph is directed, the arcs are drawn with arrow heads. It should be kept clearly in mind that two drawings of the same graph may be quite different, as shown in Figure 2.1.

People find drawings useful. Computers do not. Some of the representations of graphs that are appropriate for computers are an arc list, an incidence matrix, and an adjacency matrix.

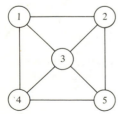
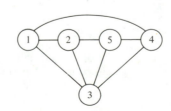

Figure 2.1   Two drawings of the same graph

An *arc list* simply contains an entry for each arc (i, j). In the case of the graph in Figure 2.1, such a list contains $(1, 2)$, $(1, 3)$, $(1, 4)$, $(2, 3)$, $(2, 5)$, $(3, 4)$, $(3, 5)$, $(4, 5)$. Arc lists may be sorted, ordered, and manipulated in various ways within the computer.

An arc (i, j) is said to be *incident* to each of the nodes i and j, and conversely. Each row of the node-arc incidence matrix is identified with a node and each column with an arc. If the arcs are numbered by the index k, then the *incidence matrix* $B = (b_{ik})$ is defined as follows:

$$b_{ik} = 1 \quad \text{if node } i \text{ is incident to arc } k,$$

$$= 0 \quad \text{otherwise.}$$

The incidence matrix of the graph in Figure 2.1 is

$$
\begin{array}{c}
1 \\ 2 \\ 3 \\ 4 \\ 5
\end{array}
\begin{pmatrix}
1 & 1 & 1 & 0 & 0 & 0 & 0 & 0 \\
1 & 0 & 0 & 1 & 1 & 0 & 0 & 0 \\
0 & 1 & 0 & 1 & 0 & 1 & 1 & 0 \\
0 & 0 & 1 & 0 & 0 & 1 & 0 & 1 \\
0 & 0 & 0 & 0 & 1 & 0 & 1 & 1
\end{pmatrix}
$$

$$
\begin{array}{cccccccc}
(1,2) & (1,3) & (1,4) & (2,3) & (2,5) & (3,4) & (3,5) & (4,5)
\end{array}
$$

Note that each column contains exactly two 1's.

In the case of a directed graph the arc (i, j), directed from i to j, is said to be *incident from i* and *incident to j*. The arc-node *incidence matrix* $B = (b_{ik})$ is defined as follows:

$$b_{ik} = +1 \quad \text{if arc } k \text{ is incident to node } i$$

$$= -1 \quad \text{if arc } k \text{ is incident from node } i$$

$$= 0 \quad \text{otherwise.}$$

The incidence matrix of the directed graph in Figure 2.2 is

$$
\begin{array}{c}
1 \\ 2 \\ 3 \\ 4
\end{array}
\begin{pmatrix}
-1 & -1 & 1 & 0 & 0 & 0 & 0 \\
1 & 0 & -1 & -1 & -1 & 1 & 0 \\
0 & 1 & 0 & 1 & 0 & -1 & 1 \\
0 & 0 & 0 & 0 & 1 & 0 & -1
\end{pmatrix}
$$

$$
\begin{array}{ccccccc}
(1,2) & (1,3) & (2,1) & (2,3) & (2,4) & (3,2) & (4,3)
\end{array}
$$

Note that each column contains exactly one $+1$ and one -1.

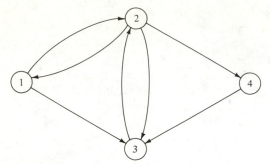

Figure 2.2   Directed graph for example

If there exists an arc (i, j) we say that nodes i and j are *adjacent*. By definition, no node is adjacent to itself. For an undirected graph, *the adjacency matrix* $A = (a_{ij})$ is defined as follows:

$a_{ij} = 1$ if there is an arc (i, j) between nodes i and j

$\quad\;\; = 0$ otherwise.

The adjacency matrix for the graph in Figure 2.1 is

$$
\begin{array}{c}
1 \\ 2 \\ 3 \\ 4 \\ 5
\end{array}
\begin{pmatrix}
0 & 1 & 1 & 1 & 0 \\
1 & 0 & 1 & 0 & 1 \\
1 & 1 & 0 & 1 & 1 \\
1 & 0 & 1 & 0 & 1 \\
0 & 1 & 1 & 1 & 0
\end{pmatrix}
$$
$$
\begin{array}{ccccc}
1 & 2 & 3 & 4 & 5
\end{array}
$$

Note that the adjacency matrix is necessarily symmetric, i.e., $a_{ij} = a_{ji}$.

In the case of a directed graph, if there is an arc (i, j) we say that node i is *adjacent to* node j and node j is *adjacent from* node i. The *adjacency matrix* $A = (a_{ij})$ is defined as follows:

$a_{ij} = 1$ if there is an arc (i, j) from i to j

$\quad\;\; = 0$ otherwise.

The adjacency matrix for the digraph in Figure 2.2 is

$$
\begin{array}{c}
1 \\ 2 \\ 3 \\ 4
\end{array}
\begin{pmatrix}
0 & 1 & 1 & 0 \\
1 & 0 & 1 & 1 \\
0 & 1 & 0 & 0 \\
0 & 0 & 1 & 0
\end{pmatrix}
$$
$$
\begin{array}{cccc}
1 & 2 & 3 & 4
\end{array}
$$

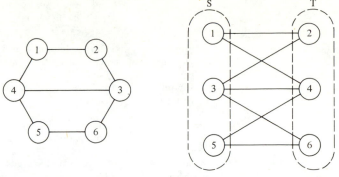

Figure 2.3   Two drawings of a bipartite graph

Of special interest is the *bipartite* graph, such as that shown in Figure 2.3. The nodes of a bipartite graph can be partitioned into two sets S and T, such that no two nodes in S or in T are adjacent, i.e., all arcs extend "between S and T." If a graph $G = (N, A)$ is bipartite, we commonly denote it as $G = (S, T, A)$ where $N = S \cup T$.

Proposition 3.1 G is a bipartite graph if and only if its nodes can be numbered in such a way that its adjacency matrix takes on the form

$$A = \left(\begin{array}{c|c} 0 & \bar{A} \\ \hline \bar{A}^T & 0 \end{array} \right) \tag{3.1}$$

In (3.1), $\bar{A}^T$ denotes the transpose of the submatrix $\bar{A}$. Thus, for a bipartite graph $G = (S, T, A)$, with $|S| = p$ and $|T| = q$, the nodes can be numbered in such a way that $\bar{A}$ is a $p \times q$ submatrix and $\bar{A}^T$ is $q \times p$. We often represent a bipartite graph simply by the adjacency submatrix $\bar{A}$.

PROBLEMS

3.1   (R. M. Karp) The following is a representative list of systems or structures for which graph models are appropriate. In each case, decide whether a graph or digraph is called for. Determine what additional mathematical structure, if any, is necessary to adequately model the more important aspects of each system. Which of the graphs, if any are bipartite?

System or Structure	Nodes	Nodes i and j Are Connected by an Arc If
Road map	Cities	i and j are connected by a road
Molecule	Atoms	There is a chemical bond between i and j

System or Structure	Nodes	Nodes i and j Are Connected by an Arc If
Electrical network	Terminals of elements	i and j are connected by a network element
Binary relation R over a set N	Elements of N	$(i, j) \in R$
Game or puzzle	Positions or configurations	i can be reached from j in one move
Discrete-state system	States	A direct transition is possible from i to j
Business organization	Employees	i is j's manager
United States national economy	Goods and services	i is required in the production of j
Computer program	Instructions	The execution of j can directly follow the execution of i
Information retrieval system	Index terms, documents	Term i is relevant to document j
Convex polyhedron	Extreme points	i is adjacent to j
System of simultaneous equations	Variables	j is an independent variable in the equation for i

3.2 If A is the adjacency matrix and B the incidence matrix of a given graph, what is the relation between A and BB^T? (Be sure to consider the relation between the diagonal elements of the two matrices.) Under what special condition is $A = BB^T$?

3.3 Devise an $O(n^2)$ algorithm to test a graph for bipartiteness. (*Hint*: Start by labeling on arbitrary node S, then label the adjacent nodes T, and so on.)

4

Subgraphs, Cliques, Multigraphs

The *degree* d_i of node i is the number of arcs incident to the node. Note that if B is the incidence matrix,

$$d_i = \sum_k b_{ik}.$$

In the case of a digraph, the *out-degree* $d_i^{(\text{out})}$ of node i is the number of arcs incident from the node, and the *in-degree* $d_i^{((\text{in})}$ is the number of arcs incident to the node. Note that

$$d_i^{(\text{out})} - d_i^{(\text{in})} = \sum_k b_{ik}.$$

The *complete graph* K_n has n nodes any two of which are adjacent. The complete graph has $n(n - 1)/2$ arcs. The *complete digraph* on n nodes has $n(n - 1)$ arcs. The *complete bipartite graph* $K_{p,q}$ is a bipartite graph $G = (S, T, A)$, with $|S| = p, |T| = q$, and $|A| = pq$.

A graph $G = (N', A')$ is called a *subgraph* of the graph $G = (N, A)$ if $N' \subseteq N$ and $A' \subseteq A$. If $N' \subseteq N$, then the *subgraph of G induced* by N' has the node set N' and all arcs (i, j) in A such that both i and j are in N'. If a subgraph of G is a complete graph it is a *complete subgraph*. A maximal complete subgraph is called a *clique*.

Given the graph $G = (N, A)$, the subgraph obtained by the deletion of the arcs $A' \subseteq A$ is simply the graph $G' = (N, A - A')$. The *complement* of the graph $G = (N, A)$ is the graph $\bar{G}$ obtained by deleting the arcs of G from the complete graph on the same nodes.

The *contraction* of an arc (i, j) is accomplished by replacing nodes i and j by a single node k. An arc (k, l) is provided in the contracted graph for each arc (i, l) or (j, l) in the original graph, except arc (i, j). The contraction of a graph may well result in a graph with multiple arcs between nodes. Such a structure we call a *multigraph*.

The above definitions are illustrated by the example in Figure 2.4.

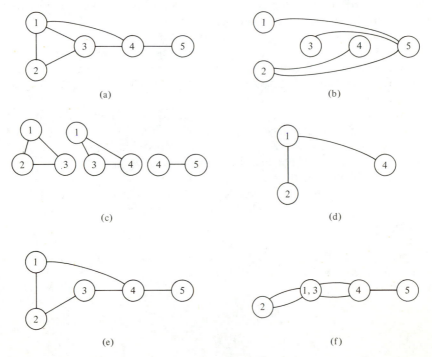

Figure 2.4   (a) Graph G. (b) Complementary graph $\bar{G}$. (c) Three cliques in G. (d) Subgraph induced by $N' = \{1, 2, 4\}$. (e) Deletion of arc (1, 3). (f) Contraction of arc (1, 3).

PROBLEMS

4.1   Prove that every graph has an even number of nodes of odd degree.

4.2   If $G = (S, T, A)$ is a bipartite graph, characterize the clique structure of G and of $\bar{G}$.

4.3   The incidence matrix of a multigraph is defined as for an ordinary graph and the adjacency matrix can be generalized so that $a_{ij} = $ the number of arcs between between i and j. What is the relation between A and BB^T? (Cf. Problem 3.2.)

5

Connectivity in Graphs

In this section we define path, cycle, component, etc., for graphs. In the next section the analogous notions for digraphs are discussed.

A *path* between s and t, or simply an (s, t) *path*, is a sequence of arcs of the form $(s, i_1), (i_1, i_2), \ldots, (i_k, t)$. If $s, i_1, i_2, \ldots, i_k, t$ are distinct nodes, we say that the path is *minimal* or *without repeated nodes*. We shall often use only the word "path," adding the words "minimal" or "without repeated nodes" where this is not clear from the context.

An (s, t) path is *open* if $s \neq t$ and *closed* if $s = t$. A *cycle* is an (s, s) path containing at least one arc, in which no node except s is repeated. In an ordinary graph (as opposed to a multigraph or a graph with loops), a cycle must contain at least three arcs. A graph which contains no cycles is *acyclic*.

Two nodes i and j are said to be *connected* if there exists an (i, j) path. A graph G is said to be *connected* if all pairs of nodes are connected. A *component* of a graph G is a maximal connected subgraph, i.e., it is not a subgraph of any other connected subgraph of G. A graph is connected if and only if it has exactly one component.

Each node or arc of G belongs to exactly one component. It follows that the components of a graph determine a unique partition of its nodes and arcs.

Proposition 5.1   If a graph G has p components, then its nodes can be numbered in such a way that its adjacency matrix takes on the block diagonal form

$$A = \begin{pmatrix} \boxed{A_1} & 0 & 0 & 0 \\ 0 & \boxed{A_2} & 0 & 0 \\ 0 & 0 & \boxed{} & 0 \\ 0 & 0 & 0 & \boxed{A_p} \end{pmatrix}$$

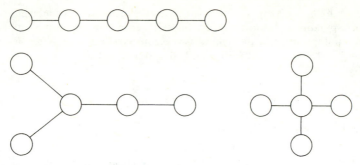

Figure 2.5   All trees on five nodes

A *tree* is a connected acyclic graph. All trees on five nodes are exhibited in Figure 2.5. The following proposition gives a number of equivalent characterizations of trees.

Proposition 5.2   The following statements are equivalent for a graph G with n nodes:

(1) G is a tree.
(2)   Every two nodes of G are connected by a unique path.
(3) G is connected and has $n - 1$ arcs.
(4) G is acyclic and has $n - 1$ arcs.
(5) G is acyclic and if any two nonadjacent nodes of G are joined by an arc e, then $G + e$ has exactly one cycle.
(6) G is connected, is not K_n for $n \geq 3$, and if any two nonadjacent nodes of G are joined by a new arc e, then $G + e$ has exactly one cycle.

A *tree* in G is a connected acyclic subgraph on the nodes of G. A *forest* in G is an acyclic subgraph on the nodes of G, i.e., each component of the forest is a tree. A maximal forest in a connected graph is a *spanning* tree. (It "spans" or connects together all nodes.) Two important theorems follow. The reader should be able to prove the first by induction. The second is difficult; its proof can be found in any standard work on graph theory.

Theorem 5.3   Every maximal forest in a graph with n nodes and p components contains $n - p$ arcs.

Theorem 5.4   (*C. W. Borchardt*) K_n contains n^{n-2} distinct spanning trees.

PROBLEMS

5.1   Show that a tree on $n \geq 2$ nodes has at least two nodes with degree one.
5.2   Prove that a graph is bipartite if and only if each of its cycles is of even length.

5.4 Show that if C is a cycle of a graph G, then the columns of the incidence matrix corresponding to the arcs in C are linearly dependent, with respect to addition and multiplication in the field of two elements. (That is, $0 + 0 = 1 + 1 = 0$, $0 + 1 = 1 + 0 = 1, 0 \cdot 0 = 0 \cdot 1 = 1 \cdot 0 = 0, 1 \cdot 1 = 1$.)

6

Connectivity in Digraphs

Each of the definitions given in the previous section is applicable to digraphs, by simply ignoring the directions of arcs. However, for every definition for graphs, there is a specialized definition for digraphs in which the directions of the arcs are taken into account.

Thus a *directed path* from s to t, or simply an (s, t) *path*, is a sequence of arcs from s to t, where the pth arc is incident to the same node from which the $(p + 1)$st arc is incident. That is, all arcs are directed from s toward t. A *directed cycle* is a minimal nonempty closed directed path. We shall often drop the word "directed" from directed paths, directed cycles, and so on, when no confusion will result.

A node i is said to be *connected to* node j, and j is said to be *connected from* i if there exists an (i, j) path. A digraph G is said to be *strongly connected* if, for all pairs of nodes i and j, i is connected to j and j is connected to i. A *strong component* of a graph G is a strongly connected subgraph of G which is maximal, i.e., it is not a subgraph of any other strongly connected subgraph of G. A graph is strongly connected if and only if it has one strong component.

Each node (but *not* each arc) of G belongs to exactly one strong component. It follows that the strong components of a graph determine a unique partition of its nodes. Suppose we contract all those arcs which lie in strong components. Then the resulting contraction digraph has the appearance of the graph in Figure 2.6. That is, each node is identified with a strong component and these nodes are, in effect, partially ordered. If there is a path from i to j, there is no path from j to i. In other words the resulting contraction digraph has no directed cycles.

Proposition 6.1 If a directed graph G has p strong components, then its nodes can be numbered in such a way that its adjacency matrix takes on the form

$$A = \begin{pmatrix} \boxed{A_1} & & & \\ 0 & \boxed{A_2} & & \\ 0 & 0 & \boxed{} & \\ 0 & 0 & 0 & \boxed{A_p} \end{pmatrix},$$

where the entries above the block diagonal submatrices are 0's and 1's.

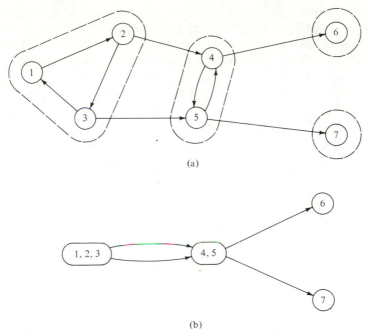

Figure 2.6   (a) Diagraph *G* and strong components. (b) *G* after contraction of strong components.

A *directed tree* is either rooted to a node or from a node. A *tree rooted from node i* is a tree in which the in-degree of *i* is zero, and the in-degree of each of the other nodes is at most one. *A tree rooted to node i* is a tree in which the out-degree of *i* is zero and the out-degree of the other nodes is at most one. A *directed spanning tree* is just as its name suggests.

A directed graph is called *acyclic* if it contains no directed cycles. Each strong component of an acyclic digraph contains exactly one node. It follows from Proposition 6.1 that there exists a numbering of the nodes such that the adjacency matrix is upper triangular, i.e., zero below the main diagonal. This observation is equivalent to the following proposition.

Proposition 6.2   A directed graph is acyclic if and only if its nodes can be numbered in such a way that for all arcs (i, j), $i < j$.

In order to show that the nodes of an acyclic graph can be so ordered, one first observes that there is at least one node with in-degree zero. Such a node is found, numbered 1, and all arcs incident from the node are deleted. A node with in-degree zero is found in the resulting subgraph. This node is numbered 2, and all arcs incident from it are deleted, and so on.

This procedure can be implemented by a computation whose complexity is $O(n^2)$. We suppose that the graph is described by its adjacency matrix A and that the rows and columns of this matrix are ordered according to the given arbitrary numbering of the nodes. Let $v(j)$ denote the new number of node j.

Initially $d_j^{(in)}$ is computed for all nodes j, by forming the sum of the entries in column j of matrix A. A node k for which $d_k^{(in)} = 0$ is found, and $v(k)$ is set to 1. The in-degrees are revised by subtracting the entries in row k of A, and the process is repeated. This is summarized below.

RENUMBERING THE NODES OF AN ACYCLIC DIGRAPH

Step 0   *(Start)*

Set $d_j^{(in)} = \sum_{i=1}^{n} a_{ij}, \qquad j = 1, 2, \ldots, n.$

Set $N = \{1, 2, \ldots, n\}.$
Set $m = 1.$

Step 1   *(Detection of Node with Zero In-Degree)*
Find $k \in N$ such that $d_k^{(in)} = 0$. If there is no such k, stop; the digraph is not acyclic.
Set $v(k) = m.$
Set $m = m + 1.$
Set $N = N - k.$
If $N = \emptyset$, stop; the computation is completed.

Step 2   *(Revision of In-Degrees)*
Set $d_j^{(in)} = d_j^{(in)} - a_{kj}, \quad$ for all $j \in N.$
Return to Step 1.//

The complexity of the computation is estimated as follows. Step 0 requires $n(n - 1)$ additions. Step 1 requires at most n comparisons to determine k, and various other operations independent of n. Step 2 requires at most $n - 1$ subtractions. Step 0, which is $O(n^2)$, is performed exactly once. Steps 1 and 2, which are both $O(n)$, are performed at most n times. It follows that the overall complexity is $O(n^2)$.

Some of the definitions given in this section are illustrated by examples in Figure 2.7.

PROBLEMS

6.1   Devise a procedure for determining the strong components of a digraph from its adjacency matrix.

6.2   Show that if C is a directed cycle of a digraph G, then the columns of the node-arc incidence matrix corresponding to the arcs in C are linearly dependent, with respect to addition and multiplication in the field of reals.

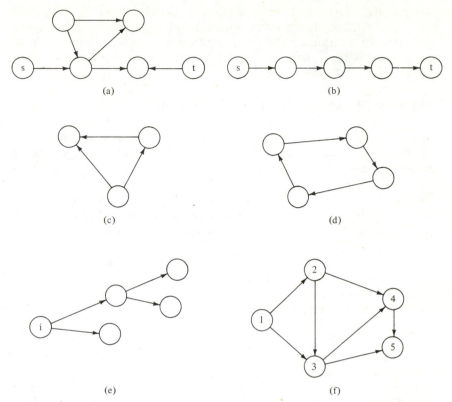

Figure 2.7   (a) (s, t) path with repeated node. (b) Minimal (s, t) directed path. (c) Cycle. (d) Directed cycle. (e) Tree rooted from i. (f) An acyclic digraph.

7
Cocycles and Directed Cocycles

Let $G = (N, A)$ be a graph, or a directed graph in which the directions of the arcs are ignored. A subset $C \subseteq A$, such that $G' = (N, A - C)$ contains more components than G, is a *separating set* of G. A minimal separating set is a *cocycle* of G. (The reason for the term "cocycle" is evident in the next section.)

For any cocycle C, there exists a partition of the nodes of the graph into two sets S and T, such that C contains just those arcs extending between S and T. The deletion of the arcs in C destroys any (s, t) path, where $s \in S$ and $t \in T$.

However, the converse is not true. That is, given an arbitrary node partition S, T, the set of arcs extending between S and T is not necessarily a cocycle. (Consider a three-node graph with arcs $(1, 2)$, $(1, 3)$. The partition $S = \{1\}$, $T = \{2, 3\}$ determines a nonminimal separating set.) We call a separating set determined by such a partition a *cutset* and we may refer to it by any one of the node partitions S, T which determines it. An (s, t)-*cutset* is any cutset (S, T), where $s \in S$ and $t \in T$.

Proposition 7.1   Every cutset is a union of disjoint cocycles.

A cutset or cocycle of a digraph in which all the arcs are oriented in the same direction, i.e., either all from S to T or all from T to S, is called a *directed cutset* or *directed cocycle*.

Theorem 7.2   (*Minty*)   Let G be a directed graph with a distinguished arc (s, t). Then, for any painting of the arcs green, yellow, and red, with (s, t) painted yellow, exactly one of the following alternatives holds:

(1) (s, t) is contained in a cycle of yellow and green arcs, in which all yellow arcs have the same direction.
(2) (s, t) is contained in a cocycle of yellow and red arcs, in which all yellow arcs have the same direction.

PROOF   Think of the graph as a network of streets, in which green arcs are two-way streets, yellow arcs are one-way streets (according to the directions of the arcs), and red arcs are streets blocked to traffic. Now starting at the street intersection represented by node t, either it is possible for traffic to move from t to s, or it is not. If there is some way, then there exists a minimal (t, s) path of yellow and green arcs, with all yellow arcs directed from t to s. This path, together with the arc (s, t), forms a cycle satisfying condition (1).

If there is no way for traffic to get from t to s then a cocycle satisfying the condition (2) can be constructed as follows. Let T be the set of all nodes accessible to traffic from t and let S be the complementary set. There can be neither yellow arcs directed from T to S nor green arcs between S and T in either direction. Otherwise, one or more of the nodes in S would be accessible to traffic from T, contrary to assumption. It follows that all arcs between S and T must be red arcs, in either direction, or yellow arcs including (s, t), directed from S to T. By Proposition 7.1, the (S, T) cutset contains a cocycle satisfying condition (2).//

8

Planarity and Duality

A graph G is called *planar* if it can be drawn so that its nodes are points in the plane and each arc (i, j) is drawn so that it intersects no other arcs and

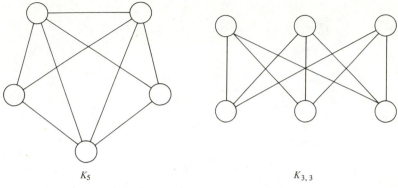

K_5 $K_{3,3}$

Figure 2.8   Kuratowski graphs

passes through no other nodes. Example of nonplanar graphs are the Kuratowski graphs K_5, $K_{3,3}$ shown in Figure 2.8. Every nonplanar graph contains one or the other of these Kuratowski graphs, in the sense that it can be obtained by contraction and deletion of arcs.

The drawing of a planar graph in the plane is called a *plane graph*. (A plane graph is not a graph; it is a drawing.) We refer to the regions defined by a plane graph as its *faces*, the unbounded region being the *exterior face*. Given a plane graph G, its geometric dual G^* is constructed as follows. Place a node in each face, including the exterior face. If two faces have an arc e in their common boundary, join the nodes of the corresponding faces by an arc e^* crossing only e. The result may be a plane graph with loops or with multiple edges, as seen in Figure 2.9. In any case, the graph or multigraph G^D for which G^* is a plane graph is said to be a *dual* of G.

The plane graph of G is not unique, and so its dual G^D is not unique, as shown in Figure 2.10. Yet we have the habit of referring to "the" dual of a graph G, and in practice there is not much harm in this.

The procedure for dualizing digraphs is essentially the same as for graphs, except that we must be able to assign directions to the arcs in the geometric dual. We do this as follows. Imagine that the arc e^* dual to the arc

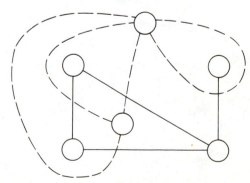

Figure 2.9   A plane graph and its geometric dual

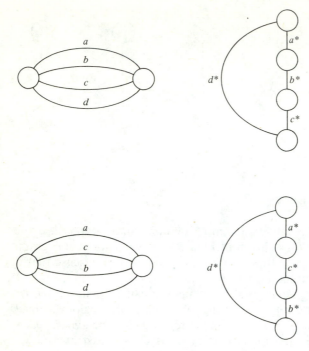

Figure 2.10   Two plane graphs of the same graph and their duals

e is rotated clockwise in the plane. Place an arrowhead on the end of e^* which would first touch the arrowhead of e. This rule is illustrated in Figure 2.11.

For our purposes, the most significant property of dualization is that it interchanges cycles and cocycles. The proof of the following theorem is quite nontrivial, and we refer the reader to the literature.

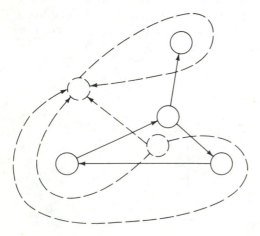

Figure 2.11   Dualization of digraph

Theorem 8.1 Let C be a subset of the arcs of G and $C*$ be the dual subset of arcs of G^D. If C is a cycle, directed cycle, cocycle, or directed cocycle in G, then $C*$ is, respectively, a cocycle, directed cocycle, cycle, or directed cycle in G^D, and conversely.

We often have occasion to deal with graphs with two designated *terminal nodes*, s and t. In some cases, it is possible to construct a dual graph with corresponding terminal nodes $s*$ and $t*$ by the following procedure.

The graph G is augmented by adding a special arc $e = (t, s)$, to obtain the graph $G + e$. (G may already have an arc (t, s), in which case e is parallel to it.) If $G + e$ is planar, then $(G + e)^D$ is obtained and the arc $e*$, dual to e, is by definition directed from $s*$ to $t*$. Now note the relationship between G^D and $(G + e)^D - e*$. The addition of e to G simply subdivides into two parts some face F of G that has nodes s and t on its boundary. Hence, G^D differs from $(G + e)^D - e*$ only in that the node in G^D corresponding to F is split into two nodes $s*$ and $t*$. See Figure 2.12.

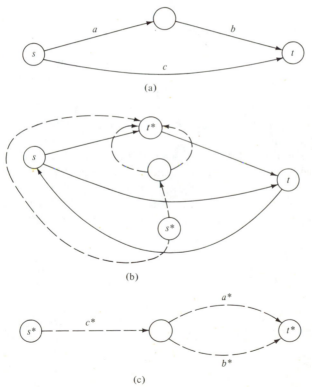

Figure 2.12   (a) Digraph G with terminals s, t. (b) Addition of (t, s) to G and dualization. (c) Dual digraph $G*$ with terminals $s*$, $t*$.

By defining e^* to be directed from s^* to t^* rather than the opposite, we obtain the following results. Suppose C is a directed path from s to t, with no repeated nodes. Then $C + e$ is a directed cycle in $G + e$ and, by Theorem 8.1, $(C + e)^* = C^* + e^*$ is a directed cocycle in $(G + e)^D$. But then C^* is a directed (s^*, t^*)-cocycle in $(G + e)^D - e^*$. Thus a directed (s, t) path in G is found to correspond to a directed (s^*, t^*) cocycle in $(G + e)^D - e^*$. The reader can employ Theorem 8.1 to work out other correspondences.

This technique of two-terminal dualization is obviously valid only if the graph G remains planar after the addition of the arc $e = (t, s)$. A graph for which this is true is said to be (s, t) *planar*.

The operations of contraction and deletion are also interchanged by dualization. That is, the contraction of an arc in G corresponds to its deletion in the dual, and vice versa. Further reference to this property is made in Chapter 7.

9

Eulerian and Hamiltonian Graphs

Graph theory is said to have been founded in 1736 when Euler settled a famous unsolved problem known as the Königsberg Bridge Problem. Two islands were linked to each other and to the banks of the Pregel River by seven bridges. The question posed was whether it was possible to begin at any of the four land areas, walk across each bridge exactly once, and return to the starting point.

The general question, for a given graph G, is whether there exists a closed path which contains each arc exactly once. Such a path, if it exists, we call an *Euler path*, and we say the graph is a *Euler graph*, or *Eulerian*. Euler was able to answer the question negatively for the specific Königsberg graph of Figure 2.13 and also to resolve the issue for all graphs, as follows.

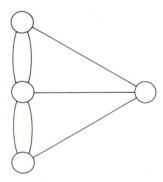

Figure 2.13   Graph of the Königsberg Bridge Problem

Theorem 9.1 A graph (or multigraph) G is Eulerian if and only if G is connected and each node of G has even degree.

PROOF If G is Eulerian, then clearly it is connected and each node has even degree. (An Euler path enters each node exactly as many times as it leaves and contains each arc exactly once, implying the degree of each node is even.)

The converse is proved by induction on the number of arcs. The theorem is true for graphs with zero arcs. Assume it is true for graphs with $m - 1$ arcs. A connected graph with $m \geq 1$ arcs and in which each node has even degree must contain a cycle C. (Show this!) The deletion of C from G produces a graph with one or more components, each of which is Eulerian by inductive assumption. An Euler path for G is formed by joining C with the Euler paths of these components. (The reader should work out a detailed plan for the order in which the various parts of the Euler path are traversed, if this is not clear to him.)//

Sir William Hamilton once investigated the existence of a cycle passing through each vertex of a dodecahedron exactly once. We call a cycle that passes through each node of a graph exactly once a *Hamilton cycle*, and the graph which contains it a *Hamilton graph*, or *Hamiltonian*. In contrast with the extremely tidy necessary and sufficient conditions for Euler graphs, Hamilton graphs seem to defy effective characterization. There are, however, a few useful sufficient conditions. For example:

Theorem 9.2 (*Chvátal*) Let G be a graph with $n \geq 3$ nodes and no loops or multiple arcs in which the nodes are numbered so that $d_1 \leq d_2 \leq \ldots \leq d_n$. G is Hamiltonian if

$$d_k \leq k \Rightarrow d_{n-k} \geq n - k, \qquad \text{for } 1 \leq k \leq \frac{n}{2}.$$

The reader is referred to Chvátal's paper for a proof.

Let S be a set and $\mathscr{S} = \{S_1, S_2, \ldots, S_n\}$ be a family of distinct non-empty subsets of S whose union is S. The *intersection graph of* $\mathscr{S}$ is a graph whose nodes are identified with sets in $\mathscr{S}$, with S_i and S_j adjacent whenever $i \neq j$ and $S_i \cap S_j \neq \emptyset$. A graph G is an *intersection graph on* S if there exists a family $\mathscr{S}$ of subsets of S, with G the intersection graph of $\mathscr{S}$.

Theorem 9.3 Every graph $G = (N, A)$ is an intersection graph.

PROOF Let $S = N \cup A$ and for every node j of G, let S_j be the union of $\{j\}$ and the set of arcs incident to j.//

Recall that an arc of a graph is defined as a subset of two nodes. Hence, for a given graph $G = (N, A)$, we can let $S = N$ and $\mathscr{S} = A$. The intersection graph of A is called the *line graph of G*, denoted $L(G)$. A graph G' is called a *line graph* if there exists a graph G, with $G' = L(G)$. Sometimes $L(G)$ is called the "arc-to-node dual" of G. Hence a line graph is a graph for which a node-to-arc dual exists. Examples of graphs and their line graphs are shown in Figure 2.14.

One characterization of line graphs is indicated by the following theorem, the proof of which is left for the reader.

Theorem 9.4 G is a line graph if and only if the arcs of G can be partitioned into complete subgraphs in such a way that no node lies in more than two of the subgraphs.

Some relations between line graphs, Euler graphs, and Hamilton graphs are indicated by the following theorems, the proofs of which are left to the reader.

Theorem 9.5 G is Eulerian if and only if $L(G)$ is Hamiltonian.

Theorem 9.6   If G is Eulerian, then $L(G)$ is Eulerian.

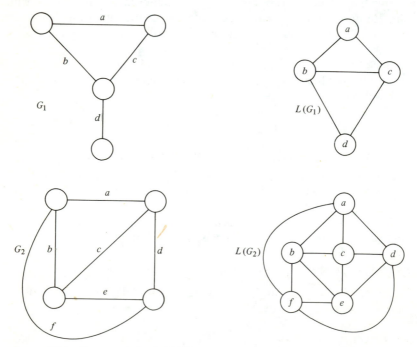

Figure 2.14   Two graphs and their line graphs

PROBLEMS

9.1   Prove that every connected graph with m arcs possesses a closed path of length not exceeding $2m$ which passes through each arc at least once.
9.2   Formulate the equivalent of Euler's conditions for digraphs.
9.3   Prove that a bipartite graph with an odd number of nodes is not Hamiltonian.
9.4   Prove Theorem 9.5.
9.5   Prove Theorem 9.6.

10
Linear Programming Problems

The general problem of linear programming is to find values for real variables $x_1, x_2, \ldots, x_n$ which will yield an extreme value (maximum or minimum) for a linear function

$$z = \sum_{j=1}^{n} c_j x_j$$

subject to the satisfaction of constraining linear relations,

$$
\left.
\begin{array}{ll}
\sum_{j=1}^{n} a_{ij} x_j \geq b_i, & i = 1, 2, \ldots, p, \\[2mm]
\sum_{j=1}^{n} a_{ij} x_j = b_i, & i = p + 1, p + 2, \ldots, m, \\[2mm]
x_j \geq 0, & j = 1, 2, \ldots, q, \\[2mm]
x_j \text{ unrestricted}, & j = q + 1, q + 2, \ldots, n.
\end{array}
\right\}
\qquad (10.1)
$$

In an econometric or operations research context, each variable x_j is identified with an "activity" within a business enterprise or economic system, e.g., the purchase of a particular raw material or the production of a certain good or service. A set of variables constitutes a "program" of operation in terms of "levels" for the various activities. (Note that it is quite natural for certain variables to be nonnegative; e.g., one cannot produce a negative amount of a good or service.) And since the constraints on the choice of a program are linear, the term "linear programming" is used. We shall, however, use the term "linear program" to refer to a linear programming problem, rather than a solution to such a problem.

The reader should be familiar with the various techniques for transforming linear programs from one form to another. For example, an inequality of the form

$$\sum_{j=1}^{n} a_{ij}x_j \geq b_i$$

is equivalent to a linear equality of the form

$$\sum_{j=1}^{n} a_{ij}x_j - s_i = b_i,$$

where $s_i \geq 0$ is introduced as a nonnegative *slack variable*. Conversely, a linear equality

$$\sum_{j=1}^{n} a_{ij}x_j = b_i$$

is equivalent to the two inequalities

$$\sum_{j=1}^{n} a_{ij}x_j \geq b_i$$

and

$$-\sum_{j=1}^{n} a_{ij}x_j \geq -b_i.$$

A variable x_j which is not sign restricted can be replaced by two variables x_j^+ and x_j^-, where

$$x_j = x_j^+ - x_j^-,$$

$$x_j^+ \geq 0,$$

and

$$x_j^- \geq 0.$$

A problem calling for the maximization of $c_1x_1 + \ldots + c_nx_n$ is the same as one calling for the minimization of $-c_1x_1 - \ldots - c_nx_n$, and conversely.

It follows that any linear programming problem is equivalent to a problem involving only equality constraints in nonnegative variables. That is, in matrix notation,

minimize

$$z = cx$$

subject to

$$Ax = b, \tag{10.2}$$

$$x \geq 0,$$

where $c = (c_1, c_2, \ldots, c_n)$ is the *cost vector*, cx is the *objective function*, $A = (a_{ij})$ is an $m \times n$ *coefficient matrix*, and $b = (b_1, b_2, \ldots, b_m)$ is the *constraint vector*. (We avoid indicating whether vectors are "row" vectors or "column" vectors, assuming that the reader will make the correct interpretation from context. Thus in (10.2), c is understood to be a $1 \times n$ row vector, x an $n \times 1$ column vector, and b an $m \times 1$ column vector.)

It is a relatively easy matter to minimize a linear function subject to linear equations. At first glance, one might think that the solution of linear programming problems should not be too much more involved, just because the variables are constrained to be nonnegative. But, in fact, the situation is very much more complicated. We will now proceed to introduce some definitions and concepts which are fundamental to the theory of linear programming, before proceeding to a description of the simplex method of solution.

A vector $\bar{x} \geq 0$ for which $A\bar{x} = b$ is said to be a *feasible solution* to (10.2). A feasible solution x^* is an *optimal solution* if there exists no other feasible solution $\bar{x}$ such that $c\bar{x} < cx^*$. There may be feasible solutions but no (finite) optimal solution. (See Problem 10.2.)

We recall from linear algebra that p vectors $x^1, x^2, \ldots, x^p$ are said to be *linearly dependent* if there exist scalars $\alpha_1, \alpha_2, \ldots, \alpha_p$, not all zero, such that

$$\alpha_1 x^1 + \alpha_2 x^2 + \ldots + \alpha_p x^p = 0. \tag{10.3}$$

Vectors which are not linearly dependent are linearly *independent*. In any linearly dependent set there is at least one vector which can be expressed as a linear combination of the others. For example, if $\alpha_1 \neq 0$ in (10.3), then

$$x^1 = -\frac{1}{\alpha_1}(\alpha_2 x^2 + \alpha_3 x^3 + \ldots + \alpha_p x^p).$$

Also recall that the maximum number of linearly independent rows of a matrix A is equal to the maximum number of linearly independent columns, and this is called the *rank* of A. Assume that the rank of the $m \times n$ matrix A is m, where $m \leq n$. If this is not so, one or more of the rows of A can be expressed as linear combinations of the others. Depending upon the coefficients b_i, the constraints represented by these rows are either redundant and can be eliminated from the problem, or else they represent inconsistencies such that the linear system $Ax = b$ has no solution.

Any m linearly independent columns of A will be referred to as a *basis* of the linear system $Ax = b$. Let B denote the submatrix of A corresponding to a given basis. The m variables identified with the columns of B are called *basic variables*; they constitute a subvector x^B of x. The remaining variables are called *secondary variables*, and they constitute the subvector x^R, complementary to x^B in x.

If, for a basis B, we suppress the $n - m$ secondary variables, the linear system $Bx^B = b$ is obtained, and this system possesses a unique solution $x^B = B^{-1}b$. The *basic solution associated with B* is defined as $x^B = B^{-1}b, x^R = 0$, but often we refer to the basic solution as simply x^B. A basic solution x^B which is feasible (i.e., $x^B \geq 0$) we call a *basic feasible solution* and a basic solution which is optimal we call a *basic optimal solution*.

Theorem 10.1 If there exists a feasible solution to (10.2), there exists a basic feasible solution.

PROOF   Similar to that of Theorem 10.2.//

Theorem 10.2 If there exists an optimal solution to (10.2), there exists a basic optimal solution.

PROOF   Suppose x^* is an optimal solution, where, without loss of generality, $x_j^* > 0$ for $j = 1, 2, \ldots, p$ and $x_j = 0$ for $j = p + 1, p + 2, \ldots, n$. If columns 1 through p of A are linearly independent, we can choose $m - p$ additional linearly independent columns so as to form a basis, and x^* is the basic solution associated with this basis.

Now suppose columns 1 through p of A are not linearly independent. Then there exists a vector α such that $A\alpha = 0$, where $\alpha_j \neq 0$ for at least one $j \leq p$, and $\alpha_j = 0, j \geq p$. Choose

$$\frac{1}{\varepsilon} = \max_{1 \leq j \leq p} \frac{|\alpha_j|}{x_j^*}.$$

Then both $x^* + \varepsilon\alpha$ and $x^* - \varepsilon\alpha$ are feasible solutions and at least one of them has at least one fewer nonzero variable than x^*. Moreover, it must be the case that $c\alpha = 0$ and both $x^* + \varepsilon\alpha$ and $x^* - \varepsilon\alpha$ are optimal solutions. (If this were not the case, one or the other would be less costly than x^*, contrary to the assumption x^* is optimal.) The procedure is repeated on whichever optimal solution has a smaller number of nonzero variables than x^*. Eventually (after no more than $p - m$ repetitions), an optimal solution is obtained in which the nonzero variables are identified with a linearly independent subset of columns of A. At this point a basic optimal solution can be constructed.//

PROBLEMS

10.1   (Diet Problem)   A dietician is concerned with no issue other than that of providing adequate nourishment at the lowest possible cost. There are n foods to choose from, and m nutrients that must be accounted for. Let c_j denote the cost of one unit of the jth food, b_i the minimum daily requirement of the ith nutrient, and a_{ij} the amount of the ith nutrient contained in one unit of the jth food. Formulate the problem as a linear program. How many foods need be purchased for a minimum-cost diet?

10.2   For each of the following linear programs, determine the number (i.e., none, one, or an unbounded number) of solutions, feasible solutions, and optimal solutions.

(a)   minimize $z = x_1$
      subject to
$$\begin{aligned} x_1 + x_2 &= 1 \\ x_1 \quad\;\; &= 2 \\ x_1, x_2 &\geq 0. \end{aligned}$$

(b)   minimize $z = x_1$
      subject to
$$\begin{aligned} x_1 + x_2 &= 1 \\ x_1 \quad\;\; &= 2 \\ x_1 &\geq 0 \\ x_2 \text{ arbitrary.} \end{aligned}$$

(c)   minimize $z = x_1$
      subject to
$$\begin{aligned} x_1 + x_2 + x_3 &= 1 \\ x_1 \quad\;\; + x_3 &= 2 \\ x_1 &\geq 0 \\ x_2, x_3 \text{ arbitrary.} \end{aligned}$$

(d)   minimize $z = -x_1$
      subject to
$$\begin{aligned} x_1 + x_2 + x_3 &= 1 \\ x_1 \quad\;\; + x_3 &= 2 \\ x_1 &\geq 0 \\ x_2, x_3 \text{ arbitrary.} \end{aligned}$$

10.3   Given any basic feasible solution x^* of the system $Ax = b$, does there exist a cost vector such that x^* is the unique optimal solution?

11
The Simplex Method

Theorem 10.2 shows that the search for an optimal solution can be narrowed to a search among basic solutions. For an $m \times n$ linear system, with $m \leq n$, there are no more than

$$\binom{n}{m} = \frac{n!}{m!(n-m)!}$$

bases, and for each basis there is a unique and readily computable basic solution. Thus we have at least succeeded in reducing the linear programming problem to a finite combinatorial problem.

The simplex method (named after the simplex, a geometric structure) of George Dantzig is a method for carrying out the search for an optimal basic solution. The computation proceeds from one basic feasible solution to another, with monotonic improvement in the objective function. When no further improvement can be made, the final basic solution is optimal.

Suppose we are given a linear program in $n - m$ variables and m constraints in inequality form, i.e.,

$$Ax \leq b,$$

where, for convenience, we assume $b_i \geq 0$, $i = 1, 2, \ldots, m$. We can introduce m slack variables to convert the constraints to equalities. For convenience, let us designate these slacks as $x_1, x_2, \ldots, x_m$, and renumber the remaining variables accordingly, Then we have a linear program in the form of (10.2):

minimize $z = \qquad c_{m+1}x_{m+1} + \ldots + c_n x_n$

subject to

$$
\left.
\begin{aligned}
x_1 \qquad\qquad + a_{1,m+1}x_{m+1} + \ldots + a_{1n}x_n &= b_1 \\
x_2 \qquad\quad + a_{2,m+1}x_{m+1} + \ldots + a_{2n}x_n &= b_2 \\
\vdots\qquad\qquad\qquad\qquad\qquad\qquad & \\
x_m + a_{m,m+1}x_{m+1} + \ldots + a_{mn}x_n &= b_m \\
x_j \geq 0, \qquad j = 1, 2, \ldots, n. &
\end{aligned}
\right\} \tag{11.1}
$$

An initial basic feasible solution is $x^B = (x_1, x_2, \ldots, x_m) = (b_1, b_2, \ldots, b_m)$. The first m columns of A are the initial basis B for the simplex computation.

We proceed to a new basic feasible solution by choosing to bring a nonbasic column s into B. As a result, we must remove some column r from B. (Thus, two successive bases in the simplex method always differ by exactly two columns.)

Intuitively, we believe that we should bring in a new column s for which $c_s < 0$, because this should result in a decrease in the value of the objective function. (As a nonbasic variable, $x_s = 0$, but as a basic variable x_s may take on a strictly positive value.) Suppose we choose such a column s, and we try to bring it into the basis in place of column r.

The change in basis is effected by a *pivot step*, for which a_{rs} is the *pivot element*. In order to make the basis change, the pivot element a_{rs} must be nonzero. If $a_{rs} = 0$, then column s is linearly dependent on the $m - 1$ columns $1, 2, \ldots, r - 1, r + 1, \ldots, m$, and the proposed change in basis is not possible.

The pivot step is carried out as follows. First divide equation r by a_{rs}. This changes the coefficient of x_s to unity in equation r. Then subtract a_{is} times equation r from the ith constraint equation, for $i \neq r$. This changes the coefficient of x_s to zero in each of these equations. Finally, subtract c_s

times equation r from the equation for the objection function

$$- z + c_{m+1}x_{m+1} + \ldots + c_n x_n = 0. \tag{11.2}$$

This changes the coefficient of x_s to zero in equation (11.2) and changes the right-hand side to the negative of the new value of z.

The result of the pivot computation is, in effect, a reformulation of the linear program:

minimize

$$z = \bar{c}_r x_r \qquad + \bar{c}_{m+1}x_{m+1} + \ldots + \bar{c}_{s-1}x_{s-1}$$

$$+ \bar{c}_{s+7}x_{s+7} + \ldots + \bar{c}_n x_n$$

subject to

$$x_1 + \bar{a}_{1r}x_r \qquad + \bar{a}_{1,m+1}x_{m+1} + \ldots + \bar{a}_{1,s-1}x_{s-1}$$

$$+ \bar{a}_{1,s+7}x_{s+7} + \ldots + \bar{a}_{1n}x_n = \bar{b}_1$$

$$\bar{a}_{rr}x_r \qquad + \bar{a}_{r,m+1}x_{m+1} + \ldots + \bar{a}_{r,s-1}x_{s-1}$$

$$+ \ \left(x_s + \bar{a}_{s,s+7}x_{s+7}\right) \tag{11.3}$$

$$+ \ldots + \bar{a}_{sn}x_n = \bar{b}_s$$

$$\bar{a}_{mr}x_r \qquad + x_m + \bar{a}_{m,m+1}x_{m+1} + \ldots + \bar{a}_{m,s-1}x_{s-1}$$

$$+ \bar{a}_{ms+2} + \ldots + \bar{a}_{mn}x_n = \bar{b}_m.$$

$$x_j \geqq 0, \qquad j = 1, 2, \ldots, n.$$

The new basic solution is feasible if and only if $\bar{b}_i \geq 0$, for all i. Notice that $\bar{b}_1, \bar{b}_2 \ \cdots$

$$\bar{b}_r = \frac{b_r}{a_{rs}}$$

and

$$\bar{b}_i = b_i - a_{is}\frac{b_r}{a_{rs}}, \qquad i \neq r.$$

We have assumed that $b_i \geq 0$, for all i. If $b_r > 0$, it is clear that a_{rs} must not be negative else $\bar{b}_r < 0$. (The annoying case in which $x_r = b_r = 0$ is discussed later.) So let us demand that a_{rs} be strictly positive. But then if

$$a_{is}\frac{b_r}{a_{rs}} > b_i,$$

$\bar{b}_i$ will be negative. Accordingly, we must demand that

$$\frac{b_r}{a_{rs}} \le \frac{b_i}{a_{is}}, \quad \text{whenever } a_{is} > 0.$$

We restate these observations as follows.

RATIO TEST

If column s is to be brought into the basis, then to preserve feasibility we must choose as our pivot element a_{rs}, where $a_{rs} > 0$ and

$$\frac{b_r}{a_{rs}} = \min_{a_{is} > 0} \left\{ \frac{b_i}{a_{is}} \right\}. \tag{11.4}$$

Now let us see how the objective function is affected by a pivot step. Equation (11.2) becomes

$$ -z + \bar{c}_r x_r + \bar{c}_{m+1} x_{m+1} + \ldots + \bar{c}_{s-1} x_{s-1} + \bar{c}_{s+7} x_{s+7} + \ldots + \bar{c}_n x_n = \bar{b}_0, $$

where

$$ \bar{b}_0 = -c_s \frac{b_r}{a_{rs}} $$

is the negative of the new value of z. Since b_r / a_{rs} can be assumed to be positive, the value of the objective function is decreased only if $c_s < 0$, as we intuitively expected. Algebraically, $\bar{c} = c - c^B B^{-1} A$, where c^B is the subvector of c identified with the new basis B.

It is now clear that we can renumber variables and constraints to put (11.3) into exactly the form of (11.1). A new pivot element a_{rs} can be chosen and we can proceed to still another basic feasible solution.

Thus, the essence of the simplex method is as follows. Start with any feasible basis. Choose a nonbasic column s for which $c_s < 0$. Choose a pivot element a_{rs} by the ratio test (11.4), and perform a pivot step to obtain a new feasible basis. Repeat the procedure until a final feasible basis is obtained for which each cost coefficient is nonnegative. This is an optimal feasible basis, since no increase in the values of the nonbasic variables can further reduce the value of z.

Each feasible basis uniquely determines a value of z. At each pivot step, z is decreased by a finite amount (provided $x_r > 0$ for that pivot step). Thus no feasible basis can be repeated. Since there are a finite number of possible bases, the procedure must terminate with an optimal solution after a finite number of pivot steps.

A number of technical questions still remain. How does one find an initial feasible basis? (Recall that we conveniently assumed that the constraints were of the form $Ax \leq b$, with $b \geq 0$.) What if there is no feasible solution at all? What if, having chosen column s, there is no positive element a_{rs}? What if the ratio test selects a pivot element a_{rs} for which $x_r = 0$? Does not this void the argument of finite convergence? Have we really proved that the final feasible basis is optimal? What if there is no finite optimal solution? How does that become apparent?

One technique for obtaining an initial feasible solution is as follows. First put the constraints into equality form. Multiply by -1 any constraint equation for which $b_i < 0$. Then introduce "artificial" variables $y_1, y_2, \ldots, y_m$, to obtain the system $Ax + Iy = b$. Give each of these variables a very large coefficient M in the objective function (assuming minimization). The artificial variables provide an initial basic feasible solution. Because of their great cost, the artificial variables eventually all become nonbasic. If this is not so, there is no feasible solution to the original problem.

The preceding is sometimes called the "big M" method. Other, more sophisticated techniques appear in the literature.

Suppose column s contains no strictly positive element a_{rs}. Then x_s can be increased without bound. That is, increasing x_s does not cause any basic variable to decrease in value. If $c_s < 0$, the problem does not have a finite optimum.

Now suppose the pivot element a_{rs} is chosen according to the ratio test, but $b_r = 0$. Then we have encountered *degeneracy*. This occurs when the constraint vector b is a linear combination of fewer than m of the basis columns (in fact, precisely those columns corresponding to nonzero basic variables.)

In this situation none of the variables change values with the basis change. It is indeed possible that the computation can "circle", repeating bases and making no progress to an optimal solution.

In practice, degeneracy seldom results in circling. Moreover, there are several schemes for insuring that no basis is repeated, so that finite convergence is assured. Possibly the mose elegant of these involves a "lexicographic" condition which is incorporated into the ratio test. However, to describe this scheme would require more space than the issue deserves here.

We should mention that nearly all of the linear programs formulated in later chapters are highly degenerate. Yet this creates no difficulty for the algorithms we shall describe.

The argument that the final feasible basis is optimal is intuitively compelling. And, indeed, our intuition is further strengthened by the geometric interpretations presented in Section 12. A proper proof is provided by duality theory in Section 13.

PROBLEMS

11.1 For any system $Ax = b, x \geq 0$, show that it is possible to pass from any given basic feasible solution x^1 to any other basic feasible solution x^2 by means of a sequence of pivot steps, each of which preserves feasibility. (*Hint*: Consider choosing a cost function for which x^2 is optimal.)

11.2 Carry out the simplex computation for each of the following:

(a)   minimize $z = -3x_1 - 2x_2$
     subject to

$$-2x_1 + x_2 \leq 1$$
$$x_1 \qquad \leq 2$$
$$x_1 + x_2 \leq 3$$
$$x_1, x_2 \geq 0.$$

(b)   minimize $z = -3x_1 - 2x_2$
     subject to

$$-2x_1 + x_2 \leq 1$$
$$x_1 - 2x_2 \leq 0$$
$$-x_1 - x_2 \leq -2$$
$$x_1, x_2 \geq 0.$$

12

Geometric Interpretation

It is often worthwhile to give a geometric interpretation to linear programming problems and the computational procedures which are applied to them. In this section we provide a very brief and intuitive introduction to this topic.

Consider the program given in Problem 11.2a.

maximize $z = 3x_1 + 2x_2$
subject to

$$\left.\begin{array}{r} -2x_1 + x_2 \leq 1 \\ x_1 \qquad \leq 2 \\ x_1 + x_2 \leq 3 \\ x_1, x_2 \geq 0. \end{array}\right\} \qquad (12.1)$$

We draw straight lines in the Euclidean plane whose equations are the constraints of the linear program (including nonnegativity constraints on x_1, x_2) in "tight" form ($\leq$ replaced by $=$). On each of these lines we indicate

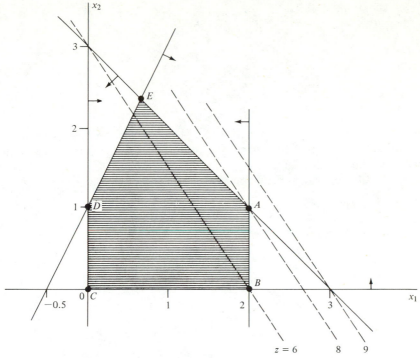

Figure 2.15   Representation of program (12.1)

by an arrow the half-plane that is feasible with respect to the constraint in question. The intersection of all these half-planes is a polygon, whose boundary and interior contain all feasible solutions to the linear program, as shown in Figure 2.15.

The object of the linear programming problem is to find a point on or within the polygon for which $3x_1 + 2x_2$ is maximum. Consider the family of parallel straight lines

$$3x_1 + 2x_2 = z,$$

where z is a parameter. The maximum value of z will be obtained if z is chosen so that the straight line passes through point A, as shown in the figure.

The coordinates of A are determined by the two tight constraints

$$\left. \begin{aligned} x_1 \quad &= 2 \\ x_1 + x_2 &= 3. \end{aligned} \right\} \tag{12.2}$$

A is an *extreme point* or *vertex* of the feasible polygon.

Now consider the program given in Problem 11.2b.

maximize $z = 3x_1 + 2x_2$
subject to

$$-2x_1 + x_2 \leq 1$$
$$x_1 - 2x_2 \leq 0$$
$$-x_1 - x_2 \leq -2$$
$$x_1, x_2 \geq 0.$$

When a similar drawing is made for this problem, the result is as shown in Figure 2.16. The region of feasible solutions is unbounded, and there is no finite maximum value for z.

Finally, consider the problem

maximize $z = 3x_1 + 2x_2$
subject to

$$2x_1 - x_2 \leq -1$$
$$-x_1 + 2x_2 \leq 0$$
$$x_1, x_2 \geq 0.$$

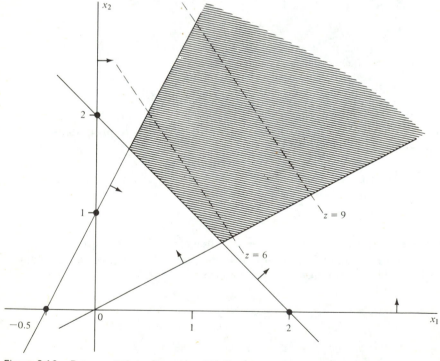

Figure 2.16   Representation of program (12.2)

When a drawing is made for this problem (a task we leave to the reader), it is seen that the feasible region is empty. The constraints are contradictory and the program has no feasible solution.

These concepts generalize naturally to problems with n variables and their representations in n-dimensional space. For $n = 2$ the tight form of a constraint defines a straight line, for $n = 3$ it defines a plane, and for $n \geq 4$ a *hyperplane*. The feasible region on one side of a hyperplane is a *half-space*. The intersection of the half-spaces defines a *convex polytope*. If the convex polytope is bounded, it is a *convex polyhedron*, the n-dimensional generalization of a convex polygon.

A set of points in n-space is said to be *convex* if, for any two points x^1 and x^2 in the set, all points on the line segment joining x^1 and x^2 are also in the set. An example of a nonconvex region in the plane is shown in Figure 2.17. Algebraically, this condition is stated as follows. A set C is convex if $x^1 \in C, x^2 \in C, 0 \leq \lambda \leq 1$ implies $\lambda x^1 + (1 - \lambda)x^2 \in C$.

A vector $\lambda x^1 + (1 - \lambda)x^2$, where $0 \leq \lambda \leq 1$, is said to be a *convex combination* of the vectors x^1 and x^2. It is easy to see that for any linear programming problem, any convex combination of two feasible solutions is also a feasible solution. Accordingly, the polytope defined by its inequality constraints is convex.

An *extreme point* of a convex set is a point that is not the convex combination of any two distinct points in the set. The extreme points of a convex polytope occur at its vertices. We shall use the terms vertex and extreme point synonomously.

Now let us investigate the correspondence between the basic feasible

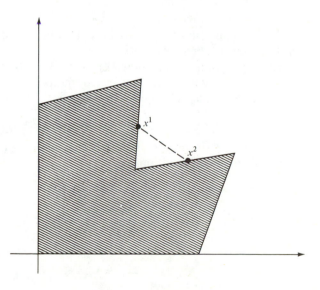

Figure 2.17   Example of nonconvex region

solutions of a linear programming problem and the extreme points of its convex polytope. Suppose, for example, we add slack variables to (12.1) to convert its constraints to equality form:

maximize $z = 3x_1 + 2x_2$
subject to

$$\left.\begin{array}{r}
-2x_1 + x_2 + s_1 \qquad\qquad = 1 \\
x_1 \qquad\qquad + s_2 \qquad\quad = 2 \\
x_1 + x_2 \qquad\qquad + s_3 = 3 \\
x_1, x_2, s_1, s_2, s_3 \qquad\qquad \geq 0.
\end{array}\right\} \qquad (12.3)$$

Then we see that the choice of x_1, x_2, s_1, as basic variables causes the equations in (12.2) to be satisfied, since the nonbasic slack variables s_2, s_3 must take on zero values. This results in the basic feasible solution $x_1 = 2, x_2 = 1, s_1 = 3$, which corresponds to vertex A of the polygon in Figure 2.15.

The following is a complete list of all basic feasible solutions, and the corresponding vertices of the polygon shown in Figure 2.15.

Basic Feasible Solution	Vertex of Polygon
$x_1 = 2, x_2 = 1, s_1 = 4$	A
$x_1 = 2, s_1 = 5, s_3 = 1$	B
$s_1 = 1, s_2 = 2, s_3 = 3$	C
$x_2 = 1, s_2 = 2, s_3 = 2$	D
$x_1 = \frac{2}{3}, x_2 = \frac{7}{3}, s_2 = \frac{4}{3}$	E

The same situation exists in higher dimensions. That is, each basic feasible solution corresponds to an extreme point of the convex polytope of the linear program. It may, however, be the case that several basic feasible solutions correspond to the same extreme point.

For example, suppose that we add to (12.1) the constraint

$$2x_1 + x_2 \leq 5. \qquad (12.5)$$

Then vertex A of the polygon is determined, not only by equations (12.2), but by two other sets of equations:

$$\left.\begin{array}{r}
x_1 \qquad = 2 \\
2x_1 + x_2 = 5
\end{array}\right\} \qquad (12.6)$$

and

$$\left.\begin{array}{r}
x_1 + x_2 = 3 \\
2x_1 + x_2 = 5.
\end{array}\right\} \qquad (12.7)$$

This is simply because there are now three nonparallel straight lines inter-secting at the point A, and any two of them are sufficient to determine A.

Equivalently, there are three distinct basic feasible solutions of the augmented linear program which correspond to the extreme point A. They are:

$$x_1 = 2, x_2 = 1, s_1 = 4, s_2 = 0,$$

$$x_1 = 2, x_2 = 1, s_1 = 4, s_3 = 0,$$

and

$$x_1 = 2, x_2 = 1, s_1 = 4, s_4 = 0.$$

This is a simple example of degeneracy.

Except when degeneracy is encountered, each pivot step of the simplex method effects a move from one vertex of the convex polytope to an adjacent vertex. The ratio test (11.4) dictates that this move is made along an edge of the polytope for which the rate of improvement in the objective function is maximal. For example, if the simplex computation for (12.3) is begun at vertex C in Figure 2.15, the first pivot step results in a move to vertex B, and the next pivot step to vertex A, which is optimal.

For a given set of linear inequalities, it is intuitively clear that if the inequalities determine an unbounded convex polytope, then there is some objective function for which a finite optimum does not exist. It is also in-tuitively clear that for each extreme point of the polytope there is an objective function for which that point is a unique optimal solution.

Sometimes we wish to show that a certain set of linear inequalities determines a convex polyhedron whose vertices are in one-to-one corre-spondence with the feasible solutions to a particular combinatorial optimi-zation problem. We probably will have formulated the linear inequality constraints in such a way that it is clear that any integer solution to the inequalities is a solution to the combinatorial problem and conversely. It then becomes of interest to know whether or not the inequalities deter-mine a convex polyhedron, all of whose vertices have integer coordinates.

Proposition 12.1   A system of linear inequalities determines a convex poly-hedron with integer vertices if and only if, for all possible choices of an objective function, there exists a finite optimal solution in integers.

13

Duality Theory

The theory of duality is one of the more interesting mathematical aspects of linear programming, and certainly the most important for our purposes.

It is essential for the understanding of many of the computational procedures presented in this book.

The basic idea of duality is that every linear programming problem has associated with it another problem, called its dual, and that the two problems bear such a close relationship that whenever one problem is solved the other problem is, in effect, solved as well.

For a given *primal* linear programming problem with n variables $x_1, x_2, \ldots, x_n$, and m constraints there is a *dual* problem with m variables $u_1, u_2, \ldots, u_m$, and n constraints, obtained as follows:

Primal Problem	Dual Problem
Minimize $z = \sum\limits_{j=1}^{n} c_j x_j$	Minimize $w = \sum\limits_{i=1}^{m} (-b_i) u_i$
Subject to	Subject to
$\sum\limits_{j=1}^{n} a_{ij} x_j \geq b_i$	$u_i \geq 0$
$\sum\limits_{j=1}^{n} a_{ij} x_j = b_i$	u_i unrestricted
$x_j \geq 0$	$\sum\limits_{i=1}^{m} (-a_{ij}) u_i \geq -c_j$
x_j unrestricted.	$\sum\limits_{i=1}^{m} (-a_{ij}) u_i = -c_j.$

Thus, for every inequality (equality) constraint in the primal problem there is a nonnegative (unrestricted) variable in the dual problem, and vice versa. (In general, changing a problem by tightening its constraints results in loosening the constraints in its dual.) The coefficient matrices of the primal and dual problems are negative transposes of each other, and the roles of the b and c vectors are reversed.

It is evident from this definition that duality is reflexive, i.e., the dual of the dual is the primal. For given pair of dual problems, the designation of one as "primal" and the other as "dual" is an essentially arbitrary matter.

We have defined duality in such a way that both problems involve minimization of the objective function and all inequality constraints are of the form "$\geq$." Of course, minimizing $-bu$ is equivalent to maximizing bu, and the direction of inequalities can be reversed. Thus, it is quite equivalent to say that the following pairs of problems are duals:

$$
\left.
\begin{array}{ll}
\text{minimize } cx & \text{maximize } ub \\
\text{subject to} & \text{subject to} \\
\quad Ax \geq b & \quad uA \leq c \\
\quad x \geq 0. & \quad u \geq 0.
\end{array}
\right\} \qquad (13.1)
$$

$$
\begin{array}{ll}
\text{minimize } cx & \text{maximize } ub \\
\text{subject to} & \text{subject to} \\
\quad Ax = b & \quad uA \leq c \\
\quad x \geq 0. & \quad u \text{ unrestricted.}
\end{array} \tag{13.2}
$$

$$
\begin{array}{ll}
\text{minimize } cx & \text{maximize } ub \\
\text{subject to} & \text{subject to} \\
\quad Ax = b & \quad uA = c \\
x \text{ unrestricted.} & \quad u \text{ unrestricted.}
\end{array} \tag{13.3}
$$

Duality relations in this form are indicated schematically in Figure 2.18, and are used in the statement of the theorems below.

Theorem 13.1 (*Weak Duality*) If $\bar{x}$ and $\bar{u}$ are feasible solutions to dual problems, then $c\bar{x} \geq \bar{u}b$.

PROOF   Suppose the problems are in the form of (13.1). Since $A\bar{x} \geq b$ and $\bar{u} \geq 0$, it follows that $\bar{u}A\bar{x} \geq \bar{u}b$. Similarly, $\bar{u}A\bar{x} \leq c\bar{x}$, so $c\bar{x} \geq \bar{u}b$.
The proof for problems not in the form of (13.1) is similar.//

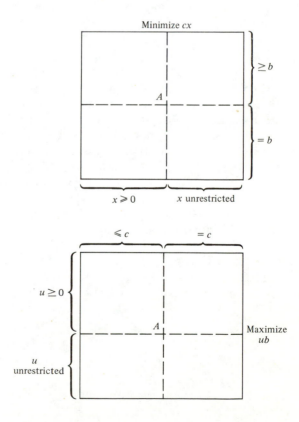

Figure 2.18   Schematic representation of duality

Corollary 13.2   If $\bar{x}$ and $\bar{u}$ are feasible solutions to dual problems and $c\bar{x} = \bar{u}b$, then $\bar{x}$ and $\bar{u}$ are optimal solutions.

We can now establish the optimality of the final basic feasible solution obtained by the simplex method. Let B be the final basis. The cost vector expressed in terms of this basis is $\bar{c} = c - c^B B^{-1} A \geq 0$. Then $\bar{u} = c^B B^{-1}$ is a feasible dual solution. (Note that u is not sign restricted, because the primal problem is in equality form.) But $c\bar{x} = c^B x^B = c^B B^{-1} b = \bar{u}b$, and so by Corollary 13.2 the final solution is optimal.

The converse of Corollary 13.2 is also true. The following theorem is the principal result of the duality theory.

Theorem 13.3   (*Strong Duality*)   If either problem of a dual pair of problems has a finite optimum, then the other does also and the two optimal objective values are equal; if either has an unbounded optimum, the other has no feasible solution.

PROOF   Assume that the dual pair of problems are in the form (13.2). Suppose that the primal problem has a finite minimum solution $\bar{x}$ achieved at a basis B. From the simplex method, we know that for an optimal basis B, $c - c^B B^{-1} A \geq 0$. Let $\bar{u} = c^B B^{-1}$. Then $c - \bar{u}A \geq 0$, and $\bar{u}$ is a feasible dual solution. Moreover, $c\bar{x} = c^B x^B = c^B B^{-1} b = \bar{u}b$. Hence, by Corollary 13.2, $\bar{u}$ is an optimal dual solution with an equal objective function value.

Suppose that $\bar{u}$ is a finite maximum solution to the dual problem in (13.2). Convert the problem to equality form with nonnegative variables. (This does not affect the optimality of the solution.) Then the argument above holds with $\bar{u}$ in the role of $\bar{x}$. This establishes the existence of an optimal primal solution with an equal objective function value.

The case of an unbounded optimum is simple. By Theorem 13.1, $cx \geq \bar{u}b$. But if $c\bar{x} \to -\infty$, this implies that $\bar{u}b$ is negative infinite no matter what $\bar{u}$ we use. Yet any feasible solution $\bar{u}$ yields a finite value for $\bar{u}b$.//

Optimal solutions to dual problems are "orthogonal", in the sense of the following theorem.

Theorem 13.4   (*Orthogonality of Optimal Solutions*)   If $\bar{x}$ and $\bar{u}$ are feasible solutions to (13.1) then $\bar{x}$ and $\bar{u}$ are optimal if and only if $(\bar{u}A - c)\bar{x} = \bar{u}(A\bar{x} - b) = 0$. That is, if and only if, for $j = 1, 2, \ldots, n$,

$$\bar{x}_j > 0 \text{ implies } \sum_{i=1}^{m} \bar{u}_i a_{ij} = c_j$$

and, for $i = 1, 2, \ldots, m$,

$$\bar{u}_i > 0 \text{ implies } \sum_{j=1}^{m} a_{ij}\bar{x}_j = b_i.$$

PROOF   It follows from $(\bar{u}A - c)\bar{x} = \bar{u}(A\bar{x} - b) = 0$ that $\bar{u}A\bar{x} = c\bar{x} = \bar{u}b$. Hence, by Corollary 13.2, if $\bar{x}, \bar{u}$ are feasible, $\bar{x}, \bar{u}$ are optimal.

Conversely, suppose $\bar{x}, \bar{u}$ are optimal. Then by Theorem 13.3, $c\bar{x} = \bar{u}b$. Since $c\bar{x} = \bar{u}b = \bar{u}A\bar{x}$, the orthogonality conditions follow immediately.//

Duality theory suggests a number of alternative procedures for solving linear programming problems. The (primal) simplex method described in the previous section proceeds from one feasible primal solution $x = B^{-1}b$ to another, with monotonic improvement of the primal objective function. The corresponding dual solutions $u = c^B B^{-1}$ are infeasible until the very end of the computation. There is also a *dual simplex method* in which row and column operations in the primal method are interchanged. This proceeds from one feasible dual solution to another, with a monotonic improvement of the dual objective function. The corresponding primal solutions are infeasible until the very end of the computation.

In addition to the primal and dual simplex methods, there are *primal-dual* methods, in which both primal and dual solutions are maintained, and at some stages of the computation changes are made in the primal solution and at others in the dual.

In the so-called *Hungarian* method, the computation is begun with feasible primal and dual solutions. (These solutions bear no special relation to each other, i.e., they do not correspond in the sense that $x = B^{-1}b$ and $u = cB^{-1}$.) The computation proceeds from one pair of feasible solutions to another, with monotonic improvement of both objective functions. Whenever there is not strict improvement in either objective function, the two solutions are made more nearly orthogonal, and improvements in orthogonality are also monotonic throughout the computation.

In the more general *out-of-kilter* method, the computation is begun with arbitrary (possibly infeasible) primal and dual solutions. Throughout the computation, there is monotonic improvement in the feasibility of the two solutions and in their relative orthogonality. There is not, however, monotonic improvement of the two objective functions, unless the initial solutions are feasible.

The out-of-kilter method is described in detail in Chapter 4, for the case of network flow computations. The Hungarian method is introduced in Chapter 5 for bipartite matchings, and is employed extensively in later chapters. These methods can be applied to general linear programming problems, but to do so is beyond the scope of this book.

PROBLEM

12.1   For each of the linear programs in Problem 10.2, formulate the dual program. Determine the relations between primal and dual problems, e.g., primal infeasible, dual unbounded, and so on.

COMMENTS AND REFERENCES

SECTIONS 3–9
Among the useful books on graph theory are the following:

C. Berge, *The Theory of Graphs and Its Applications,* John Wiley, New York, 1962.

N. Christofides, *Graph Theory, An Algorithmic Approach,* Academic Press, New York, 1975.

F. Harary, *Graph Theory,* Addison-Wesley, Reading, Mass. 1969.

O. Ore, *Theory of Graphs,* American Mathematical Society, Providence, Rhode Island, 1962.

B. Roy, *Algèbre Moderne et Théorie des graphes,* Dunod, Paris, Vol. 1, 1969 and Vol. 2, 1970. (In French.)

R. J. Wilson, *Introduction to Graph Theory,* Academic Press, New York, 1972.

The book of Harary is especially recommended.

Theorem 9.2 is from

V. Chvátal, "On Hamilton's Ideals," *J. Comb. Theory,* **12B** (April 1972) 163–168.

SECTIONS 11–13
Among the better texts on linear programming are

M. Simonnard, *Linear Programming,* Prentice Hall, Englewood Cliffs, New Jersey, 1966.

R. M. Thrall and A. Spivey, *Linear Optimization,* Holt, Rinehart and Winston, New York, 1970.

G. Hadley, *Linear Programming,* Addison-Wesley, Reading, Mass,., 1962.

G. B. Dantzig, *Linear Programming and Extensions,* Princeton Univ. Press, Princeton, New Jersey, 1962.

THREE

Shortest Paths

1
Introduction

Suppose each arc (i, j) of a directed graph is assigned a numerical "length" a_{ij}. A natural and intuitively appealing problem is to find a shortest possible directed path with no repeated nodes, from a specified origin to a specified destination.

Problems of this type are possibly the most fundamental and important of all combinatorial optimization problems. A great variety of optimization problems can be formulated and solved as shortest-path problems. In addition, a number of more complex problems can be solved by procedures which call upon shortest-path algorithms as subroutines.

One of the first observations we make in this chapter is that it appears to be as easy to compute shortest paths from a specified origin to *all* other nodes as it is to compute a shortest path from the origin to one specified destination. We shall discover that there is a very real difference between shortest-path problems in which arc lengths are restricted to positive values and problems in which arc lengths may be positive or negative. We shall also discover that, in the latter case, there is no efficient procedure known for solving the problem, if the network contains directed cycles which are negative in length. The detection of such negative cycles is an important problem in its own right.

We shall discuss several other variations of the basic shortest path problem in this chapter. Among these is the problem in which "transit times" are assigned to the arcs, and, in effect, we wish to find a directed cycle around which one can travel at the fastest possible velocity. We also describe procedures for "ranking" solutions to a shortest-path problem, i.e., finding the shortest path, the second shortest path, the third shortest path, and so on.

The dominant ideas in the solution of these shortest-path problems are those of dynamic programming. Thus, in Section 3 we invoke the "Principle of Optimality" to formulate a set of equations which must be satisfied by shortest path lengths. We then proceed to solve these equations by methods that are, for the most part, standard dynamic programming techniques.

This situation is hardly surprising. It is not inaccurate to claim that, in the deterministic and combinatorial realm, dynamic programming is primarily concerned with the computation of shortest paths in networks with one type of special structure or another. What distinguishes the networks dealt with in this chapter is that they have no distinguishing structure.

Finally, at the risk of introducing confusion where clairty prevails, we must emphasize that this chapter is concerned exclusively with shortest-path problems in *directed* networks. If all arc lengths are positive, then an undirected shortest path problem can be reduced to a directed one, by replacing each undirected arc (i, j) by a symmetric pair of directed arcs (i, j) and (j, i), each with the same length as the original. However, if the length of (i, j) is negative, such a transformation would introduce a negative directed cycle into the network.

Nevertheless, it is entirely feasible to compute shortest paths for undirected networks with positive and negative arc lengths, provided such a network contains no negative (undirected) cycles. The theory is much more sophisiticated than that of this chapter, and not at all dynamic-programming-like. See Section 2 of Chapter 6.

PROBLEM

1.1 (V. Klee) Consider an undirected network with an origin, a destination, and 100 additional nodes, with each pair of nodes connected by an arc. Show that the number of different paths (without repeated nodes, of course) from origin to destination is

$$100! + 100\,(99!) + \binom{100}{2}(98!) + \ldots + \binom{100}{98}2! + 100 + 1,$$

where the nth term counts the paths from origin to destination which omit $n - 1$ of the other nodes. Show that this sum is the greatest integer in $100!e$. Use Stirling's formula to represent $100!$ in the form $a \cdot 10^b$, where b is a positive integer, $1 \le a < 10$ and a is accurate to two significant digits. Stirling's formula asserts

$$\sqrt{2\pi}\,n^{n+1/2}e^{-n} < n! < \sqrt{2\pi}\,n^{n+1/2}e^{-n}\left(1 + \frac{1}{4n}\right).$$

2

Some Problem Formulations

Let us consider some optimization problems that can be formulated as shortest-path problems and variations.

MOST RELIABLE PATHS

In a communications network, the probability that the link from i to j is operative is p_{ij}. Hence the probability that all the links in any given path are operative is the product of the link probabilities. What is the most reliable path from one designated node to another?

   This problem becomes a shortest path problem in the conventional sense by replacing each probability p_{ij} with a "length" $a_{ij} = -\log p_{ij}$.

PERT NETWORKS

A large project is divisible into many unit "tasks." Each task requires a certain amount of time for its completion, and the tasks are partially ordered. For example, the exterior walls of a house must be framed in before the rafters can be raised.

   One can form a network in which each arc (i, j) is identified with a task and the nodes are identified with "events," i.e., the completion of various tasks. If (i, j) and (j, k) are arcs, then task (i, j) must be completed before task (j, k) is begun. (It may be necessary to insert "dummy" arcs with zero completion times in order to properly represent the partial ordering of tasks.)

   This network is sometimes called a PERT (for Project Evaluation and Review Technique) or CPM (Critical Path Method) network. Many types of analyses can be performed with such a network. For example,

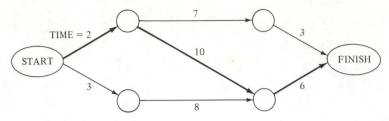

Figure 3.1   PERT network

we may determine the shortest possible time in which the entire project can be completed.

Let $a_{ij} \geq 0$ denote the length of time required to complete the task identified with arc (i, j) of the PERT network. The shortest possible completion time for the project is determined by a longest (or "critical") path from a specified origin (corresponding to the "event" of starting) to a specified destination (corresponding to the event of completion). A critical path of the PERT network shown in Figure 3.1 is indicated by bold arcs.

A PERT network is necessarily acyclic. Otherwise there would be an inconsistent ordering of the tasks; e.g., job (1,2) precedes job (2,1). Thus, the PERT problem illustrates a situation in which it is important to be able to find optimal paths in acyclic networks. It also illustrates a case in which it is desired to find a *longest* path (with respect to nonnegative arc lengths). As we shall see in Section 4, the acyclic network happens to be one exceptional type of network for which this is possible.

A TRAMP STEAMER

A tramp steamer is free to choose its ports of call and the order in which it calls on them. A voyage from port i to port j earns p_{ij} dollars profit. Presumably, $p_{ij} > 0$ if there is a cargo available at port i to be taken to port j and $p_{ij} < 0$ if the steamer must sail empty. The most profitable path from one designated node to another corresponds to a shortest path in a network in which each arc (i, j) has a "length" $a_{ij} = -p_{ij}$.

This problem illustrates a case in which it is reasonable for arc lengths to be either positive or negative. Unfortunately, the network for the tramp steamer problem is almost certain to have directed cycles which are negative in length (positive in profit), and this causes great computational difficulties.

See Section 12 for a further discussion of tramp steamers.

THE KNAPSACK PROBLEM

Suppose there are n objects, the jth object having a positive integer "weight" a_j and "value" p_j. It is desired to find the most valuable subset of objects, subject to the restriction that their total weight does not exceed b, the capacity of a "knapsack." This problem can be formulated as an integer linear programming problem of the form

maximize

$$\sum_j p_j x_j$$

subject to

$$\sum_j a_j x_j \le b,$$

where

$$x_j = 1 \quad \text{if object } j \text{ is chosen}$$

$$= 0 \quad \text{otherwise.}$$

This problem can be formulated as one of finding a longest path in an acyclic network. Let the network have $n(b+1)$ nodes denoted $j^{(k)}$, where $j = 1, 2, \ldots, n$, and $k = 0, 1, 2, \ldots, b$. The node $j^{(k)}$ has two arcs directed into it, one from $(j-1)^{(k)}$, the other from $(j-1)^{(k-a_j)}$, provided these nodes exist. The length of the first arc is zero, and that of the second is p_j. An origin node s is also provided, and it is joined to $1^{(0)}$ and $1^{(a_1)}$ by arcs of length zero and p_1. Then each path from node s to node $j^{(k)}$ corresponds to a subset of the first j objects whose total weight is exactly k, the length of the path being the value of the subset.

A destination node t is also provided, with an arc of length zero from each node $n^{(k)}$ to t. Then paths from s to t are identified with subsets of the n objects whose total weight is at most b. The length of a longest path from s to t is equal to the value of an optimal solution to the knapsack problem.

The structure of the network is suggested in Figure 3.2.

THE TRAVELING SALESMAN PROBLEM

Recall that the traveling salesman problem is to find a minimum-length Hamiltonian cycle, i.e., a cycle passing through each node exactly once.

Suppose we replace some node of the network, say node n, by two nodes s and t, where s has incident from it all of the arcs which were directed out of n, and t has incident into it all of the arcs which were directed into n. Then the traveling salesman problem becomes that of finding a shortest path from s to t, subject to the restriction that the path passes through each of the nodes $1, 2, \ldots, n-1$ *exactly once*.

Now suppose in this same network we replace a_{ij}, the length of arc (i, j), by $a_{ij} - K$ where K is a suitably large number. The problem now becomes that of finding a shortest path from s to t, subject to the restriction that the path passes through each node *at most once*. If a shortest path contains fewer than n arcs, then no Hamiltonian cycle exists.

The difficulty in finding a shortest path with no repeated nodes is

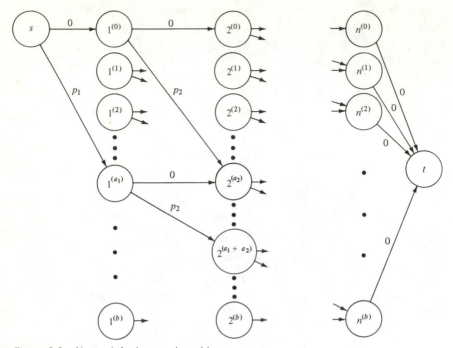

Figure 3.2   Network for knapsack problem

that the network has negative directed cycles. The problem of finding such a shortest path is a perfectly well-defined problem, and it can, of course, be "solved" by various methods. However, it cannot be solved efficiently, unless it has a very special structure.

We can, equivalently, let each arc have length $K - a_{ij}$ and view this as a longest path problem, with all arc lengths positive. But, as we have commented, there is no efficient method for solving a longest path problem, unless the network is acyclic.

PROBLEMS

2.1   What changes must be made in the network formulation of the knapsack problem if an arbitrarily large number of copies of each object can be placed in the knapsack? That is, x_j is constrained to be nonnegative integer, rather than merely 0 or 1.

2.2   Generalize the knapsack problem so as to provide two constraints, e.g., one on weight and another on volume. Formulate this problem as a longest path problem giving an explicit definition of the nodes, arcs, and arc lengths.

3

Bellman's Equations

There seems to be no really good method for finding the length of a shortest path from a specified origin to a specified destination without, in effect, finding the lengths of shortest paths from the origin to all other nodes (or, symmetrically, from all nodes to the destination). So let us suppose that we do, indeed, wish to compute shortest paths from the origin to all other nodes, and let us formulate a set of equations which must be satisfied by the shortest path lengths.

Let

a_{ij} = the (finite) length of arc (i, j), if there is such an arc

= $+\infty$, otherwise.

u_j = the length of a shortest path from the origin to node j.

Suppose the origin is numbered 1, and the other nodes are numbered $2, 3, \ldots, n$. If there are no directed cycles with negative length (and, therefore, no negative closed paths), it is clear that $u_1 = 0$. For each node j, $j \neq 1$, there must be some final arc (k, j) in a shortest path from 1 to j. Whatever the identity of k, it is certain that $u_j = u_k + a_{kj}$. This follows from the fact that the part of the path which extends to node k must be a shortest path from 1 to k; if this were not so, the overall path to j would not be as short as possible. (This is the "Principle of Optimality.") But there are only a finite number of choices for k, i.e., $k = 1, 2, \ldots, j - 1, j + 1, \ldots, n$. Clearly k must be a node for which $u_k + a_{kj}$ is as small as possible. Thus, we have established that the shortest path lengths must satisfy the following system of equations, which we refer to as Bellman's equations.

$$\left.\begin{aligned} u_1 &= 0, \\ u_j &= \min_{k \neq j} \{u_k + a_{kj}\} \qquad (j = 2, 3, \ldots, n). \end{aligned}\right\} \qquad (3.1)$$

and

We have argued that the equations (3.1) are necessarily satisfied by the shortest path lengths, provided the network contains no negative cycles. Are these equations also sufficient to determine the lengths of the shortest paths?

Assume that the network is such that there is a finite-length path from the origin to each of the other nodes. Also assume that all directed cycles are strictly positive in length. Under these conditions, it is intuitively clear that the shortest path lengths are all finite and well defined. We shall also show that under these conditions the equations (3.1) have a unique finite solution. It follows that the solution to (3.1) yields the lengths of the shortest paths.

Before proceeding to prove the uniqueness of a finite solution to (3.1) first let us indicate something of the character of such a solution. Suppose $u_1, u_2, \ldots, u_n$ satisfy (3.1). Then we can construct paths to nodes $1, 2, \ldots, n$ having these lengths, as follows. To find a path of length u_j to node j, find an arc (k, j) such that $u_j = u_k + a_{kj}$. Then find an arc (l, k) such that $u_k = u_l + a_{lk}$. Continue in this way until the origin is reached. The sequence of arcs must eventually reach back to the origin. If this were not the case we would have found a cycle of zero length. But, by assumption, there are no such cycles.

The reader should be able to establish that if we repeat this process for all nodes j, a total of exactly $n - 1$ arcs can be picked out for membership in the various paths and that these $n - 1$ arcs form a tree rooted from the origin. See Figure 3.3.

There is such a tree for any finite solution to Bellman's equations. And since the true shortest path lengths are such a solution, it follows that we have proved the following.

Theorem 3.1   If the network contains no nonpositive directed cycles, then there exists a tree rooted from the origin, such that the path in the tree from the origin to each of the other nodes is a shortest path. (We call such a tree a *tree of shortest paths*.)

Now let us consider the uniqueness question. Let $u_1, u_2, \ldots, u_n$ be shortest path lengths, and let $\bar{u}_1, \bar{u}_2, \ldots, \bar{u}_n$ be any other finite solution to

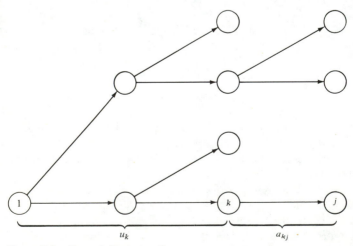

Figure 3.3   Tree of shortest paths

equations (3.1) such that $\bar{u}_j \neq u_j$, for some j. From the construction above, it follows that $\bar{u}_1, \bar{u}_2, \ldots, \bar{u}_n$ represent lengths of actual paths, although not necessarily shortest paths. Accordingly, if $\bar{u}_j \neq u_j$, it must be the case that $\bar{u}_j > u_j$. Choose j to be such that $\bar{u}_j > u_j$, but $\bar{u}_k = u_k$, where (k, j) is an arc in the tree of shortest paths. (There must be at least one such arc (k, j); note that $\bar{u}_1 = u_1$.) Then $\bar{u}_j > \bar{u}_k + a_{kj}$, contrary to the assumption that $\bar{u}_1, \bar{u}_2, \ldots, \bar{u}_n$ satisfied (3.1). We have thus proved the following.

Theorem 3.2   If the network contains no nonpositive cycles, and if there is a path from the origin to each of the other nodes, then there is a unique finite solution to the equations (3.1), where u_j is the length of a shortest path from the origin to node j.

Unfortunately, Bellman's equations do not lend themselves to solution as they stand, because they are nonlinear and imply implicit functional relationships. That is, each of the u_j's is expressed as a nonlinear function of the other u_j's. Much of the remainder of this chapter is devoted to methods for overcoming these difficulties, and to special situations in which the equations are particularly easy to solve.

In discussing these computational methods, we shall presume to have solved the shortest path problem by simply solving the equations (3.1). The actual construction of a tree of shortest paths can be carried out from the u_j values, as we have indicated above. This is facilitated by storing with each j a value of k for which $u_k + a_{kj}$ is minimal. However, in the accepted tradition of dynamic programming, we shall view such an issue as a housekeeping chore to be attended to by the computer programmer.

Finally, we note that although Theorems 3.1 and 3.2 require the network to contain no nonpositive cycles, the computational procedures we shall propose are actually effective for networks which contain no negative cycles. That is, although the solution to Bellman's equations is not unique, the computation will terminate with the correct solution. (See Problem 3.3.)

PROBLEMS

3.1   Rewrite equations (3.1) for each of the following cases:

(a) a_{ij} = the probability that arc (i, j) is intact.
     u_j = the probability associated with a "most reliable" path from the origin to node j.
(b) a_{ij} = the "capacity" of arc (i, j).
     u_j = the capacity of maximum capacity path from the origin to node j.

(The capacity of a path is the minimum of the capacities of its arcs.)

3.2   Let the arc lengths of a certain five-node network be given by the matrix:

$$A = \begin{bmatrix} 0 & -1 & 3 & \infty & 6 \\ \infty & 0 & 5 & 6 & 8 \\ \infty & \infty & 0 & \infty & 10 \\ \infty & 0 & -1 & 0 & \infty \\ \infty & 0 & 0 & -1 & 0 \end{bmatrix}.$$

Assuming that the shortest path lengths are $u_1 = 0$, $u_2 = -1$, $u_3 = 3$, $u_4 = 5$, $u_5 = 6$, construct a tree of shortest paths.

3.3   Consider the network shown in Figure 3.4. Show that for this network the equations (3.1) do not have a unique finite solution. Characterize the set of all solutions.

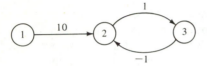

Figure 3.4   Network for Problem 3.3

4

Acyclic Networks

One special situation in which it is particularly easy to solve Bellman's equations is that in which the network is acyclic.

Recall that in the previous chapter we showed that a directed graph is acyclic if and only if there exists a numbering of its nodes such that there exists an arc directed from i to j only if $i < j$. Let us assume that the nodes of the network are so numbered. Then it is easy to see that the equations (3.1) can be replaced by

and
$$\left. \begin{array}{l} u_1 = 0, \\ u_j = \min_{k<j} \{u_k + a_{kj}\}, \quad (j = 2, 3, \dots, n). \end{array} \right\} \tag{4.1}$$

The equations (4.1) are easily solved by substitution. That is, u_1 is known, u_2 depends on u_1 only, u_3 depends on u_1 and $u_2, \dots, u_j$ depends on $u_1, u_2, \dots, u_{j-1}$, and so on. The solution of all n equations requires $0 + 1 + 2 + \cdots + n - 1 = n(n-1)/2$ additions and $0 + 0 + 1 + 2 + \cdots + n - 2 = (n-1)(n-2)/2$ comparisons. Thus the acyclic shortest path problem can be solved by an $O(n^2)$ computation. (Note that if the nodes have not been properly numbered, this task can also be accomplished in $O(n^2)$ operations. See Chapter 2, Section 6.)

Obviously, a network with no cycles can have no negative cycles, regardless of the lengths of its arcs. Thus, one can replace each arc length by its negative value and still carry out the computation successfully. This is equivalent to finding longest, rather than shortest, paths in the original network. The acyclic network is the one special type of network for which we can solve the longest path problem.

The acyclic network may seem to be an extremely special case. However, the general method we shall describe in Section 6 for solving Bellman's equations can be viewed as a technique for converting networks to acyclic form.

PROBLEMS

4.1 Solve the shortest path problem for the acyclic network in Figure 3.5, constructing the tree of shortest paths "as you go."

4.2 Repeat Problem 4.1 for the longest path problem.

4.3 Solve the shortest path problem for the network with arc lengths given by the matrix:

$$A = \begin{bmatrix} 0 & 4 & 3 & 5 & \infty & 9 & 6 \\ \infty & 0 & -1 & \infty & 6 & 4 & 0 \\ \infty & \infty & 0 & 2 & -10 & 3 & -9 \\ \infty & \infty & \infty & \infty & 8 & 2 & 8 \\ \infty & \infty & \infty & \infty & 0 & 1 & 6 \\ \infty & \infty & \infty & \infty & \infty & 0 & 3 \\ \infty & \infty & \infty & \infty & \infty & \infty & 0 \end{bmatrix}$$

Carry out the computations "algebraically," i.e., as they would be in the computer, without attempting to draw the network.

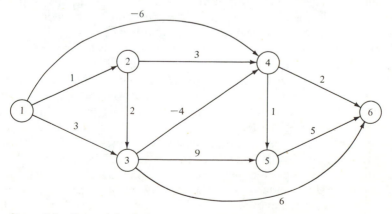

Figure 3.5   Network for Problem 4.1

4.4 Let

$$a_{ij} = 1 \quad \text{if there is an arc } (i, j)$$
$$= 0 \quad \text{otherwise.}$$

Revise the equations (4.1) for each of the following cases:

(a) U_j = the set of all paths from the origin to node j.
(b) $u_j = |U_j|$
    = the number of distinct paths from the origin to node j.

5

Networks with Positive Arcs: Dijkstra's Method

Another situation in which it is especially easy to solve the shortest path problem is that in which all arc lengths are positive. The $O(n^2)$ algorithm we shall describe for this case is due to Dijkstra.

We shall apply "labels" to the nodes of the network. At each stage of the computation, some of the labels will be designated as "permanent" and the others as "tentative." A permanent label on a node represents the true length of a shortest path to that node. A tentative label represents an upper bound on the length of a shortest path.

Initially, the only permanently labeled node is the origin, which is given the label $u_1 = 0$; each of the other nodes j is given the tentative label $u_j = a_{1j}$. The general step of the procedure is as follows. Find the tentatively labeled node k for which u_k is minimal (if there is a tie, break it arbitrarily). Declare node k to be permanently labeled, and revise the remaining tentative labels u_j by comparing u_j with $u_k + a_{kj}$, and replacing u_j by the smaller of the two values. The procedure terminates when all nodes are permanently labeled. (Note that if one wishes to find a shortest path to some designated node, the procedure can be terminated at the moment at which a permanent label is assigned to that node.)

The proof of the validity of the method is inductive. At each stage the nodes are partitioned into two sets, P and T. Assume that the label of each node in P is the length of a shortest path from the origin, whereas the label of each node j in T is the length of a shortest path, subject to the restriction that each node in the path (except j) belongs to P. Then the node k in T with the smallest label can be transferred to P, because if a shorter path from the origin existed, it would have to contain a first node that is in T. However, that node must be further away from the origin than k, since its label exceeds that of node k. The subsequent use of node k to reduce the labels of adjacent nodes belonging to T restores to T the property assumed above.

Dijkstra's algorithm can be summarized as follows.

SHORTEST PATH COMPUTATION FOR NETWORKS WITH POSITIVE ARC LENGTHS

Step 0   (*Start*)
    Set $u_1 = 0$.
    Set $u_j = a_{1j}$,   for $j = 2, 3, \ldots, n$.
    Set $P = \{1\}$, $T = \{2, 3, \ldots, n\}$.

Step 1   (*Designation of Permanent Label*)
    Find $k \in T$, where $u_k = \min_{j \in T} \{u_j\}$.
    Set $T = T - k$, $P = P + k$.
    If $T = \emptyset$, stop; the computation is completed.

Step 2   (*Revision of Tentative Labels*)
    Set $u_j = \min \{u_j, u_k + a_{kj}\}$ for all $j \in T$.
    Go to Step 1.//

Note that the first time Step 1 is executed, $n - 2$ comparisons are called for, the second time $n - 3$, the third time $n - 4$, and so on, for a total of $(n - 1)(n - 2)/2$ comparisons. The first time Step 2 is executed, $n - 2$ comparisons and $n - 2$ additions are required, then $n - 3$ comparisons and $n - 3$ additions, for a total of $(n - 1)(n - 2)/2$ comparisons and the same number of additions. An overall total of $(n - 1)(n - 2)$ comparisons and $(n - 1)(n - 2)/2$ additions is necessary, and the method is clearly $O(n^2)$ in complexity.

It is perhaps interesting to make some comparisons between Dijkstra's method and the method for acyclic networks.

Suppose that the nodes of the network happen to be numbered in such a way that $u_1 \leq u_2 \leq u_3 \leq \ldots \leq u_n$. (Of course, we have no way to so number the nodes in advance of the calculation. For the moment, suppose a "birdie" provided this numbering.) If all arc lengths are positive, we can again replace Bellman's equations by equations (4.1) used for solving acyclic networks.

Thus, if we knew how to order the nodes, an $O(n^2)$ computation would be possible. There are two important points involved in Dijkstra's procedure. The first is that it is possible to order the nodes by maintaining the sets P and T, such that at each stage of the computation,

$$\max_{j \in P} \{u_j) \le \min_{j \in T} \{u_j\}.$$

The second is that it is possible to determine each successive node in the ordering of the nodes (i.e., to transfer one node at a time from T to P), by means of $O(n)$ additions and comparisons, thereby implying an overall $O(n^2)$ computation.

Of course, Dijkstra's procedure does not simply determine an ordering of the nodes and then apply equations (4.1). However, the Dijkstra algorithm does suggest the following alternative computation for the acyclic shortest path problem.

$$\left.\begin{aligned}
&u_1^{(1)} = 0, \\
&u_j^{(2)} = a_{1j}, \qquad\qquad\qquad j = 2, 3, \ldots, n, \\
&u_j^{(k+1)} = \min \{u_j^{(k)}, u_k^{(k)} + a_{kj}\}, \qquad k = 2, 3, \ldots, n-1; \; j \ge k+1.
\end{aligned}\right\} \qquad (5.1)$$

We can view $u_j^{(1)} \ge u_j^{(2)} \ge \ldots \ge u_j^{(j)}$ as successive approximations of u_j, with $u_j^{(j)} = u_j$, for all j. Note that these equations imply exactly the same number of additions and comparisons as (4.1).

We combine the computational procedure of Chapter 2, Section 6 for ordering the nodes of an acyclic network with the computation implied by equations (5.1) in the algorithm below. We let

$$\bar{a}_{ij} = 1 \quad \text{if} \quad a_{ij} < \infty, \quad \text{i.e., there is an arc } (i, j),$$

$$= 0, \quad \text{otherwise.}$$

ALTERNATIVE SHORTEST PATH COMPUTATION FOR ACYCLIC NETWORKS

Step 0   *(Start)*
     Set $u_1 = 0$.
     Set $u_j = a_{1j}$,   for $j = 2, 3, \ldots, n$.
     Set $P = \{1\}$, $T = \{2, 3, \ldots, n\}$.

     Set $d_j = \sum_{i=2}^{n} \bar{a}_{ij}$,   for $j = 2, 3, \ldots, n$.

Step 1   *(Designation of Permanent Label)*
     Find a $k \in T$, such that $d_k = 0$. If there is no such k, stop; the network is not acyclic.
     Set $T = T - k$, $P = P + k$.
     If $T = \varnothing$, stop; the computation is completed.

Step 2   (*Revision of Tentative Labels*)
Set $u_j = \min\{u_k, u_k + a_{kj}\}$,   for all $j \in T$.
Set $d_j = d_j - \bar{a}_{kj}$,   for all $j \in T$.
Go to Step 1. //

PROBLEMS

5.1   Solve the shortest path problem for the network in Figure 3.6, using Dijkstra's method. Construct the tree of shortest paths "as you go."

5.2   Resolve Problem 4.3, using equations (5.1).

5.3   Devise a Dijkstra-like procedure for finding a shortest path from some node in a specified subset A of nodes to some node in a specified subset B. (Origin node and destination node are to be chosen optimally.) How many additions and how many comparisons are required?

5.4   Suppose the network is sparse with $m \ll n(n-1)$ arcs. Carry out a detailed estimate of the number of additions and comparisons required by Dijkstra's algorithm, as a function of m and n.

5.5   (P. Spira)   Show how to use the Dijkstra algorithm to find a shortest path from node 1 to node n in only $(n-2)^2$ comparisons (instead of $(n-1)(n-2)$ comparisons). *Hint*: First find shortest paths from node 1 to nodes $2, 3, \ldots, n-1$.

5.6   (V. Klee)   Let G be any function defined for all sequences of nonnegative numbers such that

(i) $G(a_1, a_2, \ldots, a_n, a_{n+1}) = G\big(G(a_1, a_2, \ldots, a_n), a_{n+1}\big)$,

(ii) $G(a_1, a_2, \ldots, a_n, a_{n+1}) \geq G(a_1, a_2, \ldots, a_n)$.

Let each path in a network with nonnegative arc lengths be given a G-value determined by the sequence of arc lengths in the path. Show that paths of minimum G-value can be found by a Dijkstra-like procedure, provided that G satisfies conditions (i) and (ii).

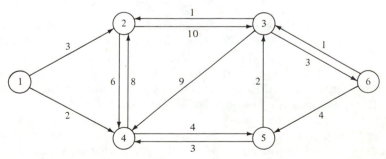

Figure 3.6   Network for Problem 5.1

6

Solution by Successive Approximations:
Bellman-Ford Method

We now consider a general method of solution to Bellman's equations. That is, we neither assume that the network is acyclic nor that all arc lengths are positive. (We do, however, continue to assume that there are no negative cycles.) The method can be attributed to Bellman and to Ford, and possibly others.

We propose to solve the equations (3.1) by successive approximations. That is, initially we set

$$u_1^{(1)} = 0,$$
$$u_j^{(1)} = a_{1j}, j \neq 1,$$
(6.1a)

and then compute the $(m + 1)$st order approximations from the mth order, as follows:

$$u_j^{(m+1)} = \min \{u_j^{(m)}, \min_{k \neq j} \{u_k^{(m)} + a_{kj}\}\}.$$
(6.1b)

Clearly, for each node j, successive approximations of u_j are monotone nonincreasing:

$$u_j^{(1)} \geq u_j^{(2)} \geq u_j^{(3)} \geq \dots.$$

How are we assured that the successive approximations converge to the correct value of u_j? Or, for that matter, that they converge to any value at all?

A simple intuitive argument can be made as follows. Apply the interpretation that

$u_j^{(m)}$ = the length of a shortest path from
the origin to j, subject to the condition
that the path contains no more than m arcs.

Clearly this interpretation is valid for $u_j^{(1)}$. Either a shortest path of no more than $m + 1$ arcs from the origin to node j has no more than m arcs, in which case its length is $u_j^{(m)}$, or else it contains $m + 1$ arcs and has some final arc, say (k, j). The portion of the path from the origin to node k contains no more than m arcs and its length is $u_k^{(m)}$. The final arc contributes length a_{kj}. Hence, minimizing $u_k^{(m)} + a_{kj}$ over all possible choices of k, one obtains $u_j^{(m+1)}$.

If the network contains no negative cycles, then there exists a shortest path from the origin to each node j with no repeated nodes. In the case of a network with n nodes, this means that there will exist shortest paths with no more than $n - 1$ arcs. In other words, we can be assured that, for all j, $u_j^{(n-1)} = u_j$.

The equations (6.1b) must be solved for $m = 1, 2, \ldots, n - 2$. For each value of m there are n equations to be solved. The solution of each equation requires $n - 1$ additions and minimization over n alternatives. It follows that approximately n^3 additions and n^3 comparisons are required overall, and the computation is clearly $O(n^3)$. (Note that the computation may be terminated whenever $u_j^{(m+1)} = u_j^{(m)}$ for *all* values of j. In this case, we are fortunate to have obtained early convergence to u_j.)

We should point out that this computational approach can be viewed as recasting the general n-node network problem into the form of an acyclic network problem with $n^2 - n + 1$ nodes, as indicated in Figure 3.7. That is, the acyclic network can be imagined to have n copies, $1^{(0)}, 1^{(1)}, \ldots, 1^{(n-1)}$, of the origin and $n - 1$ copies $j^{(1)}, j^{(2)}, \ldots, j^{(n-1)}$ of each of the other nodes j. For each arc $(1, j)$ of the original network, there are n arcs $(1^{(0)}, j^{(1)})$, $(1^{(2)}, j^{(3)}), \ldots, (1^{(n-2)}, j^{(n-1)})$, each with length a_{1j}. For each arc (i, j), $i \neq 1$, there are $n - 1$ arcs $(i^{(1)}, j^{(2)}), (i^{(2)}, j^{(3)}), \ldots, (i^{(n-1)}, j^{(n-1)})$, each with length a_{ij}. In addition, there are arcs of the form $(j^{(m)}, j^{(m+1)})$ with zero length. The length of a shortest path from the origin to $j^{(m)}$ is $u_j^{(m)}$. The equations (6.1) are essentially the same as equations (4.1), suitably modified to take into account the special structure of the acyclic network.

PROBLEMS

6.1 Solve the shortest path problem for the network with arc lengths given by the matrix:

$$
A = \begin{bmatrix}
0 & \infty & 4 & 10 & 3 & \infty & \infty \\
\infty & 0 & -1 & -3 & 2 & 11 & 0 \\
\infty & 9 & 0 & 8 & 3 & 2 & 1 \\
\infty & 4 & 0 & 0 & 8 & 6 & 3 \\
\infty & 0 & 1 & 2 & 0 & 3 & -1 \\
\infty & -1 & -1 & 3 & 2 & 0 & 0 \\
\infty & 4 & 3 & \infty & \infty & 2 & 0
\end{bmatrix}
$$

Organize your computations as you think they would be carried out in the computer. Construct the tree of shortest paths.

6.2 Suppose we want to let $u_j^{(m)}$ denote the length of a shortest path from 1 to j, subject to the condition that the path contains *exactly* m arcs. (Repeated nodes, and possibly repeated arcs, are permitted.) How should equations (6.1) be modified?

6.3 Assume that the in-degree of the origin is zero and that there is a path from the origin to each of the other nodes. Show that such a network contains a negative cycle if and only if $u_j^{(n)} < u_j^{(n-1)}$, for some j.

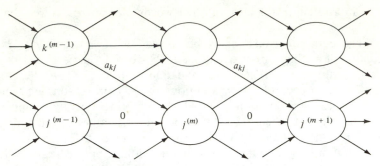

Figure 3.7   Acyclic network obtained from construction

7

Improvements in Efficiency: Yen's Modifications

A close examination of the computations implied by equations (6.1) reveals that these computations may not be as efficient as they could be. They do not make use of the best information available at each iteration. For example, $u_j^{(m+1)}$ is computed as a function of $u_1^{(m)}, u_2^{(m)}, \ldots, u_n^{(m)}$, even though $u_1^{(m+1)}$, $u_2^{(m+1)}, \ldots, u_{j-1}^{(m+1)}$ have presumably already been computed. Making use of these $(m+1)$st order approximations, when available, might accelerate convergence. This is the idea behind an improvement suggested by J. Y. Yen.

Suppose we call an arc (i, j) *upward* if $i < j$ and *downward* if $i > j$. (Cf. Figure 3.7.) A path is said to contain a *change in direction* whenever a downward arc is followed by an upward arc, or vice-versa. Note that because node 1 is the first node of any path, the first arc is upward and the first change in direction (if any) must be up to down.

Let us assign a new interpretation to the mth order approximation of u_j. Let

$u_j^{(m)}$ = the length of a shortest path from the origin to node j, subject to the condition that it contains no more than $m - 1$ changes in direction.

The appropriate equations for $u_j^{(m)}$ are as follows:

$$u_1^{(0)} = 0,$$

$$u_j^{(0)} = a_{1j}, \quad j \neq 1 \text{ (by definition)},$$

$$u_j^{(m+1)} = \min \{u_j^{(m)}, \min_{k<j} \{u_k^{(m+1)} + a_{kj}\}\}, \quad m \text{ even},$$

and

$$u_j^{(m+1)} = \min \{u_j^{(m)}, \min_{k>j} \{u_k^{(m+1)} + a_{kj}\}\}, \quad m \text{ odd}.$$

(7.1)

There exists a shortest path to any node j with no more than $n - 1$ arcs and hence no more than $n - 2$ changes in direction. It follows that $u_j^{(n-1)} = u_j$, as before.

Each of the equations (7.1) is solved by a minimization over about $n/2$ alternatives, on the average, instead of n, as in (6.1). Accordingly, the length of the computation is reduced by a factor of approximately two: about $n^3/2$ additions and $n^3/2$ comparisons are required.

Another, possibly less important, advantage is that storage requirements are also reduced by a factor of approximately two, since not both $u_j^{(m+1)}$ and $u_j^{(m)}$ must be stored. (As soon as $u_j^{(m+1)}$ is computed, it replaces $u_j^{(m)}$.)

Yen has pointed out that the computation can be reduced even further, to approximately $n^3/4$, by exploiting the fact that, at each iteration, one additional $u_j^{(m)}$ becomes a correct shortest path length and thereafter ceases to affect the calculations. Let

$$K_1 = \{2, 3, \ldots, n\},$$

and

$$K_{m+1} = \{k \mid u_k^{(m+1)} < u_k^{(m-1)}\}, \quad m \geq 1.$$

Then the minimizations indicated in equations (7.1) are taken over all $k < j$ (or $k > j$) such that $k \in K_{m+1}$. It can be shown (cf. Section 11) that $|K_{m+1}| \leq n - (m + 1)$, and that the $n^3/4$ result follows from this fact.

PROBLEMS

7.1   Resolve Problem 6.1, using equations (7.1).

7.2   Suppose Yen's computation (7.1) is applied to an acyclic network. At what iteration does the computation converge if the nodes are numbered so that all arcs are upward? What if the network is "almost" acyclic, with all arcs upward, except for p downward arcs?

7.3   Modify the acyclic network identified with the Bellman-Ford method, and pictured in Figure 3.7, to fit Yen's modification.

7.4   Investigate the statements made in the last paragraph of this section, and justify in detail.

8

Linear Programming Interpretation and Relaxation Procedures

Each of the equations (3.1),

$$u_j = \min_{k \neq j} \{u_k + a_{kj}\}, \tag{8.1}$$

implies a system of $n - 1$ inequalities. That is, for fixed j and for $k = 1, 2, \ldots, j - 1, j + 1, \ldots, n$:

$$u_j \leq u_k + a_{kj}. \tag{8.2}$$

Conversely, if $u_1, u_2, \ldots, u_{j-1}, u_{j+1}, \ldots, u_n$ are given fixed values and u_j is maximized subject to the inequalities (8.2), then the equation (8.1) is satisfied.

This suggests the following linear programming problem:

$$\left.\begin{array}{c}
\text{maximize } u_2 + u_3 + \ldots + u_n \\[4pt]
\text{subject to} \\[4pt]
u_1 = 0, \\[4pt]
\text{and, for } i = 1, 2, \ldots, n; \quad j = 2, 3, \ldots, n; \quad i \neq j, \\[4pt]
u_j - u_i \leq a_{ij}.
\end{array}\right\} \tag{8.3}$$

We assert that a finite optimal solution to (8.3) is a finite solution to Bellman's equations (3.1), and conversely.

In Chapter 4 we shall observe that the dual of (8.3) is a minimum cost flow problem, and that the dual variables identified with the inequality constraints of (8.3) have natural and intuitive interpretations in terms of arc flows. For the present we are not concerned with exploring these duality relations. We state, without proof or justification, that the basic variables of a basic feasible solution to the dual problem are identified with the arcs of a directed spanning tree rooted from the origin of the network.

We also assert that the application of the dual simplex method to the linear programming problem (8.3) can be interpreted as follows. The procedure is begun by finding any spanning tree rooted from the origin. This tree is identified with a basic feasible solution to the dual problem. Each variable u_j is set equal to the length of the path to node j in this tree. At each pivot step, an unsatisfied inequality $u_j - u_i > a_{ij}$ is identified, and the arc (i, j) is brought into the tree, replacing whatever arc (k, j) had been directed into j. (If there are no negative cycles, this exchange of

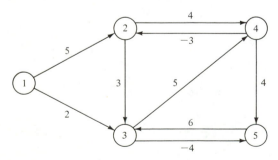

Figure 3.8   Example network

arcs results in a new spanning tree rooted from the origin.) Each variable u_j is set equal to the length of the path to node j in the new tree. Each u_j is monotone nonincreasing during the computation. An optimal solution is found when feasibility is first obtained; i.e., there are no unsatisfied inequalities. At this point, the tree rooted from the origin is a tree of shortest paths.

As an example, consider the network shown in Figure 3.8. For this network we have the problem:

$$
\begin{aligned}
&\text{maximize } u_2 + u_3 + u_4 + u_5 \\
&\text{subject to}
\end{aligned}
\left.
\begin{aligned}
u_1 &= 0 \\
u_2 - u_1 &\le 5 \\
u_2 - u_4 &\le -3 \\
u_3 - u_1 &\le 2 \\
u_3 - u_2 &\le 3 \\
u_3 - u_5 &\le 6 \\
u_4 - u_2 &\le 4 \\
u_4 - u_3 &\le 5 \\
u_5 - u_3 &\le -4 \\
u_5 - u_4 &\le 4.
\end{aligned}
\right\}
\tag{8.4}
$$

A sequence of rooted spanning trees is indicated in Figure 3.9. In each tree the arc (i, j) to be brought into the tree next is shown by a dashed line.

It is now appropriate to observe that the dual simplex method, and virtually all the other methods described in previous sections, can be considered to be specializations of a general relaxation procedure for solving the linear programming problem (8.3). The relaxation procedure is as follows.

RELAXATION PROCEDURE FOR SHORTEST PATH PROBLEM

Step 0   (*Start*)

Set $u_1 = 0$. Set u_j, $j = 2, 3, \ldots, n$, to any sufficiently large value (at least as large as the optimal value).

Step 1   (*Test Inequalities*)

If all inequalities of (8.3) are satisfied, stop; the solution is optimal.

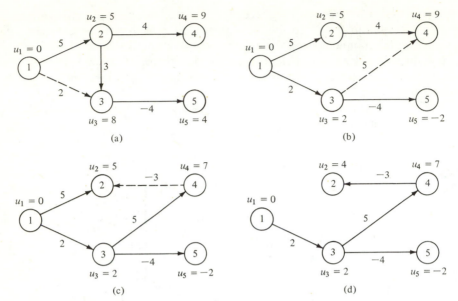

Figure 3.9   Sequence of rooted spanning trees

Otherwise, find i, j such that

$$u_j - u_i > a_{ij}.$$

Step 2   (*Relax Inequality*)
    Set $u_j = u_i + a_{ij}$.
    Return to Step 1.//

Step 1 of the relaxation procedure does not specify which inequality should be chosen for relaxation, if there are several unsatisfied inequalities in (8.3). As a practical matter, the nondeterministic character of the method actually makes it very attractive for solving small problems by hand "on the network." In this case, one can exploit intuition and insight into the structure of the network to obtain rapid convergence to an optimal solution. There is, however, a serious theoretical question of the rate of convergence to an optimal solution. This can perhaps be answered best by interpreting each of the shortest path algorithms we have studied as a specialization of the relaxation method in which the degree of nondeterminism is reduced.

Let us say that an inequality is *processed* whenever it is tested for satisfaction and then relaxed if it is not satisfied. That is, u_j is compared with $u_i + a_{ij}$ and then, if $u_i + a_{ij}$ is smaller, u_j is set equal to $u_i + a_{ij}$.

The algorithm for acyclic networks in Section 4 calls for the computation of

$$u_j = \min_{k < j} \{u_k + a_{kj}\},$$

which is equivalent to the processing of inequalities corresponding to the arcs $(1, j), (2, j), \ldots, (j - 1, j)$. The algorithm implies that it is sufficient to process each inequality of (8.3) exactly once, and the order of processing can be determined in advance of computation. In other words, at most $(n - 1)n/2$ relaxations, in predetermined order, are sufficient to solve the shortest path problem for an acyclic network.

Similarly, Dijkstra's method shows that if all a_{ij} are nonnegative, it is sufficient to process each of the $(n - 1)^2$ inequalities of (8.3) exactly once. However, the order in which the inequalities are processed cannot be predetermined (unless the relative values of the u_j's are all known in advance of computation). (Note that Dijkstra's method actually requires only $(n - 1)(n - 2)$ comparisons because each of the inequalities $u_j \leq a_{1j}$, $j = 2, 3, \ldots, n$ is satisfied initially by setting $u_j = a_{1j}$.)

The Bellman-Ford method does not lend itself to interpretation as a relaxation procedure of the type we have described, because, in effect, when a new value for u_j is determined, this value is not immediately substituted into all the inequalities of (8.3). It is precisely this fact which Yen exploited in formulating the equations (7.1). Yen's modification demonstrates that in the general case, i.e., when the network is neither acyclic nor has only positive arcs, it is sufficient to process each inequality of (8.3) only $n/2$ times. Moreover, the order of processing is predetermined.

Each pivot step of the dual simplex method is equivalent to the processing of several inequalities. When the out-of-tree arc (i, j) is exchanged for the in-tree arc (k, j) the inequality (i, j) is relaxed. This may cause a number of inequalities identified with other in-tree arcs to become unsatisfied, and these are all relaxed before the next pivot step is performed. The relaxation of these inequalities is presumably carried out by algebraic techniques quite different from the sequential processing of inequalities. Nevertheless, it is correct to conclude, as a result of the analysis of Yen's modification, that the linear programming problem (8.3) can be solved with no more than $n^3/2$ pivot steps of the dual simplex method. (Undoubtedly, this bound can be lowered substantially.)

The dual simplex method is a nondeterministic algorithm, in that there is no well-defined choice of a pivot element at each pivot step. The above-mentioned optimistic bound on the number of pivot steps is based on an intelligent choice. At the other extreme, Edmonds has shown that if one makes a pathologically poor choice, the number of pivot steps can grow exponentially with n. A fortiori, the relaxation method may require one to relax an exponentially growing number of inequalities.

Finally, we comment that if *any* feasible solution to the linear program (8.3) could be obtained in fewer than $O(n^3)$ steps, then an important result would follow. Note that if we replace a_{ij} by $\bar{a}_{ij} = a_{ij} + u_i - u_j$, for any numbers $u_1, \ldots, u_n$, then the shortest path lengths are essentially unchanged. If $u_1, \ldots, u_n$ are feasible solutions to (8.3), then $\bar{a}_{ij} \geq 0$ and Dijkstra's procedure can be applied. Thus, the shortest path problem with negative arc lengths (but no negative cycles) could be solved in fewer than $O(n^3)$ steps.

PROBLEMS

8.1   Resolve Problem 5.1 by the dual simplex method. Indicate the tree identified with each successive dual feasible solution.

8.2   Resolve Problem 5.1 by the relaxation method, working "on the network." That is, indicate initial u_j values at the nodes, and revise them downward by inspection of unsatisfied inequalities.

8.3   Let T be a spanning tree rooted from the origin and let $(i, j) \in T$, and $(k, j) \notin T$. What are necessary and sufficient conditions for $T - (i, j) + (k, j)$ also to be a tree rooted from the origin?

8.4   Suppose the network contains a negative cycle. What happens when the dual simplex method is applied? The relaxation method?

9

Shortest Paths between All Pairs of Nodes: Matrix Multiplication

Let us now turn to the problem of finding shortest paths between all pairs of nodes in the network. Instead of computing shortest paths from an origin to each of the other $n - 1$ nodes, we seek to compute shortest paths from each of the n nodes to each of the other $n - 1$ nodes, $n(n - 1)$ shortest paths in all.

We can, of course, choose n separate origins and carry out n separate computations of the type we have described in the preceding sections. However, it is more appealing to try to develop a single integrated procedure.

Let

$$u_{ij} = \text{the length of a shortest path from } i \text{ to } j.$$

$$u_{ij}^{(m)} = \text{the length of a shortest path from } i \text{ to } j, \text{ subject to the condition that the path contains no more than } m \text{ arcs.}$$

Then we have, if $a_{ii} = 0$,

$$\left. \begin{array}{l} u_{ii}^{(0)} = 0 \\[4pt] u_{ij}^{(0)} = +\infty \quad (i \neq j) \\[4pt] u_{ij}^{(m+1)} = \min_k \{u_{ik}^{(m)} + a_{kj}\}. \end{array} \right\} \tag{9.1}$$

If we carry out the indicated computations, we obtain convergence at the $(n-1)$st approximation, i.e., $u_{ij}^{(n-1)} = u_{ij}$. The overall computation is $O(n^4)$, which is just what we should expect for n repetitions of the $O(n^3)$ Bellman-Ford computation.

However, there is something which should pique our interest. Equations (9.1) are very suggestive of the definition of matrix multiplication. We are accustomed to defining the product P of two dimensionally compatible real matrices A and B as follows:

$$P = (p_{ij}) = AB,$$

where

$$p_{ij} = \sum_k a_{ik}b_{kj}.$$

Now suppose we define a new type of matrix multiplication "$\otimes$" as follows:

$$P = (p_{ij}) = A \otimes B,$$

where

$$p_{ij} = \min_k \{a_{ik} + b_{kj}\}.$$

That is, let ordinary addition take the place of multiplication and minimization take the place of addition.

Now let $U^{(m)}$ be the matrix of mth order approximations, i.e., $U^{(m)} = (u_{ij}^{(m)})$. Note that

$$U^{(0)} = \begin{bmatrix} 0 & \infty & \infty & \infty \\ \infty & 0 & \infty & \infty \\ \infty & \infty & 0 & \infty \\ \infty & \infty & \infty & 0 \end{bmatrix}$$

Let $A = (a_{ij})$ be the matrix of arc lengths. Then we see that

$$U^{(1)} = U^{(0)} \otimes A$$

$$U^{(2)} = U^{(1)} \otimes A = (U^{(0)} \otimes A) \otimes A$$

$$\vdots$$

$$U^{(n-1)} = U^{(n-2)} \otimes A = (((U^{(0)} \otimes A) \otimes A) \ldots \otimes A).$$

Two important things to know about this type of matrix multiplication are that $U^{(0)}$ is the identity matrix, i.e., $U^{(0)} \otimes A = A$, and that the multiplication is associative. Together, these facts mean that we can write

$$U^{(n-1)} = A^{n-1},$$

where by A^{n-1} we mean the $(n-1)$st power of the A matrix. It does not matter how we obtain this $n-1$ power. Since $A^{2^k} = A^{n-1}$ for any $2^k \geq n-1$, it seems appropriate simply to square A until a sufficiently high power is obtained. That is, compute $A^2 = A \otimes A$, then $A^4 = A^2 \otimes A^2$, ... A^{2^k}, for $2^k \geq n - 1$.

This method requires $\log_2 n$ matrix multiplications, each of which is an $O(n^3)$ computation. It follows that we have a computation which is $O(n^3 \log n)$ overall.

As an example, consider the network of Figure 3.10. For this network, A, A^2, etc., are as indicated.

$$
A = \begin{bmatrix}
0 & 4 & 5 & \infty & \infty & \infty & \infty \\
\infty & 0 & 6 & 3 & 10 & \infty & \infty \\
\infty & \infty & 0 & 4 & \infty & 9 & \infty \\
\infty & \infty & 3 & 0 & 6 & 3 & \infty \\
\infty & \infty & \infty & 4 & 0 & 3 & 2 \\
\infty & \infty & \infty & \infty & 2 & 0 & 2 \\
\infty & \infty & \infty & \infty & \infty & \infty & 0
\end{bmatrix}
$$

$$
A^2 = \begin{bmatrix}
0 & 4 & 5 & 7 & 14 & 14 & \infty \\
\infty & 0 & 6 & 3 & 9 & 6 & 12 \\
\infty & \infty & 0 & 4 & 10 & 7 & 11 \\
\infty & \infty & 3 & 0 & 5 & 3 & 5 \\
\infty & \infty & 7 & 4 & 0 & 3 & 2 \\
\infty & \infty & \infty & 6 & 2 & 0 & 2 \\
\infty & \infty & \infty & \infty & \infty & \infty & 0
\end{bmatrix}
$$

$$
A^4 = \begin{bmatrix}
0 & 4 & 5 & 7 & 12 & 10 & 12 \\
\infty & 0 & 6 & 3 & 8 & 6 & 8 \\
\infty & \infty & 0 & 4 & 9 & 7 & 9 \\
\infty & \infty & 3 & 0 & 5 & 3 & 5 \\
\infty & \infty & 7 & 4 & 0 & 3 & 2 \\
\infty & \infty & 9 & 6 & 2 & 0 & 2 \\
\infty & \infty & \infty & \infty & \infty & \infty & 0
\end{bmatrix}
$$

$$
U = A^8 = \begin{bmatrix}
0 & 4 & 5 & 7 & 12 & 10 & 12 \\
\infty & 0 & 6 & 3 & 8 & 6 & 8 \\
\infty & \infty & 0 & 4 & 9 & 7 & 9 \\
\infty & \infty & 3 & 0 & 5 & 3 & 5 \\
\infty & \infty & 7 & 4 & 0 & 3 & 2 \\
\infty & \infty & 9 & 6 & 2 & 0 & 2 \\
\infty & \infty & \infty & \infty & \infty & \infty & 0
\end{bmatrix}
$$

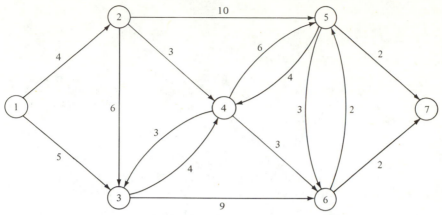

Figure 3.10   Example network

Note that it also is possible to interpret the Bellman-Ford method in terms of matrix multiplication. That is, let $u^{(m)}$ be a row vector, with

$$u^{(m)} = (u_1^{(m)}, u_2^{(m)}, \ldots, u_n^{(m)})$$

and

$$u^{(0)} = (0, \infty, \infty, \ldots, \infty).$$

Then

$$u^{(m+1)} = u^{(m)} \otimes A,$$
$$= u^{(0)} \otimes A^m.$$

PROBLEMS

9.1   Apply the matrix multiplication method to the matrix of arc lengths in Problem 5.1.

9.2   Let p_{ij} represent the probability that arc (i, j) is intact. Modify the equations (9.1) and the definition of matrix multiplication to solve the most reliable path problem. (That is, in terms of the p_{ij} values. Do not use the transformation $a_{ij} = -\log p_{ij}$.)

9.3   Let c_{ij} represent the "capacity" of arc (i, j). Modify equations (9.1) and the definition of matrix multiplication to solve the maximum capacity path problem.

9.4   Suppose we want $u_{ij}^{(m)}$ to represent the length of a shortest path from i to j, subject to the condition that the path contains *exactly* m arcs. (The path may contain repeated nodes.) How should the computation be modified?

9.5   Suppose we simply want to determine which pairs of nodes of a directed graph G are connected. How might we simplify the matrix multiplication method? Let A be the adjacency matrix. What is the form of A^{n-1}? What are necessary and sufficient conditions for G to be strongly connected, in terms of A^{n-1}?

9.6   Prove that the network contains a negative cycle if and only if $A^n \neq A^{n-1}$.

10

Floyd-Warshall Method

A computational method, due to Floyd and to Warshall, finds shortest paths between all pairs of nodes in $O(n^3)$ steps, compared with $O(n^3 \log n)$ for the matrix multiplication method.

We redefine $u_{ij}^{(m)}$ as follows:

$u_{ij}^{(m)}$ = the length of a shortest path from i to j, subject to the condition that the path does not pass through nodes $m, m + 1, \ldots, n$ (i and j excepted).

A shortest path from node i to node j which does not pass through nodes $m + 1, m + 2, \ldots, n$ either (a) does not pass through node m, in which case $u_{ij}^{(m+1)} = u_{ij}^{(m)}$ or (b) does pass through node m, in which case $u_{ij}^{(m+1)} = u_{im}^{(m)} + u_{mj}^{(m)}$.

Thus we have

$$u_{ij}^{(1)} = a_{ij},$$

and

$$u_{ij}^{(m+1)} = \min \{u_{ij}^{(m)}, u_{im}^{(m)} + u_{mj}^{(m)}\},$$

$$\left. \right\} \qquad (10.1)$$

and, clearly, $u_{ij}^{(n+1)} = u_{ij}$, the length of a shortest path from i to j.

We note that $u_{ii}^{(m)} = 0$, for all i and all m. It follows that there are exactly $n(n - 1)(n - 2)$ equations in (10.1) which require explicit solution, each by a single addition and a single comparison. (I.e., equations for which $i, j, m = 1, 2, \ldots, n$; $i \neq j$, $i \neq m$, $j \neq m$.) Thus, the Floyd-Warshall method requires exactly $n(n - 1)(n - 2)$ additions and $n(n - 1)(n - 2)$ comparisons. This is the same order of complexity as the Bellman-Ford method, which yields shortest paths only from a single origin. But, curiously, if all arc lengths are positive, and we apply the Dijkstra method n times for n separate origins, we will perform exactly the same number of comparisons and only about half as many additions as the Floyd-Warshall method. (There are other housekeeping operations which, in practice, may prevent the n-fold Dijkstra computation from being competitive with Floyd-Warshall.)

The Floyd-Warshall computation requires the storage of a single $n \times n$ array. Initially this is $U^{(1)} = A$. Thereafter, $U^{(m+1)}$ is obtained from $U^{(m)}$ by using row m and column m to revise the remaining elements. That is, u_{ij} is compared with $u_{im} + u_{mj}$ and if the latter is smaller, $u_{im} + u_{mj}$ is substituted for u_{ij} in the matrix. This is suggested schematically in Figure 3.11.

We illustrate the computation with the same example used for the

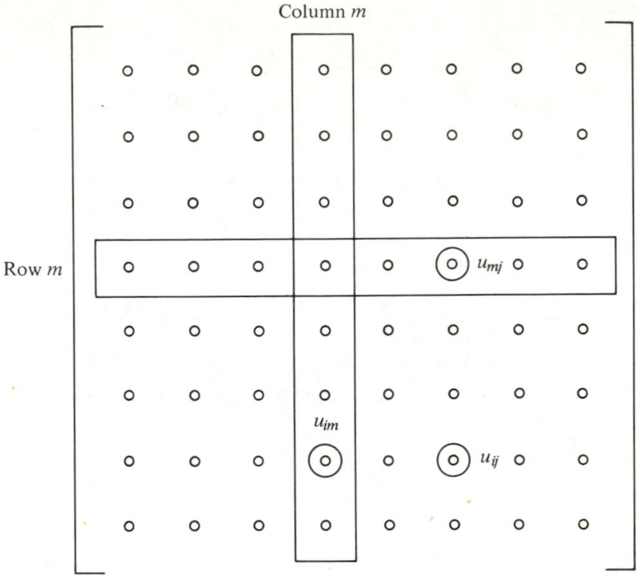

Column m

Row m u_{mj}

u_{im}

u_{ij}

Figure 3.11   Operations on matrix

matrix multiplications method. Initially, we have

$$U^{(1)} = A = \begin{bmatrix} 0 & 4 & 5 & \infty & \infty & \infty & \infty \\ \infty & 0 & 6 & 3 & 10 & \infty & \infty \\ \infty & \infty & 0 & 4 & \infty & 9 & \infty \\ \infty & \infty & 3 & 0 & 6 & 3 & \infty \\ \infty & \infty & \infty & 4 & 0 & 3 & 2 \\ \infty & \infty & \infty & \infty & 2 & 0 & 2 \\ \infty & \infty & \infty & \infty & \infty & \infty & 0 \end{bmatrix}.$$

As it turns out, $U^{(2)} = U^{(1)}$. Thereafter, we have,

$$U^{(3)} = \begin{bmatrix} 0 & 4 & 5 & 7 & 14 & \infty & \infty \\ \infty & 0 & 6 & 3 & 10 & \infty & \infty \\ \infty & \infty & 0 & 4 & \infty & 9 & \infty \\ \infty & \infty & 3 & 0 & 6 & 3 & \infty \\ \infty & \infty & \infty & 4 & 0 & 3 & 2 \\ \infty & \infty & \infty & \infty & 2 & 0 & 2 \\ \infty & \infty & \infty & \infty & \infty & \infty & 0 \end{bmatrix}$$

$$
U^{(4)} = \begin{bmatrix}
0 & 4 & 5 & 7 & 14 & 14 & \infty \\
\infty & 0 & 6 & 3 & 10 & 15 & \infty \\
\infty & \infty & 0 & 4 & \infty & 9 & \infty \\
\infty & \infty & 3 & 0 & 6 & 3 & \infty \\
\infty & \infty & \infty & 4 & 0 & 3 & 2 \\
\infty & \infty & \infty & \infty & 2 & 0 & 2 \\
\infty & \infty & \infty & \infty & \infty & \infty & 0
\end{bmatrix}
$$

$$
U^{(5)} = \begin{bmatrix}
0 & 4 & 5 & 7 & 13 & 10 & \infty \\
\infty & 0 & 6 & 3 & 9 & 6 & \infty \\
\infty & \infty & 0 & 4 & 10 & 7 & \infty \\
\infty & \infty & 3 & 0 & 6 & 3 & \infty \\
\infty & \infty & 7 & 4 & 0 & 3 & 2 \\
\infty & \infty & \infty & \infty & 2 & 0 & 2 \\
\infty & \infty & \infty & \infty & \infty & \infty & 0
\end{bmatrix}
$$

$$
U^{(6)} = \begin{bmatrix}
0 & 4 & 5 & 7 & 13 & 10 & 15 \\
\infty & 0 & 6 & 3 & 9 & 6 & 11 \\
\infty & \infty & 0 & 4 & 10 & 7 & 12 \\
\infty & \infty & 3 & 0 & 6 & 3 & 8 \\
\infty & \infty & 7 & 4 & 0 & 3 & 2 \\
\infty & \infty & 9 & 6 & 2 & 0 & 2 \\
\infty & \infty & \infty & \infty & \infty & \infty & 0
\end{bmatrix}
$$

$$
U = U^{(n+1)} = U^{(8)} = \begin{bmatrix}
0 & 4 & 5 & 7 & 12 & 10 & 12 \\
\infty & 0 & 6 & 3 & 8 & 6 & 8 \\
\infty & \infty & 0 & 4 & 9 & 7 & 9 \\
\infty & \infty & 3 & 0 & 5 & 3 & 5 \\
\infty & \infty & 7 & 4 & 0 & 3 & 2 \\
\infty & \infty & 9 & 6 & 2 & 0 & 2 \\
\infty & \infty & \infty & \infty & \infty & \infty & 0
\end{bmatrix}
$$

This is the same result as that obtained by the matrix multiplication method.

We can derive some further insight into the Floyd-Warshall method from the theorem below.

Theorem 10.1   An $n \times n$ matrix $U = (u_{ij})$ is a matrix of shortest path lengths if and only if

$$\left. \begin{array}{l} u_{ii} = 0 \\[2mm] u_{ij} \leq u_{ik} + u_{kj}, \quad \text{for all } i, j, k. \end{array} \right\} \tag{10.2}$$

The proof is left to the reader.

For any matrix A not satisfying the conditions of the theorem, but for which no negative cycles are implied, there exists a unique largest matrix $U \leq A$ which is a matrix of shortest path lengths. This fact suggests that we might formulate a linear programming problem, analogous to (8.3):

$$\left. \begin{array}{l} \text{maximize} \sum_i \sum_j u_{ij} \\[4mm] \text{subject to} \\[4mm] u_{ij} \leq a_{ij}, \\[2mm] u_{ij} - u_{ik} - u_{kj} \leq 0. \end{array} \right\} \tag{10.3}$$

We can imagine a procedure which checks a matrix U and computes the matrix of shortest path lengths, if U does not satisfy the inequalities (10.2) or (10.3). That is, one simply makes a choice of i, j, k and compares u_{ij} with $u_{ik} + u_{kj}$. If u_{ij} is larger, a relaxation is performed by reducing u_{ij} in value to $u_{ik} + u_{kj}$. When no further relaxations are necessary, the matrix of shortest path lengths has been obtained.

We call the relaxation operation which replaces u_{ij} by

$$\min \{u_{ij}, u_{ik} + u_{kj}\}$$

the *triple operation* for i, j, k. Note that the equivalent of $n(n-1)(n-2)$ triple operations are required simply to verify that a matrix U satisfies the inequalities (10.2) or (10.3), and this is exactly the number required by the Floyd-Warshall method.

The matrix squaring method can be expressed as follows:

and
$$\left. \begin{array}{l} u_{ij}^{(1)} = a_{ij} \\[3mm] u_{ij}^{(2m)} = \min_k \{u_{ik}^{(m)} + u_{kj}^{(m)}\}. \end{array} \right\} \tag{10.4}$$

In effect, this method calls for the equivalent of $n(n-1)(n-2)$ triple operations to be performed at each of $\log_2 n$ iterations.

It follows that the matrix multiplication method, in effect, calls for an inefficient ordering of triple operations. The Floyd-Warshall method prescribes a clever order of triple operations in which each such operation must be performed only once. Another ordering of this type has been proposed by G. B. Dantzig; others are possible.

PROBLEMS

10.1 Apply the Floyd-Warshall method to the matrix of arc lengths in Problem 5.1.

10.2 Resolve Problem 9.2, for the Floyd-Warshall method.

10.3 Resolve Problem 9.3, for the Floyd-Warshall method.

10.4 Prove Theorem 10.1.

10.5 (P. Spria) Show how, with appropriate preconditioning of data, one can apply the Dijkstra algorithm n times to obtain shortest paths between all pairs of nodes in only $\frac{1}{2}(n-1)(n-2)n + O(n^2 \log n)$ comparisons. (*Hint*: Sort the arc lengths first.)

10.6 Suppose that, along with the matrix U, a second $n \times n$ matrix K is maintained. Initially, $U^{(1)} = A$, the matrix of arc lengths, and $K^{(1)} = 0$, the zero matrix. Thereafter, the K matrix is updated at each iteration as follows. If the triple operation i, j, m is performed and it is found that $u_{ij}^{(m)} > u_{im}^{(m)} + u_{mj}^{(m)}$, then $k_{ij}^{(m+1)}$ is set to m. Otherwise, $k_{ij}^{(m+1)} = k_{ij}^{(m)}$. Show how to use the matrix $K^{(n+1)}$ to construct the actual sequence of arcs in a shortest path from i to j in $O(n)$ operations. (It is a very simple and clean procedure; a pushdown stack is helpful.)

10.7 Suppose the shortest path from i to j is not unique. For example, suppose there are two shortest paths: one path contains arcs $(i, 10), (10, 1), (1, j)$ and the other contains arcs $(i, 2), (2, 4), (4, j)$. Which path is chosen by the Floyd-Warshall algorithm? (Assume a path construction technique like that developed in the previous problem.) State a simple rule for answering this question in general.

11

Detection of Negative Cycles

Up to this point we have avoided the question of how negative cycles affect the various shortest path computations and how we should go about detecting negative cycles if that is our objective. This question becomes of great importance in Section 13.

Although the results we state do not strictly require it, it is reasonable to suppose that the network is strongly connected. If this is not the case, it may be best to identify the strong components and analyze the components separately.

We leave the proof of the theorem below as an exercise for the reader.

Theorem 11.1 Let the network have a path from node 1 to each of the other nodes. Then the network contains a negative cycle if and only if, in (6.1) or (7.1), $u_j^{(n)} < u_j^{(n-1)}$, for at least one $j = 1, 2, \ldots, n$.

Theorem 11.1 suggests that to detect the existence of negative cycles, all that is necessary is to carry out the Bellman-Ford or Yen computation for one additional iteration. Thus, the complexity of the computation remains at $O(n^3)$.

It may be possible to halt the computation earlier by testing for other conditions which are sufficient to indicate the existence or nonexistence of negative cycles. One condition is that $u_1^{(m)} < 0$, for any m (there is a negative cycle containing node 1). Another such condition is that $u_j^{(m+1)} = u_j^{(m)}$, for all j and for any m (there are no negative cycles). Still another set of such conditions is given by the following theorem.

Theorem 11.2   The network contains a negative cycle if, in (6.1), $u_j^{(m+1)} < u_j^{(m)}$, for some $m = 1, 2, 3, \ldots, n-1$, and for at least $n - m$ distinct nodes j.

These sufficient conditions may well enable the computation to be ended earlier, but they do not affect the worst-case bound of n^3 additions and n^3 comparisons, in the case of (6.1).

Note that Theorem 11.2 is actually a statement of the property which yields a $n^3/4$ algorithm, as described in the last paragraph of Section 7.

In the case of the matrix multiplication and Floyd-Warshall methods, we have the following theorem.

Theorem 11.3   The network contains a negative cycle if and only if, in (9.1) or (10.1), $u_{ii}^{(m)} < 0$, for some $i = 1, 2, \ldots, n$ and some $m = 1, 2, 3, \ldots, n$.

The Floyd-Warshall method has essentially the same upper bound on the number of computational steps as the (unmodified) Bellman-Ford algorithm. However, in practice, it appears that the Bellman-Ford algorithm is more likely to terminate early, and should be preferred for the detection of negative cycles.

If the network contains no negative cycles, then we can compute the length of a shortest cycle, as follows.

Theorem 11.4   If the network does not contain a negative cycle, then the length of a shortest cycle is given by

$$\min_i \{u_{ii}^{(n+1)}\},$$

where $u_{ii}^{(n+1)}$ is determined by (9.1), or (10.1), with $a_{ii} = +\infty$, for all i.

PROBLEMS

11.1   Test each of the following matrices of arc lengths for negative cycles by the Bellman-Ford method:

$$
\begin{bmatrix}
0 & 1 & 10 & \infty & \infty \\
\infty & 0 & \infty & \infty & 20 \\
\infty & -2 & 0 & -3 & \infty \\
\infty & -12 & 6 & 0 & 1 \\
\infty & \infty & 1 & \infty & 0
\end{bmatrix},
\begin{bmatrix}
0 & -8 & 1 & \infty & \infty \\
\infty & 0 & \infty & \infty & 20 \\
\infty & -3 & 0 & 0 & \infty \\
\infty & -12 & 6 & 0 & 1 \\
\infty & \infty & 1 & \infty & 0
\end{bmatrix}
$$

11.2   Prove Theorem 11.1.

11.3   Prove Theorem 11.2.

11.4   Prove Theorems 11.3 and 11.4.

11.5   Reduce the traveling salesman problem to the problem of finding a *most* negative cycle.

11.6   Obtain the proper analog of Theorem 11.2 for equations (7.1).

12
Networks with Transit Times

Suppose, in addition to a length a_{ij}, a positive integer *transit time* t_{ij} is identified with each arc (i, j). There are a number of interesting problems associated with such networks. For example, suppose we seek to find a shortest path from the origin, subject to the condition that no more than T units of time are required.
.Let

$u_j(t) =$ the length of a shortest path from the origin to node j, subject to the condition that the path requires no more than t units of time.

We can easily establish the equations

$$
\left.
\begin{aligned}
u_j(t) &= +\infty, \quad \text{for } t < 0, \\
u_1(0) &= 0 \\
u_j(t) &= \min\{u_j(t-1), \min_k\{u_k(t-t_{kj}) + a_{kj}\}\}.
\end{aligned}
\right\} \tag{12.1}
$$

The equations (12.1) can be viewed as a generalization of the Bellman-Ford equations (6.1); they imply an $O(n^2 T)$ computation to determine $u_j(T)$ for all j.

Now suppose we seek to find shortest paths between all pairs of nodes. It is possible to apply equations (12.1) n times, for n distinct origins, yielding an $O(n^3 T)$ computation. Or a single set of equations analogous to the matrix multiplication equations (9.1) can be formulated. These also imply an $O(n^3 T)$ computation. Unfortunately, however, the computation which is implied by this approach is not a simple matrix multiplication. Hence a simple matrix squaring technique, which would be $O(n^3 \log T)$ in complexity, does not seem to be feasible.

However, it is sometimes possible to do better than $O(n^3 T)$. Suppose each $t_{ij} \leq \tau$. Then we have the following proposition.

Proposition 12.2 Let P_{ij} be a path from i to j which requires no more than $2t$ units of time. Then P_{ij} can be broken into two paths P_{ik} and P_{kj} (where possibly $i = k$ or $k = j$), which respectively require no more than $t - \delta$ and $t + \delta$ units of time, for some $0 \leq \delta \leq \tau$.

Define $u_{ij}(t)$ in the obvious way, and obtain the equations

$$u_{ii}(t) = 0$$
$$u_{ij}(2t) = \min_{0 \leq \delta \leq \tau} \{ \min_k \{ u_{ik}(t - \delta) + u_{kj}(t + \delta) \} \}, \tag{12.2}$$

that may be considered to be, formally, a generalization of the matrix squaring equations (10.4).

More generally, we have

$$u_{ii}(t) = 0$$
$$u_{ij}(2t + \delta') = \min_{0 \leq \delta \leq \tau} \{ \min_k \{ u_{ik}(t + \delta' - \delta) + u_{kj}(t + \delta) \} \} \tag{12.3}$$
$$u_{ij}(2t - \delta') = \min_{0 \leq \delta \leq \tau} \{ \min_k \{ u_{ik}(t - \delta) + u_{kj}(t - \delta' + \delta) \} \}.$$

Equations (12.3) imply that $u_{ij}(T)$ can be computed for all i, j, in $O(n^3 \tau^2 \log T)$ steps. If τ is sufficiently small, i.e. $\tau^2 \ll T/\log_2 T$, this is an improvement.

As an application of these methods, consider the following problem, which requires a two-stage shortest path computation. We wish to route a vehicle through a network in which there are only certain nodes at which it can refuel. The travel time between successive refuelings must not exceed T units of time.

Suppose there are m refueling nodes, and the origin and destination for the vehicle are among them. We first apply equations (12.1) or (12.2) to obtain $u_{ij}(T)$, for all nodes i, j. We then solve a conventional (not time constrained) shortest path problem over an m-node network of refueling nodes, in which the length of arc (i, j) is $u_{ij}(T)$. The length of a shortest path in this network is the length of a shortest path in the original network, subject to refueling constraints. The overall computation is $O(n^3 T)$ or $O(n^3 \tau^2 \log T)$, depending upon whether (12.1) or (12.2) are used.

PROBLEMS

12.1 Determine the structure of an $(nT + 1)$-node acyclic network identified with equations (12.1), just as the network in Figure 3.7 is identified with the equations (6.1).

12.2 Some practical problem situations suggest that it may be useful to permit both transit times and arc lengths to be time-varying. For example, at time t_1 there may be an airline connection from city i to city j costing $a_{ij}(t_1)$ dollars and requiring $t_{ij}(t_1)$ hours. At another time t_2 there may be a train, costing $a_{ij}(t_2)$ dollars and requiring $t_{ij}(t_2)$ hours, where $a_{ij}(t_1) > a_{ij}(t_2)$ and $t_{ij}(t_1) < t_{ij}(t_2)$. One may wish to know the minimum cost to travel from city 1 to city n in time T.

To be precise, let

$$a_{ij} = \text{the length (cost) of an arc from node } i$$
$$\text{to node } j, \text{terminating at } j \text{ at time } t,$$
$$\text{if there is such an arc};$$
$$= +\infty, \text{otherwise}$$
$$t_{ij}(t) = \text{the transit time of an arc from node } i$$
$$\text{to node } j, \text{terminating at } j \text{ at time } t$$
$$\text{(and originating at } i \text{ at time } t - t_{ij}(t)).$$

In order to simplify matters, assume that for any i, j, t, there is at most one arc (i, j) directed into node j at time t. Modify the time-invariant equations (12.1) to fit the time-varying case, and show that the complexity measure remains $O(n^2 T)$.

12.3 Prove Proposition 12.2.

12.4 Justify, in detail, the complexity measure of $O(n^3 \tau^2 \log T)$ for the equations (12.3).

12.5 Suppose there is one arc in the network which has a much longer transit time than any of the others. One way to reduce the magnitude of τ, and thereby speed up the computation by equations (12.3), is to subdivide this arc into smaller arcs, each with shorter transit times. Now suppose we subdivide *all* the arcs in the network into arcs with unit transit times. Then a path requires no more than T units of time if and only if it contains no more than T arcs. Show how to apply matrix squaring to compute $u_{ij}(T)$, and obtain a bound on the length of the computation.

13

The Minimal Cost-to-Time Ratio Cycle Problem

Consider the following problem formulation due to Dantzig. A tramp steamer is free to choose its ports of call and the order in which it calls on them. A voyage from port i to port j earns p_{ij} dollars profit, and requires t_{ij} days time (including time for loading cargo at i and unloading at j).

What ports should the steamer visit, and in what order, so as to maximize its mean daily profit?

A solution to this optimization problem is found by identifying a directed cycle within the network for which the ratio of total profit to total travel time is as large as possible. The tramp steamer then sails from its starting point to any port within this cycle, and then continues to sail around the cycle indefinitely.

We are accustomed to minimizing rather than maximizing. Accordingly, we shall continue to deal with a network in which each arc (i, j) has a length or cost a_{ij} (let $a_{ij} = -p_{ij}$) and a transit time t_{ij} and we shall seek a directed cycle C for which

$$q(C) = \frac{\sum\limits_{C} a_{ij}}{\sum\limits_{C} t_{ij}} \tag{13.1}$$

is minimum. This is called the "minimal cost-to-time ratio cycle problem."

For the special case in which $t_{ij} = 1$, for all i, j, the following method suggests itself. Set $a_{ii} = +\infty$ and compute $u_{ii}^{(m)}$ for $i = 1, 2, \ldots, n$ and $m = 2, 3, \ldots, n$ by the matrix multiplication method (9.1). Then the minimum value of $q(C)$ is equal to

$$\min_{i} \min_{m} \left\{ \frac{u_{ii}^{(m)}}{m} \right\}.$$

This technique can be generalized. However, even in the special case that $t_{ij} = 1$, an $O(n^4)$ computation is implied. We shall now develop a computational procedure which is essentially $O(n^3 \log n)$.

In the following several paragraphs, we do not assume that the t_{ij} values are necessarily positive integers, or even positive. Although we may allow some t_{ij}'s to be negative (the physical interpretation of negative time is admittedly not clear), we do make the not unreasonable assumption that

$$\sum_{(i,j) \in C} t_{ij} > 0, \tag{13.2}$$

for all cycles C.

Suppose we guess a minimum value λ for the cost-to-time ratio (13.1) and give each arc (i, j) a new cost $\bar{a}_{ij} = a_{ij} - \lambda t_{ij}$. There are three situations that may exist with respect to these modified cost coefficients $\bar{a}_{ij}$:

Case 1   There is a negative cycle in the network.

Case 2   There is no negative cycle, and the cost of minimal-cost cycle is exactly zero.

Case 3   There is no negative cycle, and the cost of a minimal-cost cycle is strictly positive.

Suppose that Case 1 holds. Let C be a negative cycle. Then

$$\sum_C \bar{a}_{ij} = \sum_C (a_{ij} - \lambda t_{ij}) < 0.$$

By assumption (13.2), it follows that

$$\frac{\sum\limits_C a_{ij}}{\sum\limits_C t_{ij}} < \lambda.$$

In other words, the guessed value of λ is too large and C is a cycle for which the cost-to-time ratio is strictly smaller than λ.

By similar analysis, we see that in Case 2 the guessed value of λ is exactly equal to the minimal cost-to-time ratio, and in Case 3 λ is too small.

These observations suggest a search procedure based on the testing of successive trial values of λ. There are two principal types of searches we might conduct: "monotonic" and "binary."

One can organize a monotonic search by choosing an initial value $\lambda^{(0)}$ at least as large as the minimum cost-time ratio, and then, by successive applications of Case 1, obtain $\lambda^{(0)} > \lambda^{(1)} > \lambda^{(2)} > \ldots$, until some $\lambda^{(p)}$ is found for which Case 2 holds. This must occur in a finite number of steps, because there are only a finite number of cycles. Hence there are only a finite number of possible cost-time ratios.

Actually, it will be shown below that a monotonic search requires only $O(n^3)$ trial values of λ. Since each trial value requires an $O(n^3)$ negative cycle computation, the monotonic search procedure is $O(n^6)$ overall.

The binary search provides a much better bound and is possibly more effective in practice. The binary search proceeds as follows. Suppose we know that the optimum cost-time ratio is contained in the interval (a, b). We first try the trial value of $\lambda = (a + b)/2$. If Case 1 holds, we know that the optimum ratio is contained in the interval $(a, (a + b)/2)$. If Case 3 holds, the optimum ratio is in the interval $((a + b)/2, b)$. If Case 2 holds, we have, of course, found the optimum value of the cost-time ratio at the first try.

We continue in this way, halving the remaining interval with each trial value. After k trial values the length of the remaining interval can be no greater than $(b - a)/2^k$. Or, to put it another way, the number of trial values required to reduce the length of the interval to ε is $\log_2 (b - a) - \log_2 \varepsilon$.

We continue the interval-halving procedure until the remaining interval is so small that only one distinct cost-time ratio can be contained within the interval. Then one additional trial value of λ is sufficient to find the cycle with this minimal ratio. (The final value of λ is chosen to be equal to the largest value in the ε-interval; either Case 1 or Case 2 must hold.)

Now let us suppose that all the parameters a_{ij} and t_{ij} are integers and that $|a_{ij}| \leq \gamma$ and $|t_{ij}| \leq \tau$, for all i, j. Each cycle contains at most n arcs, and the smallest possible value for the sum of the transit times around any cycle is unity. Hence the minimum and maximum attainable cost-to-time ratios are $a = -n\gamma$ and $b = n\gamma$, respectively.

Furthermore, if the cost-to-time ratios for two cycles are unequal, those ratios must differ by at least $\varepsilon = 1/n^2\tau^2$. This can be seen as follows. Let A/T and A'/T' be two distinct cost-to-time ratios. Then

$$\left| \frac{A}{T} - \frac{A'}{T'} \right| = \left| \frac{AT' - A'T}{TT'} \right| \neq 0.$$

The difference between the ratios is minimized by letting $AT' - A'T = 1$ and $TT' = n^2\tau^2$. (It is possible that cost-to-time ratios for closed paths other than cycles may differ by less than $1/n^2\tau^2$, but this does not affect the convergence arguments.)

It immediately follows from the above observations that there can be no more than $2n^3\gamma\tau^2$ distinct ratios in all, or $O(n^3)$ distinct ratios if we assume γ and τ to be invariant with n. This yields the bound of $O(n^6)$ for monotonic search.

It also follows that the binary search procedure requires no more trial values of λ than $\log_2(b - a) - \log_2 \varepsilon = \log_2(2n\gamma) - \log_2(1/n^2\tau^2) = 1 + 3\log_2 n + \log_2 \gamma + 2\log_2 \tau$. Thus, the number of negative-cycle problems which must be solved is $0(\log n + \log \gamma + \log \tau)$.

Suppose we are concerned with networks of various sizes, but with similar cost and time parameter values. If we assume that γ and τ are invariant with n (or even if γ and τ increase as polynomial functions of n) then the number of negative cycle computations is simply proportional to $\log_2 n$ and the overall computation is $O(n^3 \log n)$.

Even if we make no assumptions about the nature of the parameters a_{ij} and t_{ij}, it is clear that the number of computational steps is bounded by a polynomial function in the number of bits required to specify an instance of the problem. In this sense, the minimal cost-to-time ratio problem can be considered to be a well-solved combinatorial optimization problem.

14
M Shortest Paths: Dreyfus Method

Sometimes it is useful to be able to compute in addition to the shortest path, the second, third, ..., Mth shortest paths between a specified pair of nodes. For example, there may be some complex set of constraints associated with paths. By simply ignoring the constraints and listing paths in order from the shortest onward, we may be able to determine the shortest path satisfying the constraints in question.

In order to simplify our analysis, we make a number of assumptions. In particular, paths containing repeated nodes are admissible paths and even the origin may be visited more than once. Two paths are considered distinct if they do not visit precisely the same nodes in the same order. This does permit two distinct paths to possess precisely the same arcs. However, all paths have different lengths. Ties are broken by a lexico-graphic ordering.

The method we shall describe, due to S. E. Dreyfus, computes the M shortest paths from an origin (node 1) to each of the other $n - 1$ nodes of the network, and does so in $O(Mn \log n)$ running time.

Let

$$u_j^{[m]} = \text{the length of the } m\text{th shortest path from the origin to node } j$$

and

$$\mu(k, j, m) = \text{the number of paths in which } (k, j) \text{ is the final arc, in the set of 1st, 2nd, ..., } m\text{th shortest paths from node 1 to node } j.$$

By definition,

$$\mu(k, j, 0) = 0.$$

During the course of the computation $\mu(k, j, m)$ will be updated quite simply:

$$\mu(k, j, m + 1) = \begin{cases} \mu(k, j, m) + 1, \text{ if } (k, j) \text{ is the final arc in the} \\ (m + 1)\text{st shortest path from the origin to } j, \\ \mu(k, j, m), \text{ otherwise.} \end{cases}$$

The $(m + 1)$st shortest path from 1 to j has some final arc (k, j). The length of this path from the origin to k must be $u_k^{[\mu(k,j,m)+1]}$. Accordingly, by minimizing over all possible choices of k, we obtain

$$u_j^{[m+1]} = \min_k \{u_k^{[\mu(k,j,m)+1]} + a_{kj}\} \tag{14.1}$$

with the initial condition

$$u_1^{[1]} = 0.$$

Equations (14.1) are clearly equivalent to Bellman's equations (3.1) for the case $m = 0$ (except that the condition $k \neq j$ is eliminated, because we permit loops). The reader will also note that, as in (3.1), there is a problem of implicit functional relationships. That is, $u_j^{[m+1]}$ may be defined in terms of $u_k^{[m+1]}$, which may in turn be defined in terms of $u_j^{[m+1]}$. We learned how to resolve this problem for $m = 0$ in Section 6, and possibly we could use a similar technique here. There is, however, a simpler solution.

Let us consider the computation of $u_j^{[2]}$, for all j. The value of $u_1^{[2]}$ (which may be infinity) is given by

$$u_1^{[2]} = \min_k \{u_k^{[1]} + a_{k1}\}.$$

For each node j whose shortest path from the origin contains only one arc, (14.1) is equivalent to

$$u_j^{[2]} = \min \{u_1^{[2]} + a_{1j}, \min_{k \neq 1} \{u_k^{[1]} + a_{kj}\}\}.$$

For each node j whose shortest path from the origin contains two arcs, say $(1, i)$ and (i, j), (14.1) is equivalent to

$$u_j^{[2]} = \min \{u_i^{[2]} + a_{ij}, \min_{k \neq i} \{u_k^{[1]} + a_{kj}\}\}.$$

We can continue, computing $u_j^{[2]}$ for nodes j whose shortest paths from the origin contain three, four, $\ldots$, $n - 1$ arcs. At no time is the value of $u_k^{[2]}$ required on the right-hand side of equations (14.1), unless it has already been computed.

In general, $u_k^{[m+1]}$ appears on the right-hand side of equations (14.1) only if the arc (k, j) is the final arc in each of the 1st, 2nd, $\ldots$, mth shortest paths from the origin to node j. But since (k, j) is the final arc of the shortest path to j, it follows that the number of arcs in a shortest path to node k is one less than the number of arcs in a shortest path to j. Therefore, if the nodes j are processed in order of the number of arcs in their shortest paths from the origin, the value of $u_k^{[m+1]}$ will be known when it is needed in the computation of $u_j^{[m+1]}$. Hence the functional relationship in (14.1) is explicit.

The initial computation of $u_j^{[1]}$, for all j, requires either $O(n^2)$ or $O(n^3)$ running time using the Dijkstra or the Bellman-Ford method, depending upon whether or not the network contains negative arcs. The computation of $u_j^{[m+1]}$ by (14.1), for a given j, seems to require $O(n)$ additions and comparisons, but this can be reduced to $O(\log n)$ running time, as described in Problem 14.2. Thus, to compute $u_j^{[M]}$, for all j, requires $O(Mn \log n)$ running time, in addition to the time required for the initial shortest path computation.

The algorithm requires that $u_k^{[m]}$ be stored, for $m = 1, 2, ..., M$, for which Mn words are needed. In addition at each iteration, $\mu(k, j, m)$ must be stored for each arc (k, j). Thus, $Mn + m'$ words of storage are required, where m' is the number of arcs in the network. This, of course, is in addition to the storage required for the specification of the network itself.

PROBLEMS

14.1   Consider the network shown in Figure 3.12, in which the tree of shortest paths is indicated with bold arcs. Use Dreyfus' method to compute fourth shortest paths to each of the nodes. How many of these paths contain repeated nodes?

14.2   (D. E. Knuth)   By using a priority queue for each node, show that it is possible to reduce the running time for each iteration of Dreyfus' method to $O(n \log n)$.

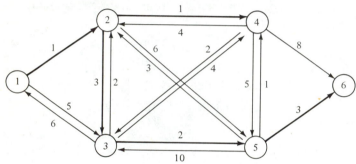

Figure 3.12   Network for Problem 14.1

15

M Shortest Paths without Repeated Nodes

We now consider the problem of computing the first, second, ..., Mth shortest paths between a specified pair of nodes, where we do not permit these paths to contain repeated nodes. The procedure is possibly conceptually simpler than that described in the previous section, but is computationally more arduous. The computation is $O(Mn^3)$ in length, and requires $O(Mn)$ words of storage, in addition to the storage ordinarily required for the shortest path problem.

Our strategy is essentially as follows. Let $\mathscr{P}$ denote the set of all paths (without repeated nodes) from node 1 to node n. Initially we find P_1, the shortest path in $\mathscr{P}$. (Here and in the sequel we assume that ties between paths of equal length are resolved by an unspecified tie-breaking rule, perhaps by lexicography. Thus P_1 is uniquely determined.) We then partition $\mathcal{P} - \{P_1\}$ into subsets $\mathcal{P}_1, \mathcal{P}_2, ..., \mathcal{P}_k$, where $k \le n - 1$, in such a way that we are able to determine the shortest path in each subset. The shortest of these shortest paths is clearly P_2, the second shortest path from node 1 to node n. Suppose $P_2 \in \mathcal{P}_j$. We then partition $\mathcal{P}_j - \{P_2\}$ into subsets, in the same way that we partitioned $\mathcal{P} - \{P_1\}$. The subsets obtained from the partitioning of $\mathcal{P}_j - \{P_2\}$, together with $\mathcal{P}_1, \mathcal{P}_2, ..., \mathcal{P}_{j-1}, \mathcal{P}_{j+1}, ..., \mathcal{P}_k$, constitute a partition of $\mathcal{P} - \{P_1, P_2\}$. The shortest of the shortest paths found in the subsets which partition $\mathcal{P} - \{P_1, P_2\}$ is clearly P_3, the third shortest path.

At the general step of the procedure, $\mathcal{P} - \{P_1, P_2, ..., P_m\}$ has been partitioned into subsets $\mathcal{P}_1, \mathcal{P}_2, ..., \mathcal{P}_k$. The shortest of the shortest paths found in any of these subsets is P_{m+1}, the $(m + 1)$st shortest path. If $P_{m+1} \in \mathcal{P}_j$, then $\mathcal{P}_j - \{P_{m+1}\}$ is partitioned into no more than $n - 1$ subsets. These subsets, together with $\mathcal{P}_1, \mathcal{P}_2, ..., \mathcal{P}_{j-1}, \mathcal{P}_{j+1}, ..., \mathcal{P}_k$, yield a partition of $\mathcal{P} - \{P_1, P_2, ..., P_{m+1}\}$.

The procedure can be visualized in terms of a rooted tree, as shown in Figure 3.13. Each node in the tree is identified with a subset of paths. A node is given the label P_m if that path was found in the corresponding subset. The arcs directed from a node point to subsets formed by further partitioning. Note that $\mathcal{P} - \{P_1, P_2, ..., P_m\}$ is partitioned into no more than $m(n - 2) + 1$ subsets, corresponding to the number of leaves of the tree at that point in the computation.

The key to the procedure is the ability to partition $\mathcal{P}_j - \{P_{m+1}\}$ into subsets in such a way that it is easy to compute the shortest path in

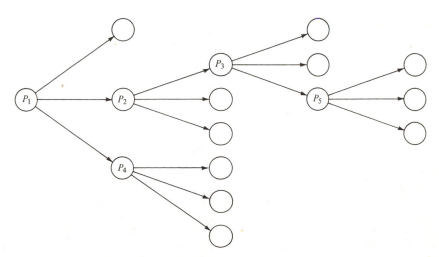

Figure 3.13   Search tree for computation

each of the subsets. This is accomplished through the forced inclusion and exclusion of arcs.

Each subset $\mathscr{P}_j$ in the partition of $\mathscr{P} - \{P_1, P_2, \ldots, P_m\}$ contains all paths which (a) include the arcs in a certain specified path from node 1 to another node p, and (b) from which certain other arcs from node p are excluded. Without loss of generality, suppose the specified path from 1 to p contains arcs $(1, 2), (2, 3), \ldots, (p - 1, p)$. A shortest path in $\mathscr{P}_j$ is found by simply finding a shortest path from p to n in the given network, after the deletion of nodes $1, 2, \ldots, p - 1$, and the arcs excluded in condition (b). Clearly, this requires nothing more than the application of an ordinary shortest path computation to the reduced network.

Now suppose $P_{m+1} \in \mathscr{P}_j$, and again without loss of generality, suppose P_{m+1} contains arcs $(1, 2), (2, 3), \ldots, (q - 1, q), (q, n)$, where $q \geq p$. If $q = p$, then $\mathscr{P}_j - \{P_{m+1}\}$ contains all paths which include the arcs $(1, 2)$, $(2, 3), \ldots, (p - 1, p)$, and from which (p, n) is excluded, along with the arcs from p excluded from $\mathscr{P}_j$. If $q > p$, then $\mathscr{P}_j - \{P_{m+1}\}$ is partitioned into $q - p + 1$ subsets $\mathscr{P}'_1, \mathscr{P}'_2, \ldots, \mathscr{P}'_{q-p+1}$. $\mathscr{P}'_1$ contains all paths which include $(1, 2), (2, 3), \ldots, (p - 1, p)$, and from which $(p, p + 1)$ is excluded, along with the arcs from p excluded from $\mathscr{P}_j$. $\mathscr{P}'_k$, $1 < k < q - p + 1$, contains all paths which include the arcs $(1, 2), (2, 3), \ldots, (p + k - 2, p + k - 1)$, and from which $(p + k - 1, p + k)$ is excluded. $\mathscr{P}'_{q-p+1}$ contains all paths which include arcs $(1, 2), (2, 3), \ldots, (q - 1, q)$, and from which (q, n) is excluded.

The reader should be able to verify that this scheme yields a valid partition of $\mathscr{P}_j - \{P_m\}$, and that the conditions defining each subset of the partition are of the same form as (a) and (b) for P_j.

The solution of the shortest path problem for each subset requires an $O(n^2)$ computation if all arc lengths are nonnegative. If this is not the case, an initial $O(n^3)$ computation suffices to determine shortest path lengths u_j from the origin, and each arc length a_{ij} can be replaced by $\bar{a}_{ij} = a_{ij} + u_i - u_j \geq 0$. (See the final paragraph of Section 8.) This trick is utilized in the summary of the algorithm below.

COMPUTATION OF M SHORTEST PATHS WITHOUT REPEATED NODES

Step 0 (Start) If all arc lengths are nonnegative, find the shortest path from node 1 to node n by Dijkstra's method. If not all arc lengths are nonnegative, find the shortest paths from node 1 to each of the other nodes, using the Bellman-Ford method, and then replace a_{ij} by $a_{ij} + u_i - u_j \geq 0$ for each arc in the network.

Place the shortest path from node 1 to node n in LIST as the only entry. Set $m = 1$.

Step 1   (*Output mth Shortest Path*)   If LIST is empty, stop; there are no more paths from 1 to n. Otherwise, remove the shortest path in LIST and output this path as P_m.

If $m = M$, stop; the computation is completed.

Step 2   (*Augmentation of LIST*)   Suppose, without loss of generality, that P_m contains arcs $(1, 2), (2, 3), \ldots, (q - 1, q), (q, n)$ and that P_m is the shortest path from node 1 to node n subject to the conditions that it is forced to include arcs $(1, 2), (2, 3), \ldots, (p - 1, p)$, where $p \leq q$, and that certain arcs from node p are excluded. (These conditions are stored with P_m as part of the same entry in LIST.)

If $p = q$, apply Dijkstra's method to find the shortest path from 1 to n, subject to the conditions that arcs $(1, 2), (2, 3), \ldots, (p - 1, p)$ are included, and that (p, n) is excluded, in addition to the arcs from p excluded for P_m. If there is such a shortest path, place it in LIST together with a record of the conditions under which it was obtained.

If $p > q$, then apply Dijkstra's method to find the shortest path from 1 to n, subject to each of the following sets of conditions:

(1)   Arcs $(1, 2), (2, 3), \ldots, (p - 1, p)$ are included and arc $(p, p + 1)$ is excluded, in addition to the arcs from p excluded for P_m.

(2)   Arcs $(1, 2), (2, 3), \ldots, (p, p + 1)$ are included, and arc $(p + 1, p + 2)$ is excluded.
$\vdots$

$(q - p - 2)$ Arcs $(1, 2), (2, 3), \ldots, (q - 2, q - 1)$ are included, and arc $(q - 1, q)$ is excluded.

$(q - p - 1)$ Arcs $(1, 2), (2, 3), \ldots, (q - 1, q)$ are included, and arc (q, n) is excluded.

Place each of the shortest paths so obtained in LIST, together with a record of the conditions under which it was obtained.

Set $m = m + 1$ and return to Step 1. //

In order to compute the Mth shortest path, $O(Mn)$ shortest path computations, each of $O(n^2)$ must be carried out. Thus $O(Mn^3)$ running time is required for these computations.

The algorithm may generate as many as $O(Mn)$ entries for LIST. If the value of M is known in advance (as is assumed in the description of of the algorithm), all but the shortest $M - m$ paths in LIST can be discarded at the mth iteration. Moreoever, even if the value of M is not known in advance (e.g., the algorithm may be allowed to run until the shortest path satisfying certain conditions is found), a storage reduction scheme can be implemented which reduces the size of list to $O(M)$ entries, but doubles the number of shortest path computations. (An explanation of this storage reduction scheme can be found in the references.) In either case, the number of entires in LIST can be assumed to be $O(M)$, and since each entry requires $O(n)$ space, the total storage requirement for LIST is $O(Mn)$.

There are various data structures that can be used for LIST. Perhaps the most appropriate is a priority queue, which permits either removal of the shortest path in LIST or the insertion of a new entry in $O(\log M)$ time. Since there are at most $O(Mn)$ entries to be removed or inserted, the time required for these operations is at worst $O(Mn \log M)$. But $\log M \leq n \log n$, since $M \leq n!$. Hence the $O(Mn \log M)$ running time for these operations is dominated by the running time for the shortest path computations, and the algorithm may fairly be said to be $O(Mn^3)$.

PROBLEM

15.1   Apply the algorithm to find the 1st, 2nd, ..., 4th shortest paths from node 1 to node 6 for the network in Figure 3.12.

COMMENTS AND REFERENCES

Much of the material in this chapter is adapted from the excellent survey paper,

S. E. Dreyfus, "An Appraisal of Some Shortest-Path Algorithms," *Operations Research,* **17** (1969) 395–412.

One topic which is not discussed in this chapter is the question of sparse networks, particularly those which lend themselves to decomposition techniques. For this further topic see

A. H. Land and S. W. Stairs, "The Extension of the Cascade Algorithm to Large Graphs," *Mgt. Sci.,* **14** (1967) 29–33.

T. C. Hu, "A Decomposition Algorithm for Shortest Paths in a Network," *Operations Research,* **16** (1968) 91–102.

D. B. Johnson, "Algorithms for Shortest Paths," Ph.D. thesis, Cornell Univ., Ithaca, New York, 1973.

SECTION 2
The formulation of the knapsack problem as a longest path problem is adapted from

D. R. Fulkerson, "Flow Networks and Combinatorial Operations Research," *Amer. Math. Monthly,* **72** (1966) 115–138.

SECTION 3

R. E. Bellman, "On a Routing Problem," *Quart. Appl. Math,* **16** (1958) 87–90.

SECTION 4

It is difficult to determine priority for the shortest path algorithm for acyclic networks. We can consider it to be part of the folklore.

SECTION 5

E. W. Dijkstra, "A Note on Two Problems in Connexion with Graphs," *Numerische Mathematik,* **1** (1959) 269–271.

The following paper is a bit earlier than Dijkstra's:

E. F. Moore, "The Shortest Path Through a Maze," *Proc. Int. Symp. on the Theory of Switching,* Part II, April 2–5, 1957. *The Annals of the Computation Laboratory of Harvard University* **30**, Harvard University Press, 1959, pp. 285–292.

It describes an essentially Dijkstra-like procedure for the special case in which, for all (i, j), $a_{ij} = a_{ji} = 1$. Moreover, Moore showed in this case that to construct the tree of shortest paths it is not necessary to compute and and store the u_j values. Instead, it is sufficient to record only two bits of information at each node.

SECTION 6

See the paper by Bellman, *op. cit.* and

L. R. Ford, Jr., "Network Flow Theory," The Rand Corp., P-923, August 1956.

SECTION 7

J. Y. Yen, "An Algorithm for Finding Shortest Routes from all Source Nodes to a Given Destination in General Network," *Quart. Appl. Math.,* **27** (1970) 526–530.

SECTIONS 8 AND 9

The interpretation of the various algorithms as variants of a relaxation procedure was developed by the author for this book, but has surely been known to other investigators. The matrix multiplication method appears to be part of the folklore.

It should be noted that the multiplication of two $n \times n$ real matrices can be carried out in $n^{2.8}$ multiplications, instead of n^3, as in the conventional method. See

V. Strassen, "Gaussian Elimination Is Not Optimal," *Numerische Mathematik,* **11** (1969) 354–356.

Although Strassen's method does not apply to the special type of matrix multiplication defined for the general shortest path problem, it can be applied to the problem of multiplying Boolean matrices. Thus, the problem of computing the transitive closure of a given binary relation is $O(n^{2.8})$. See

M. J. Fischer and A. R. Meyer, "Boolean Matrix Multiplication and Transitive Closure," *Conference Record 1971 Twelfth Annual Symposium on Switching and Automata Theory, IEEE,* New York, pp. 129–131.

I. Munro, "Efficient Determination of the Transitive Closure of a Directed Graph," *Info. Proc. Letters,* **1** (1971) 56–58.

An interesting interpretation of the various shortest path algorithms from a linear algebraic viewpoint is given by

B. A. Carré, "An Algebra for Network Routing Problems," *J. Inst. Maths. Applics,* **7** (1971) 273–294.

SECTION 10
The Floyd-Warshall method was originally published as an ALGOL algorithm,

R. W. Floyd, "Algorithm 97, Shortest Path," *Comm. ACM,* **5** (1962) 345.

and was based on a theorem of Warshall,

S. Warshall, "A Theorem on Boolean Matrices," *J. ACM,* **9** (1962) 11–12.

Another procedure, requiring exactly the same number of calculations was devised by

G. B. Dantzig, "All Shortest Routes in a Graph," Operations Research House, Stanford University, Technical Report 66-3, November 1966.

Interestingly, essentially the same type of recursion employed by Floyd and Warshall was used earlier by McNaughton and Yamada to solve a problem in automata theory. In this earlier paper, the objective was essentially to obtain a characterization of the set of all paths (with repetitions of nodes) from the origin to any one of a designated set of destinations. See

R. McNaughton and H. Yamada, "Regular Expressions and State Graphs for Automata," *IRE Trans. on Electronic Computers,* **EC-9** (1960) 39–47. Also reprinted in *Sequential Machines: Selected Papers,* edited by E. F. Moore, Addison-Wesley, Reading, Mass., 1964.

It has been shown that, for any given value of n, there exists an algorithm that will solve any n-node instance of the all-pairs shortest path problem in $O(n^{2.5})$ running time:

M. L. Fredman, "New Bounds on the Complexity of the Shortest Path Problem," *Siam J. Comput.,* **5** (1976) 83–89.

If all arc lengths are independently and identically distributed, shortest paths between all pairs of nodes can be found in $O(n^2 \log^2 n)$ time, on the average:

P. M. Spira, "A New Algorithm for Finding All Shortest Paths in a Graph of Positive Arcs in Average Time $O(n^2 \log^2 n)$," *SIAM J. Comput.* **2** (1973) 28–32.

SECTIONS 11–13

The material in these sections is taken from

E. L. Lawler, "Optimal Cycles in Doubly Weighted Directed Linear Graphs," *Theory of Graphs,* P. Rosenstiehl, editor, Dunod, Paris, and Gordon and Breach, New York, 1967, pp. 209–214.

and

E. L. Lawler, "Optimal Cycles in Graphs and the Minimal Cost-to-Time Ratio Problem," *Proceedings of a Conference on Periodic Optimization,* CISM, Udine, Italy, 1973.

See also

G. B. Dantzig, W. Blattner and M. R. Rao, "Finding a Cycle in a Graph with Minimum Cost to Times Ratio with Application to a Ship Routing Problem," *Theory of Graphs,* P. Rosenstiehl, editor, Dunod, Paris, and Gordon and Breach, New York, 1967, pp. 77–84.

I. V. Romanovskii, "Optimization of Stationary Control of a Discrete Deterministic Process," *Cybernetics,* 3 (1967) 52–62.

Some other problems that can be put into the form of the minimal cost-to-time ratio problem are industrial scheduling problems of the type described in

R. A. Cunningham-Green, "Describing Industrial Processes with Interference and Approximating Their Steady-State Behavior," *Operational Research Quarterly,* 13 (1965) 95–100.

and the determination of maximum-computation-rate periodic schedules for Karp-Miller computation graphs, as in

R. Reiter, "Scheduling Parallel Computations," *Journal ACM.,* 15 (1968) 590–599.

The procedure for the ratio problem can, of course, be generalized to solve a much wider class of combinatorial optimization problems with rational objective functions. At the same time, we should note that the standard techniques, e.g., those due to Charnes and Cooper, for solving linear programming problems with rational objective functions are unworkable for such problems. This is because of their discrete rather than continuous character.

SECTION 14

The computational procedure described in this section is from the paper by Dreyfus, *op. cit.*

SECTION 15

Many of the essential ideas in this section were presented, in the context of the assignment problem, in

K. G. Murty, "An Algorithm for Ranking all the Assignments in Increasing Order of Cost," *Operations Research,* 16 (1968) 682–687.

These same ideas were applied by to the shortest path problem by Yen in

J. Y. Yen, "Finding the K Shortest Loopless Paths in a Network," *Mgt. Sci.,* **17** (1971) 712–716.

Improvements in the efficiency of Yen's procedure, and a scheme for reducing the amount of storage, were proposed in

E. L. Lawler, "A Procedure for Computing the K Best Solutions to Discrete Optimization Problems and Its Application to the Shortest Path Problem," *Mgt. Sci.,* **18** (March 1972) 401–405.

See also

J. Marshall, "On Lawler's K Best Solution to Discrete Optimization Problem," Letter to the Editor, with reply by Lawler, *Mgt. Sci.,* **19** (1973) 834–837; also *Mgt. Sci.,* **20** (1973) 540–541.

FOUR

Network Flows

1
Introduction

Network flow problems are linear programs with the particularly useful property that they possess optimal solutions in integers. This permits a number of interesting and important combinatorial problems to be formulated and solved as network flow problems. Some of these combinatorial problems have little, if any, obvious connection with the physical reality of flows.

In this chapter we review "classical" network flow theory, including the max-flow min-cut theorem, the computation of minimum cost flows, conditions for the existence of feasible circulations, and finally, the "out-of-kilter" method of Minty and Fulkerson.

The out-of-kilter method is of special interest to us because of the way in which it exploits the concepts of linear programming duality. Many of the algorithms in this book can be viewed as specializations, variations, or extensions of this computational procedure.

We conclude this chapter with a discussion of some important applications of network flow theory, e.g., the PERT, or critical path method, of project scheduling. Some further topics, such as multiterminal and multicommodity flow problems, are also indicated.

2
Maximal Flows

why?

Suppose that each arc (i, j) of a directed graph G has assigned to it a non-negative number c_{ij}, the *capacity* of (i, j). This capacity can be thought of as representing the maximum amount of some commodity that can "flow" through the arc per unit time in a steady-state situation. Such a flow is permitted only in the indicated direction of the arc, i.e., from i to j.

Consider the problem of finding a maximal flow from a *source* node s to a *sink* node t, which can be formulated as follows. Let

$$x_{ij} = \text{the amount of flow through arc } (i, j).$$

Then, clearly,

$$0 \le x_{ij} \le c_{ij}. \tag{2.1}$$

A *conservation law* is observed at each of the nodes other than s or t. That is, what goes out of node i,

$$\sum_j x_{ij},$$

must be equal to what comes in,

$$\sum_j x_{ji}.$$

So we have

$$\sum_j x_{ji} - \sum_j x_{ij} = \begin{cases} -v, & i = s \\ 0, & i \ne s, t \\ v, & i = t. \end{cases} \tag{2.2}$$

We call any set of numbers $x = (x_{ij})$ which satisfy (2.1) and (2.2) a *feasible flow*, or simply a *flow*, and v is its *value*. The problem of finding a maximum value flow from s to t is a linear program in which the objective is to maximize v subject to constraints (2.1) and (2.2).

Let P be an undirected path from s to t. An arc (i, j) in P is said to be a *forward* arc if it is directed from s toward t and *backward* otherwise. P is said to be a *flow augmenting path* with respect to a given flow $x = (x_{ij})$ if $x_{ij} < c_{ij}$ for each forward arc (i, j) and $x_{ij} > 0$ for each backward arc in P.

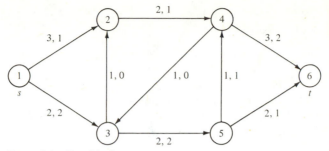

Figure 4.1   Feasible flow

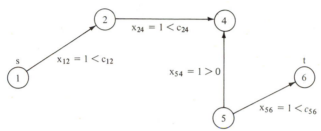

Figure 4.2   Augmenting path

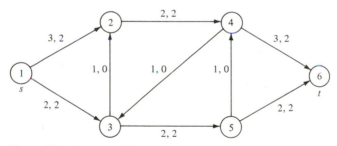

Figure 4.3   Augmented flow

Consider the network shown in Figure 4.1. The first number beside each arc (i, j) indicates its capacity c_{ij} and the second number indicates the arc flow x_{ij}. It is easily verified that the flow satisfies conditions (2.1) and (2.2), with $s = 1$ and $t = 6$, and that the flow value is 3.

An augmenting path with respect to the existing flow is indicated in Figure 4.2. We can increase the flow by one unit in each forward arc in this path and decrease the flow by one unit in each backward arc. The result is the augmented flow, with a value of 4, shown in Figure 4.3. Note that the conservation law (2.2) is again satisfied at each internal node.

Recall from Chapter 2 that an (s, t)-cutset is identified by a pair

(S, T) of complementary subsets of nodes, with $s \in S$ and $t \in T$. The *capacity* of the cutset (S, T) is defined as

$$c(S, T) = \sum_{i \in S} \sum_{j \in T} c_{ij},$$

i.e., the sum of the capacities of all arcs which are directed from S to T.

The value of any (s, t)-flow cannot exceed the capacity of any (s, t)-cutset. Suppose $x = (x_{ij})$ is a flow and (S, T) is an (s, t)-cutset. Sum the equations (2.2) identified with nodes $i \in S$ to obtain

$$\begin{aligned} v &= \sum_{i \in S} \left(\sum_j x_{ij} - \sum_j x_{ji} \right) \\ &= \sum_{i \in S} \sum_{j \in S} (x_{ij} - x_{ji}) + \sum_{i \in S} \sum_{j \in T} (x_{ij} - x_{ji}) \\ &= \sum_{i \in S} \sum_{j \in T} (x_{ij} - x_{ji}). \end{aligned} \tag{2.3}$$

That is, the value v of any flow is equal to the net flow through any cutset. But $x_{ij} \leq c_{ij}$ and $x_{ji} \geq 0$, so

$$v \leq \sum_{i \in S} \sum_{j \in T} c_{ij} = c(S, T). \tag{2.4}$$

In the case of the augmented flow shown in Figure 4.3, there is an (s, t)-cutset with capacity equal to the flow value. For example, $S = \{1, 2\}$, $T = \{3, 4, 5, 6\}$. It follows from the preceding analysis that the flow is maximal and that the cutset has minimal capacity. Notice that each arc (i, j) is *saturated*, i.e., $x_{ij} = c_{ij}$, if $i \in S$, $j \in T$ and *void*, i.e., $x_{ij} = 0$, if $i \in T$, $j \in S$.

We now state and prove three of the principal theorems of network flow theory. They will later be applied to prove other combinatorial results and to yield good algorithms for maximal flow problems.

Theorem 2.1 (*Augmenting Path Theorem*) A flow is maximal if and only if it admits no augmenting path from s to t.

PROOF Clearly, if an augmenting path exists the flow is not maximal. Suppose x is a flow that does not admit an augmenting path. Let S be the set of all nodes j (including s) for which there is an augmenting path from s to j, and let T be the complementary set. From the definition of augmenting path and from the definition of S and T, it follows that for all $i \in S$ and $j \in T$, $x_{ij} = c_{ij}$ and $x_{ji} = 0$. It follows from (2.3) that

$$v = \sum_{i \in S} \sum_{j \in T} c_{ij},$$

the capacity of the cutset (S, T). From (2.4) it follows that the flow is maximal. //

Theorem 2.2   (*Integral Flow Theorem*)   If all arc capacities are integers there is a maximal flow which is integral.

PROOF   Suppose all capacities are integers and let $x_{ij}^0 = 0$, for all i and j. If the flow $x^0 = (x_{ij}^0)$ is not maximal it admits an augmenting path and hence there is an integral flow x^1 whose value exceeds that of x^0. If x^1 is not maximal it admits an augmenting path, and so on. As each flow obtained in this way exceeds the value of its predecessor by at least one, we arrive eventually at an integral flow that admits no augmenting path and hence is maximal. //

Theorem 2.3   (*Max-Flow Min-Cut Theorem*)   The maximum value of an (s, t)-flow is equal to the minimum capacity of an (s, t)-cutset.

PROOF   The proofs of the previous two theorems, together with (2.4), are sufficient to establish the max-flow min-cut result for networks in which all capacities are integers and hence for those in which all capacities are commensurate (i.e., there exists some $c > 0$ such that every c_{ij} is an integral multiple of c).

   To complete the proof of the max-flow min-cut result, we must show that every network actually admits a maximal flow. (Note that the existence of a minimum capacity cutset is not open to question. There are only a finite number of (s, t)-cutsets, and at least one of them must be minimal.) We shall present an algorithm for computing maximal flows in the next section, and in Section 4 we shall prove that the algorithm always obtains a maximal flow in a finite (in fact, polynomial-bounded) number of steps, for any real number capacities. This will be sufficient to complete the proof. //

PROBLEMS

2.1   Find all minimum capacity (s, t)-cutsets of the network in Figure 4.3.
2.2   Characterize the maximal flow value v as a function of c_{24} and c_{35} for the network in Figure 4.4.
2.3   A recursive characterization of the set S of all nodes reachable from node s by augmenting paths is:

$$s \in S.$$

$$i \in S, x_{ij} < c_{ij} \Rightarrow j \in S,$$

$$i \in S, x_{ji} > 0 \Rightarrow j \in S.$$

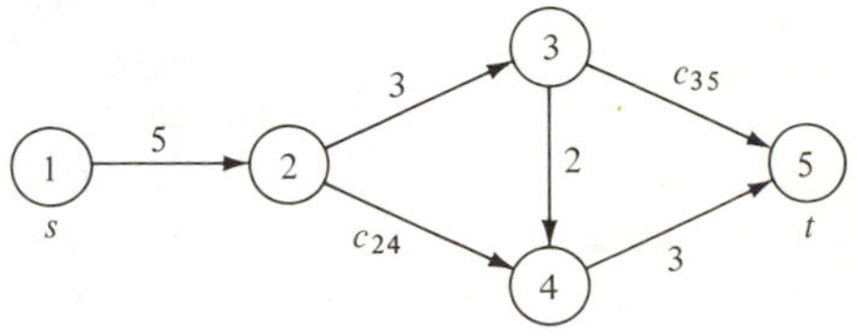

Figure 4.4   Network for Problem 2.2

Obtain a similar recursive characterization of the set T of all nodes from which node t is reachable by augmenting paths.

2.4   Which of the following statements is true?

(a) If $x = (x_{ij})$ is a maximal flow, then either $x_{ij} = 0$ or $x_{ji} = 0$.

(b) There exists a maximal flow for which either $x_{ij} = 0$ or $x_{ji} = 0$.

Explain.

2.5   If a flow network is symmetric, i.e., $c_{ij} = c_{ji}$, and (s, t)-planar, then a minimum capacity (s, t)-cutset corresponds to a shortest (s^*, t^*)-path in the dual network. What if the network is planar but not symmetric? Devise a variant of a shortest path computation to find a minimal cutset for a nonsymmetric (s, t)-planar network.

2.6   Define a *most vital arc* in a network as an arc whose deletion reduces the maximum flow value at least as much as the deletion of any other arc. *True or false*: A most vital arc is an arc of maximum capacity in an (s, t)-cutset of minimum capacity. Explain.

3

Maximal Flow Algorithm

The problem of finding a maximum capacity flow augmenting path is evidently quite similar to the problem of finding a shortest path, or, more precisely, a path in which the minimum arc length is maximum. We can make the similarity quite clear, as follows. Let

$$\bar{c}_{ij} = \max \{c_{ij} - x_{ij}, x_{ji}\},$$

where $c_{ij} = 0$, if there is no arc (i, j). Let

$u_i =$ the capacity of a maximum capacity augmenting path from node s to node i.

Then the analogues of Bellman's equations are:

$$u_s = +\infty$$

$$u_i = \max_k \min \{u_k, \bar{c}_{ki}\}, \qquad i \neq s.$$

It is clear that the u_i values and the corresponding maximum capacity paths can be found by a Dijkstra-like computation which is $O(n^2)$.

Actually, we shall be satisfied with a computation which does not necessarily compute maximum capacity paths. We propose a procedure in which labels are given to nodes. These labels are of the form (i^+, δ_j) or (i^-, δ_j). A label (i^+, δ_j) indicates that there exists an augmenting path with capacity δ_j from the source to the node j in question, and that (i, j) is the last arc in this path. A label (i^-, δ_j) indicates that (j, i) is the last arc in the path, i.e., (j, i) will be a backward arc if the path is extended to the sink t. Initially only the source node s is labeled with the special label $(-, \infty)$. Thereafter, additional nodes are labeled in one of two ways:

If node i is labeled and there is an arc (i, j) for which $x_{ij} < c_{ij}$, then the unlabeled node j can be given the label (i^+, δ_j), where

$$\delta_j = \min \{\delta_i, c_{ij} - x_{ij}\}.$$

If node i is labeled and there is an arc (j, i) for which $x_{ji} > 0$, then the unlabeled node j can be given the label (i^-, δ_j), where

$$\delta_j = \min \{\delta_i, x_{ji}\}.$$

When the procedure succeeds in labeling node t, an augmenting path has been found and the value of the flow can be augmented by δ_t. If the procedure concludes without labeling node t, then no augmenting path exists. A minimum capacity cutset (S, T) is constructed by letting S contain all labeled nodes and T contain all unlabeled nodes.

A labeled node is either "scanned" or "unscanned." A node is scanned by examining all incident arcs and applying labels to previously unlabeled adjacent nodes, according to the rules given above.

MAXIMAL FLOW ALGORITHM

Step 0 (Start)   Let $x = (x_{ij})$ be any integral feasible flow, possibly the zero flow. Give node s the permanent label $(-, \infty)$.

Step 1 (Labeling and Scanning)

(1.1)   If all labeled nodes have been scanned, go to Step 3.

(1.2)   Find a labeled but unscanned node i and scan it as follows: For each arc (i, j), if $x_{ij} < c_{ij}$ and j is unlabeled, give j the label (i^+, δ_j), where

$$\delta_j = \min \{c_{ij} - x_{ij}, \delta_i\}.$$

For each arc (j, i), if $x_{ji} > 0$ and j is unlabeled, give j the label (i^-, δ_j), where

$$\delta_j = \min \{x_{ji}, \delta_i\}.$$

(1.3)   If node t has been labeled, go to Step 2; otherwise go to Step 1.1.

Step 2 (Augmentation)   Starting at node t, use the index labels to construct an augmenting path. (The label on node t indicates the second-to-last node in the path, the label on that node indicates the third-to-last node, and so on.) Augment the flow by increasing and decreasing the arc flows by δ_t, as indicated by the superscripts on the index labels. Erase all labels, except the label on node s. Go to Step 1.

Step 3 (*Construction of Minimal Cut*)   The existing flow is maximal. A cutset of minimum capacity is obtained by placing all labeled nodes in S and all unlabeled nodes in T. The computation is completed. //

We can estimate the complexity of the computation as follows. Let m be the number of arcs. At most $2m$ arc inspections, followed by possible node labelings, are required each time an augmenting path is constructed. If all capacities are integers, at most v augmentations are required, where v is the maximum flow value. Thus the algorithm is $O(mv)$ in complexity.

PROBLEMS

3.1   Apply the max-flow algorithm to the network with capacity matrix

$$
C = \begin{bmatrix}
- & 1 & 3 & 2 \\
4 & - & 2 & 1 \\
6 & 3 & - & 5 \\
7 & 2 & 1 & -
\end{bmatrix}
$$

Let $s = 1, t = 4$ and start with the zero flow.

3.2   Modify Step 1 of the max-flow algorithms so that a maximum capacity augmenting path is found. (*Note*: In the Dijkstra shortest path computation a node i is, in effect, "scanned" at the time it is placed in the set P of permanently labeled nodes. The scanning operation consists of comparing $u_i + a_{ij}$ with u_j for all tentatively labeled nodes j in the set T.)

3.3   Modify the labeling procedure of the maximal flow algorithm to permit each arc to have a lower bound l_{ij} on flow as well as an upper bound c_{ij}. Assume Step 0 begins with a feasible flow, i.e., $l_{ij} \le x_{ij} \le c_{ij}$.

3.4   Develop an efficient procedure for finding all of the minimum capacity (s, t)-cutsets of a network and estimate its complexity as a function of m, n, and M, the number of minimal cutsets. Assume a maximal flow $x = (x_{ij})$ is available as input data. (*Suggestion*: Consult Chapter 3, Section 15. An $O(Mn)$ procedure is possible.)

4

Efficiency of the Maximal Flow Algorithm

The complexity of the maximal flow computation was shown to be $O(mv)$, but this is an unsatisfactory result in that it depends on the integer character of the arc capacities as well as the underlying digraph structure. Or, to put it differently, this bound depends on the very quantity v that the algorithm is intended to determine. We would greatly prefer a bound depending only on the number of nodes and arcs in the network.

We also need to establish that the algorithm obtains a maximum flow even when capacities are irrational, in order to complete the proof of the max-flow min-cut theorem. This is no trivial matter. For example, Ford and Fulkerson have devised an example to show that with irrational capacities a nonconvergent sequence of flow augmentations is possible. That is, with a pathologically poor choice of augmenting paths, an infinite sequence of finite augmentations is possible, without converging to the maximum flow value.

Even in the case that arc capacities are integers, a poor choice of augmenting paths can produce an exasperatingly lengthy computation. For example, if starting with zero flow one alternately chooses the alternating paths $(1, 2)$, $(2, 3)$, $(3, 4)$ and $(1, 3)$, $(2, 3)$, $(2, 4)$ in the network in Figure 4.5, two million augmentations of one unit each are required. By contrast, the augmenting paths $(1, 2)$, $(2, 4)$ and $(1, 3)$, $(3, 4)$ yield the same result with only two augmentations.

It is therefore reassuring, and somewhat surprising, to learn that the maximal flow computation is $O(m^2 n)$, provided each flow augmenting path contains as few arcs as possible. Moreover this can be accomplished quite simply by modifying Step 1.2 of the algorithm so that nodes are scanned in the same order in which they receive labels, i.e., "first labeled, first scanned."

The computation of each augmenting path is $O(m)$. The overall efficiency of $O(m^2 n)$ is assured by the following theorem of Edmonds and Karp, which holds without regard to arc capacities, which may be irrational.

Theorem 4.1 (*Edmonds and Karp*) If each flow augmentation is made along an augmenting path with a minimum number of arcs, then a maximal flow is obtained after no more than $mn/2 \leq (n^3 - n^2)/2$ augmentations, where m is the number of arcs in the network and n is the number of nodes.

Before attempting a proof of the theorem, we provide the following lemma. Let

$$\sigma_i^{(k)} = \text{the minimum number of arcs in an augmenting path}$$
from s to i after k flow augmentations

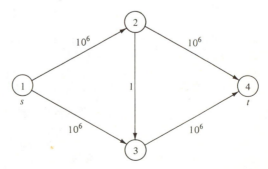

Figure 4.5   Example network

and

$$\tau_i^{(k)} = \text{the minimum number of arcs in an augmenting path}$$
$$\text{from } i \text{ to } t \text{ after } k \text{ flow augmentations.}$$

Lemma 4.2 If each flow augmentation is made along an augmenting path with a minimum number of arcs, then

$$\sigma_i^{(k+1)} \geq \sigma_i^{(k)}$$

and

$$\tau_i^{(k+1)} \geq \tau_i^{(k)}$$

for all i, k.

PROOF OF LEMMA 4.2   Assume that $\sigma_i^{(k+1)} < \sigma_i^{(k)}$, for some i, k. Moreover, let

$$\sigma_i^{(k+1)} = \min_j \{\sigma_j^{(k+1)} | \sigma_j^{(k+1)} < \sigma_j^{(k)}\}. \tag{4.1}$$

Clearly $\sigma_i^{(k+1)} \geq 1$ (only $\sigma_s^{(k+1)} = 0$), and there must be some final arc (i, j) or (j, i) in a shortest augmenting path from s to i after the $(k + 1)$st flow augmentation. Suppose this arc is (j, i), a forward arc, with $x_{ji} < c_{ji}$ (the proof is similar for (i, j)). Then $\sigma_i^{(k+1)} = \sigma_j^{(k+1)} + 1$ and because of (4.1), $\sigma_i^{(k+1)} \geq \sigma_j^{(k)} + 1$. It must have been that $x_{ji} = c_{ji}$ after the kth augmentation; otherwise $\sigma_i^{(k)} \leq \sigma_j^{(k)} + 1 \leq \sigma_i^{(k+1)}$, contrary to the assumption. But if $x_{ji} = c_{ji}$ after the kth augmentation and $x_{ji} < c_{ji}$ after the $(k + 1)$st augmentation, it follows that (j, i) was a backward arc in the $(k + 1)$st flow augmenting path. Since that path contained a minimum number of arcs, $\sigma_j^{(k)} = \sigma_i^{(k)} + 1$, and as we have seen $\sigma_j^{(k)} + 1 \leq \sigma_i^{(k+1)}$, so $\sigma_i^{(k)} + 2 \leq \sigma_i^{(k+1)}$, contrary to the assumption. The assumption that $\sigma_i^{(k+1)} < \sigma_i^{(k)}$ is therefore false.

The proof that $\tau_i^{(k+1)} \geq \tau_i^{(k)}$ parallels the above. //

PROOF OF THEOREM 4.1   Each time an augmentation is made, at least one arc in the augmenting path is *critical* in the sense that it limits the amount of augmentation. The flow through such an arc (i, j) is either increased to capacity or decreased to zero. Suppose (i, j) is a critical arc in the $(k + 1)$st augmenting path. The number of arcs in the augmenting path is $\sigma_i^{(k)} + \tau_i^{(k)} = \sigma_j^{(k)} + \tau_j^{(k)}$.

The next time arc (i, j) appears in an augmenting path, say the $(l + 1)$st, it will be with the opposite orientation. That is, if it was a forward arc in the $(k + 1)$st, it is a backward arc in the $(l + 1)$st, and vice versa. If (i, j) was a forward arc in the $(k + 1)$st path,

$$\sigma_j^{(k)} = \sigma_i^{(k)} + 1$$

and

$$\sigma_i^{(l)} = \sigma_j^{(l)} + 1.$$

Because of the lemma, $\sigma_j^{(l)} \geq \sigma_j^{(k)}$, and $\tau_i^{(l)} \geq \tau_i^{(k)}$, so that $\sigma_i^{(l)} + \tau_i^{(l)} \geq \sigma_i^{(k)} + \tau_i^{(k)} + 2$. It follows that each succeeding augmenting path in which (i, j) is a critical arc is at least two arcs longer than the preceding one.

No flow augmenting path may contain more than $n - 1$ arcs. Therefore, no arc may be a critical arc more than $n/2$ times. But each augmenting path contains a critical arc. There are $m \leq n^2 - n$ distinct arcs. Therefore there can be no more than $mn/2 \leq n(n^2 - n)/2$ flow augmenting paths and this completes the proof. //

N. Zadeh has been able to characterize a class of networks for which $O(n^3)$ augmentations are necessary, when each flow augmentation is made along a shortest augmenting path. Thus the upper bound in Theorem 4.1 cannot be improved upon except for a linear scale factor. (*Note:* Edmonds and Karp obtained a bound of $mn/4$, instead of $mn/2$, by, in effect, considering each symmetric pair of arcs (i, j), (j, i) to be a single arc.)

Edmonds and Karp have also obtained, by different reasoning, a comparable result for the case in which each augmenting path is chosen to produce a maximum increase in the flow value. A maximum flow is obtained after no more than about $O(\log v)$ augmentations if the arc capacities are integers. Except when the arc capacities are very large, this is a better bound than that given by Theorem 4.1, so there may be some advantage in computing maximum capacity augmenting paths.

It is conceivable that there may be better ways to choose augmenting paths than by either of the two policies we have mentioned, i.e., minimum number of arcs of maximum flow increment. In fact, if one is sufficiently clever in the choice of augmenting paths and in the choice of δ for each of them, no more than m flow augmentations are necessary to achieve a maximal flow.

Theorem 4.3 For any flow network (with possibly nonintegral capacities), there exists a sequence of no more than m (s, t)-flow augmenting paths, augmentation along which yields a maximal flow. Moreover, all of these augmenting paths contain only forward arcs.

PROOF An alternative linear programming formulation of the maximal flow problem is obtained as follows. Suppose we list all the possible (s, t) directed paths and form an arc-path incidence matrix $P = (p_{(i,j),k})$, where

$$p_{(i,j),k} = \begin{cases} 1 & \text{if arc } (i, j) \text{ is contained in path } k, \\ 0 & \text{otherwise.} \end{cases}$$

Let

$$\delta_k = \text{the amount of flow through path } k,$$

and $\delta = (\delta_k)$ be the vector of these flow values. Let $c = (c_{ij})$ be the vector of arc capacities. Then the maximal flow problem is

maximize

$$v = \sum_k \delta_k$$

subject to

$$P\delta \leq c$$

$$\delta \geq 0.$$

There are m constraints to this problem, one for each arc, hence there exists an optimal basic solution in which at most m of the δ_k are strictly positive. These nonzero variables are identified with the flow augmenting paths of the theorem, and the δ_k values indicate the amount of augmentation through each of them. //

Of course, Theorem 4.3 gives us no insight at all into how an appropriate sequence of augmenting paths might be found. It does suggest, however, there might exist a max-flow algorithm that is as good as, say $O(m^2)$. And, of course, there might be still better algorithms based on some other concept than that of successive flow augmentation.

PROBLEM

4.1   Suppose not all augmentations through the kth are made along shortest augmenting paths, but the $(k + 1)$st is. Does the proof of Lemma 4.2 remain valid?

5

Combinatorial Implications of Max-Flow Min-Cut Theorem

A number of combinatorial results can be viewed as consequences of the max-flow min-cut theorem. In order to show this, it is helpful to provide a generalization of the original theorem.

Let us consider a flow network in which there are arc capacities $c_{ij} \geq 0$ and, in addition, node capacities $c_i \geq 0$. Flows are required to satisfy not only the conservation conditions and arc constraints $(0 \leq x_{ij} \leq c_{ij})$ but also the node constraints,

$$\sum_j x_{ij} \leq c_i, \qquad i \neq s, t.$$

That is, the outflow (and hence the inflow) at any interior node does not exceed the capacity of the node. (If all node capacities are infinite, the situation is as before.)

It is natural to impose node capacities in certain applications. For example, nodes might be points of transhipment (transportation of goods), supply points (movement of troops), cleansing stations (overland pipelines), or relay stations (communication networks).

For a node having node capacities as well as arc capacities, we define an (s, t)-*cut* as a set of arcs and nodes such that any path from s to t uses at least one member of the set. The *capacity* of a cut is the sum of the capacities of its members.

As this notion of an (s, t)-cut appears to be different from the previous one of an (s, t)-cutset, it is necessary to show that in a network whose node capacities are all infinite, the minimum cut capacity in the new sense is equal to the minimum cutset capacity in the old sense. Let (S, T) be a cutset and let C be the set of all arcs directed from a node in S to a node in T. Then C is a cut in the new sense and its capacity is equal to that of (S, T). Let C be a cut, consisting entirely of arcs, let S be the set of all nodes that can be reached by directed paths from s not using any member of C, and let T be the remaining nodes. Then (S, T) is a cutset and C contains every arc from S to T, so the capacity of (S, T) is at most that of C.

Theorem 5.1 (*Generalized Max-Flow Min-Cut Theorem*) In a network having node capacities as well as arc capacities, the maximum value of an (s, t)-flow is equal to the minimum capacity of an (s, t)-cut. Moreover, if all capacities are integers, there is a maximal flow that is integral.

PROOF   Expand the network by replacing each interior node i by an *in-node* i', an *out-node* i'', and an arc (i', i'') of capacity c_i. For each arc (i, j) of the original network, there is an arc (i'', j') of capacity c_{ij} in the expanded network. (Let $s' = s'' = s$, $t' = t'' = t$.) An example of such an expansion is shown in Figure 4.6.

In the expanded network, nodes are uncapacitated and hence the original version of the max-flow min-cut theorem applies. As all flow entering i' must go to i'', and all flow leaving i'' must come from i', there is a natural one-to-one correspondence between flows in one network and flows in the other. The theorem follows readily by applying the original max-flow min-cut theorem to the expanded network. //

A celebrated result of graph theory, and a precursor of many other duality theorems, is a theorem of K. Menger. This theorem was originally stated in terms of undirected graphs, but for convenience we give a formulation in terms of digraphs.

A digraph G is said to be *k-connected from s to t* if for any set C of

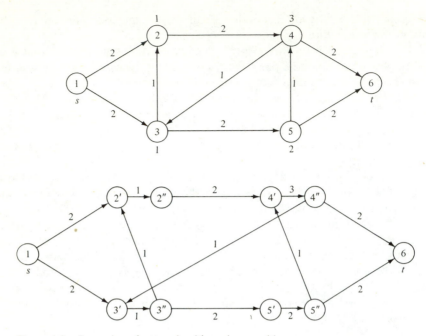

Figure 4.6   Expansion of network with node capacities

$k - 1$ nodes missing s and t there is a directed path from s to t missing C. In other words, it is not possible to disconnect s from t by removing any fewer than k nodes.

Two (s, t) paths are said to be *independent* if they have no nodes in common except s and t.

Theorem 5.2   (*Menger*)   If digraph G is k-connected from s to t and does not contain arc (s, t), then G admits k independent directed paths from s to t.

PROOF   Give each node a capacity of one and each arc an infinite capacity. Because of the nonexistence of arc (s, t), the minimum cut capacity is finite. From the k-connectivity of the digraph, it follows that the minimum cut capacity is at least k.

From Theorem 5.1, it follows that there is an integral maximal flow of value at least k. The structure of the flow network is such that this flow yields k pairwise independent directed paths from s to t. //

Although network flows theory appears to be concerned solely with digraphs, it also yields a good deal of information about the structure of undirected graphs.

Theorem 5.3   The maximum number of arc-disjoint (s, t) paths in an undirected graph G is equal to the minimum number of arcs in an (s, t)-cutset.

PROOF   Construct from G a flow network in which for each arc of G there is a symmetric pair of arcs (i, j) and (j, i), each with unit capacity. An integral maximal (s, t) flow exists in which at least one arc of each symmetric pair is void. Accordingly, such a flow yields a maximum number of disjoint (s, t) paths in G. Application of the max-flow min-cut theorem completes the proof. //

By applying Theorem 5.3 to the dual of G and reinterpreting the results in the original graph, we obtain the following.

Theorem 5.4   If G is (s, t) planar, then the minimum number of arcs in an (s, t) path is equal to the maximum number of disjoint (s, t)-cutsets.

6
Linear Programming Interpretation of Max-Flow Min-Cut Theorem

The max-flow min-cut theorem can be viewed as a consequence of linear programming duality and specifically, as a corollary of Theorem 13.3 of Chapter 2. The primal linear programming problem is

maximize v

subject to

$$\sum_j x_{ji} - \sum_j x_{ij} = \begin{cases} -v, & i = s \\ 0, & i \neq s, t \\ +v, & i = t. \end{cases}$$

$$x_{ij} \leq c_{ij}$$

$$x_{ij} \geq 0.$$

Let u_i be a dual variable identified with the ith node equation and w_{ij} be a dual variable identified with the capacity constraint on arc (i, j). Then the dual problem is minimize

$$\sum_{i,j} c_{ij} w_{ij}$$

subject to

$$
\left.
\begin{aligned}
u_j - u_i + w_{ij} &\geq 0 \\
u_s - u_t \quad\quad &\geq 1 \\
w_{ij} &\geq 0
\end{aligned}
\right\} \tag{6.1}
$$

u_i unrestricted.

For any (s, t)-cutset there is a feasible solution to the dual problem whose value is equal to the capacity of the cutset. Let (S, T) be such a cutset, and let

$$
\begin{aligned}
u_i &= 1, \quad \text{if } i \in S \\
&= 0, \quad \text{if } i \in T \\
w_{ij} &= 1, \quad \text{if } i \in S, j \in T \\
&= 0, \quad \text{otherwise.}
\end{aligned}
$$

Moreover, there is an optimal solution to the dual problem which corresponds to an (s, t)-cutset. For such an optimal solution, we may assume that $u_t = 0$. This is equivalent to dropping the redundant equation for node t from the primal problem. Also assume $u_s = 1$. (The reader can verify that there is no reason for u_s to be greater.) Then the remaining variables are forced to take on 0, 1 values. For each arc (i, j), it is the case that $w_{ij} = 1$ if and only if $u_i = 1$ and $u_j = 0$. (Note that $c_{ij} > 0$.) Then let

$$
\begin{aligned}
S &= \{i \,|\, u_i = 1\}, \\
T &= \{j \,|\, u_j = 0\}.
\end{aligned}
$$

The capacity of the cutset (S, T) is exactly equal to the value of the optimal dual solution.

Thus, the dual problem, in effect, finds a minimum capacity (s, t)-cutset. The max-flow min-cut theorem follows immediately from Theorem 13.3 of Chapter 2.

From Theorem 13.4 of Chapter 2, it follows that primal and dual solutions are optimal if and only if

$$
\begin{aligned}
x_{ij} > 0 &\Rightarrow u_j - u_i + w_{ij} = 0 \\
w_{ij} > 0 &\Rightarrow x_{ij} = c_{ij}.
\end{aligned}
$$

Suppose we view u_i as a "node potential." e.g., altitude or fluid pressure. Then, for an optimal pair of primal and dual solutions, exactly one of three cases exists for each arc (i, j):

Case 1   The potential at i is less than at j. There is zero flow in (i, j).

Case 2   The potential at i is equal to that at j. There may or may not be positive flow in (i, j).

Case 3   The potential at i is greater than at j. The flow in (i, j) is equal to its capacity c_{ij}.

These conditions correspond very well indeed with our intuitive notion of the relationships that should exist between node potentials and arc flows. These ideas, in generalized form, are the basis for the out-of-kilter method presented in Section 10.

It is just as important to be able to recognize combinatorial problems that can be formulated as min-cut problems as it is to be able to recognize those which can be formulated in max-flow form. Generally speaking, one should watch for problems with constraints involving sums or differences of pairs of variables. The following problem is an excellent example.

A PROVISIONING PROBLEM

In formulating the knapsack problem of Chapter 3, Section 2, we assumed that the benefit to be gained from the selection of any given item is independent of the selection of the other items. This is clearly a simplistic view of utility. For example, the benefit to be gained from a kerosene lantern without fuel is rather small.

A more sophisticated view can be taken. Suppose there are n items to choose from, where item j costs $c_j > 0$ dollars. Also suppose there are m sets of items, $S_1, S_2, \ldots, S_m$, that are known to confer special benefits. If all of the items in set S_i are chosen, then a benefit of $b_i > 0$ dollars is gained. The sets are arbitrary and need not be related in any particular way, e.g., a given item may be contained in several different sets.

There is no restriction on the number of items that can be purchased, i.e., there is no limiting knapsack. Our objective is simply to maximize the net benefit, i.e., total benefit gained minus total cost of items purchased.

Even without any constraints on the selection of items the problem appears to be unreasonably difficult. Yet it can be cast into the mold of a min-cut problem and can therefore be solved quite easily.

Let

$$v_j = 1 \quad \text{if item } j \text{ is purchased}$$
$$\quad\;\; = 0 \quad \text{otherwise,}$$

only 1 item of each kind

and let

$$u_i = 1 \quad \text{if all of the items in set } S_i \text{ are purchased}$$

$$ = 0 \quad \text{otherwise.}$$

Then the problem is to
maximize

$$Z = \sum_i b_i u_i - \sum_j c_j v_j \tag{6.2}$$

subject to

$$v_j - u_i \geq 0 \tag{6.3}$$

for each pair i, j such that $j \in S_i$, and

$$u_i, v_j \in \{0, 1\}.$$

Because of the 0, 1 restrictions on the variables and constraints (6.3), it is not possible for a benefit b_i to be earned unless all items j in the set S_i are purchased.

Let us make matters more complex by introducing $m + n$ new variables, $w_1, w_2, \ldots, w_m$ and $z_1, z_2, \ldots, z_n$.

Consider the problem:
minimize

$$z = \sum_i b_i w_i + \sum_j c_j z_i \tag{6.4}$$

subject to

$$v_j - u_i \geq 0, \qquad j \in S_i$$

$$u_i + w_i \geq 1, \qquad i = 1, 2, \ldots, m \tag{6.5}$$

$$-v_j + z_j \geq 0, \qquad j = 1, 2, \ldots, n \tag{6.6}$$

$$u_i, v_j, w_i, z_j \in \{0, 1\}.$$

Suppose $\bar{u} = (\bar{u}_i)$, $\bar{v} = (v_j)$ is a feasible solution to the original problem. Let $\bar{w} = (1 - \bar{u}_i)$, $\bar{z} = \bar{v}$. Then $\bar{u}, \bar{v}, \bar{w}, \bar{z}$ is a feasible solution to the new problem. Moreover,

$$z = \sum_i b_i \bar{w}_i + \sum_j c_j \bar{z}_j$$

$$= \sum_i b_i (1 - \bar{u}_i) + \sum_j c_j \bar{v}_j$$

$$= \sum_i b_i - Z.$$

Now suppose $\bar{u}, \bar{v}, \bar{w}, \bar{z}$ is a minimal solution to the new problem. From (6.5) and $b_i > 0$ it follows that $\bar{w}_i = 1 - \bar{u}_i$. From (6.6) and $c_j > 0$ it follows that $\bar{z}_j = \bar{v}_j$. Clearly $\bar{u}, \bar{v}$ is a feasible solution to the original problem and again $z = \sum_i b_i - Z$. It follows that a minimal solution to the new problem yields a maximal solution to the original problem.

We need to make a few more changes to put the problem into the form of a min-cut problem. We introduce two new variables u_0 and v_{n+1} and mn new variables w_{ij}. Let K be a large number. Consider the problem:

minimize

$$z = \sum_i b_i w_i + \sum_j c_j z_j + \sum_{i,j} K w_{ij}$$

subject to

$$
\left.
\begin{aligned}
v_j - u_i + w_{ij} &\geq 0, & j &\in S_i \\
u_i - u_0 + w_i &\geq 0, & i &= 1, 2, \ldots, m \\
v_{n+1} - v_j + z_j &\geq 0, & j &= 1, 2, \ldots, n \\
u_0 - v_{n+1} &\geq 1 \\
u_i, v_j, w_i, z_j, w_{ij} &\in \{0, 1\}.
\end{aligned}
\right\}
\tag{6.7}
$$

These changes make no essential difference in the problem. Because u_0 and v_{n+1} are restricted to 0, 1 values, the constraint $u_0 - v_{n+1} \geq 1$ can be satisfied if and only if $u_0 = 1$, $v_{n+1} = 0$. If K is sufficiently large, all the variables w_{ij} are zero in a minimal solution.

Except for the 0, 1 restrictions on the variables, (6.7) is in the same form as the min-cut problem (6.1). There is only a superficial difference in the designations of variables and their indices. But we know that Problem (6.1) admits an optimal solution with 0, 1 values for its variables. It follows that we can drop the 0, 1 restrictions from equation (6.7), retaining only the nonnegativity constraints on w_i, z_j, w_{ij}.

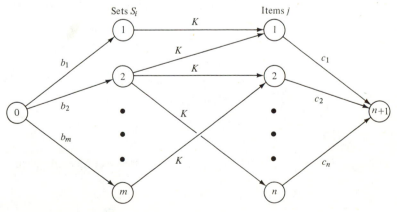

Figure 4.7   Network for provisioning problem

The network for the min-cut formulation of the provisioning problem is shown in Figure 4.7.

PROBLEMS

6.1 Solve the provisioning problem for the following data:

Item j	Cost c_j
1	4
2	5
3	12
4	6
5	10
6	5

Set S_i	Benefit b_i
1, 2	7
1, 5	4
2, 3, 4	9
3, 4	3
3, 4, 5	8
4, 6	6
5, 6	3

6.2 The provisioning problem, as formulated, does not provide any restriction on the number, weight, or cost of the items which may be purchased. Suppose, as in the knapsack problem, item j weights a_j pounds and we are restricted to a total weight b, that is,

$$\sum_j a_j v_j \leq b.$$

We might try to incorporate such a constraint into the objective function by means of a Lagrange multiplier, i.e., maximize

$$z = \sum_i b_i u_i - \sum_j (\lambda a_j + c_j) v_j.$$

What are the difficulties that might be encountered with this approach?

7

Minimum Cost Flows

Suppose in addition to a capacity c_{ij}, each arc of a flow network is assigned a *cost* a_{ij}. The *cost* of a flow $x = (x_{ij})$ is

$$\sum_{i,j} a_{ij} x_{ij}.$$

We now pose the problem of finding a minimum cost flow for a given flow value v.

ASSIGNMENT PROBLEM

There are n men and n jobs. The cost of assigning man i to job j is a_{ij}. For what man-job assignment is the total cost minimized?

Construct a directed bipartite graph with n nodes in each of its parts, and give arc (i, j) cost a_{ij} and infinite capacity. Add a source node s with an arc (s, i) to each node in the first part, and a sink node t with an arc (j, t) from each node in the second part. Set $c_{si} = 1$, $a_{si} = 0$, for all i, and $c_{jt} = 1$, $a_{jt} = 0$, for all j. A minimum cost integral flow of value n yields a solution to the problem.

The flow network for the assignment problem is shown in Figure 4.8. The first number of each arc represents its capacity and the second number is its cost.

Let us define the *cost of an augmenting path* to be the sum of the costs of forward arcs minus the sum of costs of backward arcs. Thus the cost of a path is equal to the net change in the cost of flow for one unit of augmenta-

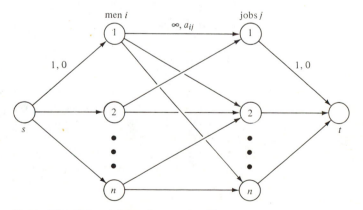

Figure 4.8   Network for assignment problem

tion along the path. An *augmenting cycle* is a closed augmenting path. The cost of an augmenting cycle is computed in the obvious way, with respect to a given orientation of the cycle, i.e., clockwise or counterclockwise.

→ total flow in s.

Theorem 7.1   A flow of value v is of minimum cost if and only if it admits no flow augmenting cycle with negative cost.

PROOF   The only if part of the theorem is obvious. For the converse, suppose that $x^0 = (x_{ij}^0)$ and $x^1 = (x_{ij}^1)$ are two flows, both of value v, where x^0 is less costly than x^1. The difference between these two flows, $y = x^0 - x^1$, can be expressed as a sum of flow augmenting cycles with respect to x^1. Because the cost of x^0 is less than that of x^1, at least one of these cycles must have negative cost. //

Theorem 7.2   (*Jewell, Busacker and Gowan*)   The augmentation by δ of a minimum cost flow of value v along a minimum cost flow augmenting path yields a minimum cost flow of value $v + \delta$.

PROOF   By Theorem 7.1, it suffices to show that the flow resulting from augmentation along a minimum cost augmenting path does not admit a negative augmenting cycle. Suppose such a cycle C were introduced. Then C must contain at least one arc (i, j) of the minimum cost augmenting path P. But then $(P \cup C) - (i, j)$, or some subset of it, would be an augmenting path with respect to the original flow, and would be less costly than P, contrary to the assumption that P is minimal. //

A minimum-cost augmenting path can be found by means of a shortest path computation. Specifically, for a given flow $x = (x_{ij})$ and arc costs a_{ij}, let

if $x_{ij} = 0$ $x_{ji} > 0$

$$\bar{a}_{ij} = \begin{cases} a_{ij}, & \text{if } x_{ij} < c_{ij}, x_{ji} = 0 \\ \min\{a_{ij}, -a_{ji}\}, & \text{if } x_{ij} < c_{ij}, x_{ji} > 0 \\ -a_{ji}, & \text{if } x_{ij} = c_{ij}, x_{ji} > 0 \\ +\infty, & \text{if } x_{ij} = c_{ij}, x_{ji} = 0, \end{cases} \qquad (7.1)$$

where we understand that $a_{ij} = +\infty$ if (i, j) is not an arc of the flow network. A shortest (s, t) directed path with respect to arc lengths $\bar{a}_{ij}$ corresponds to a minimum cost (s, t) augmenting path. A negative directed cycle corresponds to an augmenting cycle with negative cost.

We can now outline an algorithm for solving the minimum cost flow problem. This algorithm combines ideas of Klein and of Busacker and Gowen.

MINIMUM COST FLOW ALGORITHM

Step 0   (*Start*)   Let $x = (x_{ij})$ be any (s, t) flow with value $v' \leq v$, where v is the desired flow value. This initial flow can be the zero flow, or a flow of value v, perhaps determined by the max-flow algorithm. Or if a flow $x' = (x'_{ij})$ of value $v' > v$ is known, one can let $x = (v/v') x'$.

Step 1   (*Elimination of Negative Cycles*)

(1.1)   Apply a shortest path algorithm with respect to arc lengths $\bar{a}_{ij}$ with the objective of detecting negative cycles. If no negative cycle exists, go to Step 2.

(1.2)   Augment the flow around the corresponding augmenting cycle to obtain a less costly flow of the same value v', then return to Step 1.1.

Step 2   (*Minimum Cost Augmentation*)

(2.0)   If the existing flow value $v' = v$, the existing flow is optimal and the computation is completed. Otherwise, proceed to Step 2.1.

(2.1)   Apply a shortest path algorithm with respect to arc lengths $\bar{a}_{ij}$ with the objective of finding shortest path from s to t. If no shortest path exists, there is no flow of value v and the computation is halted.

(2.2)   Augment the flow by δ, where $v' + \delta \leq v$, along a minimum cost (s, t) augmenting path as determined by the shortest path computation. Return to Step 2.0. //

Note that the procedure has two phases. In the first phase negative cycles are eliminated and in the second phase a succession of minimum cost augmentations are made, until the desired flow value v is achieved. If one begins with the zero flow and no negative cycles exist with respect to the arc costs a_{ij}, then at most v augmentations are required, provided all capacities are integers. Each augmentation requires a shortest path computation which is $O(n^3)$. Hence in this situation the overall complexity is $O(n^3 v)$.

Edmonds and Karp have shown that, once negative cycles are eliminated, it can be arranged for the shortest path computation to be carried out over nonnegative arc lengths. Thus, Dijkstra's $O(n^2)$ shortest path algorithm can be applied. The complexity bound of $O(n^3 v)$ is then reduced to $O(n^2 v)$.

Suppose all arc costs a_{ij} are nonnegative. The computation is begun with an initial flow $x^0 = (0)$. An initial shortest path computation is carried out over arc lengths $\bar{a}_{ij}^{(0)} = a_{ij}$ and an initial flow augmentation is made to obtain a flow x^1.

Thereafter, let

$$u_i^{(k)} = \text{the length of a shortest path from } s \text{ to } i, \text{ with respect to arc lengths } \bar{a}_{ij}^{(k)}$$

and

$$\bar{a}_{ij}^{(k)} = \bar{a}_{ij} + \pi_i^{(k)} - \pi_j^{(k)},$$
$$\pi_j^{(k+1)} = \pi_j^{(k)} + u_j^{(k)}, \tag{7.2}$$
$$\pi_j^{(0)} = 0,$$

where $\bar{a}_{ij}$ is defined in (7.1) with respect to flow x^k.

Clearly a shortest (s, t) path with respect to $\bar{a}_{ij}^{(k)}$ is also a shortest path with respect to arc lengths $\bar{a}_{ij}$, differing in length by $\pi_s^{(k)} - \pi_t^{(k)}$. (For each node $i \neq s, t$ in an (s, t) path, $\pi_i^{(k)}$ is both added and subtracted from the path length.) It remains to be shown that each $\bar{a}_{ij}^{(k)}$ is nonnegative. We leave this as an exercise for the reader in Problem 7.4. (*Note*: In constructing a proof, it simplifies matters to assume that the network contains at most one arc, i.e., (i, j) or (j, i), between any given pair of nodes i, j.)

Even a bound of $O(n^2 v)$ is not satisfying, for the same reasons we disliked a similar bound for the max-flow algorithm. Moreover, we have not attempted to obtain a bound at all for the case in which there are negative cycles with respect to the initial flow. We shall not overcome these difficulties

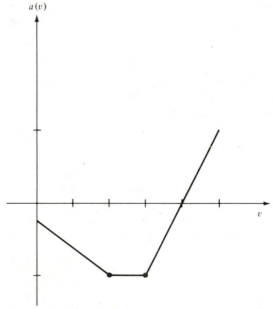

Figure 4.9   Plot of $a(v)$

for the present algorithm. However, in Sections 9 and 10 we show that the out-of-kilter algorithm can solve the minimum cost flow problem, even in the case of negative cycles, with a polynomial-bounded number of steps.

Note: It is possible to show, by a generalization of Theorem 4.3, that there exists a sequence of no more than m minimum cost augmenting paths which are sufficient to yield a minimum cost flow of any given value v. (See Problem 7.5.)

Finally, we should note that the minimum cost flow algorithm is well-suited to a parametric analysis of minimum flow cost as a function of flow value v.

Let $a(v)$ denote the minimum cost of an (s, t) flow of value v. A plot of $a(v)$ versus v, obtained from successive minimum cost augmentations, is shown in Figure 4.9. Intuitively, we expect each successive augmenting path to be at least as costly as the previous one, so the $a(v)$ curve should be convex. Indeed, the convexity of $a(v)$ is easily demonstrated. For suppose x, x' are minimum cost flows with values v, v'. Then $\lambda x + (1 - \lambda) x'$ is a feasible flow with value $\lambda v + (1 - \lambda) v'$ and its cost is $\lambda a(v) + (1 - \lambda) a(v')$, where $0 \leq \lambda \leq 1$. It follows that $a(\lambda v + (1 - \lambda) v') \leq \lambda a(v) + (1 - \lambda) a(v')$ and the function $a(v)$ is convex.

PROBLEMS

7.1 (Caterer Problem) A caterer requires $r_j \geq 0$ fresh napkins on each of n successive days, $j = 1, 2, ..., n$. He can meet his requirements either by purchasing new napkins or by using napkins previously laundered. Moreover, the laundry has two kinds of service: quick service requires p days and slow service requires q days, where, presumably, $p \leq q$. Suppose a new napkin costs a cents, quick laundering costs b cents, and slow laundering costs c cents. How should the caterer, starting with no napkins, meet his requirements with minimum cost? Formulate as a minimum cost network flow problem. (This problem had its origin as an aircraft maintenance problem, with the possibility of quick and slow overhaul of engines.)

7.2 Suppose a minimum cost flow of maximum flow value is desired. Let (S, T) be a minimum capacity cutset. Show that a maximal flow x is of minimum cost if and only if x admits a negative cost augmenting cycle within neither S nor T. (It is unnecessary to consider cycles with nodes in both S and T.) Why?

7.3 Devise a specialized version of the minimum cost flow algorithm for the assignment problem, with all operations "on the matrix." Estimate the computational complexity. (An $n \times n$ problem can be solved in $O(n^3)$ steps.)

7.4 Prove the nonnegativity of $\bar{a}_{ij}^{(k)}$, as defined in (7.2). (*Suggestion*: Try a proof similar to that of Lemma 4.2.)

7.5 Restate and prove Theorem 4.3 for minimum cost flows.

8

Networks with Losses and Gains

Suppose that flow is not necessarily conserved within arcs. If x_{ij} units of flow go into the tail of arc (i, j), then $m_{ij}x_{ij}$ comes out at the head, where m_{ij} is a nonnegative flow *multiplier* associated with that arc. If $0 < m_{ij} < 1$, the arc is *lossy*, and if $1 < m_{ij} < \infty$, the arc is *gainy*. In a conventional flow network, of course, $m_{ij} = 1$ for all arcs. (The case $m_{ij} = \pm 1$ is a "bidirected" flow and is discussed in Chapter 6.)

Let

$$x_{ij} = \text{the amount of flow into arc } (i, j).$$

We require the satisfaction of capacity constraints,

$$0 \le x_{ij} \le c_{ij}$$

and the satisfaction of conservation conditions at each node other than s or t:

$$\sum_j m_{ji}x_{ji} - \sum_j x_{ij} = \begin{cases} -v_s, & i = s \\ 0, & i \ne s, t \\ +v_t, & i = t. \end{cases}$$

Note that v_s is not necessarily equal to v_t, because of flow losses and gains within arcs. All of the equations above are necessary; none of them is implied by the others, unless the rank of the coefficient matrix is less than n.

Define $v_s - v_t$ to be the *loss* of the flow. We shall be concerned with the problem of finding a minimum loss flow for a given flow value v_s or v_t. That is, given v_s maximize v_t, or given v_t minimize v_s.

CURRENCY CONVERSION

An exchange rate has been established such that for each unit of currency i one receives m_{ij} units of currency j. There is a bound c_{ij} on the number of units of currency i that one can so convert.

The network in Figure 4.10 exemplifies a hypothetical currency conversion problem, in which the first number on arc (i, j) is its capacity c_{ij} and the second number is its multiplier m_{ij}. The largest number of rubles that can be purchased with \$10,000 is given by a minimum loss flow of value $v_s = 10,000$. What would be the significance of a directed cycle for which the product of the multipliers is greater than unity?

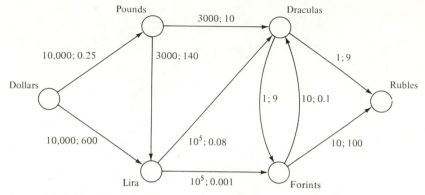

Figure 4.10   Hypothetical currency conversion network

WORK ASSIGNMENT

There are p men and q jobs. Any man is capable of performing all the work on any given job, or the work can be apportioned among several men. One hour of time by man i is sufficient to complete a fraction m_{ij} of job j. Man i is available to work no more than c_i hours. How should the men be assigned to the jobs so that the jobs can be completed with the smallest possible total number of man-hours of labor?

Let x_{ij} = the number of hours man i works on job j. The problem is to

$$\text{minimize} \sum_{i,j} x_{ij}$$

subject to

$$\sum_j x_{ij} \le c_i \quad i = 1, 2, \ldots, p,$$

$$\sum_i m_{ij} x_{ij} = 1 \quad j = 1, 2, \ldots, q,$$

and

$$x_{ij} \ge 0.$$

This is equivalent to finding a minimum loss flow of value $v_t = q$ for the network shown in Figure 4.11.

The theory of minimum loss flows is quite parallel to the theory of minimum cost flows, and we can develop a computational procedure parallel to that presented in the previous section.

A *flow augmenting path* is defined as before. That is, $x_{ij} < c_{ij}$ for

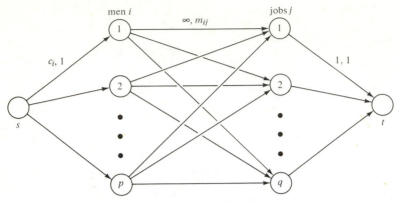

Figure 4.11   Work assignment network

each forward arc (i, j) and $x_{ij} > 0$ for each backward arc. The *multiplier* of a path is the product of the multipliers for forward arcs and the reciprocals of multipliers for backward arcs. A *minimum loss* (s, t) augmenting path is one for which the multiplier is maximum.

The *capacity* of an (s, t) augmenting path, i.e., the amount of augmentation that is permissible, is determined as follows. The capacity at node s is $\delta_s = +\infty$. If (i, j) is a forward arc and the capacity at node i is δ_i, then the capacity at node j is

$$\delta_j = m_{ij} \min \{\delta_i, c_{ij} - x_{ij}\}.$$

If (j, i) is a backward arc, then

$$\delta_j = \min \left\{ \frac{1}{m_{ji}} \delta_i, x_{ji} \right\}. \tag{8.1}$$

The (overall) capacity of the path is δ_t.

A peculiar feature of networks with losses and gains is that a directed cycle can act as a source or as a sink, depending upon whether the product of the multipliers in the cycle is greater than unity or less than unity.

Let C be an augmenting cycle, i.e., an augmenting path from some node i to itself, and let the multiplier of this cycle be greater than unity. Let P be an augmenting path, arc disjoint from C, from any node of C to the source s or to the sink t. Then $C \cup P$ is said to be an *endogenous* flow augmenting path.

Two endogenous augmenting paths are illustrated in Figure 4.12. The first number by each arc represents its multiplier m_{ij} and the second number is an increment δ_{ij} to arc flow x_{ij}. (We ignore capacities in this figure.) Note that the multiplier of each flow-generating cycle is 2, and that conservation conditions at all nodes other than s or t are observed.

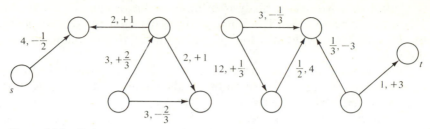

Figure 4.12   Endogenous augmenting paths

The following theorems are analogous to Theorems 7.1 and 7.2 and admit similar proofs.

Theorem 8.1   In a network with losses and gains, a flow of source value v_s is of minimum loss if and only if it admits no endogenous flow augmenting path to t. A flow of sink value v_t is of minimum loss if and only if it admits no endogenous flow augmenting path to s.

Theorem 8.2   In a network with losses and gains, the augmentation of a minimum loss flow of sink value v_t along a minimum loss augmenting path of capacity δ_t yields a minimum loss flow of value $v_t + \delta_t$.

A minimum loss augmenting path can be found by means of a shortest path computation. Let

$$
\bar{a}_{ij} = \begin{cases}
-\log m_{ij}, & \text{if } x_{ij} < c_{ij}, x_{ji} = 0 \\
\min\{-\log m_{ij}, +\log m_{ji}\}, & \text{if } x_{ij} < c_{ij}, x_{ji} > 0 \\
+\log m_{ji}, & \text{if } x_{ij} = c_{ij}, x_{ji} > 0 \\
+\infty, & \text{if } x_{ij} = c_{ij}, x_{ji} = 0.
\end{cases}
$$

Then a shortest (s, t) directed path with respect to arc lengths $\bar{a}_{ij}$ corresponds to a minimum-loss (s, t) augmenting path. A negative directed cycle from which the source or the sink is reachable yields an endogenous flow augmenting path.

There may of course be many augmenting cycles with multipliers greater than unity from which the source or sink is not reachable. It is the reachability condition which enables endogenous augmenting paths to be obtained effectively by shortest path algorithms which compute shortest paths from a single origin. Except that to find endogenous paths to s or to t one should compute shortest paths *to s* or *to t*, rather than *from* these nodes as origins.

We leave it to the reader to provide the outline of a minimum-loss flow algorithm, parallel to the algorithm in Section 7. When this algorithm is applied to a parametric analysis of flow, a plot of minimum loss, $l(v_t)$ versus v_t, can be obtained. The function $l(v_t)$ is piecewise linear and convex, by the same arguments used for the convexity of $a(v)$ for minimum cost flows.

Up to this point, there has been a fairly close parallel with the theory of minimum cost flows. The question of algorithmic complexity is, however, much more bleak than before.

Reference to (8.1) shows that although the existing flow $x = (x_{ij})$ is integral and all capacities c_{ij} and multipliers m_{ij} are integers, an augmentation may necessarily be fractional. Thus, unfortunately, successive augmentations may increase the flow value v_s or v_t by very small increments. Can we even be assured that the procedure obtains an optimal solution with a finite number of augmentations?

There are a finite number of possible augmenting paths (but a very large number, of order $n!$). If we can insure that no augmenting path is used more than once, then at least the algorithm is finite.

There are at least two ways to accomplish this objective. One (messy) way is to perturb the arc multipliers slightly so that no two augmenting paths can have exactly the same multiplier. Another, essentially equivalent, way is to use lexicography to break ties between augmenting paths with equal multipliers. This can be implemented easily as part of the shortest path computation.

In any case, it is not possible to obtain a bound as attractive as $O(n^2 v_t)$. The minimum loss flow problem appears to be decidedly non-polynomial bounded, in spite of the fact that it can be shown that m augmentations are sufficient. (See Problem 8.1.)

PROBLEM

8.1   Restate and prove Theorem 4.3 for minimum loss flows in networks with losses and gains.

9

Lower Bounds and Circulations

Some combinatorial problems can be successfully formulated as network flow problems only if lower bounds on arc flow are imposed. That is, in addition to a capacity c_{ij} for each arc (i, j) we may designate a *lower bound* l_{ij} and require that $l_{ij} \le x_{ij} \le c_{ij}$.

As an example, consider the following problem.

AIRCRAFT SCHEDULING

An airline wishes to use the smallest possible number of planes to meet a fixed flight schedule. A digraph is constructed with two nodes i, i' and an arc (i, i') for each flight. An arc (i', j) is provided if it is feasible for a plane to return from the destination of flight i to the starting point for flight j and be ready in time for its scheduled departure. (Planes are assumed to be identical and capable of making any of the flights.) In addition, there are dummy nodes s' and t, with arcs (s', i) and (i', t), for all i and i'.

Set $l_{ii'} = c_{ii'} = 1$, for all arcs (i, i') and $l_{i',j} = 0$, $c_{i',j} = 1$ for all other arcs (i', j). The minimum number of airplanes required to meet the flight schedule is determined by an integral (s', t)-flow of *minimum* value.

Up to this point in our study of network flows we have not had to be concerned with the existence of feasible flows. The zero flow, if no other, always satisfied arc capacity constraints. Now, however, the nonexistence of a feasible flow is a distinct possibility. For example, a network with only two arcs, $(s, 1)$, $(1, t)$, with $c_{s1} < l_{1t}$, has no feasible (s, t)-flow.

It is useful to approach the feasibility problem through the study of "circulations." A *circulation* is simply a flow in a network in which conservation conditions are observed at all nodes. That is, there is no source or sink.

To convert a conventional flow problem to circulation form, add an arc (t, s) to the network, with $l_{ts} = 0$, $c_{ts} = +\infty$. Then a maximal (s, t) flow is simply a circulation for which x_{ts} is maximum.

Here is how to find a feasible circulation in a network with both lower bounds and capacities, if such a circulation exists. Begin with the zero circulation. If all lower bounds are zero, this circulation is feasible. Otherwise, find an arc (p, q) for which $x_{pq} < l_{pq}$. Construct a flow augmenting path from q to p where this path is of the conventional type, except that we require $x_{ij} > l_{ij}$ for each backward arc and δ is chosen such that $\delta \le x_{ij} - l_{ij}$. Augment the flow from q to p by δ, and repeat until $x_{pq} \ge l_{pq}$. Then repeat for another arc for which the arc flow is infeasible. Eventually a feasible circulation is obtained, if the network admits such a circulation.

But suppose at some point an augmenting path cannot be found. Let (t, s), with $x_{ts} < l_{ts}$, be the arc for which the augmenting path cannot be found. Let S be the set of nodes which can be reached from s by an augmenting path, and T those which cannot. For each arc (i, j) directed from S to T, $x_{ij} = c_{ij}$, and for each arc directed from T to S, $x_{ij} \le l_{ij}$. (See Figure 4.13.) The net flow across the cutset (S, T) is zero, i.e.,

$$\sum_{i \in S, j \in T} x_{ij} = \sum_{i \in T, j \in S} x_{ij}.$$

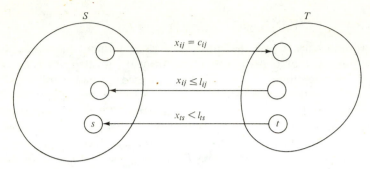

Figure 4.13   Infeasibility of circulation

But

$$\sum_{i\in S, j\in T} x_{ij} = \sum_{i\in S, j\in T} c_{ij}$$

and

$$\sum_{i\in T, j\in S} x_{ij} < \sum_{i\in T, j\in S} l_{ij},$$

with strict inequality because of arc (t, s). We have constructed a cutset (S, T) for which

$$\sum_{i\in S, j\in T} c_{ij} < \sum_{i\in T, j\in S} l_{ij}.$$

We have thus proved the following theorem.

Theorem 9.1   (*Hoffman*)   In a network with lower bounds and capacities a feasible circulation exists if and only if

$$\sum_{i\in T, j\in S} l_{ij} \leq \sum_{i\in S, j\in T} c_{ij} \qquad (9.1)$$

for all cutsets (S, T).

Corollary 9.2   (*Generalized Max-Flow Min-Cut Theorem*)   Let G be a flow network with lower bounds and capacities and which admits a feasible (s, t)-flow. The maximum value of an (s, t)-flow in G is equal to the minimum capacity of an (s, t)-cutset, where the capacity of cutset (S, T) is defined as

$$c(S, T) = \sum_{i\in S, j\in T} c_{ij} - \sum_{i\in T, j\in S} l_{ij}.$$

PROOF   Convert the flow problem to circulation form by adding an arc (t, s) to the network, with $l_{ts} = v$, $c_{ts} = +\infty$. Because a feasible (s, t)-flow exists in the original network, a feasible circulation exists in the new network for sufficiently small (s, t)-flow values v. By Theorem 9.1, the largest value of v for which there exists a feasible circulation is that which satisfies the inequalities (9.1) for all (s, t)-cutsets, with strict equality in the case of at least one (s, t)-cutset. But this value of v is precisely the minimum capacity of an (s, t)-cutset, as defined in the statement of the corollary. //

As we noted in the statement of the aircraft scheduling problem, it is sometimes desired to find a *minimum* value flow, rather than a maximum value flow.

Corollary 9.3 (*Min-Flow Max-Cut Theorem*) Let G be a flow network with lower bounds and capacities and which admits a feasible (s, t)-flow. The minimum value of an (s, t)-flow in G is equal to the maximum of

$$\sum_{i \in S, t \in T} l_{ij} - \sum_{i \in T, j \in S} c_{ij}$$

over all (s, t)-cutsets (S, T), or equivalently, the negative of the minimum capacity of a (t, s)-cutset.

PROOF Repeat the construction for the preceding corollary, this time letting $l_{ts} = 0$, $c_{ts} = v$. //

We can use Corollary 9.3 to prove a well-known theorem of Dilworth. This theorem concerns the minimum number of paths in an acyclic directed graph which are sufficient to cover a specified subset of arcs. (A set of paths "covers" a set of arcs A if each arc in A is contained in at least one path.)

Theorem 9.4 (*Dilworth*) Let G be an acyclic directed graph and let A be a subset of its arcs. The minimum number of directed paths required to cover the arcs in A is equal to the maximum number of arcs in A, no two of which are contained in a directed path in G.

PROOF Add nodes s and t to G, and arcs (s, i), (i, t), for all $i \neq s, t$. For each arc $(i, j) \in A$, set $l_{ij} = 1$, $c_{ij} = +\infty$, and for all other arcs set $l_{ij} = 0$, $c_{ij} = +\infty$. A minimum value (s, t)-flow yields the minimum number of directed paths required to cover all the arcs in A. (Note that if the graph contained directed cycles, some of the arcs in A could be covered by flow circulating around those cycles.) Apply Corollary 9.3 and the result follows immediately. //

When the Dilworth Theorem is applied to the aircraft scheduling problem, it yields the result that the minimum number of planes required by the flight schedule is equal to the maximum number of flights, no two of which can be made by the same plane.

Let A be the entire set of arcs of G, apply the Dilworth Theorem to the dual of G, and reinterpret the results in the original graph. Then the following theorem is obtained, parallel to Theorem 5.4.

Theorem 9.5 If G is an acyclic, (s, t) planar digraph, then the maximum number of arcs in an (s, t) directed path is equal to the minimum number of (s, t) directed cutsets covering all the arcs of G.

PROBLEMS

9.1   Using the Edmonds-Karp results, obtain a polynomial bound (in n) on the number of steps required by the procedure for constructing a feasible circulation. Also obtain a bound in n and $L = \sum_{i,j} l_{ij}$. (Assume all lower bounds and capacities are integers.)

9.2   Sometimes the Dilworth Theorem is stated in terms of partial orderings. For a given partial ordering $(S, \leq)$, a *chain* of elements is a sequence $s_1, s_2, \ldots, s_m$, where $s_i \leq s_{i+1}$. Apply Theorem 9.4 to show that the minimum number of chains, such that every element is contained in at least one chain, is equal to the maximum number of incomparable elements. (Elements s_i and s_j are incomparable if neither $s_i \leq s_j$ nor $s_j \leq s_i$.)

9.3   Suppose, hypothetically, the Dilworth Theorem could be generalized to apply to digraphs with cycles. For example "The minimum number of directed paths required to cover the arcs in A is equal to the maximum number of arcs in a subset $A^D \subseteq A \ldots$ [where A^D has some specified dual structure] ..." Show that such a theorem would yield necessary and sufficient conditions for the existence of a Hamiltonian cycle in an arbitrary digraph.

10
The Out-of-Kilter Method

We shall now describe a general computational procedure, developed independently by Fulkerson and Minty, for finding minimum cost circulations.

The minimum cost circulation problem is to

$$\text{minimize} \sum_{i,j} a_{ij} x_{ij}$$

subject to

$$\left.\begin{array}{c} \sum_{j} x_{ji} - \sum_{j} x_{ij} = 0, \quad \text{all } i \\[2mm] 0 \leq l_{ij} \leq x_{ij} \leq c_{ij}, \quad \text{all } i, j. \end{array}\right\} \tag{10.1}$$

All of the flow problems we have studied so far, and many others, can be cast into the form of (10.1). For example:

MAXIMAL FLOW PROBLEM

To the given flow network with source s and sink t add a return arc (t, s) with $l_{ts} = 0$, $c_{ts} = +\infty$ and $a_{ts} = -1$. For all other arcs (i, j), the lower bounds (if any) and capacities are as given and $a_{ij} = 0$. (For a minimum flow problem, set $a_{ts} = 1$.)

MINIMUM COST FLOW PROBLEM

Add a return arc (t, s) with $l_{ts} = 0$, $c_{ts} = v$, and $a_{ts} = 0$. The lower bounds, capacities, and costs of all other arcs are as given.

FEASIBLE CIRCULATION PROBLEM

Set $a_{ij} = 0$ for all arcs (i, j).

SHORTEST PATH PROBLEM

To find a shortest path from s to t in a network with arc lengths a_{ij}, add a return arc (t, s) with $l_{ts} = c_{ts} = 1$. For all other arcs (i, j), $l_{ij} = 0$, $c_{ij} = +\infty$, and a_{ij} is as given.

To find shortest paths from s to all other nodes, add return arcs (j, s) from all nodes $j \neq s$, with $l_{js} = c_{js} = 1$.

The out-of-kilter algorithm is a primal-dual linear programming method. The problem dual to (10.1) is:

maximize

$$\sum_{i,j} l_{ij}\lambda_{ij} - \sum_{i,j} c_{ij}\gamma_{ij}$$

subject to

$$u_j - u_i + \lambda_{ij} - \gamma_{ij} \leq a_{ij} \tag{10.2}$$

$$\lambda_{ij}, \gamma_{ij} \geq 0$$

u_i unrestricted.

The dual variables λ_{ij} and γ_{ij} are identified with the primal constraints $x_{ij} \geq l_{ij}$ and $-x_{ij} \geq -c_{ij}$. (The variable γ_{ij} is analogous to w_{ij} in (6.1), but there the primal constraints were of the form $x_{ij} \leq c_{ij}$, hence the change in sign in the inequalities of (10.2).) The dual variables u_i are identified with primal node equations, as in (6.1).

Applying Theorem 13.4 of Chapter 2, we obtain the following orthogonality conditions which are necessary and sufficient for optimality of primal and dual solutions:

$$x_{ij} > 0 \Rightarrow u_j - u_i + \lambda_{ij} - \gamma_{ij} = a_{ij}$$

$$\lambda_{ij} > 0 \Rightarrow x_{ij} = l_{ij}$$

$$\gamma_{ij} > 0 \Rightarrow x_{ij} = c_{ij}.$$

The nonnegative variables λ_{ij} and γ_{ij} can effectively be dispensed with by noting that the above conditions are equivalent to the following:

$$\left.\begin{array}{r} x_{ij} = l_{ij} \Rightarrow u_j - u_i \leq a_{ij} \\ l_{ij} < x_{ij} < c_{ij} \Rightarrow u_j - u_i = a_{ij} \\ x_{ij} = c_{ij} \Rightarrow u_j - u_i \geq a_{ij}. \end{array}\right\} \tag{10.3}$$

For example, suppose $x = (x_{ij})$ is a primal solution and for some arc $(i, j), 0 < l_{ij} = x_{ij} < c_{ij}$. Then

$$x_{ij} > 0 \Rightarrow u_j - u_i + \lambda_{ij} - \gamma_{ij} = a_{ij}.$$

But

$$x_{ij} < c_{ij} \Rightarrow \gamma_{ij} = 0$$

and from the nonnegativity of λ_{ij} it follows that $u_j - u_i \leq a_{ij}$. A similar analysis of other cases establishes that conditions (10.3) are satisfied if and only if the primal and dual solutions are optimal.

We refer to conditions (10.3) as *kilter conditions* and represent them by a *kilter diagram* for each arc as shown in Figure 4.14. Points $(x_{ij}, u_j - u_i)$ on the crooked line are *in kilter* and those which are not are *out of kilter*. To each point $(x_{ij}, u_j - u_i)$ we assign a kilter number $K(x_{ij})$ equal to the absolute value of the change in x_{ij} necessary to bring the arc into kilter. Thus,

$$K(x_{ij}) = \begin{cases} |x_{ij} - l_{ij}|, & \text{if } u_j - u_i < a_{ij} \\ l_{ij} - x_{ij}, & \text{if } x_{ij} < l_{ij}, u_j - u_i = a_{ij} \\ x_{ij} - c_{ij}, & \text{if } x_{ij} > c_{ij}, u_j - u_i = a_{ij} \\ 0, & \text{if } l_{ij} \leq x_{ij} \leq c_{ij}, u_j - u_i = a_{ij} \\ |x_{ij} - c_{ij}|, & \text{if } u_j - u_i > a_{ij}. \end{cases}$$

The objective of the out-of-kilter method is to obtain a circulation $x = (x_{ij})$ and a set of node numbers $u = (u_i)$ for which the kilter conditions (10.3) are satisfied. As conditions (10.3) are satisfied if and only if all kilter numbers are zero, the sum of the kilter numbers can be used as a measure of progress toward an optimal pair of solutions.

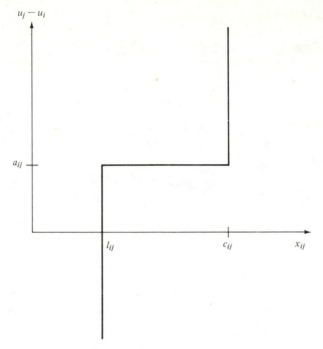

Figure 4.14   Kilter diagram

The out-of-kilter computation is begun with any circulation, feasible or not, provided node conservation conditions are satisfied, and with any set of node numbers whatsoever. At each iteration a change is made either in the circulation or in the node numbers. The type of change that is made is determined by the application of Minty's painting theorem, described as follows.

Recall the statement of the painting theorem, Theorem 7.2, Chapter 2. For any green-yellow-red coloring of the arcs of a digraph, and any given yellow arc (t, s), there exists exactly one of the following: A yellow-green cycle containing (t, s) and in which all yellow arcs are oriented in the same direction as (t, s), or a yellow-red cocycle containing (t, s) and in which all yellow arcs are oriented in the same direction as (t, s). We shall color the arcs according to a scheme described below and then focus our attention on an out-of-kilter yellow arc (t, s). Then if we find a yellow-green cycle, we shall modify the circulation around that cycle. If we find a yellow-red cocycle, we shall use that cocycle as a basis for revising the node numbers.

Here is how we propose to color the arcs, and also change the directions of some of them:

(10.4) Paint an arc *green* if it is in kilter and it is possible to either increase or decrease the arc flow without throwing the arc out of kilter. For such an arc,

$$l_{ij} < x_{ij} < c_{ij} \quad \text{and} \quad u_j - u_i = a_{ij}.$$

(10.5) Paint an arc *yellow* if it is possible to increase the arc flow, but not to decrease it, without increasing the arc kilter number. For such an arc, either

$$x_{ij} < c_{ij} \quad \text{and} \quad u_j - u_i > a_{ij}$$

or

$$x_{ij} \le l_{ij} \quad \text{and} \quad u_j - u_i = a_{ij}$$

or

$$x_{ij} < l_{ij} \quad \text{and} \quad u_j - u_i < a_{ij}.$$

(10.6) Paint an arc *yellow* and also reverse its direction if it is possible to decrease the arc flow, but not to increase it, without increasing the arc kilter number. For such an arc, either

$$x_{ij} > c_{ij} \quad \text{and} \quad u_j - u_i > a_{ij}$$

or

$$x_{ij} \ge c_{ij} \quad \text{and} \quad u_j - u_i = a_{ij}$$

or

$$x_{ij} > l_{ij} \quad \text{and} \quad u_j - u_i < a_{ij}.$$

(10.7) Paint an arc *red* if the arc flow can be neither increased nor decreased without increasing the kilter number. For such an arc, either

$$x_{ij} = c_{ij} \quad \text{and} \quad u_j - u_i > a_{ij}$$

or

$$x_{ij} = l_{ij} \quad \text{and} \quad u_j - u_i < a_{ij}.$$

These cases account for all possibilities and are summarized in Figure 4.15. Note that all green and red arcs are in kilter. A yellow arc (i, j) is in kilter only if $(x_{ij}, u_j - u_i)$ is a "corner" point in the kilter diagram for the arc.

Let us focus attention on an out-of-kilter yellow arc (t, s) and apply the painting theorem. Suppose there is a yellow-green cycle C, in which all yellow arcs are oriented in the same direction as (t, s). Reorient all arcs

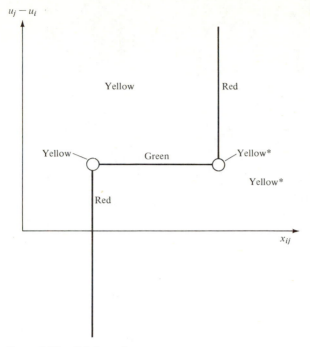

Figure 4.15   Painting of arcs

whose directions were reversed at the time they were painted yellow. An increase by a small amount $\delta > 0$ in the flow through (t, s) will decrease its kilter number by a like amount, assuming the kilter number is finite. (If (t, s) is one of the yellow arcs whose direction was reversed, we mean to *decrease* the flow through (s, t), and the discussion below must be appropriately modified.) An increase by δ in the flow through the arcs of C oriented in the same direction as (t, s) and a decrease by δ in the other arcs will not increase the kilter number of any arc, and may decrease the kilter numbers of some. In other words $C - (t, s)$ describes an augmenting path from s to t.

As an example, consider the cycle shown in Figure 4.16a. After reorientation of the yellow arc $(1, 2)$, the cycle is as shown in Figure 4.16b. Changes in the kilter diagrams for arcs in this cycle are indicated in Figure 4.17. Note that the largest permissible value for δ is determined by the yellow arc $(2, 1)$.

An analysis of cases shows that the kilter diagrams of the yellow and green arcs in the cycle can be affected only in the manner suggested by the arrows in Figure 4.18. There is no increase in the kilter number of the arc, provided δ is sufficiently small. Let us now consider such a choice of δ.

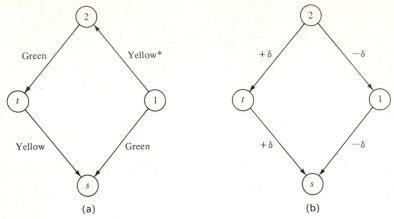

Figure 4.16   (a) Typical yellow-green cycle. (b) Flow increments after re-orientation.

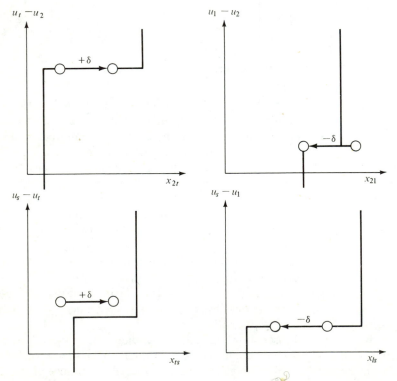

Figure 4.17   Kilter diagrams for yellow-green cycle

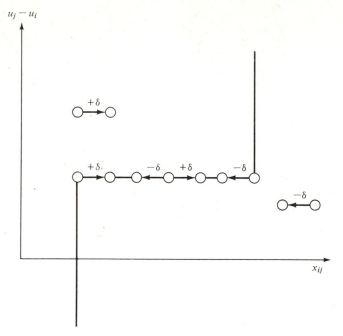

Figure 4.18   Possible changes in kilter diagrams of arcs in yellow-green cycle

For a given yellow-green cycle C, let Y, G denote the subsets of yellow and green arcs in C. Let superscripts $+$ and $-$ indicate subsets of Y, G for which arc flow is to be respectively incremented and decremented by δ. No in-kilter arc will be thrown out of kilter if δ is no greater than δ_1, δ_2, where

$$\delta_1 = \min \{c_{ij} - x_{ij} | (i, j) \in Y^+ \cup G^+, u_j - u_i = a_{ij}\},$$

$$\delta_2 = \min \{x_{ij} - l_{ij} | (i, j) \in Y^- \cup G^-, u_j - u_i = a_{ij}\}.$$

The increment δ will not be any greater than necessary to bring an out-of-kilter arc into kilter if δ is chosen to be no greater than

$$\delta_3 = \min \{|c_{ij} - x_{ij}| | (i, j) \in Y^+ \cup Y^-, u_j - u_i > a_{ij}\},$$

$$\delta_4 = \min \{|x_{ij} - l_{ij}| | (i, j) \in Y^+ \cup Y^-, u_j - u_i < a_{ij}\}.$$

Accordingly, we choose

$$\delta = \min \{\delta_1, \delta_2, \delta_3, \delta_4\}. \tag{10.8}$$

If in (10.8) δ is unbounded, i.e. each of $\delta_1, ..., \delta_4$ is determined by minimization over an empty set, there is no finite optimal circulation.

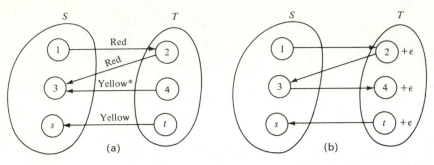

Figure 4.19   (a) Typical yellow-red cocycle. (b) Reorientation of yellow arc and increments to node numbers.

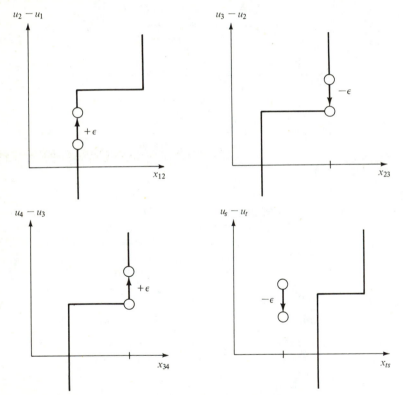

Figure 4.20   Kilter diagrams for yellow-red cocycle

This can occur when capacities of arcs in the cycle are infinite and the net cost of circulation around the cycle is negative.

Now suppose there is a yellow-red cocycle (S, T) with $s \in S$, $t \in T$, in which all yellow arcs are oriented in the same direction as (t, s). Reorient all arcs whose directions were reversed at the time they were painted yellow.

An increase by a small amount $\varepsilon > 0$ in the node numbers of all nodes i in T affects the value of $u_j - u_i$ only for the arcs in the cocycle. Moreover, such a change will not increase the kilter number of any arc, and may decrease the kilter numbers of some.

As an example, consider the cocycle shown in Figure 4.19a. After reorientation of the yellow arc (4, 3), the cocycle is as shown in Figure 4.19b. Changes in the kilter diagrams for arcs in this cocycle are indicated in Figure 4.20. Note that the largest permissible value for ε is determined by the red arc (2.3), which will be colored yellow, and its direction reversed, the next time it is painted.

An analysis of cases shows that the kilter diagrams of the yellow and red arcs in such the cocycle can be affected only in the manner suggested by the arrows in Figure 4.21. In each case, there is no increase in the kilter number of an arc, provided ε is chosen sufficiently small. Let us now consider such a choice of ε.

For a given yellow-red cocycle C let Y, R denote the subsets of yellow and red arcs in the cocycle. Let superscripts $+, -$ indicate subsets of arcs for which $u_j - u_i$ will be respectively increased and decreased by the ε-increment to the node numbers. No in-kilter arc will be thrown out of kilter if ε is no greater than $\varepsilon_1, \varepsilon_2$, where

$$\varepsilon_1 = \{u_j - u_i - a_{ij} \,|\, (i, j) \in R^-, x_{ij} = c_{ij}\}$$
$$\varepsilon_2 = \{a_{ij} - u_j + u_i \,|\, (i, j) \in R^+, x_{ij} = l_{ij}\}.$$

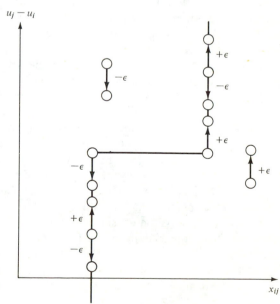

Figure 4.21   Possible changes in kilter diagrams of arcs in yellow-red cocycle

The increment ε will not be any greater than necessary to bring an out-of-kilter arc into kilter if ε is chosen to be no greater than ε_3, ε_4, where

$$\varepsilon_3 = \{u_j - u_i - a_{ij} | (i, j) \in Y^-, l_{ij} \leq x_{ij} < c_{ij}\}$$

$$\varepsilon_4 = \{a_{ij} - u_j + u_i | (i, j) \in Y^+, l_{ij} < x_{ij} \leq c_{ij}\}.$$

Accordingly, we choose

$$\varepsilon = \min \{\varepsilon_1, \varepsilon_2, \varepsilon_3, \varepsilon_4\}. \tag{10.9}$$

There are three possible cases:

Case 1 ε is unbounded, i.e., each of $\varepsilon_1, \dots, \varepsilon_4$ is determined by minimization over an empty set. This can occur only if $x_{ij} \geq c_{ij}$ for all arcs from S to T and $x_{ij} \leq l_{ij}$ for all arcs from T to S and $x_{ts} < l_{ts}$. Net flow from S to T is zero, so

$$\sum_{i \in S, j \in T} l_{ij} > \sum_{i \in T, j \in S} c_{ij}.$$

It follows from Theorem 9.1 that no feasible circulation exists.

Case 2 ε is finite and equal to either ε_3 or ε_4. At least one out-of-kilter arc is brought into kilter. No kilter numbers are increased and some may be decreased.

Case 3 ε is finite and less than both ε_3 and ε_4. No out-of-kilter arc is brought into kilter. No kilter numbers are increased and some may be decreased. At least one red arc will be colored yellow the next time it is painted. For such an arc (i, j), if $i \in S$, $j \in T$, then $l_{ij} = x_{ij} < c_{ij}$ and if $i \in T$, $j \in S$, then $l_{ij} < x_{ij} = c_{ij}$. In addition, some arcs may change color from yellow to red. For each of these arcs, $i \in S, j \in T$ implies $l_{ij} < x_{ij} = c_{ij}$ and $i \in T, j \in S$ implies $l_{ij} = x_{ij} < c_{ij}$. No green arcs, of course, are affected.

A labeling procedure can be used, as in the proof of the painting theorem, to construct a yellow-green cycle or a yellow-red cocycle. The node s is initially labeled, and all nodes reachable from s are successively labeled. To use the analogy of the proof of the painting theorem, green arcs are viewed as two-way streets, yellow arcs as one-way streets, and red arcs as streets blocked in both directions. If t is reachable from s, backtracing from the label on t yields a yellow-green cycle. If t is not reachable, let S contain all labeled nodes and T the remaining nodes. The desired yellow-red cocycle is (S, T). (Actually, (S, T) is a cutset not necessarily a cocycle, but this is just as good for our purposes.)

We are now ready to establish the convergence of the algorithm, provided all lower bounds and capacities are integers and the initial circulation is integral.

Each discovery of a yellow-green cycle results in the reduction of at least one kilter number by some $\delta \geq 1$. Thus, no more than K revisions of the circulation are necessary, where K is the sum of the kilter numbers for the initial circulation.

Assuming a feasible circulation exists, each time a yellow-red cocycle is discovered, either an out-of-kilter arc is brought into kilter (Case 2) or at least one red arc changes color to yellow (Case 3). The former case reduces at least one positive kilter number to zero, so this cannot occur more than min (m, K) times in all. The latter case cannot occur more than $n - 1$ times in succession, by the the following reasoning.

Suppose the same arc (t, s) is used for the application of the painting theorem until a yellow-green cycle is discovered. Then each time a cocycle is discovered and Case 3 occurs, at least one red arc changes color to yellow in such a way that an additional node i in T will become reachable from s the next time the labeling procedure is applied. All nodes reachable from s remain reachable. (Changes from yellow to red are of no consequence.) Thus Case 3 can occur at most $n - 1$ times in succession before either a cycle is discovered or else an out-of-kilter arc is brought into kilter (Case 2).

To summarize: K is an upper bound on the total number of discoveries of either a yellow-green cycle or a yellow-red cocycle for which Case 2 applies. There can be no more than $n - 1$ discoveries in succession of a yellow-red cocycle for which Case 3 applies. Thus the labeling procedure is applied at most nK times overall. Since the labeling procedure requires $O(m)$ time, and no other operations require more time, it follows that $O(mnK)$ is an upper bound on the running time of the out-of-kilter algorithm.

The algorithm can be made more efficient by exploiting the fact that labels can be preserved after the discovery of a cocycle for which Case 3 applies. (Recall that all nodes reachable from s remain reachable.) This means that we can, in effect, make one application of the labeling procedure serve for each succession of Case 3 cocycles. Thus at most K complete labelings are required, yielding a bound of $O(mK)$.

A little cleverness is required in order to obtain this result. We shall apply two types of labels: "permanent" and "tentative." A permanent label indicates that the node to which it is applied can be reached from s by means of a yellow-green path, with all yellow arcs oriented in the forward direction. A tentative label indicates that the node will be reachable by a yellow-green path, once the node numbers are revised by a sufficient value ε. This value of ε will be indicated by a number π_j associated with a tentatively labeled node j.

The procedure is summarized as follows.

OUT-OF-KILTER ALGORITHM

Step 0 (*Start*)   Let $x = (x_{ij})$ be any circulation, possibly infeasible, but satisfying conservation conditions, and let $u = (u_i)$ be any set of node numbers. It is desirable to start with x, u such that the sum of the kilter numbers is small, but $x = (0), u = (0)$ will do.

Step 1   (*Painting and Labeling*)

(1.0)   If all arcs are in kilter, halt; the existing circulation is optimal and u is an optimal dual solution. Otherwise paint the arcs green, yellow, and red, in accordance with rules (10.4) through (10.7). Set $\pi_i = +\infty$ for all nodes i. Choose any arc (t, s) which is out of kilter and apply the permanent label "$\varnothing$" to s. No other nodes have labels.

(1.1)   If all permanently labeled nodes have been scanned, go to Step 3. Otherwise, find a permanently labeled but unscanned node i and scan it as follows: For each yellow or green arc (i, j) and for each green arc (j, i), if j does not already have a permanent label, give j the permanent label "i" (replacing any existing tentative label). For each red arc (i, j), if $x_{ij} = l_{ij}$ and $u_j - u_i - a_{ij} < \pi_j$ give j the tentative label "i" (replacing any existing label) and set $\pi_j = u_j - u_i - a_{ij}$. For each red arc (j, i), if $x_{ji} = c_{ji}$ and $a_{ji} + u_j - u_i < \pi_j$ give j the tentative label "i" (replacing any existing label) and set $u_j = a_{ji} + u_j - u_i$.

(1.2)   If node t has been given a permanent label, go to Step 2; otherwise, go to Step 1.1.

Step 2   (*Change in Circulation*)   Identify a yellow-green cycle C by using the label on t to backtrace to s. Determine δ by (10.8). If δ is unbounded, there is no finite optimal solution and the computation is terminated. Otherwise, increment or decrement the flow in each arc in C by δ. Erase all labels on nodes and go to Step 1.0.

Step 3   (*Change in Node Numbers*)   Let S contain the all permanently labeled nodes and T contain the remaining nodes. (S, T) is a yellow-red cutset. Determine ε by (10.9). If ε is unbounded, no feasible circulation exists and the computation is terminated. Otherwise, add ε to u_i for each node i in T. If Case 2 applies, go to Step 1.0. If Case 3 applies, subtract ε from π_i for each node i in T and make the labels permanent on all nodes for which $\pi_i = 0$. Then go to Step 1.1. //

The out-of-kilter method is easily adapted to handle piecewise linear convex arc costs. A typical arc cost curve of this type and its corresponding kilter diagram are shown in Figure 4.22. It is left to the reader

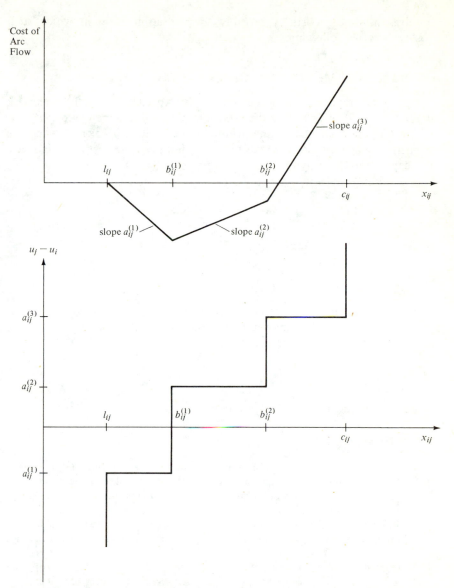

Figure 4.22   Typical arc cost function and its kilter diagram

in Problem 10.2 to determine how the algorithm should be generalized and to show that the order of complexity of the computation is unaffected, provided lower bounds, capacities, and breakpoints b_{ij} are integers.

In Section 13, it will be seen that a problem in project scheduling involves nonlinear costs. A possibly simpler application in which such costs arise is the following.

OPTIMAL AUGMENTATION OF CAPACITY

Suppose that it is desired to augment the arc capacities of a flow network in the least costly way, so that the maximum flow value is increased to $v' > v$, where v is the existing maximum flow value. If the cost of increasing the capacity of each arc is linear and there is a nonnegative cost a_{ij} to increase the capacity of (i, j) by one unit, then the problem is

$$\text{minimize} \sum_{i,j} a_{ij} y_{ij}$$

subject to

$$\sum_j x_{ji} - \sum_j x_{ij} = \begin{cases} -v', & i = s \\ 0, & i \neq s, t \\ v', & i = t. \end{cases}$$

$$0 \leq x_{ij} \leq c_{ij} + y_{ij}.$$

Add a return arc (t, s) to the network with $l_{ts} = c_{ts} = v'$, and the problem becomes one of finding a minimum cost circulation, where the cost of flow in arc (i, j) is $\bar{a}_{ij}(x_{ij})$, where

$$\bar{a}_{ij}(x_{ij}) = \begin{cases} 0, & x_{ij} \leq c_{ij} \\ a_{ij}(x_{ij} - c_{ij}), & x_{ij} > c_{ij}. \end{cases}$$

Since $a_{ij} \geq 0$, the function $\bar{a}_{ij}(x_{ij})$ is convex.

PROBLEMS

10.1 Try to relate the $u_j^{(k)}$ variables in the Edmonds-Karp technique for solving the minimum cost flow problem to the dual variables in the linear programming formulation of the problem. Do the final values of these variables yield an optimal dual solution?

10.2 Indicate how the out-of-kilter algorithm should be generalized to accommodate convex arc cost functions. How should arcs be colored with reference to Figure 4.22?

10.3 (For electrical engineers) Let u_i denote potential, $u_j - u_i$ voltage drop, and x_{ij} current. The plot of the "$e - i$ characteristic" of a network element is equivalent to a kilter diagram. What are the kilter diagrams for ideal batteries, resistors, diodes? Determine how you could employ the out-of-kilter algorithm to compute the characteristics of two-terminal networks composed of such devices. What types of devices cannot be accommodated? (See paper by Minty on electrical network computations.)

10.4 Try to generalize the out-of-kilter method to networks with losses and gains. What difficulties arise?

11

Theoretical Improvement in Efficiency of Out-of-Kilter Method

We concluded the discussion of the out-of-kilter method by establishing a bound of $O(Km)$ on the number of steps, where K is the sum of the arc kilter numbers for the initial primal and dual solutions. If $x = 0$, $u = 0$ are taken as initial solutions, then K may be as large as the sum of all arc capacities, which are assumed to be integers.

In order to qualify as a bona fide polynomial-bounded computation, the number of steps required by the out-of-kilter method should be polynomial not in the magnitudes of the arc capacities but in their logarithms, i.e., the number of bits required to specify them as input data. A similar observation holds for the minimum cost flow computation of Section 7, for which a bound of $O(mv)$ was obtained. It is quite possible that the desired flow value v could approximate the sum of the arc capacities.

We shall not show that either algorithm is polynomial bounded (in fact, they are not). Instead we shall describe a "scaling" technique due to Edmonds and Karp whereby the out-of-kilter algorithm is applied to a series of problems which provide successively closer approximations to the given problem. A polynomial bound of the desired type is then obtained.

Suppose we wish to apply the out-of-kilter method to a problem with integer lower bounds and capacities and for which the maximum arc capacity is no greater than 2^p. We first replace the original problem by a problem (0) in which

$$c_{ij}^{(0)} = \left\lceil \frac{c_{ij}}{2^p} \right\rceil,$$

$$l_{ij}^{(0)} = \left\lfloor \frac{l_{ij}}{2^p} \right\rfloor,$$

and arc costs are as given. (Here "$\lceil\ \rceil$" means "least integer no less than" and "$\lfloor\ \rfloor$" means "greatest integer no greater than.") All lower bounds and capacities are 0 or 1.

This 0-order approximation of the original network admits a feasible circulation, if a feasible circulation was possible in the original, for note that

$$2^p c_{ij}^{(0)} \geq c_{ij},$$
$$2^p l_{ij}^{(0)} \leq l_{ij}.$$

If we take $u = 0$, $x = 0$ as an initial circulation, in this crude approximation of the original network, all kilter numbers are 0 or 1. Hence $K \leq m$, where m is the number of arcs. Accordingly, the out-of-kilter method requires no more than $O(m^2)$ steps to obtain optimal primal and dual solutions x^0, u^0.

We now construct a problem (1) in which

$$c_{ij}^{(1)} = \left\lceil \frac{c_{ij}}{2^{p-1}} \right\rceil,$$

$$l_{ij}^{(1)} = \left\lfloor \frac{l_{ij}}{2^{p-1}} \right\rfloor,$$

and arc costs remain as given. All lower bounds and capacities are either 0, 1, or 2. If we take $2x^{(0)}$, $u^{(0)}$ as an initial primal and dual solutions, all arc kilter numbers are again 0 or 1 and again $K \leq m$. The out-of-kilter method requires no more than $O(m^2)$ steps to obtain primal and dual solutions $x^{(1)}, u^{(1)}$.

We continue in this way, passing from problem (k) to problem $(k + 1)$, taking $2x^{(k)}$, $u^{(k)}$ as initial solutions for problem $(k + 1)$. Finally, problem (p) is for a network identical to the original and we will have obtained a circulation for it in $O(m^2 p)$ steps overall. Since $p = \lceil \log_2 c_{ij} \rceil$ for the largest c_{ij}, we have obtained the desired result.

Kilter diagrams for a typical arc with $l_{ij} = 7$, $c_{ij} = 20$ are shown in Figure 4.23. The diagrams for successive problems are rescaled so at to best display their relationship with the original. The reader can verify that the $l_{ij}^{(k)}$ and $c_{ij}^{(k)}$ values are easily determined from the binary representation of l_{ij} and c_{ij}.

It does not seem possible to apply this scaling technique to the minimum cost flow algorithm, unless the algorithm is generalized in some way. That is, if $x^{(k)}$ is an optimal solution to problem (k), then $2x^{(k)}$ may exceed capacity constraints for problem $(k + 1)$. Some technique must be used to restore feasibility before problem $(k + 1)$ can be solved. Edmonds and Karp proposed a limited number of iterations of the out-of-kilter method, but this seems a bit devious.

We should conclude by saying that this scaling technique, although easy enough to implement, is probably of very limited practical importance. Its significance appears to be largely theoretical, but in this realm it provides a very satisfying result.

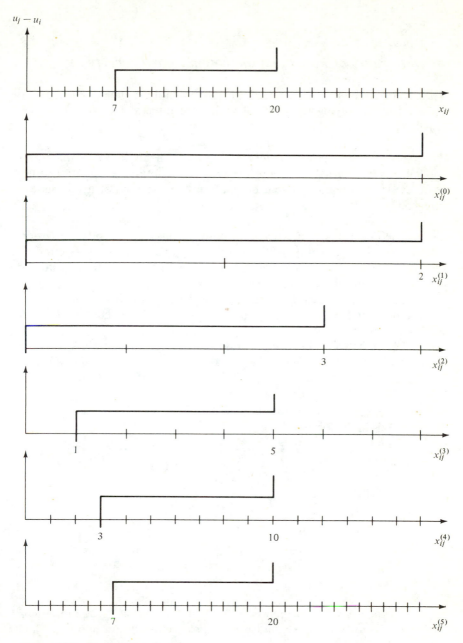

Figure 4.23   Scaled kilter diagram

12
Integrality of Flows and the Unimodular Property

The nature of the out-of-kilter method is such that it provides a constructive proof of the following theorem, of which the integral flow theorem is a corollary:

Theorem 12.1 (*Integral Circulation Theorem*)   If all lower bounds and capacities are integers and there exists a finite optimal circulation, then there exists an integral optimal circulation (whether or not arc costs are integers).

The integrality of optimal circulations is in contrast to the situation encountered for networks with losses and gains, studied in Section 8. One is not assured of an integral minimum loss flow, even though all arc capacities and multipliers are integers.

Some insight into Theorem 12.1 is obtained by an examination of the algebraic structure of the circulation problem from the viewpoint of linear programming.

Let us convert the lower bound and capacity constraints in (10.1) to equality form by introducing nonnegative slack variables r_{ij} and s_{ij}:

$$-x_{ij} + r_{ij} = -l_{ij},$$

$$x_{ij} + s_{ij} = c_{ij}.$$

Then (10.1) is in the form
    minimize ax
    subject to

$$A(x, r, s) = b$$

$$x, r, s \geq 0,$$

where A and b are structured as below

$$A = \left(\begin{array}{c|c|c} G & 0 & 0 \\ \hline -I_m & I_m & 0 \\ \hline I_m & 0 & I_m \end{array} \right) \qquad b = \left(\begin{array}{c} 0 \\ \hline -l \\ \hline c \end{array} \right) \qquad (12.1)$$

Here G is the arc-node incidence matrix of the network, I_m, I_n are $m \times m$ and $n \times n$ identity matrices, and l and c are vectors of lower bounds and capacities.

It so happens that the matrix A is *totally unimodular*, meaning that every subdeterminant of A is either $+1$, -1, or 0. From this unimodular property it follows that every basis inverse B^{-1} is integral and so $x^B = B^{-1}b$ is integral if b is integral. Thus, no matter what integral lower bounds and capacities are chosen, all basic feasible solutions, including a basic optimal solution, are integral.

Theorem 12.2 (*Hoffman and Kruskal*) Let a linear program have constraints $Ax = b$, $x \geq 0$, where A is an integer matrix with linearly independent rows and b is an integer vector. The following three conditions are equivalent:

(12.2)   The determinant of every basis B is ± 1.
(12.3)   The extreme points of the convex polytope C defined by $Ax = b$, $x \geq 0$ are integral, for all integer vectors b.
(12.4)   The inverse B^{-1} of every basis B is integer.

PROOF   This proof is due to Veinott and Dantzig. (12.2) implies (12.3). Let $x = (x^B, x^R)$ be an extreme point of the convex polytope C and B be the associated basis. By Cramer's rule, $\det B = \pm 1$ implies that B^{-1} is integral. Hence if b is integral, $x^B = B^{-1}b$ is integral.
(12.3) implies (12.4). Let B be a basis and y be any integer vector such that $y + B^{-1}e_i \geq 0$, where e_i is the ith unit column vector. Let $z = y + B^{-1}e_i \geq 0$. Then $Bz = By + e_i$ is an integer vector since B, y, and e_i are all integral. Because b can be any integer vector, we shall let $b = Bz$. Now $Bz = b$ and $z \geq 0$, which shows that z is an extreme point of the convex polytope C defined by $Ax = b$, $x \geq 0$. By (12.3), z is an integer vector. But $z - y = B^{-1}e_i$, from which it follows that $B^{-1}e_i$ is integral. The vector $B^{-1}e_i$ is the ith column vector of B^{-1}, and the argument can be repeated for $i = 1, 2, \ldots, m$ to show that B^{-1} is an integer matrix.
(12.4) implies (12.2). Let B be a basis. By assumption B is an integer matrix and $\det B$ is an integer. By condition (12.4) B^{-1} is an integer matrix so $\det B^{-1}$ is also an integer. But $(\det B)(\det B^{-1}) = 1$ which implies that $\det B = \det B^{-1} = \pm 1$.

Corollary 12.3   Let C' be the convex polytope defined by the inequality constraints $A'x \leq b$, $x \geq 0$, where A' is an integer matrix. The following three conditions are equivalent:

(12.2′) A' is totally unimodular.
(12.3′)   The extreme points of C' are all integral for any integer vector b.
(12.4′)   Every nonsingular submatrix of A' has an integer inverse.

PROOF   Let $A = (A', I)$. It is not hard to establish the equivalence of (12.2) to (12.2′), (12.3) to (12.3′), and (12.4) to (12.4′). For example, if M is any submatrix of A' of rank $m - k$, then a basis of A can be found, after permuting rows, of the form

$$B = \begin{pmatrix} M & 0 \\ N & I_k \end{pmatrix},$$

where I_k is a $k \times k$ identity matrix. Then $\det B = \det M$, so that $\det B = \pm 1$. Similar transformations suffice to establish other equivalences. //

If we can establish that the coefficient matrix A in (12.1) is totally unimodular, then Theorem 12.1 follows from Theorem 12.2. We will then have an algebraic, rather than algorithmic proof of the integrality of optimal circulations.

Unfortunately, there do not seem to be any easily tested necessary and sufficient conditions for total unimodularity. Perhaps the most elegant such conditions are due to Camion, which we state without proof.

A matrix is said to be *Eulerian* if the sum of the elements in each row and in each column is even.

Theorem 12.4   (*Camion*)   A $(0, +1, -1)$ matrix is totally unimodular if and only if the sum of the elements in each Eulerian square submatrix is a multiple of four.

There is also an easily tested set of sufficient (but not necessary) conditions for total unimodularity.

Theorem 12.5   A $(0, +1, -1)$ matrix A is totally unimodular if both of the following conditions are satisfied:

(12.5)   Each column contains at most two nonzero elements.
(12.6)   The rows of A can be partitioned into two sets A_1 and A_2 such that two nonzero entries in a column are in the same set of rows if they have different signs and in different sets of rows if they have the same sign.

PROOF   A submatrix of a $(0, +1, -1)$ matrix satisfying the conditions of the theorem must also satisfy the same conditions. Hence it is sufficient to prove that $\det A = 0, \pm 1$, for all square matrices satisfying the conditions. For any 1×1 matrix A, clearly $\det A = 0, \pm 1$. Now suppose, by inductive hypothesis, that $\det A = 0, \pm 1$ for all $(n - 1) \times (n - 1)$ matrices A. Let A be $n \times n$. If A contains a zero column, $\det A = 0$. If some column of A contains exactly one nonzero entry, then $\det A = \pm \det A' = 0, \pm 1$, where A' is the cofactor of that entry. If every column of A contains exactly two nonzero entries, then

$$\sum_{i \in A_1} a_{ij} = \sum_{i \in A_2} a_{ij}, \quad \text{for } j = 1, 2, \ldots, n.$$

This implies that $\det A = 0$ and the proof is complete. //

Corollary 12.6   A $(0, +1, -1)$ matrix A is totally unimodular if it contains no more than one $+1$ and no more than one -1 in each column.

The incidence matrix G is a $(0, +1, -1)$ matrix with exactly one $+1$ and one -1 matrix in each column. It follows immediately from Corollary 12.6 and G is totally unimodular.

Theorem 12.7   A matrix A is totally unimodular if and only if any one of the matrices $A^T, -A, (A, A), (A, I)$ is totally unimodular.

PROOF   The proof is left to the reader. //

We thus see, from any one of several possible sequences of transformations, using Theorem 12.7, that the matrix

$$\begin{pmatrix} G & I_n & 0 & 0 \\ -I_m & 0 & I_m & 0 \\ I_m & 0 & 0 & I_m \end{pmatrix}$$

is totally unimodular. The matrix A in (12.1) is a submatrix of this last matrix and hence is also totally unimodular. We have thus established the desired result.

A linear programming problem with a totally unimodular coefficient matrix yields an optimal solution in integers for any objective vector and any integer vector on the right-hand side of the constraints. There are nonunimodular problems which yield integral optimal solutions for any objective vector but only certain integer constraint vectors. Nearly all the problems studied in Chapters 6 through 8 are of this variety. There are still other nonunimodular problems which yield integral optimal solutions for any integer constraint vector but only certain objective vectors. As an example of the latter type consider the following problem.

As we noted in Section 4, any (s, t)-flow can be expressed as a sum of flows in (s, t) directed paths and circulations around directed cycles. Let us suppose the network we are dealing with is acyclic, so that we need not be concerned with cycles. Let $P = (p_{(i,j),k})$ be an incidence matrix of arcs and (all possible) directed paths from s to t, where

$$p_{(i,j)k} = \begin{cases} 1 & \text{if arc } (i, j) \text{ is contained in path } k \\ 0 & \text{otherwise.} \end{cases}$$

This is an $m \times p$ matrix, where p is a very large number. Then the max-flow problem is equivalent to a linear program of the form:

maximize

$$v = \sum_k y_k$$

subject to

(12.8)

$$\sum_k p_{(i,j),k} y_k \le c_{ij}, \quad \text{for all arcs } (i, j)$$

$$y_k \ge 0,$$

where the arc flows identified with a solution to (12.8) are in the relation

$$x_{ij} = \sum_k p_{(i,j),k} y_k.$$

Consider the network shown in Figure 4.24. There are eight (s, t) paths in this network and the path incidence matrix is:

$$
\begin{array}{c}
(1, 2) \\
(1, 3) \\
(2, 3) \\
(3, 4) \\
(3, 5) \\
(4, 5) \\
(5, 6) \\
(5, 7) \\
(6, 7)
\end{array}
\begin{bmatrix}
0 & 1 & 0 & 1 & 0 & 1 & 0 & 1 \\
1 & 0 & 1 & 0 & 1 & 0 & 1 & 0 \\
0 & 1 & 0 & 1 & 0 & 1 & 0 & 1 \\
0 & 0 & 1 & 0 & 0 & 1 & 1 & 0 \\
1 & 1 & 0 & 1 & 1 & 0 & 0 & 1 \\
0 & 0 & 1 & 0 & 0 & 1 & 1 & 0 \\
1 & 0 & 0 & 0 & 0 & 1 & 1 & 1 \\
0 & 1 & 1 & 1 & 1 & 0 & 0 & 0 \\
1 & 0 & 0 & 0 & 0 & 1 & 1 & 1
\end{bmatrix}
$$
$$P_1 \; P_2 \; P_3 \; P_4 \; P_5 \; P_6 \; P_7 \; P_8$$

This matrix is not totally unimodular, since the determinant of the submatrix

$$
\begin{array}{c}
(1, 3) \\
(3, 5) \\
(5, 7)
\end{array}
\begin{bmatrix}
1 & 0 & 1 \\
1 & 1 & 0 \\
0 & 1 & 1
\end{bmatrix}
$$
$$P_1 \; P_2 \; P_3$$

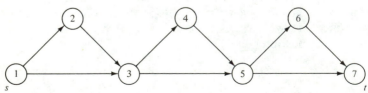

Figure 4.24   Flow network for example

is two. Nevertheless (12.8) does admit an optimal solution in integers, for any choice of integer arc capacities. Moreover, for any choice of arc costs whatsoever, we can let c_k denote the negative sum of the costs in path P_k. Maximization of $\sum_k c_k y_k$ yields an optimal solution in integers.

The coefficient matrix P is not totally unimodular. Yet for any choice of arc costs and integer arc capacities an integral optimal solution is obtained. This result seems to be in conflict with Corollary 12.3. What is the reason?

The answer is simply that we can construct an objective function that does not correspond to any assignment of arc costs. For example, let all capacities be unity and let $c_1 = c_2 = c_3 = +1$, $c_k = 0$, $4 \leq k \leq 8$. Then maximization of $\sum c_k y_k$ yields the unique optimal solution $y_1 = y_2 = y_3 = \frac{1}{2}$, $y_k = 0, 4 \leq k \leq 8$.

PROBLEMS

12.1   Try to devise an efficient procedure for testing an arbitrary matrix for total unimodularity, using the conditions of Theorem 12.4.

12.2   Prove Theorem 12.7.

12.3   Prove that a graph is bipartite if and only if its arc-node incidence matrix is totally unimodular.

13

Application to Project Scheduling

One of the more celebrated and useful applications of network flow theory is in the area of project scheduling. Various techniques have been developed under such titles as CPM (Critical Path Method) and PERT (Project Evaluation and Review Technique). We outline here the basic ideas of this application.

Suppose that a large project can be broken into a number of *tasks*. The precedence relations between these tasks are indicated by identifying the tasks with the arcs of a directed graph. All tasks directed into a node must be completed before any task directed out is begun. (It may be necessary to insert "dummy" tasks having zero completion time, in order to be able to adequately model all the precedence relations of a given set of tasks.)

Associated with each task (i, j) are its "normal" completion time a_{ij}, its "crash" completion time b_{ij} and the cost c_{ij} of shortening the task by one time unit (presumably by the application of overtime or a larger work force). Thus if t_{ij} is the actual duration of the task, then $b_{ij} \leq t_{ij} \leq a_{ij}$, and the cost required to complete the task in that time is $c_{ij}(a_{ij} - t_{ij})$.

Associate a variable u_i with each node i of the project network, where u_i denotes the time at which the "event" i occurs. We let node s mark the initial event of the project, and node t mark the final event. Then the problem of finding the minimum cost C of shortening the project to a given duration T is:

minimize
$$C = \sum_{i,j} c_{ij}(a_{ij} - t_{ij}) \tag{13.1}$$

or, equivalently,

maximize
$$\sum_{i,j} c_{ij}t_{ij} \tag{13.2}$$

subject to

$$\left. \begin{array}{l} u_t - u_s \qquad \leq T \\ u_i - u_j + t_{ij} \leq 0 \\ b_{ij} \leq t_{ij} \leq a_{ij} \end{array} \right\} \quad \text{for all arcs } (i, j)$$

$$u_i, t_{ij} \text{ unrestricted.}$$

Associate nonnegative variables v, x_{ij}, α_{ij}, β_{ij} with constraints $u_t - u_s \leq T$, $u_i - u_j + t_{ij} \leq 0$, $t_{ij} \leq a_{ij}$, $-t_{ij} \leq -b_{ij}$ and the dual of this linear programming problem is:

minimize
$$c = \sum_{i,j} a_{ij}\alpha_{ij} - \sum_{i,j} b_{ij}\beta_{ij} + Tv \tag{13.3}$$

subject to

$$\sum_j x_{ji} - \sum_j x_{ij} = \begin{cases} -v & i = s \\ 0 & i \neq s, t \\ v & i = t \end{cases}$$

$$x_{ij} + \alpha_{ij} - \beta_{ij} = c_{ij} \tag{13.4}$$

$$x_{ij}, \alpha_{ij}, \beta_{ij} \geq 0.$$

From $a_{ij} \geq b_{ij} \geq 0$ and (13.4) it follows that an optimal solution must satisfy the conditions

$$x_{ij} \leq c_{ij} \Rightarrow \alpha_{ij} = c_{ij} - x_{ij}, \; \beta_{ij} = 0$$

$$x_{ij} > c_{ij} \Rightarrow \alpha_{ij} = 0, \; \beta_{ij} = x_{ij} - c_{ij}.$$

Accordingly, an equivalent flow problem is

minimize
$$c = \sum_{i,j} T_{ij}(x_{ij}) + Tv \tag{13.5}$$

subject to

$$\sum_j x_{ji} - \sum_j x_{ij} = \begin{cases} -v & i = s \\ 0 & i \neq s, t \\ v & i = t \end{cases}$$

$$x_{ij} \geq 0,$$

where $T_{ij}(x_{ij})$ has the form shown in Figure 4.25.

Note that we dropped a constant in passing from (13.1) to (13.2) and restored the same constant in going from (13.3) to (13.5). Accordingly for optimal solutions the objective functions (13.1) and (13.5) are in the relation $C = -c$.

We can visualize each task (i, j) of the project as being represented by two parallel arcs from i to j in the flow network, one with cost $-a_{ij}$ and capacity c_{ij} and the other with cost $-b_{ij}$ and unbounded capacity. If there existed directed cycles in the project network the flow problem would not have a finite optimal solution, for any flow value v. But of course the task precedence relations are such that the network is necessarily acyclic.

We can add to the flow network a return arc (t, s) with unbounded capacity and cost T, the flow through this arc being v. For any specified T, the circulation problem can be solved by the out-of-kilter method. The kilter diagram for a typical arc (i, j) is as shown in Figure 4.26. As we noted in Problem 10.2, the out-of-kilter method is easily adapted to handle such kilter diagrams.

We propose to vary the parameter T and observe the optimal circula-

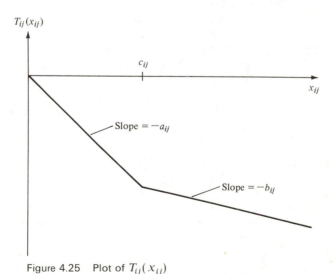

Figure 4.25   Plot of $T_{ij}(x_{ij})$

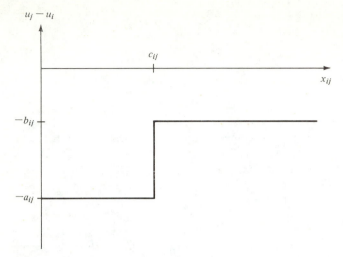

Figure 4.26   Kilter diagram

tions which result. If T is chosen very large, we expect that the zero circulation will be optimal, reflecting the fact that if the project duration is permitted to be sufficiently long, no money should be spent to shorten tasks. This will be true for any T as large as a critical or longest path from s to t with respect to arc lengths a_{ij}. (Recall the discussion in Chapter 3, Section 4.)

On the other hand, if T is chosen sufficiently small, we expect that there will be no finite optimal circulation, corresponding to the fact that no finite expenditure of money can reduce the project duration below a certain point. This will be the case for any value of T smaller than the length of a longest path from s to t with respect to arc lengths b_{ij}.

We begin the parametric analysis by solving a longest path problem with respect to arc lengths a_{ij}. The node numbers u_i so determined together with the zero circulation provide optimal primal and dual solutions for $T \geq u_t$. The parameter T is then reduced. All arcs remain in kilter except arc (t, s). The out-of-kilter method is then applied to bring (t, s) back into kilter. The procedure is repeated for successively smaller values of T until no finite optimal circulation exists.

The product of this computation is a project cost curve, such as that shown in Figure 4.27. This curve is piecewise linear and convex, since v increases as T decreases and we know that plots of minimum flow cost against v have this characteristic. The negative slope at T is equal to the marginal cost of decreasing the project duration by one time unit, and we should expect this marginal cost to increase as T is decreased.

The physical interpretations of the variables u_i, event times, and t_{ij}, task durations, are obvious. Not so obvious, however, is the interpreta-

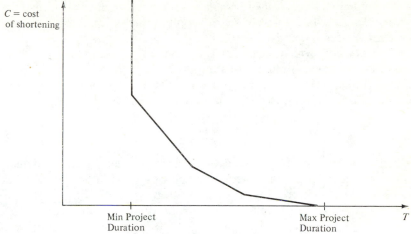

Figure 4.27   Typical project cost curve

tion of x_{ij}. The variable x_{ij} represents the amount we are willing to spend to shorten t_{ij} by one unit. Thus if $0 < x_{ij} < c_{ij}$ we are not willing to spend at a rate sufficient to shorten t_{ij}. If $x_{ij} = c_{ij}$ we are willing to spend at exactly the rate necessary to shorten t_{ij}. And if $x_{ij} > c_{ij}$ we would be willing to spend at a rate greater than c_{ij} to reduce t_{ij}, but it is impossible to reduce t_{ij} any further since $x_{ij} = b_{ij}$, the crash duration.

14

Transhipment and Transportation Problems

A *transhipment problem* is a form of minimum cost flow problem in which for each node i there is a given number b_i and instead of the ordinary conservation condition it is required that

$$\sum_j x_{ji} - \sum_j x_{ij} \geq b_i.$$

If $b_i < 0, > 0, = 0$, then node i is respectively a *supply* node, a *demand node*, or a *transhipment* node. Each arc (i, j) has an assigned flow cost a_{ij}, and arc capacities are assumed to be infinite. If this is not the case, then the problem is said to be *capacitated*.

A *Hitchcock-Koopmans transportation problem* is a transhipment problem on a bipartite graph $G = (S, T, A)$ with all supply nodes in S, all source nodes in T, and all arcs directed from S to T. (Transhipment nodes are eliminated.) The *assignment problem* is a special case of the transportation problem in which the number of supply nodes is equal to the number of demand nodes and each b_i is ± 1.

It is quite evident that the transhipment problem can be reduced to a conventional minimum cost flow problem with a single source-sink pair s, t. First, notice that if the problem is to be feasible, the sum of the supplies must be no less than the sum of the demands. That is,

$$-\sum_{b_i < 0} b_i \geq \sum_{b_i > 0} b_i = v.$$

Assume that the cost of any directed path from a supply node to a demand node is nonnegative, so that there exists an optimal solution in which demands are met with equality. Provide a source node s with an arc (s, i), $c_{si} = -b_i$, $a_{si} = 0$ to each supply node i and a sink node t with an arc (j, t), $c_{jt} = b_j$, $a_{jt} = 0$ from each demand node j. Restablish conservation conditions at all nodes. Then a minimum cost flow of value v yields a solution to the transhipment problem. (If some supply-demand paths are negative, it is necessary to introduce lower bounds on the arcs (j, t).)

It is also quite clear that the minimum cost flow problem is a capacitated transhipment problem (For a desired flow value v, set $b_s = -v$, $b_i = v$.) What is really surprising is that *the capacitated transhipment problem, and therefore the minimum cost flow problem, can be reduced to the uncapacitated Hitchcock-Koopmans transportation problem*. There are many transformations that provide this reduction and any of them serves to prove the dictum that "network programming is bipartite programming." This is the basis upon which the theory of bipartite matching presented in the next chapter can be considered to be coextensive with the theory of network flows we have developed to this point.

In the remainder of this section we indicate the reduction of the capacitated transhipment problem to the uncapacitated Hitchcock-Koopmans problem and conclude with some observations about the application of the out-of-kilter method to the latter type of problem.

REDUCTION OF CAPACITATED TRANSHIPMENT PROBLEM TO CAPACITATED HITCHCOCK-KOOPMANS PROBLEM

First note that, without loss of generality, we may assume that all supplies and demands in the transhipment problem must be satisfied with strict equality, i.e., the sum of the supplies is equal to the sum of the capacities. If this is not so, introduce an additional demand node with arcs directed to it from the sources, each such arc having large capacity and zero cost. This yields a problem of the form

minimize

$$a_{ij}x_{ij}$$

subject to

$$\sum_j x_{ji} - \sum_j x_{ij} = b_i$$

$$0 \le x_{ij} \le c_{ij},$$

where b_i is either negative, positive or zero, depending upon whether node i is a supply, demand, or transhipment node.

Now create a new $2n$-node network $\bar{G}$, in which each node i of the transhipment network G is represented by two nodes i, i' and an arc (i, i'), with $\bar{c}_{ii'} = +\infty$, $\bar{a}_{ii'} = 0$. For each arc (i, j) of G there is an arc (i, j') in $\bar{G}$, with $\bar{c}_{ij'} = c_{ij}$ and $\bar{a}_{ij'} = a_{ij}$. Assign values $\bar{b}_i$ to the nodes in the new network such that the absolute value of each $\bar{b}_i$ is suitably large and $\bar{b}_i + \bar{b}_{i'} = b_i$.

As an example, consider the transhipment network G shown in Figure 4.28a and the equivalent transportation network $\bar{G}$ in Figure 4.28b. The first number on each arc is its capacity and the second number is its cost. Numbers on nodes are b_i and $\bar{b}_i$ values.

The reader can verify that this transformation is generally effective and yields a correct result for the networks in Figure 4.28.

ELIMINATION OF CAPACITY CONSTRAINTS

Capacity constraints are removed from the network $\bar{G}$ by the following simple trick. Subdivide each arc (i, j) of $\bar{G}$ into three arcs (i, k) $(k'. k)$, (k', j), where k and k' are new nodes introduced by the subdivision. (Notice that k has out-degree zero and k' has in-degree zero.) Set $\bar{\bar{b}}_i = b_i$, $\bar{\bar{b}}_k = \bar{c}_{ij}$, $\bar{\bar{b}}_{k'} = -\bar{c}_{ij}$, $\bar{\bar{b}}_j = b_j$. Set $\bar{\bar{a}}_{ik} = \bar{a}_{ij}$, and all other arc costs to zero. All arc capacities are infinite. See Figure 4.29.

If $\bar{G}$ is bipartite with n nodes and m arcs, then $\bar{\bar{G}}$ is bipartite with $n + 2m$ nodes and $3m$ arcs. The reader can easily verify that $\bar{\bar{G}}$ is equivalent to $\bar{G}$, provided the numbers $\bar{b}_i$ in $\bar{G}$ are sufficiently large.

APPLICATION OF OUT-OF-KILTER METHOD TO HITCHCOCK-KOOPMANS TRANSPORATION PROBLEM

The transportation problem, in capacitated or uncapacitated form, is easily converted to a circulation problem by introducing a source s with arcs (s, i), $c_{si} = -b_i$, $a_{si} = 0$ to each supply node i, a sink t with arcs (j, t), $c_{jt} = b_j$, $a_{jt} = 0$ from each demand node, and a return arc (t, s), with $a_{ts} = 0$, $l_{ts} = c_{ts} = v$, where v is the sum of the supplies (= the sum of the demands).

For this circulation network, the primal and dual solutions $x = (0)$, $u = (0)$ are feasible and only arc (t, s) is out of kilter (with kilter number v). As the out-of-kilter computation proceeds, arc (t, s) is the only arc that is

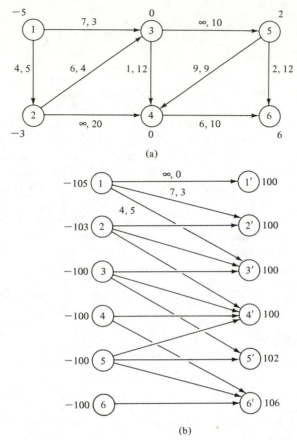

Figure 4.28   (a) Transhipment network G. (b) Corresponding transportation network $\bar{G}$.

ever out of kilter, just as was the situation with respect to the project scheduling problem in the previous section.

The principal point we want to make is that virtually all existing computational procedures for the transportation problem can be interpreted

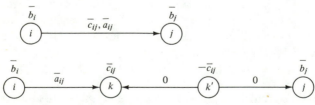

Figure 4.29   Elimination of arc capacity

as adaptations, variations, or specializations of the out-of-kilter method when it is applied in this way.

PROBLEM

14.1   In the transformation from the transhipment problem to the transportation problem, what does "suitably large" mean in the definition of $\bar{b}_i$? What, in general, is the smallest value which can be given to $\bar{b}_i$?

15

Multiterminal and Multicommodity Flows

Up to this point, we have been concerned exclusively with network problems involving the flow of a single commodity. Thus, for example, in the Hitchcock transportation problem any source of supply can be used to satisfy the demand at any sink (given requisite capacities and network structure). This enabled us to reduce the transportation problem to a flow problem with one source and one sink, and then to transform it to a circulation problem.

It is obvious that many real world problems involve flows of multiple, differentiated commodities. For some of these problems, the generalization of single-commodity flow theory is simple and direct. For others, rather severe complications arise. In this section we attempt a brief survey of both types of problems.

Generally speaking there are two ways in which multiple commodities may flow in a network. At any point in time, a network can be dedicated to the flow of a single commodity. For example, a railroad train may cross a switchyard from point 1 to point 2. Then switches can be thrown and a second train cross from point 3 to point 4. Problems with this characteristic have come to be known as *multiterminal flow* problems. On the other hand, several commodities may flow in the network simultaneously. For example, a telephone network is expected to handle a great multiplicity of messages simultaneously, each message with distinct source-sink pair. Such problems are referred to as *multicommodity flow* problems.

In engineering terminology, multiterminal flows involve time-sharing of the network and multicommodity flows, space-sharing. Mixed time- and space-sharing is, of course, also possible but is not our concern here.

We can also differentiate problems of *analysis* and problems of *synthesis*. Up to this point we have been primarily concerned with analysis, i.e., finding an optimal flow within a given network with certain fixed capacities, and so on. Many of these analysis techniques can also be applied to network synthesis, e.g., the problem of minimum cost augmentation of capacity discussed in Section 10.

Let us consider the four types of analysis and synthesis problems.

MULTITERMINAL ANALYSIS

For a given network, we may wish to know the maximum value flow, or the minimum cost flow, between all pairs of nodes, or some specified set of node pairs. This can, of course, be accomplished by carrying out a separate max-flow or min-cost computation for each node pair. However, some shortcuts are possible. For example, Gomory and Hu have shown that $p - 1$ max-flow computations, instead of $p(p - 1)/2$, are sufficient to determine maximum flow values between all pairs of a specified set of p nodes in a symmetric n-node network.

The following realizability result has also been obtained. For a given network, let

v_{ij} = the maximum value of a flow from node i to node j.

Then $V = (v_{ij})$ is the *flow matrix* of the network.

Theorem 15.1 (*Gomory and Hu*)   A necessary and sufficient condition for there to exist a network with a given symmetric matrix $V = (v_{ij})$ as its flow matrix is that

$$v_{ij} \geq \min \{v_{ik}, v_{kj}\},$$

for i, j, k.

PROOF

Necessity   by considering i to be the source and j to be the sink, it follows from the max-flow min-cut theorem that there is a cutset (S, T), $i \in S$, $j \in T$, with

$$v_{ij} = \sum_{i \in S} \sum_{j \in T} c_{ij} = C_{ij}.$$

If $k \in S$, then

$$v_{kj} \leq C_{ij} = v_{ij}, \qquad (15.1)$$

and if $k \in T$, then

$$v_{ik} \leq C_{ij} = v_{ij}. \qquad (15.2)$$

Since either (15.1) or (15.2) must hold,

$$v_{ij} \geq \min \{v_{ik}, v_{kj}\}.$$

Sufficiency   It can be shown that there exists a network in the form of a tree which realizes the flow values indicated by the matrix. This tree network can be constructed by means of the maximal spanning tree algorithm discussed in Chapter 7. The reader is invited to supply a proof. //

MULTITERMINAL SYNTHESIS

Let $R = (r_{ij})$ be a given matrix of flow requirements, and $A = (a_{ij})$ be a given matrix of arc costs. The cost of providing c_{ij} units of capacity in arc (i, j) is $a_{ij}c_{ij}$. What assignment of capacities to arcs will provide a minimum cost network with flow matrix $V \geq R$?

For the special case that R is symmetric and each $a_{ij} = 1$, Gomory and Hu have devised an efficient algorithm, discussed in Chapter 7. The more general case can be solved by linear programming, but vastly less efficiently.

MULTICOMMODITY ANALYSIS

We wish to induce a flow of one commodity between one specified pair of nodes, a flow of a second commodity between a second pair of nodes, and so on. Find a flow which satisfies certain specified node-pair flow values, subject to the constraint that the sum of the flows of all commodities through any given arc does not exceed its capacity. Or, in another version of the problem, maximize the sum of the commodity flow values.

These problems can be formulated and solved as linear programming problems. However, for one special case of the two-commodity flow problem, Hu has obtained a more effective procedure.

Suppose the sum of the flows of the two commodities in either direction cannot exceed the given capacity of an arc. That is, if x_{ij} is the flow of the first commodity from i to j and y_{ij} is the flow of the second, then

$$x_{ij} + x_{ji} + y_{ij} + y_{ji} \leq c_{ij} = c_{ji}.$$

The objective is to maximize the sum $v_1 + v_2$, where v_1 is the value of flow of the first commodity from node 1 to node 1' and v_2 is the value of the flow of the second commodity from 2 to 2'.

Let σ_1 be the minimum capacity of a cutset separating 1 and 1', σ_2 be the same for 2 and 2', and σ_{12} be the minimum capacity of a cutset separating both 1 and 1' and 2 and 2' (1 and 2 may be on one side of the cutset and 1' and 2' may be on the other, or else 1 and 2' on one side and 1' and 2 on the other).

The necessity of the conditions in the theorem below is obvious. Sufficiency is proved constructively by Hu's algorithm, which we do not present.

Theorem 15.2 (*Hu*) A two-commodity flow of amount v_1 in the first commodity and v_2 in the second is attainable if and only if

$$v_1 \leq \sigma_1,$$

$$v_2 \leq \sigma_2,$$

and

$$v_1 + v_2 \leq \sigma_{12}.$$

We note that $\sigma_1 + \sigma_2 \geq \sigma_{12}$, and this enables us to obtain a two-commodity max-flow min-cut theorem as a corollary.

Corollary 15.3 The maximum total value of a two-commodity flow is σ_{12}, i.e.,

$$\max \{v_1 + v_2\} = \sigma_{12}.$$

It should be noted, however, that integer capacities are not sufficient to guarantee integer flows. Two conditions which are sufficient are that all capacities are even, and that the sum of the capacities of the arcs incident to each node is even.

MULTICOMMODITY SYNTHESIS

As in the case of multiterminal synthesis, let $R = (r_{ij})$ be a given matrix of flow requirements and $A = (a_{ij})$ be a given matrix of arc costs. The cost of providing c_{ij} units of capacity in arc (i, j) is $a_{ij}c_{ij}$. What assignments of capacities to arcs will provide a minimum cost network which admits multicommodity flows as large as those specified by R?

The problem as stated is quite simple. Compute shortest paths between all pairs of nodes, with respect to arc costs a_{ij}. If P_{st} a shortest path from s to t provide r_{st} units of capacity in each arc $(i, j) \in P_{st}$ for the flow of the commodity from s to t. The total capacity that should be provided for each arc is the sum of the capacities needed for the individual commodities. That is, obtain a superposition of the shortest paths.

Things become immensely more difficult when additional constraints are placed on the problem, such as bounds on total arc capacities, nonlinearities of arc costs, and so on. A problem of enormous economic significance, and also of enormous complexity, is the so-called TELPAK problem. A reasonable approximation of this problem is that of a multicommodity network synthesis problem with concave arc capacity costs, i.e., there is economy of scale in the construction of arc capacity.

Much remains to be done in this area.

COMMENTS AND REFERENCES

The standard reference on network flow theory is

L. R. Ford, Jr. and D. R. Fulkerson, *Flows in Networks,* Princeton University Press, Princeton, New Jersey, 1962.

in which a number of results of combinatorial significance are emphasized. See also

C. Berge and A. Ghouila-Houri, *Programming, Games and Transportation Networks,* John Wiley, New York, 1965.
R. G. Busacker and T. L. Saaty, *Finite Graphs and Networks,* McGraw-Hill, New York, 1964.
H. Frank and I. Frisch, *Communication, Transportation and Flow Networks,* Addison-Wesley, Reading, Mass., 1972.
T. C. Hu, *Integer Programming and Network Flows,* Addison-Wesley, Reading, Mass., 1969.
Masao Iri, *Network Flows, Transportation and Scheduling,* Academic Press, New York, 1969.

SECTION 2
The max-flow min-cut theorem was established independently by

P. Elias, A. Feinstein, and C. E. Shannon, "Note on Maximum Flow Through a Network," *IRE Trans. on Information Theory,* **IT-2** (1956) 117–119.
L. R. Ford, Jr. and D. R. Fulkerson, "Maximal Flow Through a Network," *Canad. J. Math.* **8** (1956) 399–404.

SECTION 3
The maximum flow computation was presented in

L. R. Ford, Jr. and D. R. Fulkerson, "A Simple Algorithm for Finding Maximal Network Flows and an Application to the Hitchcock Problem," *Canad. J. Math.* **9** (1957) 210–218.

SECTION 4
J. Edmonds and R. M. Karp, "Theoretical Improvements in Algorithmic Efficiency for Network Flow Problems," *J. ACM,* **19** (1972) 248–264.
N. Zadeh, "Theoretical Efficiency of the Edmonds-Karp Algorithm for Computing Maximal Flows," *J. ACM,* **19** (1972) 184–192.
N. Zadeh, "More Pathological Examples for Network Flow Problems," *Math. Programming,* **5** (1973) 217–224.

Some of the Edmonds-Karp results were anticipated by Dinic, who also showed how to make further improvements in efficiency by, in effect, using one application of the labeling procedure to obtain all augmenting paths of a given length.

E. A. Dinic, "Algorithm for Solution of a Problem of Maximum Flow in a Network with Power Estimation," *Sov. Math. Dokl.*, **11** (1970) 1277–1280.

SECTION 5

G. A. Dirac, "Short Proof of Menger's Theorem," *Mathematiks*, **13** (1966) 42–44.

SECTION 6

J. Rhys, "Shared Fixed Cost and Network Flows," *Mgt. Sci.*, **17** (1970) 200–207.
M. L. Balinski, "On a Selection Problem," *Mgt. Sci.*, **17** (1970) 230–231.

SECTION 7

Theorem 7.2 was stated by

W. S. Jewell, "Optimal Flow through Networks," Interim Technical Report No. 8, Massachusetts Institute of Technology, 1958.
R. G. Busacker and P. J. Gowen, "A Procedure for Determining a Family of Minimal-Cost Network Flow Patterns," O. R. O. Technical Paper 15, 1961.

According to Fulkerson, the theorem is implicit in the computational procedure of

M. Iri, "A New Method of Solving Transporation-Network Problems," *J. Op. Res. Soc. Japan,* **3** (1960) 27–87.

See also

M. Klein, "A Primal Method for Minimal Cost Flows," *Mgt. Sci.*, **14** (1967) 205–220.
T. C. Hu, "Minimum Convex Cost Flows," *Naval Res. Logist. Quart.*, **13**, (1966) 1–9.

SECTION 8

Flow networks with losses and gains have been studied independently by operations research specialists and by electrical engineers, with each group being largely ignorant of the other's activity. Among the contributions on the operations research side are

H. Markowitz, "Concepts and Computing Procedures for Certain x_{ij} Programming Problems," *Proceedings of the 2nd Symposium on Linear Programming,* Directorate of Management Analysis, DCS/comptroller, Headquarters, U.S. Air Force, Washington, D.C., 1955, pp. 509–566.
J. Abadie, *Revue de Recherche Operationnelle,* **2** (1958) 94.
W. S. Jewell, "Optimal Flow through Networks with Gains," *Operations Research,* **10** (1962) 476–499.
W. Oettli and W. Prager, "Flow Networks with Amplification and Coupling," *Unternehmensforschung,* **10** (1966) 42–49.
J. J. Jarvis and A. M. Jezior, "Maximal Flow with Gains through a Special Network," *Operations Research,* **20** (1972) 678–688.
J. F. Maurras, "Optimization of the Flow through Networks with Gains," *Math. Programming,* **3** (1972) 135–144.

R. C. Grinold, "Calculating Maximal Flows in a Network with Positive Gains," *Operations Research,* **21** (1973) 528–541.

K. Truemper, "An Efficient Scaling Procedure for Gains Networks," to appear in *Networks.*

Work on the electrical engineering side includes

M. Iri, S. Amari, and M. Takata, *R.A.A.G. Research Note,* 3rd Series, No. 47, Tokyo, April 1961.

T. Fujisawa, "Maximal Flow in a Lossy Network," *Proc. Allerton Conference on Circuit and System Theory,* 1963, pp. 385–393.

W. Mayeda and M. E. Valkenburg, "Properties of Lossy Communication Nets," *IEEE Trans. Circuit Theory,* **CT-12** (1965) 334–338.

K. Onaga, "Dynamic Programming of Optimum Flows in Lossy Communication Nets," *IEEE Trans. Circuit Theory,* **CT-13** (1966) 282–287.

K. Onaga, "Optimal Flows in General Communication Networks," *Journal Franklin Instit.* **283** (1967) 308–327.

Onaga appears to have been the first to have explicitly pointed out the correspondence between the minimum cost flow problem in a conventional network and the minimum loss flow problem in a lossy network.

SECTION 9

The aircraft scheduling problem was solved by

G. B. Dantzig and D. R. Fulkerson, "Minimizing the Number of Tankers to Meet a Fixed Schedule," *Naval Res. Logist. Quart.,* **1** (1954) 217–222.

Theorem 9.1 on feasibility of circulations is due to

A. J. Hoffman, "Some Recent Applications of the Theory of Linear Inequalities to Extremal Combinatorial Analysis," *Proc. Symposium on Appl. Math.,* **10,** 1960.

For Dilworth's theorem, see

R. P. Dilworth, "A Decomposition Theorem for Partially Ordered Sets," *Annals of Math.,* **51** (1950) 161–166.

SECTION 10

The out-of-kilter method was developed independently by

G. J. Minty, "Monotone Networks," *Proc. Roy. Soc. London,* Ser. A, **257** (1960) 194–212.

and by

D. R. Fulkerson, "An Out-of-Kilter Method for Minimal Cost Flow Problems," *SIAM J. Appl. Math.,* **9** (1961) 18–27.

It appears that many of the ideas of the out-of-kilter method were anticipated by

M. A. Yakovleva, "Problem of Minimum Transporation Expense," in *Applications of Mathematics to Economics Research,* ed. by V. S. Nemchinov, Moscow, 1959, pp. 390–399.

Minty formulated his version of the algorithm for convex cost functions, and illustrated the application of his method to steady-state electrical network calculations in

G. J. Minty, "Solving Steady-State Nonlinear Networks of 'Monotone' Elements," *I.R.E. Trans. Circuit. Theory,* **CT-8** (1961) 99–104.

For other discussions of electrical analogs of network flows see

J. B. Dennis, *Mathematical Programming and Electrical Networks,* John Wiley, New York, 1959.
W. Prager, "Problems of Network Flow," *J. Appl. Math. and Physics (ZAMP),* **16** (1965) 185–190.

SECTION 11
See the Edmonds-Karp paper cited for Section 4.

SECTION 12
A. J. Hoffman and J. B. Kruskal, "Integral Boundary Points of Convex Polyhedra," in H. W. Kuhn and A. W. Tucker (eds.) *Linear Inequalities and Related Systems,* Annals of Mathematics Study No. 38, Princeton Univ. Press, Princeton, New Jersey, 1956, pp. 233–246.
A. F. Veinott, Jr. and G. B. Dantzig, "Integer Extreme Points," *SIAM Review,* **10** (1968) 371–372.
P. Camion, "Modules Unimodulaires," *J. Comb. Theory,* **4** (1968) 301–362.
P. Camion, "Characterization of Totally Unimodular Matrices," *Proc. Amer. Math. Soc.,* **16** (1965) 1068–1073.

SECTION 13
There is a very large body of literature on project scheduling. Among the first papers are

J. E. Kelley, Jr. and M. R. Walker, "Critical Path Planning and Scheduling," *Proc. Eastern Joint Computer Conference,* Boston, 1959.
D. R. Fulkerson, "A Network Flow Computation for Project Cost Curves," *Mgt. Sci.,* **7** (1961) 167–178.
B. Roy, "Cheminement et Connexité dan les Graphes, Application aux Problémes d'Ordonnancement," Paris, 1962.

SECTION 14
The transhipment problem, or related problems, seems to have a long history. Berge cites

Monge, "Déblai et Remblai," *Mem. Avad. Sci.,* 1781.
P. Apell, "Le Problème Géométrique des Deblais et Remblais," *Mem. des Sciences Math.,* Paris, **27**, 1928.

The "modern" literature on transhipment and transportation problem seems to begin with

F. L. Hitchcock, "The Distribution of a Product from Several Sources to Numerous Localities," *J. Math. Phys.,* **20** (1941) 224–230.
L. Kantorovitch, "On the Translocation of Masses," *Compt. Rend. (Doklady) Acad. Sci.,* **37** (1942) 199–201.

The simplex method was specialized to the transportation problem in the form of the "stepping stone" method

G. B. Dantzig, "Application of the Simplex Method to a Transportation Problem," *Activity Analysis of Production and Allocation,* Cowles Commission Monograph 13, John Wiley, New York, 1951, pp. 359–373.

The "primal-dual" method (which amounts to a specialization of the out-of-kilter method) was introduced in

L. R. Ford, Jr. and D. R. Fulkerson, "A Primal-Dual Algorithm for the Capacitated Hitchcock Problem, *"Naval Res. Logist. Quart.,* **4** (1957) 47–54.

The primal-dual method amounted to an extension of

H. W. Kuhn, "The Hungarian Method for the Assignment Problem," *Naval Res. Logist. Quart.,* **3** (1955) 253–258.

See the following, for other transhipment-transportation transformations:

H. M. Wagner, "On a Class of Capacitated Transportation Problems" *Mgt. Sci.,* **5** (1959) 304–318.
A. Orden, "The Transhipment Problem," *Mgt. Sci.,* **3** (1956) 276–285.

SECTION 15

L. R. Ford, Jr. and D. R. Fulkerson, "A Suggested Computation for Maximal Multi-Commodity Network Flows," *Mgt. Sci.,* **5** (1958) 97–101.
R. E. Gomory and T. C. Hu, "Multi-terminal Network Flows," *SIAM J. Appl. Math.,* **9** (1961) 551–570.
R. E. Gomory and T. C. Hu, "An Application of Generalized Linear Programming to Network Flows," *SIAM J. Appl. Math.,* **10** (1962) 260–283.
T. C. Hu, "Multi-Commodity Network Flows," *Operations Research,* **11** (1963) 344–360.

FIVE

Bipartite Matching

1
Introduction

Let $G = (S, T, A)$ be an undriected bipartite graph. A subset $X \subseteq A$ is said to be a *matching* if no two arcs in X are incident to the same node. The term "matching" derives from the idea that nodes in S are matched with nodes in T. For example, the nodes in S may be identified with men and those in T with jobs. Hence men are matched with jobs.

With respect to a given matching X, a node j is said to be *matched* or *covered* if there is an arc in X incident to j. If a node is not matched, it is said to be *unmatched* or *exposed*. A matching that leaves no nodes exposed is said to be *complete*.

In this chapter we are concerned with methods for obtaining matchings that are optimal in one sense or another. In particular, we consider the following problems.

CARDINALITY MATCHING PROBLEM

Given a bipartite graph, find a matching containing a maximum number of arcs.

MAX-MIN MATCHING PROBLEM

Given an arc-weighted bipartite graph, find a maximum-cardinality matching for which the minimum of weights of the arcs in the matching is maximum. (This is sometimes called the "bottleneck" problem.)

WEIGHTED MATCHING PROBLEM

Given an arc-weighted bipartite graph, find a matching for which the sum of the weights of the arcs is maximum.

Matchings in bipartite graphs have long been a subject of investigation in both operations research and classical combinatorial analysis, although with rather different terminology and different motivations by investigators. One of the earliest optimization problems to be studied in the field of operations research was the assignment problem. Recall that this problem was introduced in Chapter 4, and was defined as follows. Given an $n \times n$ matrix, find a subset of elements in the matrix, exactly one element in each column and one in each row, such that the sum of the chosen elements is minimal. The reader should have little difficulty in establishing the equivalence of this problem to the weighted matching problem. We do not hesitate to refer to the weighted matching problem and the assignment problem almost interchangeably, when that seems appropriate.

An important topic in combinatorial analysis is that of "systems of distinct representatives." Let $Q = \{q_i; i = 1, 2, \ldots, m\}$ be a family of (not necessarily distinct) subsets of a set $E = \{e_j; j = 1, 2, \ldots, n\}$. A set $T = \{e_{j(1)}, \ldots, e_{j(t)}\}$, $0 \le t \le n$, is called a *partial transversal* of Q if T consists of distinct elements in E and if there are distinct integers $i(1), \ldots, i(t)$, such that $e_{j(k)} \in q_{i(k)}$ for $k = 1, \ldots, t$. Such a set is called a *transversal* or a *system of distinct representatives* (SDR) of Q if $t = m$.

Typical of the viewpoint of combinatorial analysis is a classic theorem of Philip Hall which states necessary and sufficient conditions for the existence of an SDR. (Not surprisingly, the Philip Hall Theorem can be shown to follow from the max-flow min-cut theorem of network flows.)

From our point of view, the problem of determining an SDR is equivalent to the cardinality matching problem. Consider a bipartite graph in which nodes correspond to subsets q_i and elements e_j. There is an arc (i, j)

between q_i and e_j if and only if $e_j \in q_i$. A matching in this graph yields a partial transversal. If the cardinality of the matching is m, the matching is an SDR. (More precisely, the set of nodes e_j covered by the matching is the SDR.)

It should come as no surprise to the reader that the network flow algorithms of the previous chapter are quite sufficient to solve the matching problems we have defined above. The cardinality matching problem can be solved as a maximal flow problem and the weighted matching problem yields to a minimal cost flow computation. Thus, from a theoretical point of view, we break no new ground in this chapter.

We propose to study bipartite matching problems because they are important and interesting in their own right, and also because the special computational procedures we shall develop for them are a helpful introduction to later topics. The algorithms described in the remainder of this book, including the matroid computations, are patterned after the bipartite matching algorithms of this chapter.

In Section 2 we first attempt to clarify the relationship between bipartite matchings and network flows. We then indicate exact counterparts, for matchings, of the augmenting path theorem, the integrality theorem, and the max-flow min-cut theorem of network flows. We then proceed to develop algorithms for solving the cardinality, max-min, and weighted matching problems. The chapter concludes with a discussion of a matching problem with a novel and interesting optimization criterion, due to Gale and Shapely.

PROBLEM

1.1   Demonstrate explicitly the equivalence of the weighted matching problem and the assignment problem. Specifically, if a weighted matching problem is defined for a graph $G = (S, T, A)$, with $|S| < |T| = n$, show how to add dummy nodes and arcs so that an equivalent $n \times n$ assignment problem can be obtained.

2

Problem Reductions and Equivalences

We propose to show the following. For every cardinality matching problem on $m + n$ nodes, there is a corresponding maximal flow problem in an $(m + n + 2)$-node flow network. Similarly, for every $n \times n$ assignment problem, there is a corresponding min-cost flow problem in a $(2n + 2)$-node flow network. Accordingly, there is a polynomial-bounded reduction of weighted matching problems to network flow problems and, indirectly, to the shortest path problem.

Conversely, we shall show that for every maximal flow problem there is a reduction to a cardinality matching problem, and a reduction of every min-cost flow problem to a weighted matching problem. Thus, network flow theory and bipartite matching theory are, for our purposes, essentially equivalent.

REDUCTION OF CARDINALITY MATCHING PROBLEM TO MAXIMAL FLOW PROBLEM

The reduction of the cardinality matching problem to the maximal flow problem is simple and direct. Consider the bipartite graph shown in Figure 5.1. From it, we construct the flow network with capacities as indicated on the arcs. These capacities permit at most one unit of flow to enter each of the nodes 1, 2, 3 and at most one unit to leave each of the nodes 4, 5, 6. From the integrality theorem of network flows it follows that there exists a maximal value solution in which the flow through each arc is either 0 or 1. The arcs (i, j), $i \neq s$, $j \neq t$, assigned flow values of unity, are identified with the arcs of a maximum cardinality matching in the original bipartite graph.

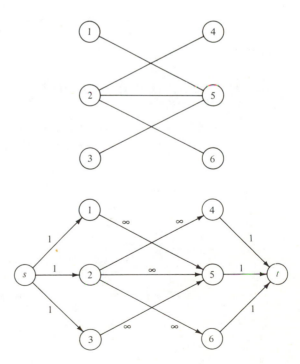

Figure 5.1   Bipartite graph and corresponding flow network

It is important to note that the integrality theorem plays an essential role in each of the problem reductions even though we may not explicitly mention that fact.

REDUCTION OF ASSIGNMENT PROBLEM TO MIN-COST FLOW PROBLEM

We have already referred to the fact that the weighted matching problem is equivalent to the assignment problem. The assignment problem can itself be reduced to a min-cost flow problem by a construction similar to that used for the cardinality matching problem. For example, if an assignment problem is defined by the 3×3 matrix

$$A = \begin{bmatrix} 4 & 6 & -3 \\ 2 & 1 & 0 \\ \infty & 5 & 2 \end{bmatrix},$$

we obtain the flow network shown in Figure 5.2. As before, the first number on each arc denotes its capacity and the second its cost. It should be clear that a min-cost flow of value 3 corresponds to an optimal solution to the assignment problem.

We know that the min-cost flow problem corresponding to an $n \times n$ assignment problem can be solved with exactly n flow augmentations. Each augmentation can be determined by a shortest path computation of $O(n^2)$ complexity. Thus, the assignment problem is, at worst, $O(n^3)$ in complexity.

REDUCTION OF SHORTEST PATH PROBLEM TO ASSIGNMENT PROBLEM

Conversely, and not surprisingly, any algorithm for solving the assignment problem can be used to solve the shortest path problem. Suppose we wish

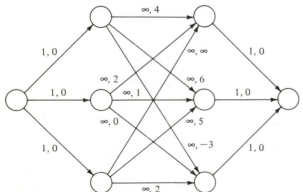

Figure 5.2   Flow network for assignment problem

to find a shortest path from node 1 to node n in an n-node directed network. Let A be the $n \times n$ matrix of arc lengths, with $a_{ii} = 0$, for all i. We delete column 1 and row n from this matrix. Any feasible solution to the $(n - 1) \times (n - 1)$ assignment problem, so defined, selects arcs forming a path from node 1 to node n, plus a number of other node-disjoint directed cycles, some of which may be loops. If there are no negative cycles in the network, then an optimal solution to the assignment problem yields a shortest path from node 1 to node n, plus directed cycles, each of zero length.

REDUCTION OF MIN-COST FLOW PROBLEM TO WEIGHTED MATCHING PROBLEM

We recall that in Chapter 4 the general min-cost flow problem was reduced to the transportation problem. By reducing the transportation problem to the weighted matching problem, we provide a reduction of the general min-cost flow problem to the weighted matching problem.

Every (uncapacitated) transportation problem is equivalent to a weighted matching problem on $2v$ nodes, where v is the sum of the demands at the sinks (assuming supplies and demands are in equality form). To show this, we merely replace each node i of the transportation network by $|b_i|$ copies of the node, where b_i is the integer-valued supply or demand at that node. An undirected arc with cost $K - a_{ij}$ (where K is sufficiently large) is furnished between each copy of node i and each copy of node j, provided (i, j) existed in the transportation network. A feasible solution to the transportation problem exists if and only if there is a complete matching in the bipartite graph, and an optimal solution corresponds to a maximum weight matching.

PROBLEMS

2.1   Suppose an n-node graph contains negative cycles. What interpretation can be given to an optimal solution to the assignment problem defined by the $n \times n$ matrix A of arc lengths? Suppose there is some node i, such that every negative

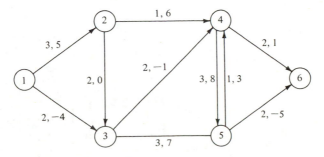

Figure 5.3   Flow network for Problem 2.2

cycle contains node i. Can we solve the "most negative" cycle problem under this condition?

2.2   Consider the flow network shown in Figure 5.3. Transform the min-cost flow problem for this network, with node 1 as source and node 6 as sink, to an uncapacitated transportation problem. Transform the transportation problem to a weighted matching problem.

2.3   Is the reduction of the min-cost flow problem to the weighted matching problem of such a form that the existence of a polynomial-bounded algorithm for the matching problem implies the existence of a polynomial-bounded algorithm for the flow problem? Discuss.

3

Counterparts of Network Flow Theorems

We propose to restate the essential theorems of network flow theory in the context of bipartite matchings. We are concerned particularly with the augmenting path theorem, the integrality theorem, and the max-flow min-cut duality theorem.

With respect to a given matching X, an *alternating path* is an (undirected) path of arcs which are alternately in X and not in X. An *augmenting path* is an alternating path between two exposed nodes.

AUGMENTING PATH THEOREM

A matching X contains a maximum number of arcs if and only if it admits no augmenting path.

When we formulate the weighted matching problem as a minimal cost flow problem, the integrality theorem of network flows assures us that there is an optimal solution in which the flow through each arc is either zero or one. This is equivalent to saying that there exists an optimal solution to the linear programming problem

maximize

$$\sum_{i,j} w_{ij} x_{ij} \tag{3.1}$$

subject to

$$\left.\begin{array}{l} \sum_{j} x_{ij} \leq 1, \quad (i = 1, 2, \ldots, m) \\[2mm] \sum_{i} x_{ij} \leq 1 \quad (j = 1, 2, \ldots, n) \\[2mm] x_{ij} \geq 0, \end{array}\right\} \tag{3.2}$$

in which each variable x_{ij} takes on the value zero or one, regardless of the coefficients in the objective function (3.1). This establishes the following theorem.

INTEGRALITY THEOREM FOR BIPARTITE MATCHING

The "matching" polyhedron defined by the constraints (3.2) has only $(0, 1)$ vertices.

If $m = n$, then any feasible solution $X = (x_{ij})$ which satisfies constraints (3.2) with equality is a *doubly-stochastic matrix*, i.e., a nonnegative matrix in which the sum of the entries in each row and in each column is unity. A feasible solution of zeros and ones is in the form of a *permutation matrix*, i.e., a $(0, 1)$ matrix with exactly one 1 in each row and in each column. Thus, we obtain the following as a corollary of the integrality theorem.

BIRKHOFF-VON NEUMANN THEOREM

Any doubly-stochastic matrix is a convex combination (cf. Chapter 2, Section 12) of permutation matrices.

The Birkhoff-von Neumann theorem has been cited as a "proof" that monogamy is the best of all possible systems of marriage. Suppose we have a society of n men and n women. Let w_{ij} represent the benefit to be derived from full-time cohabitation of man i with woman j, and let x_{ij} denote the fraction of time that man i actually cohabitates with woman j. If the objective is to maximize total benefit, so the argument goes, there is an optimal solution in which each x_{ij} is 0 or 1, i.e., a solution in which marriage is monogamous. (It has been pointed out by cynics that the Birkhoff-von Neuman theorem also shows that monogamy can result in a *minimization* of total benefit.)

We shall restate the max-flow min-cut theorem in terms of "coverings" of arcs by nodes. A subset of the nodes of a graph is said to *cover* the arcs if each arc of the graph is incident to at least one of the nodes in the subset. (It is essential to distinguish between a covering of arcs by nodes and a covering of nodes by arcs!)

The relationship between matchings and coverings may be a bit obscure, and it is perhaps helpful to refer to the graph and the flow network in Figure 5.1 as an example. By inspection, we see that the arcs $(1, 5)$ and $(2, 6)$ constitute a maximum cardinality matching in the graph. This matching corresponds to unit flows in the paths $(s, 1), (1, 5), (5, t)$ and $(s, 2), (2, 6), 6, t)$ in the flow network, all other arcs having zero flows. The minimal capacity cut corresponding to this maximal flow is shown in Figure 5.4.

The minimal cut has a capacity of two: the sum of the capacities of

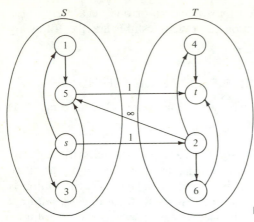

Figure 5.4   Minimum capacity cutset

arcs $(5, t)$ and $(s, 2)$. We next observe that if (i, j) is an arc, where both i and j belong to S, then either $i = s$, and (i, j) does not correspond to an arc of the bipartite graph, or else $j = 5$, and the arc is covered by node 5. A similar situation holds for arcs, both ends of which are in T; node 2 is the covering node in that case. The only arc (i, j) with i in T and j in S is $(2, 5)$. This arc is clearly covered by both nodes 2 and 5. Thus, nodes 2 and 5 cover all arcs of the bipartite graph from which the flow network was constructed.

For the example, we have constructed a covering of arcs by nodes that is equal in cardinality to that of a maximal cordinality matching. We observe that this can be done more generally. That is, such a covering contains all nodes i and j, where (s, j) and (i, t) are arcs in a minimal capacity cut of the flow network. This gives us the desired duality theorem for matchings:

KÖNIG-EGERVARY THEOREM

For any bipartite graph, the maximum number of arcs in a matching is equal to the minimum number of nodes in a covering of arcs by nodes.

An equivalent statement of this theorem is as follows. Consider any $m \times n$ matrix of 0's and 1's. Refer to a row or a column of the matrix by the common term "line." A set of lines "covers" the 1's of the matrix if each 1 belongs to some line of the set. A subset of the 1's is "independent" if no two 1's lie in the same line. The König-Egervary Theorem states that the maximum cardinality of an independent set of 1's is equal to the minimum number of lines that cover all 1's.

PROBLEMS

3.1   For a given bipartite graph, let X_p and X_{p+1} be matchings with p and $p + 1$ arcs, respectively. Consider the form of $X_p \oplus X_{p+1}$, i.e., the set of arcs contained in

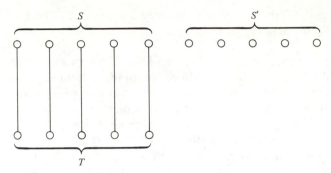

Figure 5.5   Graph for Problem 3.4

one matching but not the other. ($X_p \oplus X_{p+1}$ consists of alternating paths and cycles.) What observations are necessary to provide a "direct" proof of the augmenting path theorem for matchings?

3.2   Provide a direct proof of the Birkhoff-von Neumann theorem. Specifically, show that any given doubly-stochastic matrix which is not a permutation matrix can be expressed as a convex combination of two other doubly-stochastic matrices, each of which contains fewer nonzero elements than the original. This provides the key step for an inductive proof.

3.3   Provide a simple demonstration that the number of nodes in any covering of arcs by nodes must be at least as great as the number of arcs in any matching. (This proof should be valid for nonbipartite graphs.)

3.4   (V. Klee) The König-Egervary equality holds for some graphs which are not bipartite. Prove that a graph G is such that the maximum number of arcs in a matching is equal to the minimum number of nodes in a covering if and only if G is of the form shown in Figure 5.5, plus some other arcs (not shown), where the cardinalities of S and S' are unrestricted, the cardinality of T is of course equal to that of S, and the other arcs all go from $S \cup S'$ to T or from T to T, but not from $S \cup S'$ to $S \cup S'$.

4

Mendelsohn-Dulmage Theorem

An interesting theorem about bipartite matchings follows.

Theorem 4.1   (*Mendelsohn-Dulmage*)   Let $G = (S, T, A)$ be a bipartite graph and let X_1, X_2 be two matchings in G. Then there exists a matching $X \subseteq X_1 \cup X_2$, such that X covers all the nodes of S covered by X_1 and all the nodes of T covered by X_2.

PROOF   Form the symmetric difference $X_1 \oplus X_2$. It consists of the five types of paths and cycles shown in Figure 5.6. In each case it is possible to select a matching $X' \subseteq X_1 \oplus X_2$ such that X' covers all the nodes of S covered by

$X_1 - X_2$ and all the nodes of T covered by $X_2 - X_1$. Then $X = X' \cup (X_1 \cap X_2)$ is the desired matching. //

As an application of the theorem, let S, T represent men and jobs to be matched, where the arcs denote the compatibility relation. It is not possible to match all men to all the jobs. But suppose the union proposes a matching which employs as many men as possible, subject to a system of seniority. And suppose management proposes a matching which assigns men to jobs according to a system of job priorities. It is gratifying that there is a matching which will be satisfactory to both union and management. This matching gives jobs to all the men the union wants employed and will assign men to all the jobs management wants done.

The following theorem and corollary follow directly from Theorem 4.1.

Theorem 4.2   Let X be any matching in $G = (S, T, A)$. Then there exists a maximum cardinality matching X^* which covers all the nodes of G covered by X.

Corollary 4.3   For any nonisolated node i (degree greater than zero), there exists a maximum cardinality matching which covers i.

Suppose that a factory manager has made a feasible assignment of men to machines. It then follows from Theorem 4.2 that there exists a maximum cardinality ("full production") matching in which all the men and machines employed under the manager's solution remain employed.

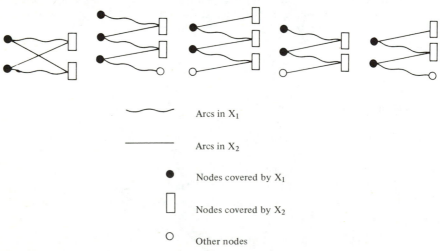

~~~~~~   Arcs in X_1

————   Arcs in X_2

●   Nodes covered by X_1

▯   Nodes covered by X_2

○   Other nodes

Figure 5.6   Symmetric difference $X_1 \oplus X_2$

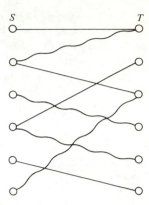

Figure 5.7   Graph for Problem 4.1

PROBLEMS

4.1   In the bipartite graph shown in Figure 5.7, let X_1 be represented by wavy lines and X_2 by straight lines. Find a matching $X \subseteq X_1 \cup X_2$ that covers all the nodes of S covered by X_1 and all the nodes of T covered by X_2.

4.2   (a)   Use Theorem 4.1 to prove Theorem 4.2.
      (b)   Use the augmenting path theorem to Prove Theorem 4.2.

5

Cardinality Matching Algorithm

The computational procedure for cardinality matching corresponds exactly to the maximal flow computation for the problem. However, we introduce some terminology which is appropriate for matching.

For a given bipartite graph $G = (S, T, A)$ and a given matching $X \subseteq A$, we define an *alternating tree* relative to the matching to be a tree which satisfies the following two conditions. First, the tree contains exactly one exposed node from S, which we call its *root*. Second, all paths between the root and any other node in the tree are alternating paths. (Cf. Section 3.)

The computational procedure is begun with any feasible matching, possibly the empty matching. Each exposed node in S is made the root of an alternating tree and nodes and arcs are added to the trees by means of a labeling technique. Eventually, one or the other of two events must occur. Either an exposed node in T is added to one of the trees, or else it is not possible to add more nodes and arcs to any of the trees. In the former case, the matching is augmented and the tree-building procedure is repeated with respect to the new matching. In the latter case, the trees are said to be *Hungarian* and can be used to construct an optimal dual solution consisting of the union of all out-of-tree nodes in S and all in-tree nodes in T.

As an example, consider the matching shown in Figure 5.8, in which wavy lines represent arcs in the matching, and straight lines those which are not. Alternating trees are constructed, with the exposed S-nodes 1 and 5 as roots, as shown in Figure 5.9. An augmenting path is found, as indicated in the figure. (Note that several different sets of alternating trees could have been constructed. For example, the tree rooted to node 1 could have contained the arc (2.8).)

The augmented matching is shown in Figure 5.10. When an alternat-

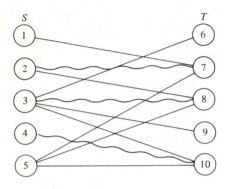

Figure 5.8   Graph for example

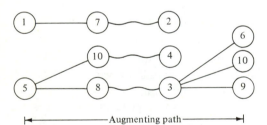

Augmenting path

Figure 5.9   Alternating trees

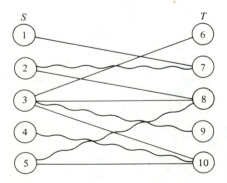

Figure 5.10   Augmenting matching

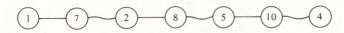

Figure 5.11   Alternating tree for augmented matching

ing tree is constructed for the augmented matching, as shown in Figure 5.11, it becomes Hungarian. It follows that the matching in Figure 5.4 can be used to construct an optimal dual solution. The only out-of-tree node in S is 3. The in-tree nodes in T are 7, 8, and 10. The reader can verify that these four nodes do indeed cover all the arcs of the graph.

The cardinality matching algorithm is summarized as follows. (We leave it as an exercise for the reader to show that the computation is $O(m^2n)$, where $|S| = m, |T| = n, m \leq n$.)

BIPARTITE CARDINALITY MATCHING ALGORITHM

Step 0 *(Start)*   The bipartite graph $G = (S, T, A)$ is given. Let X be any matching, possibly the empty matching. No nodes are labeled.

Step 1   *(Labeling)*

(1.0)   Give the label "$\emptyset$" to each exposed node in S.

(1.1)   If there are no unscanned labels, go to Step 3. Otherwise, find a node i with an unscanned label. If $i \in S$, go to Step 1.2; if $i \in T$, go to Step 1.3.

(1.2)   Scan the label on node i ($i \in S$) as follows. For each arc $(i, j) \notin X$ incident to node i, give node j the label "i," unless node j is already labeled. Return to Step 1.1.

(1.3)   Scan the label on node i ($i \in T$) as follows. If node i is exposed, go to Step 2. Otherwise, identify the unique arc $(i, j) \in X$ incident to node i and give node j the label "i." Return to Step 1.1.

Step 2   *(Augmentation)*   An augmenting path has been found, terminating at node i (identified in Step 1.3). The nodes preceding node i in the path are identified by "backtracing." That is, if the label on node i is "j," the second-to-last node in the path is j. If the label on node j is "k," the third-to-last node is k, and so on. The initial node in the path has the label "$\emptyset$." Augment X by adding to X all arcs in the augmenting path that are not in X and removing from X those which are. Remove all labels from nodes. Return to Step 1.0.

Step 3   *(Hungarian Labeling)*   The labeling is Hungarian, no augmenting path exists, and the matching X is of maximum cardinality. Let $L \subseteq S \cup T$ denote the set of labeled nodes. Then $C = (S - L) \cup (T \cap L)$ is a minimum cardinality covering of arcs by nodes, dual to X. Halt.//

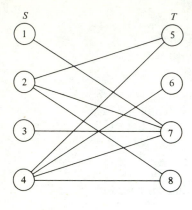

Figure 5.12   Graph for Problem 5.1

PROBLEM

5.1   Apply the algorithm to obtain a maximum cardinality matching, and a minimum cardinality covering of arcs by nodes, for the bipartite graph shown in Figure 5.12.

6

A Special Case: Convex Graphs

The cardinality matching problem is particularly easy to solve for a special type of graph which F. Glover calls "convex." A bipartite graph $G = (S, T, A)$ is said to be *convex* if it has the property that if (i, j) and (k, j) are arcs, where $i < k$, then $(i + 1, j), (i + 2, j), \ldots, (k - 1, j)$ are also arcs. Such a graph is shown in Figure 5.13.

As an example, suppose a certain product requires one machined part from a set S and a second from a set T. An S-part of length a_i can be fitted

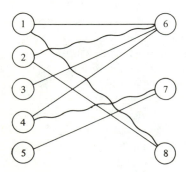

Figure 5.13   Convex bipartite graph

with a *T*-part of length b_j if and only if

$$|a_i - b_j| \le \varepsilon,$$

where ε is some specified tolerance. This situation leads to a convex matching problem, and, in fact, to a "doubly-convex" problem. (See Problem 6.3.)

The cardinality matching problem can be solved by the following procedure. For each node $j \in T$, let

$$\pi_j = \max \{i | (i, j) \in A\}.$$

Start with the empty matching and iterate over $i = 1, 2, \ldots, m$. If there are any arcs (i, j), where j is an exposed node, add to the matching the arc (i, j) for which π_j is as small as possible.

Application of this procedure to the convex graph in Figure 5.13 results in the matching indicated by wavy lines.

PROBLEMS

6.1   Prove the validity of Glover's computational procedure.

6.2   Show that Glover's procedure is $O(mn)$, where $|S| = m$, $|T| = n$.

6.3   A doubly-convex bipartite graph is one which is convex "in both *S* and *T*." Determine how Glover's procedure can be made more efficient for this case, and estimate the computational complexity.

7

Max-Min Matching

A commonly cited example of max-min or "bottleneck" matching is the following. There are *n* workers to be assigned to *n* stations on a conveyorized production line. Let w_{ij} denote the rate at which worker *i* can perform the task at station *j*. The rate at which production can proceed is limited by the rate of the slowest worker. What assignment of workers to work stations will maximize the production rate?

This problem calls for the computation of a maximum cardinality matching for which the minimum arc weight is maximum. A procedure which computes max-min matchings for all possible cardinalities, including the maximum cardinality, is as follows.

Start with the empty matching and a suitably large "threshold" *W*. At the general step of the algorithm, a max-min matching of cardinality *k* has been obtained. One then tries to find an augmenting path in the subgraph containing all arcs (i, j) for which $w_{ij} \ge .W$. If augmentation is possible, a max-min matching of cardinality $k + 1$ results. If augmentation is not possible, the threshold W is reduced just enough to permit augmentation to occur.

The number of threshold values which must be considered certainly does not exceed the number of distinct arc weights, i.e., mn, where $|S| = m$, $|T| = n$. For each threshold value, the augmentation computation is $O(mn)$. Thus, this naive thresholding procedure is $O(m^2n^2)$.

However, it is possible to do better. In particular, it is foolish to throw away the alternating trees which have been constructed as part of an unsuccessful augmentation computation. The same alternating trees must simply be reconstructed after the threshold is reduced.

In the algorithm that is summarized here, a number π_j is associated with each node j in T. This number indicates the level to which the threshold must be reduced, so that j may be added to an alternating tree. In other words, π_j is set equal to the largest w_{ij}, such that (i, j) is an arc and node i is in an alternating tree. Nodes are labeled fully, but no labeled node j in T is scanned unless $\pi_j \geq W$. When there are no further nodes eligible for scanning, W is reduced to the maximum value of π_j strictly less than W. This permits at least one additional node to be added to a tree. Eventually either augmentation must occur, or the trees become Hungarian.

The algorithm also yields the construction of a solution dual to the max-min matching. Let X_k denote any matching containing k arcs. Let H_{k-1} denote any subgraph obtained from G by deleting $k-1$ nodes.

Theorem 7.1 *(Gross)* For any bipartite graph G,

$$\max_{X_k} \min \{w_{ij}|(i,j) \in X_k\} = \min_{H_{k-1}} \max \{w_{ij}|(i,j) \in H_{k-1}\}.$$

Note that the dual of the empty matching is undefined.

The proof of the theorem follows directly from the König-Egervary theorem. (See the proof of Theorem 7.3 in Chapter 6 for a more general case.)

We leave it as an exercise for the reader to verify that the algorithm requires $O(m^2n)$ steps, the same as for cardinality matching.

THRESHOLD METHOD FOR MAX-MIN MATCHING

Step 0 *(Start)* The bipartite graph $G = (S, T, A)$ and a weight w_{ij} for each arc $(i, j) \in A$ are given. Set $X = \emptyset$, $W = +\infty$, and $\pi_j = -\infty$ for each node $j \in T$. No nodes are labeled.

Step 1 *(Labeling)*

(1.0) Give the label "$\emptyset$" to each exposed node in S.

(1.1) If there are no unscanned labels, go to Step 3. If there are unscanned labels, but each unscanned label is on a node i in T for which $\pi_i < W$, then set $W = \max \{\pi_i | \pi_i < W\}$.

(1.2)   Find a node i with an unscanned label, where either $i \in S$ or else $i \in T$ and $\pi_i \geq W$. If $i \in S$, go to Step 1.3; if $i \in T$, go to Step 1.4.

(1.3)   Scan the label on node i ($i \in S$) as follows. For each arc $(i, j) \notin X$ incident to i, if $\pi_j < w_{ij}$ and $\pi_j < W$, then give node j the label "i" (replacing any existing label) and set $\pi_j = w_{ij}$. Return to Step 1.1.

(1.4)   Scan the label on node i ($i \in T$) as follows. If node i is exposed, go to Step 2. Otherwise, identify the unique arc $(i, j) \in X$ incident to node i and give node j the label "i." Return to Step 1.1.

Step 2   (*Augmentation*)   An augmenting path has been found, terminating at node i (identified in Step 1.4). The nodes preceding node i in the path are identified by "backtracing" from label to label. Augment X by adding to X all arcs in the augmenting path that are not in X, and removing from X those which are. Remove all labels from nodes. Set $\pi_j = -\infty$, for each node j in T. Return to Step 1.0.

Step 3   (*Hungarian Labeling*)   No augmenting path exists, and the matching X is a max-min matching of maximum cardinality. Let $L \subseteq S \cup T$ denote the set of labeled nodes. Let $(i', j') \in X$ be such that

$$w_{i'j'} = \min \{w_{ij} | (i, j) \in X\}.$$

The subgraph obtained by deleting the nodes in $(S - L) \cup (T \cap L) - \{i', j'\}$ is a min-max solution dual to X. Halt.//

We should mention that an alternative, and perhaps conceptually simpler, approach to max-min matching is as follows. Given a max-min matching X_k, one obtains X_{k+1} by means of an augmenting path for which the minimum of the weights of the arcs is maximized. Such a path can be computed by an adaptation of the shortest path techniques described in Chapter 3. (Cf. comments about "maximum capacity" paths.) In particular one can develop a Dijkstra-like computation for this purpose. Once this is done, however, it is discovered that the algorithm looks remarkably like the threshold method. Specifically, Step 1.1 of the threshold method corresponds to the operation of finding the largest "tentative" label in the Dijkstra method, for the purpose of making the label permanent.

The two approaches to the max-min matching problem lead to essentially similar algorithms. However, to the extent that they are conceptually different, we can draw something of a parallel between the threshold method for max-min matching and the Hungarian method for weighted matching on the one hand, and the max-min (Dijkstra-like) augmenting path and the "primal" method for weighted matching on the other. This question is discussed further in Section 8.

PROBLEMS

7.1 Apply the max-min matching algorithm to the weighted bipartite graph shown in Figure 5.14. Find both a max-min matching of maximum cardinality and a min-max dual solution.

7.2 Prove Theorem 7.1.

7.3 Write out, in detail, the steps of a max-min matching algorithm based on the approach of max-min augmenting paths. Make a detailed comparison with the threshold algorithm.

7.4 (Klein and Takamori) Consider the following generalization of the production line problem. There are n workers to be assigned to stations on two parallel lines, with a total of n stations. As before, let w_{ij} denote the rate at which worker i can perform the task at station j. The rate at which production can proceed on each line is determined by the rate of the slowest worker on that line. The total rate of production is the sum of the rates of production for the two lines. What assignment of workers to work stations will maximize the total production rate?

   As a generalization of the above, suppose that each arc of a bipartite graph on $2n$ nodes is colored either red or green. The problem is to find a complete matching which maximizes the sum of the minimum weight red arc and the minimum weight green arc in the matching.

   One way to solve the matching problem is to establish two thresholds, W_r and W_g, for red and green arcs, respectively. One can then test for the existence of a complete matching in the subgraph composed of all red arcs (i, j) for which $w_{ij} \geq W_r$ and all green arcs for which $w_{ij} \geq W_g$. If a complete matching exists, then clearly there is a feasible solution with a value of $W_r + W_g$. By testing for all possible combinations of W_r and W_g, one can obtain an optimal solution.

   The process of testing for choices of W_r and W_g is greatly accelerated by taking advantage of an obvious dominance relation. Namely, if $W_r + W_g$ is feasible, then so is $W_r' + W_g'$, for any $W_r' \leq W_r$ and $W_g' \leq W_g$. And if $W_r + W_g$ is infeasible, then so is $W_r' + W_g'$, for $W_r' \geq W_r$ and $W_g' \geq W_g$. Moreover, the total number of W_r and W_g values which must be tested cannot possibly exceed the number of distinct arc weights w_{ij}, which is n^2 at most. Thus, an

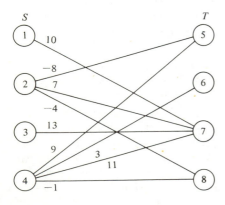

Figure 5.14   Network for Problem 7.1

optimal value of $W_r + W_g$ must occur at one of the corners of the "staircase" boundary separating the "feasible" and "infeasible" regions in Figure 5.15.

There are no more than n^2 points on this staircase boundary. The staircase points can be identified by a search procedure which moves from one corner point to another. Each move requires a single augmenting path computation which is $O(n^2)$ in complexity. Hence the entire staircase boundary can be determined, and an optimal solution located, with an $O(n^4)$ computation. (*Hint*: If $W_r + W_g$ is infeasible, move "down" in the diagram of Figure 5.15 by reducing W_g until a feasible solution is found. Then move "right" by increasing the value of W_r until infeasibility results.)

(a)   Work out the details of this computational procedure, and write out the steps of the algorithm.

(b)   Attempt to generalize the procedure to three or more parallel production lines. What computational complexity seems to be required?

7.5   For Problem 7.4, find, and prove, an appropriate generalization of the duality theorem for max-min matching.

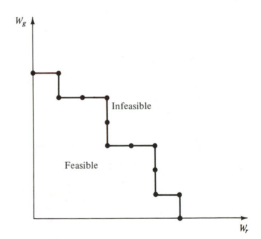

Figure 5.15   Feasible and infeasible regions

8

The Hungarian Method for Weighted Matching

The procedure we propose for the weighted matching problem is a primal-dual method, called "Hungarian" by H. W. Kuhn in recognition of the mathematician Egervary.

For simplicity, assume a complete bipartite graph $G = (S, T, S \times T)$, with $|S| = m$, $|T| = n$, $m \leq n$. A linear programming formulation of the weighted matching problem is:

maximize $\sum\limits_{i,j} w_{ij}x_{ij}$

subject to

$$\sum_j x_{ij} \le 1,$$

$$\sum_i x_{ij} \le 1,$$

$$x_{ij} \ge 0,$$

with the understanding that

$$x_{ij} = 1 \Rightarrow (i,j) \in X,$$

$$x_{ij} = 0 \Rightarrow (i,j) \notin X.$$

The dual linear programming problem is:

minimize $\sum\limits_i u_i + \sum\limits_j v_j$

subject to

$$u_i + v_j \ge w_{ij},$$
$$u_i \ge 0,$$

$$v_j \ge 0.$$

Orthogonality conditions which are necessary and sufficient for optimality of primal and dual solutions are:

$$x_{ij} > 0 \Rightarrow u_i + v_j = w_{ij}, \tag{8.1}$$

$$u_i > 0 \Rightarrow \sum_j x_{ij} = 1, \tag{8.2}$$

$$v_j > 0 \Rightarrow \sum_i x_{ij} = 1. \tag{8.3}$$

The Hungarian method maintains primal and dual feasibility at all times, and in addition maintains satisfaction of all orthogonality conditions, except conditions (8.2). The number of such unsatisfied conditions is decreased monotonically during the course of the computation.

The procedure is begun with the feasible matching $X = \emptyset$ and with the feasible dual solution $u_i = W$, where $W \ge \max \{w_{ij}\}$, and $v_j = 0$, for all i, j. These initial primal and dual solutions clearly satisfy all of the conditions (8.1) and (8.3), but not the conditions (8.2).

At the general step of the procedure, X is feasible, u_i and v_j are dual feasible, all conditions (8.1) and (8.3) are satisfied, but some of the conditions (8.2) are not. One then tries, by means of a labeling procedure, to find an augmenting path within the subgraph containing only arcs (i, j) for which $u_i + v_j = w_{ij}$. In particular, an augmenting path is sought from an exposed node i in S for which (necessarily) $u_i > 0$. If such a path can be found, the new matching will be feasible, all conditions (8.1) and (8.3) continue to be satisfied, and one more of the conditions (8.2) will be satisfied than before. If augmentation is not possible, then a change of δ is made in the dual variables, by subtracting $\delta > 0$ from u_i for each labeled S-node i and adding δ to v_j to each labeled T-node j.

It is always possible to choose δ so that at least one new arc can be added to an alternating tree, while maintaining dual feasibility, unless the choice of δ is restricted by the size of u_i at some S-node. But u_i takes on its smallest value at the exposed S-nodes. The exposed nodes have been exposed at each step since the beginning of the algorithm, and hence their dual variables have been decremented each time a change in dual variables has been made. It follows that when u_i is reduced to zero at these nodes, the conditions (8.2) are satisfied, and both the primal and dual solutions are optimal.

The augmentation computation is such that only arcs (i, j) for which $u_i + v_j = w_{ij}$ are placed in the alternating trees. If the construction of the alternating trees concludes without an augmenting path being found, then one of two things has occurred. Either the trees are truly Hungarian and the matching is of the maximum cardinality, or else it is not possible to continue adding to the trees because all arcs (i, j) available for that purpose are such that $u_i + v_j > w_{ij}$.

Let us deal with the latter case first. Any arcs which we should like to add to the alternating trees are arcs not in the matching X. (Because condions (8.1) are satisfied, arcs in X are such that $u_i + v_j = w_{ij}$.) Such arcs are incident to an S-node in an alternating tree and a T-node not in any tree. In the max-min problem, we lowered the threshold in the comparable situation, thereby permitting at least one arc to be added to an alternating tree. In the present case, we manipulate the values of the dual variables so as to achieve the desired effect.

Suppose we subtract $\delta > 0$ from u_i for each S-node i in a tree and add δ to v_j for each T-node j in a tree. Such a change in the dual variables affects the net value of $u_i + v_j$ only for arcs which have one end in a tree and the other end out. If such an arc is incident to a T-node of the tree, $u_i + v_j$ is increased by δ, which is of no consequence (note that such an arc cannot be in the current matching). If the arc is incident to an S-node of a tree, $u_i + v_j$ is decreased by δ, possibly to w_{ij}, in which case it can be added to the tree.

The effect of the changes in the dual variables is summarized in Figure 5.16. Under each node in that figure is indicated the change in u_i or v_j. On each arc is indicated the net change in $u_i + v_j$ for that arc. All possibilities are accounted for. (Note that it is not possible for an arc in the matching to have one end in an alternating tree and the other end out.)

If the alternating trees are truly Hungarian, then the choice of δ is

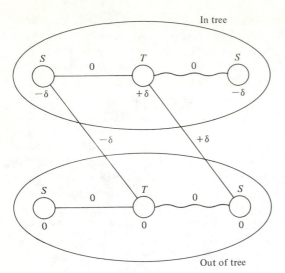

Figure 5.16 . Effect of change in dual variables

indeed determined by the value of u_i at the exposed S-nodes. In this case, the values of the dual variables are changed, as indicated above, conditions (8.2) are satisfied, and both the primal and dual solutions are optimal.

The algorithm begins with the empty matching, X_0, and then produces matchings $X_1, X_2, \ldots, X_k$, containing $1, 2, \ldots, k$ arcs. Each of these matchings is of maximum weight, with respect to all other matchings of the same cardinality, as is shown below. (Incidentally, note that the maximum weight matching existing at the end of the computation does not necessarily have maximum cardinality.)

Suppose we were to demand a maximum weight matching, subject to the constraint that it contains no more than k arcs. Then we could add a single constraint to the primal linear programming problem:

$$\sum_{ij} x_{ij} \le k.$$

This constraint is identified with a dual variable λ and, after appropriate modifications in the dual problem, the orthogonality conditions become

$$x_{ij} > 0 \Rightarrow u_i + v_j + \lambda = w_{ij},$$

$$u_i > 0 \Rightarrow \sum_j x_{ij} = 1,$$

$$v_j > 0 \Rightarrow \sum_i x_{ij} = 1,$$

$$\lambda > 0 \Rightarrow \sum_{i,j} x_{ij} = k.$$

Let X_k be the matching of cardinality k obtained by the algorithm, and $\bar{u}_i$, $\bar{v}_j$ be the dual solution. Choose $\lambda = \min\{\bar{u}_i\}$. Then $X_k, \bar{u}_i - \lambda, \bar{v}_j, \lambda$ are feasible primal and dual solutions for the k-cardinality problem and satisfy the new orthogonality conditions indicated above. It follows that X_k is of maximum weight, with respect to all matchings containing k arcs.

As in the case of the threshold algorithm for max-min matching, a number π_j is associated with each node j in T. This number indicates the value of δ by which the dual variables must be changed, in order that j may be added to an alternating tree. The labeling procedure progressively decreases π_j until π_j is equal to the smallest value of $u_i + v_j - w_{ij}$, for arcs (i, j) with $i \in S$ labeled. A node j in T may receive a label if $\pi_j > 0$, but its label is scanned only if $\pi_j = 0$. In other words, j is "in tree" if and only if $\pi_j = 0$.

The algorithm is summarized below. We leave it as an exercise for the reader to verify that the number of computational steps required is $O(m^2 n)$, the same as for cardinality matching and max-min matching.

BIPARTITE WEIGHTED MATCHING ALGORITHM

Step 0 (*Start*) The bipartite graph $G = (S, T, A)$ and a weight w_{ij} for each arc $(i, j) \in A$ are given. Set $X = \varnothing$. Set $u_i = \max\{w_{ij}\}$ for each node $i \in S$. Set $v_j = 0$ and $\pi_j = +\infty$ for each node $j \in T$. No nodes are labeled.

Step 1 (*Labeling*)

(1.0) Give the label "$\varnothing$" to each exposed node in S.

(1.1) If there are no unscanned labels, or if there are unscanned labels, but each unscanned label is on a node i in T for which $\pi_i > 0$, then go to Step 3.

(1.2) Find a node i with an unscanned label, where either $i \in S$ or else $i \in T$ and $\pi_i = 0$. If $i \in S$, go to Step 1.3; if $i \in T$, go to Step 1.4.

(1.3) Scan the label on node i ($i \in S$) as follows. For each arc $(i, j) \notin X$ incident to node i, if $u_i + v_j - w_{ij} < \pi_j$, then give node j the label "i" (replacing any existing label) and set $\pi_j = u_i + v_j - w_{ij}$. Return to Step 1.1.

(1.4) Scan the label on node i ($i \in T$) as follows. If node i is exposed, go to Step 2. Otherwise, identify the unique arc $(i, j) \in X$ incident to node i and give node j the label "i." Return to Step 1.1.

Step 2 (*Augmentation*) An augmenting path has been found, terminating at node i (identified in Step 1.4). The nodes preceding node i in the path are identified by "backtracing" from label to label. Augment X by adding to X

all arcs in the augmenting path that are not in X and removing from X those which are. Set $\pi_j = +\infty$, for each node j in T. Remove all labels from nodes. Return to Step 1.0.

Step 3 (*Change in Dual Variables*) Find

$$\delta_1 = \min\{u_i | i \in S\},$$

$$\delta_2 = \min\{\pi_j | \pi_j > 0, j \in T\},$$

$$\delta = \min\{\delta_1, \delta_2\}.$$

Subtract δ from u_i, for each labeled node $i \in S$. Add δ to v_j for each node $j \in T$ with $\pi_j = 0$. Subtract δ from π_j for each labeled node $j \in T$ with $\pi_j > 0$. If $\delta < \delta_1$ go to Step 1.1. Otherwise, X is a maximum weight matching and the u_i and v_j variables are an optimal dual solution. Halt. //

There is an alternative, "primal" approach to weighted matching. This is to perform successive augmentations of the matching X by means of a maximum weight augmenting path (where the weight of arc (i, j) is taken to be w_{ij} if $(i, j) \in X$ and $-w_{ij}$ if $(i, j) \notin X$). This approach is essentially the same as that used in the previous chapter to compute min-cost flows by successive min-cost augmentations. We refer to this as a "primal" method because it involves no dual variables or other considerations of duality.

It is easy to devise a procedure for determining maximum weight augmentations. In fact, a method essentially like that of Bellman and Ford can be implemented very nicely within the framework of a labeling procedure. The computation of a maximum weight augmenting path requires $O(m^2 n)$ steps, when carried out in this way. Since $O(m)$ augmentations are called for, the overall complexity is $O(m^3 n)$, compared with $O(m^2 n)$ for the Hungarian method.

The efficiency of the primal method can be improved, by making use of node numbers, as described in the previous chapter. The number π_i^k indicates the weight of a maximum weight alternating path from an exposed S-node to node i, relative to matching X_k. These node numbers are used to modify the arc weights, so that all arc weights are negative when a maximum weight augmentation is sought, relative to matching X_{k+1}. (Negative arc weights are desired, since a maximum weight path is sought.) It follows that a Dijkstra-like procedure can be used to find an optimal augmenting path.

When the details have been worked out, it is discovered that the Dijkstra-like procedure looks very much like the Hungarian method. Specifically, the computation of δ_2 in Step 3 of the Hungarian method corresponds to the operation of finding, in the Dijkstra computation, that "tentative" label which is next to be made permanent. Thus, the Hungarian method and the modified primal method are essentially similar.

We noted a similar situation in the previous section, with respect to the threshold method and the max-min augmenting path method for max-min matching. The reader is referred to that discussion.

PROBLEMS

8.1 Apply the Hungarian algorithm to the weighted bipartite graph shown in Figure 5.14 to find a maximum weight matching and an optimal dual solution.

8.2 Interpret each step of the Hungarian algorithm, as nearly as possible, as a step of the out-of-kilter method. Where do the two algorithms differ?

8.3 Generalize the algorithm to the case

$$\sum_j x_{ij} \leq a_i,$$

$$\sum_i x_{ij} \leq b_j.$$

8.4 (D. Gale) There are m potential house buyers and n potential house sellers, where $m \leq n$. Buyer i evaluates house j and decides that its value to him is w_{ij} dollars. If seller j puts a price of v_j on his house, buyer i will be willing to buy only if $w_{ij} \geq v_j$. Moreover, if there is more than one house j for which $w_{ij} \geq v_j$, he will prefer to buy a house for which $w_{ij} - v_j$ is maximal. A set of prices is said to be "feasible" if it is such that for every buyer i there is at least one house j for which $w_{ij} \geq v_j$. Show that, with respect to all other feasible sets of prices, there is one set of prices which maximizes both the sum of the total profits to the buyers,

$$\sum (w_{ij} - v_j)$$

and total proceeds to the sellers, $\sum v_j$.

8.5 Devise a simple example of a matching problem in which a maximum weight matching does not have maximum cardinality. (All arc weights are to be strictly positive.) How should the Hungarian method be modified so as to produce a maximum cardinality matching which is of maximum weight (relative to all other such matchings)?

8.6 Write out, in detail, the steps of a weighted matching algorithm based on the approach of finding maximum-weight augmenting paths by a Dijkstra-like procedure. Make a detailed comparison with the Hungarian algorithm.

9

A Special Case: Gilmore-Gomory Matching

Consider two examples of weighted matching problems which have particularly simple solutions.

SKIES AND SKIERS

A ski instructor has n pairs of skis to assign to n novice skiers. The length of the skis assigned to a skier should be proportional to his height, and for simplicity, we assume that the constant of proportionality is unity. How should the instructor match skis to skiers so that the resulting differences between ski length and height of skier are as small as possible?

The obvious solution to this problem is optimal. The shortest pair of skies should be assigned to the shortest skier, the second shortest pair to the second shortest skier, ..., the kth shortest pair to the kth shortest skier, and so on. This assignment minimizes the sum of the absolute differences of ski length and skier height. Perhaps more importantly, it also minimizes the maximum of the differences.

SCHOOL BUSING (R. B. POTTS)

A bus company has n morning runs and n afternoon runs to assign to n bus drivers. The runs vary in duration, and if a driver is given a morning run and an afternoon run whose total duration exceeds T hours, he is to be paid a premium on the overtime hours. The problem, from management's point of view, is to match morning runs with afternoon runs so as to minimize the total number of overtime hours. This is accomplished by matching the kth longest morning run with the kth shortest afternoon run, for $k = 1, 2, \ldots, n$.

The bus drivers' union has different optimization criteria. One of the union demands is that the minimum number of hours worked by any driver should be maximized. And, more generally, that the number of hours worked by the various drivers should be as uniform as possible.

As it turns out, management's solution to the problem also happens to maximize the minimum number of hours and minimize the maximum number of hours worked by any driver. Thus, there exists a solution which is both management-optimal and union-optimal. (Recall that a similar situation was discussed in Section 4.)

Both of these weighted matching problems can be formulated as follows. Let $G = (S, T, S \times T)$ be a complete bipartite graph with $|S| = |T| = n$. Each node $i \in S$ has associated with it a real number α_i and each node $j \in T$ a real number β_j. For all i, j, the weight of arc (i, j) is taken to be

$$
\left.
\begin{aligned}
w_{ij} &= \int_{\alpha_i}^{\beta_j} f(y)\, dy, \qquad (\alpha_i \le \beta_j) \\
&= \int_{\beta_j}^{\alpha_i} g(y)\, dy, \qquad (\beta_j < \alpha_i),
\end{aligned}
\right\}
\tag{9.1}
$$

where $f(y)$ and $g(y)$ are given integrable functions. A matching problem with arc weights determined as in (9.1) will be referred to as a *Gilmore-Gomory* matching problem.

In the example of skies and skiers, let α_i be the length of the ith pair of skies, β_j be the height of the jth skier, and $f(y) = g(y) = 1$. This yields, by (9.1), the weights

$$w_{ij} = |\alpha_i - \beta_j|.$$

It is desired to find a complete matching for which the sum of these weights is minimized.

In the case of school busing let a_i and b_j denote the length of the ith morning run and the jth afternoon run respectively. Then let $\alpha_i = T - a_i$, $\beta_j = b_j$, $f(y) = 1$ and $g(y) = 0$. By (9.1),

$$w_{ij} = \max \{0, a_i + b_j - T\},$$

is the amount of overtime occasioned by a matching of morning run i with afternoon run j. Management seeks a complete matching for which the sum of these weights is minimized.

For the union's problem, let $\alpha_i = -a_i$, $\beta_j = b_j$, and $f(y) = g(y) = 1$. Then, by (9.1), $w_{ij} = a_i + b_j$, and a complete matching is sought for which the minimum of the weights is maximized.

The optimality of the solutions to the example problems can be shown by applying the theorems below. In the statement of each of these theorems, we assume that $\alpha_1 \geq \alpha_2 \geq \ldots \geq \alpha_n$ and $\beta_1 \geq \beta_2 \geq \ldots \geq \beta_n$. In each case, we demand a complete matching which is optimal with respect to all other complete matchings.

Theorem 9.1

$$X = \{(i, i) | i = 1, 2, \ldots, n\}$$

is a minimum-weight complete matching, if $f(y) + g(y) \geq 0$ for all y.

Theorem 9.2

$$X = \{(i, n - i + 1) | i = 1, 2, \ldots, n\}$$

is a maximum-weight complete matching, if $f(y) + g(y) \geq 0$ for all y.

Theorem 9.3

$$X = \{(i, i) | i = 1, 2, \ldots, n\}$$

is a min-max optimal complete matching, if $f(y) \geq 0$, $g(y) \geq 0$, for all y.

Theorem 9.4

$$X = \{(i, i) | i = 1, 2, \ldots, n\}$$

is a max-min optimal complete matching if either $f(y) \geq 0$, $g(y) \leq 0$, for all y, or $f(y) \leq 0$, $g(y) \geq 0$, for all y.

It helps to visualize Gilmore-Gomory matchings if the nodes of the graph are arranged on two vertical axes, with the nodes in S and T positioned according to the values of α_i and β_j. If a complete matching differs from $X = \{(i, i)\}$, then it contains at least one pair of "crossed" arcs (i, j), (k, l), as illustrated in Figure 5.17. The proof of Theorem 9.1 is based on the effect of "uncrossing" such pairs of arcs.

PROOF OF THEOREM 9.1   Let X^1 be a complete matching. If $X^1 \neq X = \{(i, i)\}$, then X^1 contains arcs (i, j) and (k, l), with $i < k$, $j > l$. Let

$$X^2 = X^1 + (k, j) + (i, l) - (i, j) - (k, l),$$

and let $w(X^1)$, $w(X^2)$ denote the weights of the matchings X^1, X^2. It can be shown that

$$w(X^2) = w(X^1) - \int_{y_1}^{y_2} (f(y) + g(y))\, dy, \quad \text{if } y_1 < y_2,$$

$$= w(X^1), \quad \text{if } y_1 \geq y_2,$$

where $\quad y_1 \doteq \max \{\alpha_i, \beta_l\}$, $y_2 = \min \{\alpha_k, \beta_j\}$.

Since $f(y) + g(y) \geq 0$, clearly $w(X^2) \leq w(X^1)$. If $X^2 \neq X$, repeat the pro-

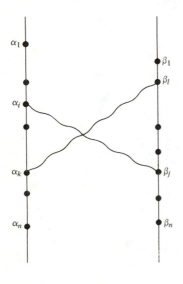

Figure 5.17   "Crossed" arcs

cedure a finite number of times, obtaining matchings $X^3, X^4, \ldots, X^p = X$, showing that $w(X^1) \geq w(X)$.//

We leave the proofs of the other theorems as problems for the reader.

In Problem 9.5 we suggest a method for solving Gilmore-Gomory problems for graphs in which $|S| \neq |T|$.

PROBLEMS

9.1 Let $a = (a_1, a_2, \ldots, a_n)$ and $b = (b_1, b_2, \ldots, b_n)$ be positive real vectors. We wish to permute the elements of a in such a way that the inner product

$$a \cdot b = \sum_i a_i b_i$$

is minimized. Formulate the problem as a Gilmore-Gomory matching problem.

9.2 Prove Theorem 9.2.

9.3 Prove Theorem 9.3.

9.4 Prove Theorem 9.4.

9.5 Let $G = (S, T, A)$ be a bipartite graph with an arbitrary (not necessarily Gilmore-Gomory) weighting of the arcs. Suppose we seek to find a maximum weight matching, subject to the conditions that it contains no crossed arcs (with respect to a given numbering of the nodes in S and in T). Let

$W(p, q) = $ the maximum weight of an uncrossed matching containing only arcs (i, j), where $i \leq p, j \leq q$.

(a) Obtain a recursion formula for $W(p, q)$ which can be used to find a maximum-weight uncrossed matching in $O(mn)$ computational steps, where $|S| = m, |T| = n$.

(b) Obtain a similar recursion formula which can be used to find a minimum-weight uncrossed matching with exactly m arcs, assuming $m \leq n$, also in $O(mn)$ steps.

(c) Now suppose that the graph is complete and that arc weights are determined by formula (9.1), with $f(y) + g(y) \geq 0$. Generalize Theorem 9.1 by showing that there exists a minimum weight matching with exactly m arcs in which no arcs are crossed.

(d) Obtain results parallel to those of parts (b) and (c), for the case of maximum weight matching.

10

A Novel Optimization Criterion:
Gale-Shapley Matching

D. Gale and L. S. Shapley have proposed a novel optimization criterion for matching which does not depend in any way on arc weights. We can perhaps illustrate their approach best with their own example.

A certain community consists of n men and n women. Each person ranks those of the opposite sex in accordance with his or her preferences for a marriage partner. For example, suppose there are three men, α, β, and γ, and three women, A, B, and C. Their preferences can be illustrated by a "ranking matrix" such as that below:

	A	B	C
α	1,3	2,2	3,1
β	3,1	1,3	2,2
γ	2,2	3,1	1,3

The first number of each pair in the matrix gives the ranking of women by men, the second number gives the ranking of men by women. Thus α ranks A first, B second, C third, while A ranks β first, γ second, and α third.

There are as many possible sets of marriages as there are complete matchings of three men and three women, (i.e., 3!). Some of these matchings are unstable. For suppose α marries B, β marries A, and γ marries C. Under such an arrangement, β would like to leave A, his third choice, in favor of C, his second choice, while C would be willing to break up with γ, her third choice, in order to join β, also her second choice.

Definition   A complete matching of men and women is said to be *unstable* if under it there are a man and a woman who are not married to each other but prefer each other to their assigned mates.

It is by no means clear that a stable matching need exist. However, not only does a stable matching exist, for any set of rankings, but also a matching which is optimal, in a very strong sense.

Definition   A stable matching of men and women is said to be (*man*) *optimal* if every man is at least as well off under it as under any other stable matching.

Theorem 10.1   (*Gale, Shapley*)   For any set of rankings, there exists a (man) optimal matching of men and women.

The following algorithm yields a man-optimal matching, and thereby provides the basis of a constructive proof of Theorem 10.1. To quote Gale and Shapley:

To start, let each boy propose to his favorite girl. Each girl who receives more than one proposal rejects all but her favorite from among those who have proposed to her. However, she does not accept him yet, but keeps him on a string to allow for the possibility that someone better may come along later.

We are now ready for the second stage. Those boys who are rejected now propose to their second choices. Each girl receiving proposals chooses her favorite from the group consisting of the new proposees and the boy on her string, if any. She rejects all the rest and again keeps the favorite in suspense.

We proceed in the same manner. Those who are rejected at the second stage propose to their second choices, and the girls again reject all but the best proposal they have had so far.

Eventually (in fact in at most $n^2 - 2n + 2$ stages) each girl will have received a proposal, for as long as any girl has not been proposed to there will be rejections and new proposals, but since no boy can propose to the same girl more than once, every girl is sure to get a proposal in due time. As soon as the last girl gets her proposal, the 'courtship' is declared over, and each girl is now required to accept the boy on her string.

We first must show that the algorithm yields a stable set of marriages. This is easy. "Namely, suppose John and Mary are not married to each other, but John prefers Mary to his own wife. Then John must have proposed to Mary at some stage and subsequently been rejected in favor of someone that Mary liked better. It is now clear that Mary must prefer her husband to John and there is no instability."

Now let us show that the set of marriages is (man) optimal. We call a woman "possible" for a man if there is a stable matching that marries him to her. The proof is by induction. Assume that up to a given point in the procedure no man has as yet been rejected by a woman that is possible for him. At this point suppose that a woman A, having received a proposal from a man β she prefers, rejects man α. We must show that A is impossible for α. We know that β prefers A to all the others, except for those who have previously rejected him, and hence (by assumption) are impossible for him. Consider a hypothetical matching in which α is married to A, and β is married to a woman who is possible for him. Under such an arrangement β is married to a woman who is less desirable to him than A. But such a hypothetical matching is unstable since β and A could upset it to the benefit of both. The conclusion is that the algorithm rejects men only from women that they could not possibly be married to under any stable matching. The resulting matching is therefore optimal.

Note that, by symmetry, a woman-optimal matching is obtained by having the women propose to the men. (Women's lib take note.)

The procedure is easily generalized to match students with colleges or football players with professional teams. However, it is not possible to apply the procedure to obtain optimal marriages for a group of homosexuals. In fact, no stable set of homosexual marriages may exist. (One is free to draw whatever sociological conclusions one will.) See Problem 10.4.

PROBLEMS

10.1 Find a (man) optimal matching for the ranking matrix below.

	A	B	C	D
α	1,3	2,3	3,2	4,3
β	1,4	4,1	3,3	2,2
γ	2,2	1,4	3,4	4,1
δ	4,1	2,2	3,1	1,4

Verify that the optimal assignment is the only stable assignment.

10.2 Verify Gale and Shapley's statement that at most $n^2 - 2n + 2$ iterations of their procedure are required. Estimate the overall computational complexity of the algorithm.

10.3 Modify the algorithm for the case of college admissions. That is, suppose $\alpha, \beta, \ldots, \omega$ are prospective students and $A, B, \ldots, Z$ are colleges, where each college can accept q students. Deal with both student-optimal and college-optimal matchings.

10.4 The Gale-Shapley results hold only for bipartite matchings. To quote Gale and Shapley:

A problem similar to the marriage problem is the "problem of the room-mates." An even number of boys wish to divide up into pairs of roommates. A set of pairings is called *stable* if under it there are no two boys who are not roommates and who prefer each other to their actual roommates. An easy example shows that there can be situations in which there exists no stable pairing. Namely consider boys α, β, γ, and δ, where α ranks β first, β ranks γ first, γ ranks α first, and α, β, γ all rank δ last . . . .

Show that regardless of δ's preferences, there can be no stable pairing.

10.5 Show that a set of marriages is both man-optimal and woman-optimal if and only if it is the only stable set of marriages.

COMMENTS AND REFERENCES

SECTION 2

Some further relations between the assignment problem and the shortest path problem are discussed in

A. J. Hoffman and H. M. Markowitz, "A Note on Shortest Path, Assignment, and Transportation Problems," *Naval Res. Logist. Quart.*, **10** (1963) 375–380.

We deal with systems of distinct representatives from a matroid theoretic point of view in Chapter 8. See that chapter for further comments and references.

SECTION 4

N. S. Mendelsohn and A. L. Dulmage, "Some Generalizations of the Problem of Distinct Representatives," *Canad. J. Math.*, **10** (1958) 230–241.

A matroid generalization of the Mendelsohn-Dulmage theorem is presented in Chapter 8.

SECTION 5

The cardinality matching algorithm appeared in publications of Ford and Fulkerson, circa 1956. However, it is difficult to assign priority for the first efficient solution method. For example, the reader may be interested in comparing the procedure described in the text with the procedure in

M. Hall, Jr., "An Algorithm for Distinct Representatives," *Amer. Math. Monthly,* **63** (1956) 716–717.

It is undoubtedly possible to produce earlier references.

Recently it has been shown that the cardinality matching problem can be solved in essentially $O(n^{2.5})$ steps. This involves a careful study of the lengths of successive augmenting paths, and the intelligent use of data structures for computation. See

J. E. Hopcroft and R. M. Karp, "A $n^{5/2}$ Algorithm for Maximum Matchings in Bipartite Graphs," *SIAM J. Comput.*, **2** (1973) 225–231.

Unfortunately the Hopcroft-Karp techniques do not seem to lend themselves to extension to the weighted matching problem.

SECTION 6

This material is from

F. Glover, "Maximum Matching in a Convex Bipartite Graph," *Naval Res. Logist. Quart.*, **14** (1967) 313–316.

SECTION 7

The bottleneck assignment problem seems first to have been given attention by

D. R. Fulkerson, I. Glicksberg, and O. Gross, "A Production Line Assignment Problem," The RAND Corp., RM-1102, May 1953.

O. Gross, "The Bottleneck Assignment Problem: An Algorithm," *Proceedings, Rand Symposium on Mathematical Programming,* Rand Publication R-351, Philip Wolfe, editor, 1960, pp. 87–88.

The duality theorem for max-min matchings can be viewed as a corollary of a more general theorem concerning "blocking systems." See

J. Edmonds and D. R. Fulkerson, "Bottleneck Extrema," *J. Combinatorial Theory* **8** (1970) 299–306.

Problem 7.4 is drawn from material in

M. Klein and H. Takamori, "Parallel Line Assignment Problems," *Mgt. Sci.,* **19** (1972) 1–10.

SECTION 8

This type of primal-dual algorithm originated with

H. W. Kuhn, "The Hungarian Method for the Assignment Problem" *Naval Res. Logist. Quart.,* **2** (1955) 83–97.

H. W. Kuhn, "Variants of the Hungarian Method for Assignment Problems," *Naval Res. Logist. Quart.,* **3** (1956) 253–258.

Typical of later work on algorithms is

M. L. Balinski and R. E. Gomory, "A Primal Method for the Assignment and Transportation Problems," *Mgt. Sci.,* **10** (1964) 578–593.

Problem 8.4 is taken from

D. Gale, *The Theory of Linear Economic Models,* McGraw-Hill, New York, 1958.

SECTION 9

The Gilmore-Gomory matching problem is a byproduct of research on the traveling salesman problem. See

P. C. Gilmore and R. E. Gomory, "Sequencing a One State-Variable Machine: A Solvable Case of the Traveling Salesman Problem." *Operations Research,* **12** (1964) 655–679.

The example of the bus drivers and runs is from unpublished material of R. B. Potts.

SECTION 10

This material is extracted from the entertaining paper

D. Gale and L. S. Shapley, "College Admissions and the Stability of Marriage," *Amer. Math. Monthly,* **69** (1962) 9–14.

SIX

Nonbipartite Matching

1
Introduction

The theory and algorithmic techniques of the previous chapter have been generalized by Edmonds to apply to matchings in nonbipartite graphs. This also provides a proper generalization of network flow theory to "bidirected" network flow theory.

As we shall see, the augmenting path theorem can be extended to nonbipartite matchings. However, the computational problems involved in finding augmenting paths are more formidable than in the bipartite case, and can be solved only by the proper treatment of "blossoms," as shown by Edmonds. Nevertheless, the nonbipartite cardinality matching problem, the max-min problem, and the weighted problem can all be solved in $O(n^3)$ steps, as in the bipartite case.

The nonbipartite matching problem is a special case of an apparently more general type of problem that we refer to as the *degree-constrained subgraph problem*. This is the problem of finding an optimal subgraph of a given graph, subject to the constraint that the subgraph observes certain constraints on the degrees of its nodes. If there is a lower and upper bound on the permissible degree of each node, but no other restrictions, the problem is reducible to the ordinary matching problem. This reduction, similar to the reduction of the transportation problem to the assignment problem, is explained in Section 3. A degree-constrained subgraph problem in which the lower and upper degrees are equal is sometimes called a *factors* problem.

2

Problem Formulations

Nonbipartite matching problems arise in a variety of contexts. We indicate below some applications for cardinality, max-min, and weighted matching algorithms.

OPTIMAL SCHEDULING OF TWO PROCESSORS

There are two identical processors and n jobs, each requiring one unit of processing time. A partial ordering relation "$\leq$" is given, which prescribes precedence constraints for the jobs. For example, if $i \leq j$, then job i must be completed before job j can be begun by either processor. How should the jobs be scheduled on the two processors, so that all the jobs can be completed at the earliest possible time?

A simple set of precedence constraints on seven jobs is indicated by the acyclic directed graph in Figure 6.1. Each node is identified with a job. Job i must precede job j if there is a directed path from i to j.

For any acyclic directed graph G representing precedence constraints on jobs, we can construct a "compatibility" graph G^*, as follows. G^* has the same nodes as G, and there is an (undirected) arc (i, j) in G^* if and only if there is no directed path from i to j or from j to i in G. In other words, if i and j are adjacent in G^*, then jobs i and j can be processed at the same time.

A maximum cardinality matching in G^* indicates the maximum number of pairs of jobs that can be simultaneously processed and therefore yields a lower bound on the total processing time. Fujii et al., have shown that a maximum matching can be used to obtain a schedule that meets this lower bound and is therefore optimal.

As an example, the nonbipartite compatibility graph in Figure 6.1 permits a matching of three arcs. Hence a lower bound on the length of a schedule is four. But suppose the matching contains arcs $(1, 6)$, $(2, 5)$, and

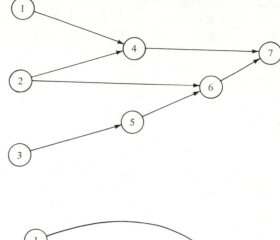

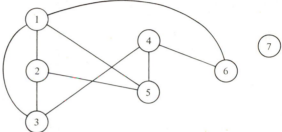

Figure 6.1 Precedence constraints on jobs and associated compatibility graph

(3, 4). It is not possible to process both jobs 1 and 6 and jobs 3 and 4 simultaneously. However, it is possible to effect an interchange of jobs between the pairs (1, 6) and (3, 4) to obtain the pairs (1, 3) and (4, 6). and these pairs, together with (2, 5), constitute a feasible arrangement. Fujii et al. show such an interchange of jobs can always be carried out. (See Problem 2.1.)

SYMMETRIC BIPARTITE MATCHING

There are situations in which an optimal bipartite matching is sought, subject to the condition that it be symmetric. That is, arc (i, j), $i \in S, j \in T$, is to be in the matching if and only if (j, i), $j \in S, i \in T$, is in the matching.

Consider the following situation. Each of n workers has a regular job. However, the factory manager believes that each worker should be able to perform a second job should the need arise. He decides that the best plan is to arrange a "buddy" system, where worker A trains worker B in A's regular job, and B does the same for A.

Clearly, the factory manager's problem is one of symmetric bipartite matching (cardinality, max-min, or weighted, as the case may be). But symmetric matching in a $2n$-node bipartite graph is really no different from matching in an n-node nonbipartite graph. (The reader should be clear on this point.) Or, to put it another way: Just as the weighted bipartite matching problem is equivalent to the assignment problem, so is the weighted nonbipartite matching problem equivalent to the symmetric assignment problem. Some of the difficulties resulting from symmetry are discussed in the following.

HOMOSEXUAL MARRIAGE

The (heterosexual) marriage problem was discussed in the previous chapter in connection with the integrality theorem of bipartite matching. It was shown that there exists a monogamous set of marriages that maximizes total happiness in the community.

We may consider the analogous situation with respect to a community of homosexuals. Let there be n individuals, and let w_{ij} represent the benefit to be derived from full-time cohabitation of individual i with individual j. Let x_{ij} denote the fraction of time that i spends with j. We must require that $x_{ij} = x_{ji}$. Or in other words, we seek a *symmetric* doubly-stochastic matrix $X = (x_{ij})$ such that $\sum w_{ij}x_{ij}$ is maximal.

The fact is that the Birkhoff-von Neumann theorem does not apply to symmetric matrices. That is, a symmetric doubly-stochastic matrix is not necessarily a convex combination of symmetric permutation matrices. In other words, it is not necessarily true that there exists a monogamous set of homosexual marriages that is optimal. (It is, however, true that there exists an optimal solution to the problem in which each x_{ij} is either 0, $\frac{1}{2}$, or 1.)

This is the second "proof" of the instability of monogamous homosexual marriages. (See also Chapter 5, Section 10.) We need not assign any particular social significance to these results in order to conclude that matching in nonbipartite graphs is rather different from matching in bipartite graphs.

UNDIRECTED SHORTEST PATHS

Suppose we wish to find a shortest path between two nodes in an undirected network. If all arc lengths are nonnegative, it is possible to replace each undirected arc (i, j) by a pair of directed arcs (i, j) and (j, i), each with the same length as the original arc, and solve as a conventional shortest path problem in $O(n^2)$ steps. However, if any of the arc lengths are negative, this transformation creates negative directed cycles, and even the $O(n^3)$ procedures of Chapter 3 are inapplicable.

It is possible to solve the undirected shortest path problem as a nonbipartite weighted matching problem. Negative arc lengths are permissible, but there must be no undirected cycles which are negative in length. We illustrate the transformation to a matching problem by the example network shown in Figure 6.2.

By inspection, a shortest undirected path from node 1 to node 6 contains arcs (1, 2) (2, 3) (3, 5) and (5, 6), and has length -6. This path is

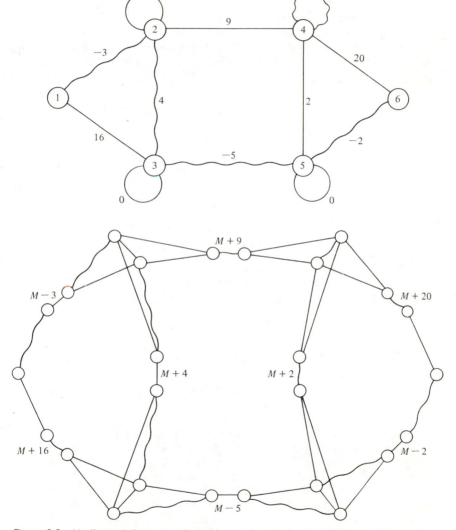

Figure 6.2   Undirected shortest path problem and equivalent weighted matching problem

obtained by solving a degree-constrained subgraph problem in which each of the nodes 2, 3, 4, 5 is provided with a loop of length zero. Lengths are interpreted as costs, and a minimum-cost subgraph is sought, in which nodes 1 and 6 are to have degree one and each of the other nodes is to have degree two. Such a subgraph is in the form of a path between nodes 1 and 6, plus a node-disjoint set of cycles (some of which may be loops). If there are no negative cycles in the network, the path contained in such a minimum cost subgraph is a shortest path.

The reduction of the degree-constrained subgraph problem to a weighted matching problem is indicated by the network in the lower portion of Figure 6.2. All arc weights are zero, unless otherwise indicated. The solution to the minimum cost degree-constrained subgraph problem indicated by wavy lines in the original network corresponds to the maximum weight matching indicated in a like manner in the second network.

A general procedure for transforming degree-constrained subgraph problems to ordinary matching problems is described in the next section.

THE CHINESE POSTMAN'S PROBLEM

A postman delivers mail along a set of streets represented by the arcs of a connected graph G. He must traverse each street at least once, in either direction. He starts at the post office (one of the nodes of G) and must return to this starting point. What route enables the postman to walk the shortest possible distance?

This problem, dubbed "Chinese" by Edmonds in recognition of the mathematician Mei-ko Kwan who proposed it, can be solved efficiently by a procedure which employs the weighted nonbipartite matching algorithm as a subroutine. The problem is discussed in Section 11.

PROBLEMS

2.1   Describe a systematic technique for interchanging jobs between the pairs determined by a maximum cardinality matching in the compatibility graph of a two-processor scheduling problem. In particular, consider the case where i, j and k, l are paired, and there is a conflict because $i \leq k$ and $l \leq j$. Then show that there is no conflict in pairing i with l and k with j. Show that the interchange problem can be completely avoided by solving a weighted matching problem on the compatibility graph, for a suitably chosen set of arc weights.

2.2   Verify that the Birkhoff-von Neumann Theorem does not apply to the symmetric assignment problem. That is, show that a symmetric, doubly-stochastic permutation matrix is not necessarily a convex combination of symmetric permutation matrices. (A 3×3 counterexample suffices to show this.)

2.3   (Norman and Rabin) A maximum cardinality matching can be used to obtain a minimum cardinality covering of nodes by arcs. Prove that, given a maximum cardinality matching which leaves a certain set of nodes exposed, one can add one arc at each exposed node to achieve a minimal covering. Prove that, conversely, given a minimum cardinality covering, one can retain one arc from each component of the solution to achieve a maximal matching. (The problem of covering nodes with arcs should not be confused with the problem of covering arcs with nodes. There is no known polynomial-bounded algorithm for the latter problem, except in special cases.)

2.4 Show that a minimum cardinality covering of nodes by arcs in G yields a minimum cardinality covering of arcs by nodes in $L(G)$. In other words, there is a polynomial-bounded reduction of the covering problem for line graphs to the cardinality matching problem for nonbipartite graphs.

3

Bidirected Flows

We noted in the previous chapter that bipartite matching theory is essentially coextensive with network flow theory. Edmonds has observed that non-bipartite matching theory is coextensive with "bidirected" network flow theory.

A directed graph is a graph in which each arc has both a "head" and a "tail." A *bidirected graph* is a graph in which each arc can have a head or a tail, or two heads or two tails. The node-arc incidence matrix of a bidirected graph is, as for a directed graph, a matrix $A = (a_{ij})$, where

$$a_{ij} = \begin{cases} 1, & \text{if arc } j \text{ has a tail at node } i \\ -1, & \text{if arc } j \text{ has a head at node } i \\ 0, & \text{otherwise.} \end{cases}$$

(We can also provide for arcs which have two tails or two heads at the same node, by setting $a_{ii} = 2$ or -2, respectively. However, this is not necessary for our present development.)

A *bidirected network flow problem* is an integer linear programming problem of the form

minimize

$$\sum_j a_j x_j$$

subject to

$$Ax = b$$

$$x \le c$$

x_j nonnegative integer,

where A is the incidence matrix of a bidirected graph, a_j is the cost of one unit of "flow" through arc j, $c = (c_1, c_2, \ldots, c_m)$ is a vector representing arc "capacities," and $b = (b_1, b_2, \ldots, b_n)$ is a vector in which b_i represents the net supply (if $b_i \geq 0$) or demand (if $b_i \leq 0$) at node i. (Hopefully, it does not cause confusion to let a_j denote the unit cost of flow in arc j, to let a_{ij} be an element of the incidence matrix A, nor to refer to arcs by a single index j, where elsewhere double indices are used.)

Nonbipartite matching problems are reduced to bidirected flow problems by a simple procedure. If the number of nodes is odd, a dummy node is added to the graph. Then "slack" arcs with zero weight are added to convert the matching problem to a degree-constrained subgraph problem in which each node of the subgraph is to have degree one (a "one-factor" problem). Each undirected arc becomes a bidirected arc with two tail ends and unit capacity. Arc weights are converted to costs, b_i is set to unity at each node i, and the transformation is complete.

The reduction of bidirected flow problems to matching problems requires a few more steps. First, the bidirected flow problem is transformed to a problem involving an undirected network. For each node i in the bidirected network G, let there be two nodes, i and i' in the undirected network G^*. Let all the bidirected arcs which have tails at i be identified with undirected arcs which are incident to i in G^*, and all the arcs which have heads at i be identified with arcs which are incident to i' in G^*, and let their costs and capacities be as they were before. Let there also be arcs of the form (i, i'), for all i, each with zero cost and infinity capacity. Let b_i^* and $b_{i'}^*$ be appropriately large, and such that $b_i^* - b_{i'}^* = b_i$.

We now have a problem of the form

minimize

$$\sum_j a_j x_j$$

subject to

$$A^* x = b^*$$

$$x \leq c^*$$

x_j nonnegative integer,

where A^* is the node-arc incidence matrix of the $2n$-node undirected graph we have just constructed. The construction at this point is parallel to that described in Chapter 4 for transforming transhipment problems into transportation problems. The reader can verify that if the bidirected network G is directed, then G^* is bipartite.

The second step is to eliminate arc capacities, by essentially the same technique used in Chapter 4 to eliminate arc capacities in the capacitated transportation problem. Subdivide each arc (i, j) with finite capacity c_{ij}

by replacing (i, j) by (i, k), (k, k'), (k', j). where k and k' are new nodes. Set $b_k^* = b_{k'}^* = c_{ij}$, $a_{ik}^* = a_{k'j}^* = 0$, and $a_{kk'}^* = a_{ij}^*$, and leave b_i^* and b_j^* unchanged. (Note that now a_{ij}^* denotes the cost of arc (i, j); we have reverted to double index notation.)

The third step is to convert the problem to one in which a complete matching is demanded. Construct a new network G^{**} in which for each node i of G^* there are b_i^* copies of node i. For each arc (i, j), an arc with the same cost is provided between each copy of i and each copy of j. Set $b_i^{**} = 1$ at each node i. This is similar to the transformation used to convert the transportation problem to the assignment problem in Chapter 4, Section 14.

The fourth and final step is to set $w_{ij} = M - a_{ij}^{**}$ in G^{**}, for a suitably large M. A maximum weight matching is then a complete matching, if a complete matching exists, and corresponds to a minimal cost flow in the original network G. If no complete matching exists, there is no feasible solution to the original bidirected flow problem.

It has been shown that a bidirected flow problem can, in principle, be solved as a nonbipartite matching problem. However, it would probably be unwise to do so, just as it would be unwise to solve a transhipment problem by first transforming it into an assignment problem. Although we shall not discuss computation procedures for the bidirected flow problem, we note that such procedures have been developed and successfully programmed for a computer. They make use of essentially the same ideas as those presented in this chapter.

PROBLEMS

3.1   In the transformation of the network G to G^*, what does it mean for b_i^* and $b_{i'}^*$ to be "suitably large?" Is the reduction to a matching problem really a polynomial-bounded reduction?

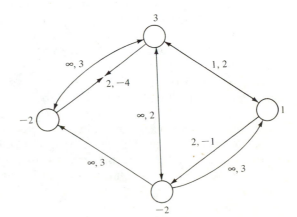

Figure 6.3   Bidirected flow network (Problem 3.5)

3.2   How large does M have to be, in order to insure that a maximum weight matching is a complete matching?

3.3   In the reduction of the undirected shortest path problem to a matching problem, some simplifications were made in the final network, in order to obtain the graph shown in Figure 6.2. Trace through the reduction, according to the rules presented in this section. Determine the nature of the simplification, and verify that it is valid.

3.4   Consider a weighted matching problem in a graph in the form of a three-cycle, with arc weights $-1, 2, 5$. Reduce this problem to a bidirected flow problem.

3.5   Reduce the bidirected flow problem for the network shown in Figure 6.3 to a matching problem. The numbers by each arc represent its capacity and cost. The number by each node i is the value of b_i.

4

Augmenting Paths

It has been pointed out that the (bipartite) integrality theorem and the König-Egervary theorem do not apply to nonbipartite graphs. However, some of the theory of bipartite matching does carry over intact. In particular, the concepts of "alternating paths," "augmenting paths," and the augmenting path theorem generalize without change.

Theorem 4.1   (*Berge, Norman and Rabin*)   A matching X in a nonbipartite graph contains a maximum number of arcs if and only if it admits no augmenting path.

PROOF   If there exists an augmenting path with respect to X, then clearly X does not contain a maximum number of arcs. Conversely, suppose X and X^* are matchings and that $|X| < |X^*|$. The arcs in the symmetric difference $X \oplus X^*$ form a subgraph with a number of components. Each component is either an alternating path or an alternating cycle, as indicated in Figure 6.4. Each cycle must contain an equal number of arcs from X and from X^*. And since $|X| < |X^*|$, it follows that there must be at least one alternating path that contains more arcs from X^* than from X. Such a path extends between two nodes that are exposed by X, and is therefore an augmenting path with respect to X. //

Augmentation of a matching X by means by an augmenting path does not expose any nodes covered by X. It follows that successive augmentations of X results in a maximum-cardinality matching which covers all nodes covered by X. Thus, Theorem 4.2 of Chapter 5 generalizes to nonbipartite graphs.

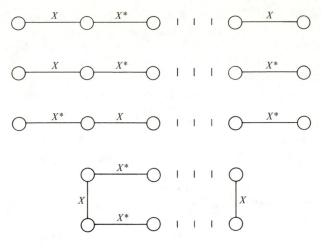

Figure 6.4   Components of $X \oplus X*$

Theorem 4.2   Let X be any matching in the nonbipartite graph $G = (N, A)$. Then there exists a maximum cardinality matching $X*$ which covers all the nodes of G covered by X.

Corollary 4.3   For any nonisolated node i, there exists a maximum cardinality matching which covers i.

Theorem 4.1 was at one time thought sufficient by itself to provide a solution to the nonbipartite matching problem. Indeed, for small graphs it is not at all difficult to discover augmenting paths, or to solve matching problems "by inspection." However, it seems that when one tries to devise a systematic procedure for discovering augmenting paths, all the "obvious" approaches either contain pitfalls or else involve an exponentially growing amount of computation. The following indicates some of these inadequate approaches.

One way to solve the problem is to partition to the nodes into an "S" set and a "T" set, making sure that each arc of the matching extends between an S-node and a T-node. One can then apply the procedures of the bipartite matching algorithm to the induced bipartite subgraph. If there exists an augmenting path, then there exists an S, T partition for which the path can be discovered in this way. However, the number of partitions grows exponentially with the number of nodes, and to test all possible partitions clearly requires a nonpolynomial-bounded number of computational steps.

Another approach is to assign S and T designations to nodes, as dictated by a labeling procedure. Thus one can start by giving an exposed node the label "$S : \emptyset$." Thereafter, when an S-label on node i is scanned, for each arc $(i, j) \notin X$ incident to i, the label "$T : i$" is given to node j, unless node j already has a T-label. When a T-label is scanned, the unique arc $(i, j) \in X$ is identified, and the label "$S : i$" is given to node j. The procedure is continued until either an exposed node is given a T-label or no further labels can be applied. In the first case an augmenting path has presumably been found. In the latter case, the "tree" of labeled nodes is Hungarian, and another tree can be grown from another exposed node.

This procedure, which, of course, works perfectly well for bipartite graphs, can lead to the false discovery of an augmenting path as shown in Figure 6.5.

One might suspect that the labeling procedure fails because nodes are permitted to take on both S-labels and T-labels. It is quite simple to

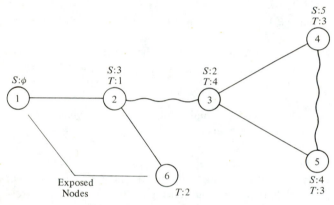

Figure 6.5   False discovery of augmenting path

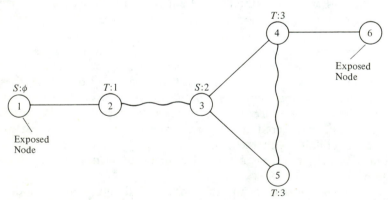

Figure 6.6   Failure to discover augmenting path

add the restriction that once a node is given one type of label, it cannot be given the other. This does, indeed, eliminate the possibility of false paths. But it may also prohibit the discovery of valid augmenting paths, as shown in Figure 6.6.

A still further refinement would be to permit double labeling of nodes but in such a way that the sequence of labels so generated does not "loop back" on itself. For example, nodes 4 and 5 in Figures 6.5 and 6.6 would be permitted to have double labels, but not node 3.

This last refinement is actually fairly close to a solution to the problem, but is still not quite sufficient to permit the discovery of all valid augmenting paths. In the next section we indicate a solution to this problem.

PROBLEM

4.1   Suppose there exists an augmenting path with respect to a matching X in a nonbipartite graph $G = (N, A)$. Show that an augmenting path can be found by applying the bipartite labeling procedure to the bipartite subgraph obtained by appropriately partitioning the nodes into sets S and T, and deleting all arcs that do not extend between an S-node and a T-node.

5

Trees and Blossoms

An elegant solution to the problem of finding augmenting paths has been devised by Edmonds. Briefly, Edmonds' approach involves the construction of alternating trees (much as in bipartite matching), the detection of certain odd cycles called "blossoms," and the "shrinking" of these blossoms by contraction of the graph.

Definition 5.1   Let X be a matching in the graph $G = (N, A)$. Let $N_B \subseteq N$ be a subset of $2r + 1$ nodes, $r \geq 1$, and let B be the set of all arcs, both ends of which are incident to nodes in N_B. B is said to be a *blossom* with respect to the matching X if

(5.1a)
$$|X \cap B| = r,$$

i.e., the matching X is maximal within B. The unique node b of N_B left exposed by $X \cap B$ is the *base* of the blossom.

(5.1b)   There exists an alternating path S, called the *stem* of the blossom, where $|S|$ is even and $S \cap B = \emptyset$, extending between the base of the blossom and a node exposed by X, called the *root* of the stem.

(5.1c)   For each node $i \in N_B$, there is an alternating path $S_{b,i} \subseteq B$, where

$|S_{b,i}|$ is even, between node i and the base of the blossom. It follows that there is an alternating path of the form S, $S_{b,i}$ between the root of the stem and node i.

The simplest form of blossom is one in which B is an odd cycle. Thus the arcs $(3, 4)$, $(3, 5)$, $(4, 5)$ form a blossom in Figures 6.5 and 6.6, with arcs $(1, 2)$, $(2, 3)$ as its stem and node 3 as its base.

The stem of the blossom may be empty, in which case we say that the blossom is *rooted*. If the stem is not empty, it contains an arc in X incident to the base. Thus, the base of a blossom is exposed if and only if the blossom is rooted.

Suppose we use a labeling procedure to construct alternating trees, approximately as suggested in the previous section. Then a blossom is formed whenever there is an arc $(i, j) \notin X$ between two nodes with S-labels or an arc $(i, j) \in X$ between two nodes with T-labels. (The two nodes are assumed to be in the same tree.) Whenever a blossom B is detected, we propose to "shrink" it by replacing the graph G with G ctr B. The node corresponding to B in G ctr B is referred to as a *pseudonode*, and is given an S-label for the purpose of further tree construction.

The tree construction process may involve a number of shrinking operations. In fact, blossoms may be shrunk within blossoms several levels deep. However, if an augmenting path is found in the (blossomless) alternating trees which ultimately result, there is an augmenting path in the original graph G. The existence of such a path is guaranteed by the transitive application of Theorem 5.2.

Theorem 5.2   Let B be a blossom with respect to X in G. There exists an augmenting path in G ctr B with respect to $X - B$, if and only if there exists an augmenting path in G with respect to X.

PROOF   Let P be an augmenting path in G ctr B. If P does not pass through the pseudonode corresponding to B, then clearly P is also an augmenting path in G. If P does pass through the pseudonode, and the pseudonode is not exposed, then P is of the form P_1, (i, b), P_2, where $(i, b) \in X$ is the arc of the matching incident to the base b of the blossom in G. Then there exists an alternating path $S' \subseteq B$ such that P_1, (i, b), S', P_2 is an augmenting path in G. Similarly, if the pseudonode is exposed, there exists an $S' \subseteq B$ such that S', P is an augmenting path in G. (An example is indicated in Figure 6.7.)

Conversely, suppose there is an augmenting path P in G. It is possible, by a rather complicated case analysis, to show that there exists an augmenting path in G ctr B. However, it is easier to show, as a consequence of Theorem 7.1, that if there does not exist an augmenting path in G ctr B then there does not exist an augmenting path in G. This line of reasoning

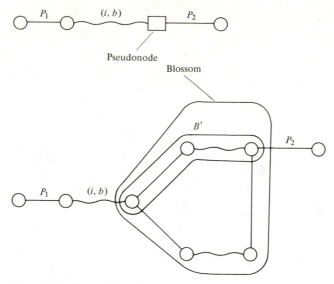

Figure 6.7   Example for Theorem 5.2

is analogous to invoking the König-Egervary theorem to prove the augmenting path theorem for bipartite graphs. //

The outlines of an algorithm, which we will illustrate by an example, have now been sketched out. Consider the matching in the graph shown in Figure 6.8. There exists an augmenting path from node 1 to nodes 3, 5, 9, 8, 7, 6, 4, 2, and then 10. Our task is to construct this path systematically.

We begin by establishing node 1 as the root of an alternating tree, with the label "$S:\varnothing$." Nodes 2 and 3 are given the label "$T:1$," and so on. Eventually nodes 6 and 7 are given T-labels, and an arc of the matching is discovered between them, as shown in the first diagram of Figure 6.9.

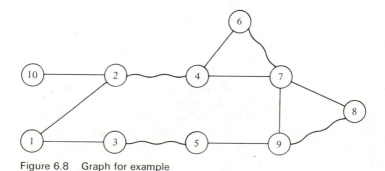

Figure 6.8   Graph for example

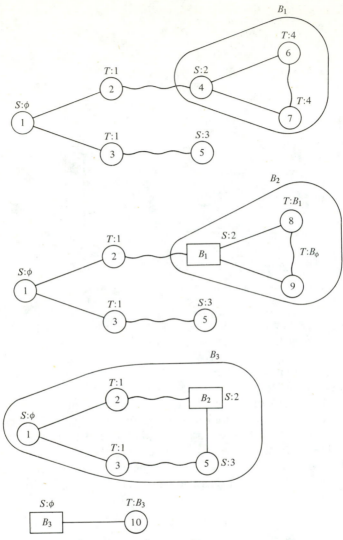

Figure 6.9   Alternating trees for example

Thus, the blossom B_1 is formed and replaced by a pseudonode, B_1, as indicated in the second diagram. The pseudonode B_1 is given the same S-label as the base of B_1, and this label is considered to be unscanned. Continuation of the labeling procedure results in the detection and shrinking of blossoms B_2 and B_3, as shown in the third diagram. Finally, an augmenting path is found in G ctr B_1 ctr B_2 ctr B_3, as shown in the fourth diagram.

The construction of an augmenting path in the original graph G, starting from the augmenting path in $G \operatorname{ctr} B_1 \operatorname{ctr} B_2 \operatorname{ctr} B_3$, proceeds as follows. First, backtracing in the final graph yields the sequence of nodes B_3, 10. It is then necessary to find an alternating path through B_3 in the graph $G \operatorname{ctr} B_1 \operatorname{ctr} B_2$. The appropriate alternating path passes through nodes 1, 3, 5, B_2, 2. The desired path through B_2 in $G \operatorname{ctr} B_1$ is B_1, 8, 9, and the path through B_1 in G is 7, 6, 4. Putting all these pieces together, we obtain the desired sequence 1, 3, 5, 9, 8, 7, 6, 4, 2, 10.

It is seen that there are two principal elaborations required of the bipartite cardinality matching algorithm. First, it is necessary to detect and shrink blossoms. Second, it must be possible to discover appropriate alternating paths through shrunken blossoms, so that an augmenting path in the original graph can be reconstructed. The detection of blossoms is simple, and shrinking is really no problem. (The reader should be able to think of more than one way to write a subroutine for graphical contraction.) However, it is a nontrivial matter to perform these operations in the most efficient manner.

In the next section, we go into some details of implementation of the algorithm, and we carry out an analysis of its complexity. We show that the algorithm can be programmed in such a way that its complexity is $O(n^3)$, as in the case of bipartite matching.

6

Cardinality Matching Algorithm

We now concern ourselves with the implementation of Edmonds' algorithm for the computer. We shall develop a labeling procedure that does not require the actual contraction of blossoms in the graph; instead blossoms are treated "as though" they were shrunk. The labeling technique provides a systematic and efficient method for backtracing through blossoms.

RECORDING OF BLOSSOMS

We need to keep a record only of outermost blossoms, and these blossoms are identified by their base nodes. Associated with each node i is an index $b(i)$ indicating the base node of the (outermost) blossom in which it is contained. If a node i is not contained in a blossom, then $b(i) = i$. Thus two nodes i, j are in the same outermost blossom if and only if $b(i) = b(j)$.

When a new blossom is formed, the base node b of the new blossom is identified, and $b(i)$ is set to b, for all nodes i in the blossom. This means that it is necessary to maintain a listing of all the nodes within a given blossom, and it must be possible to merge these listings efficiently.

DETECTION OF AUGMENTING PATHS AND BLOSSOMS

It is possible to grow one alternating tree at a time, and when one tree becomes Hungarian to begin another at a new root node. Or, we may begin by rooting an alternating tree at each exposed node and grow all alternating trees simultaneously. There are technical reasons, concerning the modification of dual variables, why the latter alternative is preferable for the weighted matching problem. Hence we adopt this plan here.

Initially the label "$S:\varnothing$" is given to all exposed nodes. Thereafter, S-labels and T-labels are applied to nodes. An S-label indicates the existence of an even-length alternating path to the root node, and a T-label indicates the existence of an odd-length path. (A node receives both types of labels if and only if it is a nonbase node of an outermost blossom.) Augmenting paths extend between the root nodes of two different trees, as suggested in Figure 6.10.

Now, suppose the labeling procedure discovers an arc $(i, j) \notin X$ where i and j have S-labels or an arc $(i, j) \in X$, where i and j have T-labels. Assume $b(i) \neq b(j)$, i.e., nodes i and j are not contained within the same blossom. Then an augmenting path has been found if i and j are in different alternating trees, and a new outermost blossom has been formed if i and j are in the same tree. The question of which one of these situations exists is resolved by backtracing from the labels on i and j. If different root nodes are reached, then an augmenting path has been found. If the same root node is reached in both cases, then a blossom has been formed.

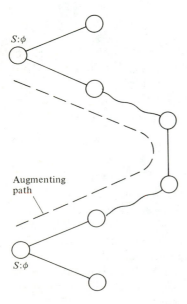

Figure 6.10   Example of augmenting path

LABELING PROCEDURE

Rules covering the detection of augmenting paths and blossoms, in accordance with the preceding paragraph, are incorporated into the labeling procedure. Other than these, the rules for labeling are quite similar to those for bipartite matching.

That is, when an S-label on node i is scanned, the following procedure is carried out for each arc $(i, j) \notin X$ incident to i. If $b(i) = b(j)$, then nothing is done, because i and j are contained within the same blossom. (All possible labels are applied within a blossom at the time the blossom is formed; see below.) Otherwise, if node j has an S-label, backtracing is carried out from i and from j to detect either an augmenting path or a blossom. If node j has neither an S-label nor a T-label, then the label "$T : i$" is applied to j.

When a T-label on node i is scanned the unique arc $(i, j) \in X$ incident to i is found. If $b(i) = b(j)$, then nothing is done. Otherwise, if node j has a T-label, backtracing is carried out from i and from j to detect either an augmenting path or a blossom. If node j has neither an S-label nor a T-label, then the label "$S : i$" is applied to j.

CONSTRUCTION OF BLOSSOMS

Once a new blossom has been detected, it is necessary to determine its membership and the identity of its base node. This is done as follows.

Backtracing from nodes i and j produces two sequences of nodes

$$i_1, i_2, \ldots, i_p,$$

$$j_1, j_2, \ldots, j_q,$$

where $i_1 = j_1$ (the root node of the alternating tree) and $i_p = i, j_q = j$ (where backtracing began). Since $i_1 = j_1$ and $i_p \neq j_q$, there is some index m, such that $i_1 = j_1, i_2 = j_2, \ldots, i_m = j_m$, and either $i_m = i$ or $j_m = j$, or $i_{m+1} \neq j_{m+1}$. The base of the new blossom is $i_l, l \leq m$, where $i_l = b(i_m)$, and its stem passes through the nodes $i_1, i_2, \ldots, i_l$.

The new blossom contains all nodes k, such that

$$b(k) \in \{b(i_m), b(i_{m+1}), \ldots, b(i_p), b(j_{m+1}), b(j_{m+2}), \ldots, b(j_q)\}. \tag{6.1}$$

Accordingly, $b(k)$ is set to i_l for all nodes k in the new blossom. This, plus the addition of missing labels to nodes within the blossom (to be described below), is all that is necessary to "shrink" the blossom.

As an example consider the situation shown in Figure 6.11. There are T-labels on nodes 8 and 9, and $(8, 9) \in X$. Hence a blossom has been

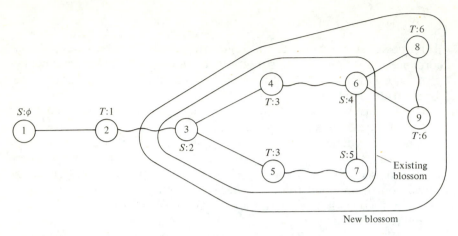

Figure 6.11   Example of blossom construction

detected. Backtracing from nodes 8 and 9 yields the sequences

$$1, 2, 3, 4, 6, 8$$

and

$$1, 2, 3, 4, 6, 9.$$

In this case, $i_m = j_m = 6$ and $b(6) = 3$, since node 6 is already part of a blossom, with node 3 as its base. The nodes 3, 4, 5, 6, 7, 8, and 9 are in the new blossom, node 3 is its base, and nodes 1, 2, and 3 are in its stem.

LABELING OF NODES IN BLOSSOMS

Between each nonbase node in the new blossom and the root of the alternating tree there exists both an even-length and an odd-length alternating path. This fact should be indicated by the existence of both an S-label and a T-label on each such node.

    Suppose the blossom was detected by backtracing from nodes $i = i_p$ and $j = j_q$, where i and j have S-labels and $(i, j) \notin X$. (We leave it to the reader to supply rules for the case i and j have T-labels and $(i, j) \in X$.) We concern ourselves only with nodes $i_{m+1}, i_{m+2}, \ldots, i_p$. (The rules for nodes $j_{m+1}, j_{m+2}, \ldots, j_q$ are, of course, similar.) The S-labels on $i_p, i_{p-2}, \ldots, i_{m+2}$, and the T-labels on $i_{p-1}, i_{p-3}, \ldots, i_{m+1}$ were actually used in backtracing. Hence any missing labels must be T-labels on $i_p, i_{p-2}, \ldots, i_{m+2}$, or S-labels on $i_{p-1}, i_{p-3}, \ldots, i_{m+1}$. The label assigned to any node i_r will be such that backtracing from that label yields the sequence of nodes $i_r, i_{r+1}, \ldots, i_p$, $j_q, j_{q-1}, \ldots, j_1$.

    Let us assign missing labels to $i_{m+1}, i_{m+2}, \ldots, i_p$ in order. Suppose i_r lacks an S-label. We assert that necessarily $(i_r, i_{r+1}) \in X$ and that i_{r+1}

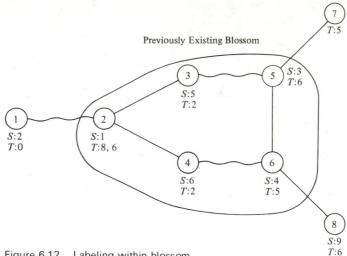

Figure 6.12   Labeling within blossom

lacks a T-label. We give i_r the label "$S:i_{r+1}$". The T-label we shall assign to i_{r+1} will cause backtracing to be carried out correctly.

Now suppose i_r lacks a T-label. We assert that necessarily $(i_r, i_{r+1}) \notin X$. If also i_{r+1} lacks an S-label, then we give the label "$T:i_{r+1}$," to i_r. The S-label we shall assign to i_{r+1} will cause backtracing to be carried out correctly.

But now suppose i_r lacks a T-label and i_{r+1} has an S-label already. Then i_r must be the base node of a previously existing blossom, containing i_{r+1}, and backtracing from the S-label on i_{r+1} will lead back to i_r. It is therefore quite wrong to give the label "$T:i_{r+1}$" to node i_r.

What we do to resolve this problem is to find the last node i_k in the sequence $i_{r+1}, i_{r+2}, \ldots, i_p$ that is contained in this previously existing outermost blossom with i_r as base. Necessarily $k \geq r + 2$. We then assign a special label "$T:i_{k+1}, i_k$" to i_r. This label is interpreted as follows: There exists an odd-length alternating path between i_r and the root node. To find this path, backtrace from the S-label on node i_{k+1} to the root, and also from node i_k to i_r itself. The arcs thus discovered, together with the arc (i_k, i_{k+1}), properly ordered, constitute the desired alternating path.

An example of the application of labels within a blossom is shown in Figure 6.12.

BACKTRACING ROUTINE

The introduction of special T-labels with double indexes does complicate backtracing a bit, and a recursive routine is called for. For example, in backtracing one may encounter the label "$T:i, j$" at node k. Backtracing from j to k, one may then encounter "$T:i_1, j_1$" at k_1. Backtracing from j_1 to k_1, one may encounter "$T:i_2, j_2$" at k_2, and so on. This may continue for as many levels as blossoms are nested. Suffice it to say that the backtracing routine can be efficiently and elegantly implemented on a computer, and that backtracing from a given node to the root of the alternating tree is no more than $O(n)$ in running time.

The complete cardinality matching algorithm can now be summarized as follows.

NONBIPARTITE CARDINALITY MATCHING ALGORITHM

Step 0 (*Start*)   The graph $G = (N, A)$ is given. Let X be any matching, possibly the empty matching. Set $b(i) = i$, for all nodes $i \in N$. No nodes are labeled.

Step 1 (*Labeling*)

(1.0)   Apply the label "$S: \emptyset$" to each exposed node.
(1.1)   If there are no unscanned labels, go to Step 4. Otherwise, find a node i with an unscanned label. If the label is an S-label, go to Step 1.2: if it is a T-label, go to Step 1.3.
(1.2)   Scan the S-label on node i by carrying out the following procedure for each arc $(i, j) \notin X$ incident to node i. If $b(i) = b(j)$, do nothing. Otherwise, if node j has an S-label, backtrace from the S-labels on nodes i and j and if different root nodes are reached, go to Step 2; if the same root node is reached, go to Step 3. If node j has neither an S-label nor a T-label, apply the label "$T:i$" to j.
When the scanning of node i is complete, return to Step 1.1.
(1.3)   Scan the T-label on node i as follows. Find the unique arc $(i, j) \in X$ incident to node i. If $b(i) = b(j)$, do nothing. Otherwise, if node j has a T-label, backtrace from the T-labels on nodes i and j and if different root nodes are reached, go to Step 2; if the same root node is reached, go to Step 3. If node j has neither an S-label nor a T-label, apply the label "$S:i$" to j.
Return to Step 1.1.

Step 2 (*Augmentation*)   An augmenting path has been found in Step 1.2 or 1.3. Augment the matching X. Remove all labels from nodes and set $b(i) = i$, for all i. Return to Step 1.0.

Step 3 (*Blossoming*)   A blossom has been formed in Step 1.2 or 1.3. Determine the membership and base node of the new blossom, as described in the text. Supply missing labels for all nonbase nodes in the new blossom.

Reset $b(i)$ for all nodes i in the new blossom. Return to Step 1.2 or 1.3, as appropriate.

Step 4   (*Hungarian Labeling*)   The labeling is Hungarian. No augmenting path exists, and the matching X is of maximum cardinality. The labels and blossom numbers can be used to construct an optimal dual solution (cf. Section 7). Halt.//

Let us consider the complexity of the algorithm. For a graph with n nodes, there can be no more than $O(n)$ augmentations and applications of the labeling procedure. Each application of the labeling procedure calls for the labels on each of the n nodes to be scanned at most once, and each scanning operation requires at most $O(n)$ steps (ignoring backtracing, and so on). Hence simple scanning and labeling contributes $O(n^3)$ steps overall to the algorithm.

There can be no more than $O(n)$ blossoms formed per augmentation, or $O(n^2)$ overall. Each augmentation and each blossom requires backtracing, which is $O(n)$ in complexity. Hence backtracing contributes $O(n^3)$ steps overall. The other operations for blossom construction, including the determination of blossom membership by (6.1) and the application of missing labels, require $O(n)$ steps per blossom or $O(n^3)$ steps overall. The complexity of other operations is dominated by those mentioned above. Hence we conclude that the overall running time of the algorithm is $O(n^3)$.

7

Duality Theory

We now wish to formulate and prove a duality theorem for nonbipartite matching, generalizing the König-Egervary theorem for bipartite matching. The appropriate dual structure is suggested by the notion of blossoms, and the cardinality intersection algorithm provides a constructive proof for the duality theorem.

Let $G = (N, A)$ be a given graph and let $\mathcal{N} = \{N_1, N_2, \ldots, N_p\}$ be a family of subsets of nodes, i.e., $N_i \subseteq N$, where each N_i contains an odd number of elements. If $|N_i| = 1$, then N_i is said to *cover* all arcs incident to the node in N_i, and the *capacity* of N_i is one. If $|N_i| = 2r + 1$, $r \geq 1$, then N_i is said to *cover* all arcs, both ends of which are incident to nodes in N_i, and the *capacity* of N_i is r. The family $\mathcal{N}$ is said to be an *odd-set cover* if each arc of the graph is covered by at least one subset $N_i \in \mathcal{N}$. The *capacity* of $\mathcal{N}$, denoted $c(\mathcal{N})$, is the sum of the capacities of the odd sets contained within it.

We assert that $|X| \leq c(\mathscr{N})$ for any matching X and any odd-set cover $\mathscr{N}$. (Prove this.) We now seek to show that $\max |X| = \min c(\mathscr{N})$.

Consider the situation at the conclusion of the matching computation, as described in Section 5. There is a Hungarian tree rooted at each exposed node. Whatever pseudonodes exist have been given S designations. A typical case is shown in Figure 6.13, in which pseudonodes are drawn as squares. We assert that, for any given arc of the graph, exactly one of the following cases holds:

(1) The arc is incident to a T-labeled node in a tree.
(2) The arc is contained within a blossom, shrunken to a pseudonode.
(3) Both ends of the arc are incident to unlabeled (out-of-tree) nodes.

Hence we can construct an odd-set cover, $\mathscr{N}$, with capacity equal to the number of arcs in the matching, as follows. Each T-labeled node becomes a singleton set in $\mathscr{N}$. There are exactly as many such nodes as there are arcs of the matching in the Hungarian trees. The nodes in each blossom become an odd set in $\mathscr{N}$, and its capacity is equal to the number of arcs of the matching contained within it. There are $2k$ unlabeled (out-of-

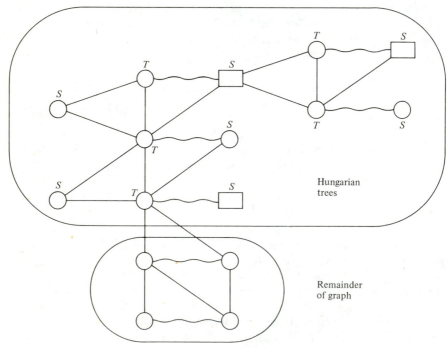

Figure 6.13   Example for duality theorem

tree) nodes and k arcs of the matching between them. If $k = 0$, the cover $\mathcal{N}$ is complete, and $|X| = c(\mathcal{N})$, as claimed. If $k = 1$, one of the out-of-tree nodes is chosen arbitrarily as a singleton set, and this completes the odd-set cover. If $k \geq 2$, one of the out-of-tree nodes is arbitrarily chosen as a singleton set, and the remaining $2k - 1$ nodes are chosen as an odd set with capacity $k - 1$. This completes the cover.

We have thus proved the following theorem.

Theorem 7.1 (*Edmonds*) For any graph G, the maximum number of arcs in a matching is equal to the minimum capacity of an odd-set cover.

An older theorem of Tutte giving necessary and sufficient conditions for the existence of a complete matching can be obtained from Theorem 7.1 as a corollary. Let $S \subseteq N$ be a subset of the nodes of $G = (N, A)$. Let $c(S)$ denote the number of components of G del S which contain an odd number of nodes.

Corollary 7.2 (*Tutte*) $G = (N, A)$ contains a complete matching if and only if there does not exist an $S \subseteq N$ such that $c(S) > |S|$.

PROOF   The proof is left to the reader as an exercise.//

Theorem 7.1 also enables us to prove a max-min duality theorem for nonbipartite matching, just as the König-Egervary Theorem could be used to prove Gross's max-min duality theorem in the bipartite case.

Let H_{k-1} denote any graph obtained from G by contracting odd sets of three or more nodes and deleting single nodes, where the capacity of the family of odd sets (not necessarily a cover of G) is $k - 1$. Let X_k denote any matching containing k arcs. Each arc (i, j) has a weight w_{ij}.

Theorem 7.3

$$\max_{X_k} \min \{w_{ij} | (i, j) \in X_k\} = \min_{H_{k-1}} \max \{w_{ij} | (i, j) \in H_{k-1}\}.$$

PROOF   Let X_k^* be max-min optimal, with respect to matchings with k arcs. Let $(p, q) \in X_k$ be such that

$$w_{pq} = \min \{w_{ij} | (i, j) \in X_k^*\},$$

where the weights of the arcs are assumed to be distinct. Let G_{k-1}^* contain all arcs (i, j) such that $w_{ij} > w_{pq}$. Clearly a maximum cardinality matching in G_{k-1}^* contains at most $k - 1$ arcs, and G_{k-1}^* can be covered by an odd-set cover with capacity $k - 1$. Appropriate contraction and deletion operations with respect to this odd-set cover of G_{k-1}^* yields an H_{k-1} such that

$$w_{pq} = \max \{w_{ij} | (i, j) \in H_{k-1}\}.//$$

PROBLEMS

7.1   Prove the assertion that the maximum cardinality of a matching cannot exceed the minimum capacity of an odd-set cover.

7.2   Prove Corollary 7.2.

8

Linear Programming Formulation of Weighted Matching Problem

The matching duality theorem gives an indication of how the matching problem should be formulated as a linear programming problem. That is, the theorem suggests a set of linear inequalities which are satisfied by any matching, and it is anticipated that these inequalities describe a convex polyhedron with integer vertices corresponding to feasible matchings.

Let
$$x_{ij} = 1 \quad \text{if arc } (i, j) \text{ is chosen for the matching}$$
$$= 0 \quad \text{otherwise.}$$

Let R_k be any set of $2r_k + 1$ nodes. Then it is clear that the inequality

$$\sum_{i \in R_k} \sum_{j \in R_k} x_{ij} \leq r_k$$

must be satisfied by any matching. We represent the set of all possible constraints of this form by

$$Rx \leq r,$$

where R denotes the incidence matrix of odd sets of nodes vs. arcs. That is, the kth row of R is the incidence vector of R_k; when necessary, we also denote this incidence vector by R_k. The vector $r = (r_1, r_2, \ldots, r_m)$ is such that $|R_k| = 2r_k + 1$; r_k is the capacity of the set R_k.

Let us proceed to investigate the linear programming problem

maximize
$$wx$$

subject to
$$Ax \leq 1,$$
$$Rx \leq r,$$
$$x \geq 0,$$

where, as before, A is the node vs. arc incidence matrix of the graph for which the matching is to be computed, and the vector w represents the weights on the arcs.

We know, from Edmonds' theorem, that the linear programming problem yields an integer solution for the case of unit weights, i.e., the cardinality problem. *However, it has not been established that it yields an integer solution in the more general case.* We will prove that it does, by developing a procedure that computes an integer primal solution and an orthogonal dual solution for any given set of arc weights.

The dual to the linear programming problem above is
minimize

$$\sum_i u_i + \sum_k r_k z_k$$

subject to

$$A^T u + R^T z \geq w,$$

$$u, z \geq 0.$$

The dual variables u_i and z_k are identified with node i and the odd set of nodes R_k, respectively.

Orthogonality conditions which are necessary and sufficient for the optimality of primal and dual solutions are

$$x_{ij} > 0 \Rightarrow u_i + u_j + \sum_{R_k \supseteq \{(i,j)\}} z_k = w_{ij}, \tag{8.1}$$

$$u_i > 0 \Rightarrow \sum_j x_{ij} = 1, \tag{8.2}$$

$$z_k > 0 \Rightarrow R_k x = r_k. \tag{8.3}$$

As in the bipartite case, the computational procedure maintains primal and dual feasibility at all times, and in addition maintains satisfaction of all orthogonality conditions, except conditions (8.2). The number of such unsatisfied conditions, i.e., the number of exposed nodes i for which u_i is strictly positive, is decreased monotonically during the course of the computation.

The computation is begun with the feasible matching $X = \emptyset$ and with the feasible dual solution

$$u_i = W, \quad \text{for all } i,$$

$$z_k = 0, \quad \text{for all } k,$$

where W is suitably large, say

$$W = \tfrac{1}{2} \max_{i,j} \{w_{ij}\}.$$

These initial primal and dual solutions clearly satisfy all of the conditions (8.1) and (8.3), but not the conditions (8.2).

At the general step of the procedure, X is feasible, all conditions (8.1) and (8.3) are satisfied, but some of the conditions (8.2) are not. One then tries, in effect, to find an augmenting path within the subgraph obtained by shrinking all blossoms k for which $z_k > 0$ and from which all arcs (i, j) are deleted for which $u_i + u_j + \sum z_k > w_{ij}$.

If an augmenting path is found, it extends between two exposed nodes i and j for which $u_i = u_j > 0$. Thus, after augmentation of the matching two less of the conditions (8.2) fail to be satisfied. Changes in the matching within each of the shrunken blossoms are such that the matching continues to be maximal within each blossom. Thus, each of the conditions (8.3) continues to be satisfied after augmentation. Because the augmenting path involves only arcs (i, j) for which $u_i + u_j + \sum z_k = w_{ij}$, all of the conditions (8.1) continue to be satisfied.

If augmentation is not possible, then an appropriate value $\delta > 0$ is chosen, and the following changes are made in the dual variables. For each node i with an S-label and each node i contained within an outermost blossom whose pseudonode is given a S-label, δ is subtracted from u_i. For each node i with an T-label and each node i contained within an outermost blossom whose pseudonode is given a T-label, δ is added to u_i. For each outermost blossom k whose pseudonode is given an S-label, 2δ is added to z_k, and for each outermost blossom k whose pseudonode is given a T-label, 2δ is subtracted from z_k.

If an arc (i, j) is contained within a blossom, there is no effect at all on $u_i + u_j + \sum z_k$ caused by the changes in the values of the dual variables. But if i given an S-label or i is contained within an outermost blossom whose pseudonode has an S-label and j is unlabeled, then the net effect is $-\delta$. Other cases are indicated in Figure 6.14. As before, square boxes are used to represent pseudonodes.

Recall that in the case of bipartite matching there were two constraints on the maximum value of δ. First, for all S-nodes i, it was required that $u_i - \delta \geq 0$. Second, for each arc (i, j) where i was a labeled S-node and j an unlabeled T-node, it was required that $(u_i - \delta) + v_j \geq w_{ij}$. Now there are no less than the following four constraints:

(8.4)   If i is a node with an S-label or is contained within an outermost blossom whose pseudonode has an S-label, it is required that $u_i - \delta \geq 0$.

(8.5)   If (i, j) is an arc such that both i and j either have S-labels or are contained within different outermost blossoms whose pseudonodes have S-labels, it is required that

$$(u_i - \delta) + (u_j - \delta) \geq w_{ij}.$$

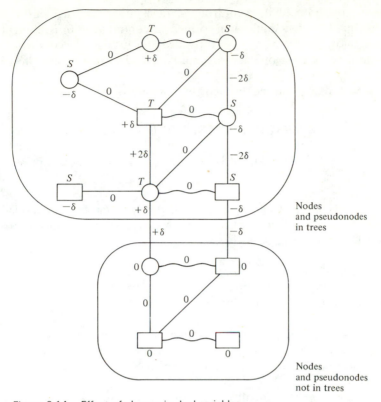

Figure 6.14   Effect of change in dual variables

(8.6) If the pseudonode for an outermost blossom k has a T-label, then it is required that

$$z_k - 2\delta \geq 0.$$

(8.7) If (i, j) is an arc such that i is a node with an S-label or is contained within an outermost blossom whose pseudonode has an S-label, whereas node j is either unlabeled or contained within an outermost blossom whose pseudonode is unlabeled, then it is required that

$$(u_i - \delta) + u_j \geq w_{ij}.$$

Suppose δ is chosen to be as large as possible subject to conditions (8.4) through (8.7). If condition (8.4) is controlling, then the new dual solutions is such that all of the conditions (8.2) are satisfied. Both the primal and dual solutions are optimal, and a maximum matching has been obtained. (Recall that uniform initial values were chosen for the u_i variables. Hence the same minimum value of u_i exists at each exposed node i.)

If condition (8.5) is controlling, then either an augmenting path can be found or a new blossom formed. If condition (8.6) is controlling, an outermost blossom can be expanded (unshrunk). If condition (8.7) is controlling, at least one new arc can be added to one of the alternating trees.

We can now outline the algorithm as follows:

SUMMARY OF WEIGHTED MATCHING ALGORITHM

Step 0   (Start)   Start with $X = \varnothing$ and $u_i = \frac{1}{2} \max \{w_{ij}\}$ as primal and dual solutions.

Step 1   (Labeling)   Root an alternating tree at each exposed node, and proceed to construct alternating trees by labeling, using only arcs (i, j) for which

$$u_i + u_j + \sum z_k = w_{ij}.$$

If an augmenting path is found, go to Step 2. If a blossom is formed, go to Step 3. If the trees become Hungarian, go to Step 4.

Step 2   (Augmentation)   Find the augmenting path, tracing the path through shrunken blossoms. Augment the matching, remove all labels from nodes and pseudonodes, and return to Step 1.

Step 3   (Blossoming)   Identify the blossom and shrink it in the graph. The pseudonode representing the blossom receives an S-label, and its z-variable is set to zero. Return to Step 1.

Step 4   (Change in Dual Variables)   Determine the maximum value of δ, according to conditions (8.4) through (8.7), and make the appropriate changes in the dual variables. If condition (8.4) is controlling, halt; the matching and the dual solution are optimal. Otherwise, expand outermost blossoms for which $z_k = 0$ and return to Step 1. //

PROBLEMS

8.1   Using the linear programming formulation of the weighted matching problem as a guide, obtain a linear programming formulation of the symmetric matching problem. Start with the problem

maximize

$$\sum_{i,j} w_{ij} x_{ij}$$

subject to

$$\sum_j x_{ij} \leq 1$$

$$\sum_i x_{ij} \leq 1$$

$$x_{ij} = x_{ji}$$

$$x_{ij} = 0 \quad \text{or } 1.$$

What linear inequality constraints must be added to insure that there exists an optimal solution in integers when each x_{ij} is simply required to be non-negative?

8.2   Show that each successive augmentation yields a matching which is of maximum weight relative to all other matchings with the same number of arcs. (Consider the addition of a constraint of the form $\sum_{i,j} x_{ij} = k$ into the linear programming formulation, and the role of the dual variable identified with this constraint.)

9

An $O(n^4)$ Weighted Matching Algorithm

We now consider the implementation of the weighted matching algorithm outlined in the previous section. In this section we detail only those features which are necessary to attain $O(n^4)$ running time. In the next section we shall describe additional elaborations necessary to reduce the complexity to $O(n^3)$.

RECORDING OF BLOSSOMS

The management of blossoms is much more involved than in the case of cardinality matching. It is not sufficient to record only the outermost blossoms. When an outermost blossom is expanded, it is necessary to know which blossoms are nested immediately within it, so that these blossoms can be restored to the status of outermost blossoms. When augmentation occurs, blossoms with strictly positive dual variables must be maintained for use in the next application of the labeling procedure.

It follows that it is necessary to maintain an explicit record of all blossoms, their base nodes, and their nesting relationships. It seems unnecessary to specify the exact form in which these records are to be maintained. A variety of data structures are appropriate. It is necessary only that the reader be convinced that the necessary record-keeping tasks can be accomplished in a manner consistent with the asserted complexity estimates.

As before, we identify the base node of the outermost blossom in which a given node i is contained by $b(i)$. Nested blossoms may have the same base node (hence blossoms are not uniquely identified by their base nodes), but two distinct outermost blossoms cannot have the same base.

For brevity, we call a node i a *base node* if $b(i) = i$, even though such a node may not be contained within a blossom. Similarly, we may speak of "nodes contained in the same outermost blossom as i," even though i is not in a blossom. In this case, we refer only to the node i itself.

TYPES OF BLOSSOMS

In cardinality matching only outermost blossoms are of consequence, and the base nodes of these blossoms have S-labels but not T-labels. There are now four distinct types of blossoms:

(1) *Unlabeled blossoms*, corresponding to unlabeled pseudonodes. The base node has no label. The blossom is outermost, and its dual variable is strictly positive.

(2) *S-blossoms*, corresponding to S-labeled pseudonodes. The base node has an S-label, but not a T-label. The blossom is outermost, and its dual variable may be either zero or positive.

(3) *T-blossoms*, corresponding to T-labeled pseudonodes. The base node has a T-label, but not an S-label. The blossom is outermost, and its dual variable is strictly positive.

(4) *Inner blossoms*, corresponding to pseudonodes shrunken inside pseudonodes. The base node may have both an S-label and a T-label and the dual variable is strictly positive.

LABELING OF T-BLOSSOMS

Suppose the S-label on node i is scanned and an arc $(i, j) \notin X$ is found, where $u_i + u_j - w_{ij} = 0$, $b(j) \neq b(i)$, $b(j) \neq j$, and $b(j)$ is unlabeled. In this situation, j is contained in an unlabeled blossom which should receive a T-label from i. Accordingly, we apply the label "$T:i, j$" to $b(j)$, where this label has exactly the same interpretation as in Section 6.

For ease of description, we shall place the label "$T:i, j$" on node $b(j)$, even when $b(j) = j$. This is harmless, the second index being ignored in backtracing.

CORRECTION OF LABELS FOLLOWING AUGMENTATION

After each augmentation, blossoms must be retained for use in the next application of the labeling procedure. We also wish to retain labels on nodes within blossoms. But the labels on nodes through which the augmenting path passes are no longer valid, and must be corrected.

We carry out this task as follows. First, identify *all* the blossoms (not just the outermost ones) through which the augmenting path passes. For each blossom, find its new base node. (The augmenting path extends between the old base node and the new base node of each blossom through which it passes.)

For all nodes in the augmenting path which are neither new base nodes nor old base nodes, simply interchange the indices of the labels. That is, if the labels on such a node are "$S:i$" and "$T:j$," the new labels are "$S:j$" and "$T:i$."

For a node b that is a new base node, find the innermost blossom in which it is contained and the old base node b' of this blossom. Find arcs (b, i) and (b', j) of the augmenting path, where i, j are not contained in the blossom. The new labels for b are "$S:i$" and "$T:j, b'$."

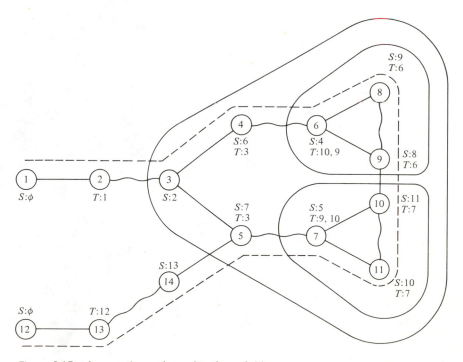

Figure 6.15   Augmenting path passing through blossoms

For a node b' that is an old base node, find the innermost blossom in which it is contained, and the new base node b of this blossom. If $b = b'$, simply interchange the indices of the labels on b'. Otherwise, backtrace from the (old) T-label on b, to discover an arc $(b', j) \notin X$, where j is in the blossom. Let (b', i) be the arc of the augmenting path, where i is in the blossom, incident to b'. The new labels for b' are "$S:i$" and "$T:j$."

An example of the effect of the label correction procedure is shown in Figures 6.15 and 6.16. An augmenting path extends between nodes 1 and 10 in Figures 6.15. After augmentation and correction of labels, the labels on nodes within the outermost blossom are as shown in Figure 6.16.

It should be clear that the procedure requires no more than $O(n^2)$ running time, which is all that is required to attain the overall level of complexity of $O(n^3)$ asserted for the algorithm developed in the next section.

Δ-VARIABLE

A variable Δ is introduced and updated by the labeling procedure. This variable is to indicate the maximum value of δ which can be chosen, consistent with conditions (8.5) and (8.7).

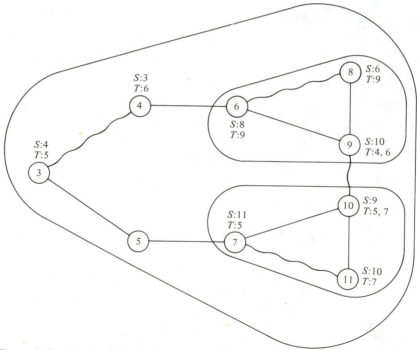

Figure 6.16   Corrected labels after augmentation

Finally we should note that, for conciseness, $\bar{w}_{ij}$ is used to represent $u_i + u_j - w_{ij}$. Each time $\bar{w}_{ij}$ is referred to in the computation, the values of u_i, u_j, and w_{ij} are found and $\bar{w}_{ij} = u_i + u_j - w_{ij}$ is computed. The values of $\bar{w}_{ij}$ are not maintained in storage, else they would all have to be recomputed with each revision of the dual solution, defeating the $O(n^3)$ complexity estimate sought in the next section.

$O(n^4)$ WEIGHTED MATCHING ALGORITHM

Step 0   (Start)   The graph $G = (N, A)$ is given, with a weight w_{ij} for each arc (i, j). Set $u_i = \frac{1}{2} \max \{w_{ij}\}$, for each node $i \in N$. Set $\Delta = +\infty$. Set $X = \varnothing$. There are no blossoms and no nodes are labeled.

Step 1   (Labeling)

(1.0)   Apply the label "$S : \varnothing$" to each exposed node.

(1.1)   If there are no unscanned labels, go to Step 4. Otherwise, find a node i with an unscanned label. If the label is an S-label, go to Step 1.2; if it is a T-label, go to Step 1.3.

(1.2)   Scan the S-label on node i by carrying out the following procedure for each arc $(i, j) \notin X$ incident to node i:

   If $b(i) = b(j)$, do nothing; otherwise continue.

   If node $b(j)$ has an S-label and $\bar{w}_{ij} = 0$. backtrace from the S-labels on nodes i and j. If different root nodes are reached, go to Step 2; if the same root node is reached, go to Step 3.

   If node $b(j)$ has an S-label and $\bar{w}_{ij} > 0$, set $\Delta = \min \{\Delta, \frac{1}{2}\bar{w}_{ij}\}$.

   If node $b(j)$ is unlabeled and $\bar{w}_{ij} = 0$, apply the label "$T : i, j$" to $b(j)$.

   If node $b(j)$ is unlabeled and $\bar{w}_{ij} > 0$, set $\Delta = \min \{\Delta, \bar{w}_{ij}\}$.

   When the scanning of node i is complete, return to Step 1.1.

(1.3)   Scan the T-label on node i by carrying out the following procedure for the unique arc $(i, j) \in X$ incident to node i.

   If $b(i) = b(j)$, do nothing; otherwise continue.

   If node j has a T-label, backtrace from the T-labels on nodes i and j. If different root nodes are reached, go to Step 2; if the same root node is reached, go to Step 3.

   Otherwise, give node j the label "$S : i$." The S-labels on all nodes within the outermost blossom with base node j are now considered to be unscanned.

   Return to Step 1.1.

Step 2   (Augmentation)   An augmenting path has been found in Step 1.2 or 1.3. Augment the matching X. Correct labels on nodes in the augmenting path, as described in the text. Expand blossoms with zero dual variables, resetting the blossom numbers $b(i)$. Remove labels from all base nodes. Remaining labels are set to "scanned" state. Set $\Delta = +\infty$. Go to Step 1.0.

Step 3   (*Blossoming*)   A blossom has been formed in Step 1.2 or 1.3. Determine the membership and base node of the new blossom, as described in the text. Supply missing labels for all nodes, except the base node, in the new blossom. Reset blossom numbers. Set the z-variable to zero for the new blossom.

Return to Step 1.2 or 1.3, as appropriate.

Step 4   (*Revision of Dual Solution*)   Let K_S denote the set of S-blossoms and K_T denote the set of T-blossoms.

Find

$$\delta_1 = \min \{u_i\},$$

$$\delta_2 = \tfrac{1}{2} \min \{z_k | k \in K_T\},$$

$$\delta = \min \{\delta_1, \delta_2, \Delta\}.$$

Set $u_i = u_i - \delta$, for each node i such that $b(i)$ has an S-label.
Set $u_i = u_i + \delta$, for each node i such that $b(i)$ has a T-label.
Set $z_k = z_k - 2\delta$, for each blossom $k \in K_T$.
Set $z_k = z_k + 2\delta$, for each blossom $k \in K_S$.

If $\delta = \delta_1$, halt; X is a maximum weight matching, and the values of u_i, z_k yield an optimal dual solution.

If $\delta = \delta_2$, expand each T-blossom k for which $z_k = 0$ by determining the blossoms nested immediately within the T-blossom and resetting $b(i)$ for all nodes within the blossom. Remove labels from all new base nodes within the expanded blossom.

All labels on base nodes, and S-labels on nodes within S-blossoms, are now "unscanned." Remaining labels are in a "scanned" state.

Set $\Delta = +\infty$.
Return to Step 1.1. //

10

An $O(n^3)$ Weighted Matching Algortihm

Several features must be added to the algorithm presented in the previous section, in order to reduce its complexity to $O(n^3)$. Each of these features has as its objective the avoidance of rescanning labels after revision of the dual solution.

There are three reasons why labels must be rescanned in the $O(n^4)$ algorithm:

(1) *T-labels* Suppose $\overline{w}_{ij}$ is reduced to zero for an arc $(i, j) \notin X$, where i has an S-label and $b(j)$ is unlabeled. Rescanning the S-label on node i results in the application of a T-label to $b(j)$.

(2) *Augmenting paths and blossoms* Suppose $\overline{w}_{ij}$ is reduced to zero for an arc $(i, j) \notin X$, where both i and j have S-labels. Rescanning the S-label on either i or j results in the discovery of either an augmenting path or a new blossom.

(3) *Expansion of T-blossoms* Suppose a T-blossom is expanded because its z-variable is reduced to zero. Rescanning the S-labels on nodes adjacent to the expanded blossom may result in the labeling of nodes and blossoms contained within the expanded blossom.

These three situations are provided for by the introduction of special variables π_i, γ_i, and τ_i and two arrays $C(i, j)$ and $t(i)$, as described in the following. The variable Δ is dispensed with.

π_i VARIABLES

The role of the π_i variables is exactly the same as in bipartite matching. Suppose the S-label on node i is scanned, and an arc $(i, j) \notin X$ is found, where $b(i) \neq b(j)$ and $b(j)$ has no S-label. Then if $\overline{w}_{ij} < \pi_{b(j)}$, the label $T:i, j$ is applied to node $b(j)$, and $\pi_{b(j)}$ is set to $\overline{w}_{ij}$.

In other words, if $\pi_i > 0$, then the T-label on node i is "undeserved." The value of π_i indicates the value of δ by which the dual solution must be revised, in order for the T-label on node i to become "deserved." The T-label on node i is scanned only if $\pi_i = 0$.

γ_i VARIABLES, $C(i, j)$ ARRAY

Let us call an arc $(i, j) \notin X$ *critical* if i and j are contained in different S-blossoms. Such an arc is found in the course of scanning the S-label on i or j. If $\overline{w}_{ij} = u_i + u_j - w_{ij} = 0$, either an augmenting path has been discovered or a new blossom formed. On the other hand, if $\overline{w}_{ij} > 0$, a later revision of the dual variables may reduce $\overline{w}_{ij}$ to zero, and access to arc (i, j) is needed at that time.

Critical arcs can be recovered by rescanning all S-labels after each revision of the dual variables. But, as we know, this technique causes the algorithm to be $O(n^4)$ in complexity. Clearly another strategy is called for.

We associate a variable γ_i with each node i. For each base node i, γ_i indicates the minimum value of $\overline{w}_{pq}$, for any critical arc (p, q) extending between the S-blossom containing i and any other S-blossom (or S-labeled base node). The variable γ_i is continually updated by the labeling and blossoming procedures.

When the dual solution is revised, γ_i is reduced by 2δ. (The u-variable at each end of a critical arc is decreased by δ.) If γ_i becomes zero at a base node i, then we recover the critical arc which yields either an augmenting path or a new blossom by utilizing an array $C(i, j)$ of critical arcs which is maintained for this purpose.

For each pair of base nodes i and j, $C(i, j)$ is a critical arc (p, q) extending between the S-blossoms containing i and j, and $\bar{w}_{pq}$ is minimal with respect to all such arcs. When $\gamma_i = 0$ for base node i, the desired critical arc can be found by retrieving all arcs $C(i, j) = (p, q)$, where i is fixed and j ranges over all other base nodes, and evaluating $\bar{w}_{pq}$ for each such arc. (If $C(i, j)$ does not exist, denoted $C(i, j) = \varnothing$, then $\bar{w}_{pq} = +\infty$.) For at least one of these arcs (p, q), it must be the case that $\bar{w}_{pq} = 0$. Recovering this arc requires $O(n)$ running time.

Initially, and after each augmentation, $\gamma_i = +\infty$ and $C(i, j) = \varnothing$. Updating is performed by the labeling procedure as follows. Suppose the S-label on node i is scanned and an arc $(i, j) \notin X$ is found, where $\bar{w}_{ij} > 0$, $b(i) \neq b(j)$, and $b(j)$ has an S-label. Set

$$\gamma_{b(i)} = \min\{\gamma_{b(i)}, \tfrac{1}{2}\bar{w}_{ij}\},$$

$$\gamma_{b(j)} = \min\{\gamma_{b(j)}, \tfrac{1}{2}\bar{w}_{ij}\}.$$

Find $C(b(i), b(j)) = (p, q)$ and evaluate $\bar{w}_{pq}$. If $\bar{w}_{ij} < \bar{w}_{pq}$, then set $C(b(i), b(j)) = (i, j)$. (The array is symmetric; we assume resetting $C(i, j)$ also resets $C(j, i)$.)

Now suppose a new blossom is formed, with base node b. Let I denote the set of (old) base nodes which are to be contained in this blossom, and let J be the complementary set of base nodes. We must revise γ_b and $C(b, j)$, for each $j \in J$. (γ_j, for $j \in J$, and $C(i, j)$ for all pairs $i, j \in J$ are unchanged.) This is done as follows.

For each $j \in J$, find an arc $C(i, j) = (p', q')$ for which

$$\bar{w}_{p'q'} = \min_{i \in I}\{\bar{w}_{pq} | C(i, j) = (p, q)\}, \tag{10.1}$$

and set $C(b, j) = (p', q')$. Then set

$$\gamma_b = \min_{j \in J}\{\bar{w}_{pq} | C(b, j) = (p, q)\}.$$

At first glance, it might appear that this procedure causes us trouble in attaining the desired degree of complexity for the algorithm. The revision of $C(b, j)$ by (10.1) requires $O(n^2)$ running time for any single blossom, and $O(n^2)$ blossoms may be formed overall, seeming to imply $O(n^4)$ running time for the algorithm. This is not, however the case, as we shall show.

Suppose $|I| = k_1$, $|J| = k_2$. Then $k_1 k_2$ node pairs i, j enter into the evaluation of (10.1) for all $j \in J$, and the evaluation is $O(k_1 k_2)$ in complexity. At least $(k_1 - 1) k_2$ of these pairs can never enter into any later evaluation of (10.1). (That is, not until after the next augmentation.) Also $k_1 \geq 3$. It follows that for every three node pairs entering into the evaluation of (10.1), at least two other node pairs will not enter into any later evaluation. The total number of node pairs is less than $\frac{1}{2} n^2$, hence the total number of node pairs processed by (10.1) between augmentations is bounded by

$$\tfrac{1}{2} n^2 + \tfrac{1}{6} n^2 + \tfrac{1}{18} n^2 + \ldots,$$

which is $O(n^2)$. The total running time attributable to (10.1) between augmentations is thus $O(n^2)$ or $O(n^3)$ overall. The other operations involved in maintaining the variables γ_i or array $C(i, j)$ are easily seen to have equal or less complexity.

τ_i VARIABLES, $t(i)$ ARRAY

When the z-variable identified with a T-blossom is reduced to zero, that blossom must be expanded. Any blossoms immediately within the blossom now become outermost blossoms, and the base number $b(i)$ for each node i within the blossom must be reset accordingly.

We must now take care that the base nodes of the new outermost blossoms have correct labels. This task is complicated by the fact that certain of these new base nodes would have been entitled to receive T-labels from the scanning of S-labels on nodes outside the expanded blossom, except that at the time those S-labels were scanned, the base nodes were contained within the now expanded blossom. If we were to rescan all existing S-labels, the appropriate T-labels would now be applied. However, this would not enable us to achieve the desired degree of complexity for the algorithm.

We resolve this problem by providing a variable τ_i and an index $t(i)$ for each node i. At the beginning of the labeling procedure, $\tau_i = +\infty$ and $t(i)$ is undefined. Thereafter, suppose the S-label on node i is scanned, an arc $(i, j) \notin X$ is found to exist, $b(i) \neq b(j)$, and $b(j)$ has no S-label. We compare $\bar{w}_{ij}$ with τ_j. If $\bar{w}_{ij} < \tau_j$, we set $\tau_j = \bar{w}_{ij}$ and $t(j) = i$. Then, when a T-blossom is expanded, we perform the following operations. First, any existing labels are removed from the base nodes of the new outermost blossoms. Then, for each new outermost blossom, we find the minimum of τ_j over all nodes j within the blossom. Suppose $\tau_k = \min \tau_j$ and $t(k) = i$. Then the label "$T: i, k$" is applied to the base node $b(k)$ and $\pi_{b(k)}$ is set to τ_k.

Each time a change in δ is made in the dual variables, τ_i is reduced by δ for each node i within an unlabeled blossom and is unchanged for each node within a T-blossom.

$O(n^3)$ WEIGHTED MATCHING ALGORITHM

Step 0 (*Start*) The graph $G = (N, A)$ is given, with a weight w_{ij} for each arc (i, j). Let $W = \frac{1}{2} \max \{w_{ij}\}$. Set $u_i = W$, $\gamma_i = \pi_i = \tau_i = +\infty$ and $b(i) = i$ for each node $i \in N$. For each node pair i, j set $C(i, j) = \varnothing$. Set $X = \varnothing$. There are no blossoms and no nodes are labeled.

Step 1 (*Labeling*)

(1.0) Apply the label "$S: \varnothing$" to each exposed node.

(1.1) If there is no node i with an unscanned S-label or an unscanned T-label with $\pi_i = 0$, go to Step 4. Otherwise, find such a node i. If the label is an S-label, go to Step 1.2; if it is a T-label, go to Step 1.3.

(1.2) Scan the S-label on node i by carrying out the following procedure for each arc $(i, j) \notin X$ incident to node i:

If $b(i) = b(j)$, do nothing; otherwise continue.

If node $b(j)$ has an S-label and $\overline{w}_{ij} = 0$, backtrace from the S-labels on nodes i and j. If different root nodes are reached, go to Step 2; if the same root node is reached, go to Step 3.

If node $b(j)$ has an S-label and $\overline{w}_{ij} > 0$, then carry out the following procedure. Set

$$\gamma_{b(i)} = \min \{\gamma_{b(i)}, \tfrac{1}{2}\overline{w}_{ij}\},$$

$$\gamma_{b(j)} = \min \{\gamma_{b(j)}, \tfrac{1}{2}\overline{w}_{ij}\}.$$

Find $C(b(i), b(j)) = (p, q)$. If $\overline{w}_{ij} < \overline{w}_{pq}$, then set $C(b(i), b(j)) = (i, j)$.

If node $b(j)$ has no S-label and $\overline{w}_{ij} < \pi_{b(j)}$, then apply the label "$T: i, j$" to $b(j)$, replacing any existing T-label, and set $\pi_{b(j)} = \overline{w}_{ij}$.

If node $b(j)$ has no S-label and $\overline{w}_{ij} < \tau_j$, then set $\tau_j = \overline{w}_{ij}$ and set $t(j) = i$.

When the scanning of node i is complete, return to Step 1.1.

(1.3) Scan the T-label on node i (where $\pi_i = 0$) by carrying out the following procedure for the unique arc $(i, j) \in X$ incident to node i.

If $b(i) = b(j)$, do nothing; otherwise continue.

If node j has a T-label and $\pi_j = 0$, backtrace from the T-labels on nodes i and j. If different root nodes are reached, go to Step 2; if the same root node is reached, go to Step 3.

Otherwise, give node j the label "$S:i$." The S-labels on all nodes within the outermost blossom with base node j are now considered to be unscanned.

Return to Step 1.1.

Step 2 (*Augmentation*) An augmenting path has been found in Step 1.2, 1.3, or 4.2. Augment the matching X. Correct labels on nodes in the augmenting path, as described in the text. Expand blossoms with zero dual variables, resetting the blossom numbers. Remove labels from all base nodes. The remaining labels are set to the "scanned" state. Set $\gamma_i = \pi_i = \tau_i = +\infty$, for all i, and $C(i, j) = \varnothing$, for all i, j. Go to Step 1.0.

Step 3   (Blossoming)   A blossom has been formed in Step 1.2, 1.3, or 4.2. Determine the membership and base node of the new blossom, as described in the text. Supply the missing labels for all nodes, except the base node, in the new blossom. Reset the blossom numbers. Set the z-variable to zero for the new blossom.

Let b be the base node of the new blossom, and I be the set of (old) base nodes contained in the blossom. Let J be the complementary set of base nodes. For each $j \in J$, find arc $C(i, j) = (p', q')$, for which

$$\overline{w}_{p'q'} = \min_{i \in I} \{\overline{w}_{pq} | C(i, j) = (p, q)\},$$

and set $C(b, j) = (p', q')$. Then set

$$\gamma_b = \min_{j \in J} \{\overline{w}_{pq} | C(b, j) = (p, q)\}.$$

Return to Step 1.2, 1.3, or 4.2, as appropriate.

Step 4   (Revision of Dual Solution)

(4.1)   Let K_S denote the set of S-blossoms and K_T denote the set of T-blossoms, i.e., outermost blossoms whose base nodes b have T-labels with $\pi_b = 0$.
     Find

$$\delta_1 = \min \{u_i\}$$
$$\delta_2 = \tfrac{1}{2} \min \{z_k | k \in K_T\}$$
$$\delta_3 = \min \{\gamma_i | b(i) = i\}$$
$$\delta_4 = \min \{\pi_i | \pi_i > 0\}$$
$$\delta = \min \{\delta_1, \delta_2, \delta_3, \delta_4\}.$$

Set $u_i = u_i - \delta$, for each node i such that $b(i)$ has an S-label.
Set $u_i = u_i + \delta$, for each node i such that $b(i)$ has a T-label and $\pi_{b(i)} = 0$.
Set $\gamma_i = \gamma_i - 2\delta$, for each node i such that $b(i) = i$.
Set $\pi_i = \pi_i - \delta$, if $\pi_i > 0$.
Set $\tau_i = \tau_i - \delta$, for each node i such that $\pi_{b(i)} > 0$.
Set $z_k = z_k - 2\delta$, for each blossom $k \in K_T$.
Set $z_k = z + 2\delta$, for each blossom $k \in K_S$.
     If $\delta = \delta_1$ halt; X is a maximum weight matching, and the values of u_i, z_k yield an optimal solution.

If $\delta = \delta_2$, carry out the following procedure to expand each T-blossom k for which $z_k = 0$. Determine the blossoms nested immediately within the T-blossom and reset $b(i)$ for all nodes within the blossom. Remove labels from all new base nodes within the blossom. For each new base node b, find

$$\tau_i = \min \{\tau_j | b(j) = b\},$$

and if $\tau_i < +\infty$, apply the (unscanned) label "$T : t(i), i$" to b and set $\pi_b = \tau_i$. Remaining labels on nodes within the blossom are in a "scanned" state.

(4.2)   If $\gamma_b > 0$, for all base nodes b, go to Step 1.1. Otherwise, find a base node b for which $\gamma_b = 0$ and a base node b' such that $\overline{w}_{ij} = 0$ for $(i, j) = C(b, b')$. Backtrace from the S-labels on i and j. If different root nodes are reached, go to Step 2. If the same root node is reached, go to Step 3, later returning to Step 4.2. //

We can now verify the complexity estimate of $O(n^3)$ for the algorithm. For simplicity, let us estimate running time between each of the $O(n)$ augmentations, and show that this is $O(n^2)$.

The scanning operations performed in Step 1, exclusive of backtracing, are $O(n)$ for each label scanned. At most two labels are scanned for each node, hence labeling and scanning account for $O(n^2)$ running time. (Note that new labels applied to new base nodes created by the expansion of T-blossoms replace T-labels that are in a "scanned" state, but which have not been scanned since the previous augmentation.)

The correction of labels following augmentation requires $O(n^2)$ running time.

At most $n/2$ blossoms are formed, and the backtracing and labeling operations are $O(n)$ in complexity. The revision of γ_i and $C(i, j)$ requires $O(n^2)$ running time per augmentation, as shown previously. Hence blossoming operations require $O(n^2)$ running time.

There can be at most $O(n)$ revisions of the dual solution. (Each change in the dual variables results either in a new T-label with $\pi_i = 0$, in the formation of a new S-blossom, the expansion of a T-blossom, in the discovery of an augmenting path, or in termination of the computation. None of these things can occur more than $O(n)$ times.) All operations that are required for each revison of the dual solution are $O(n)$, except for those which are $O(n^2)$ overall between augmentations, e.g., expansion of T-blossoms.

We thus conclude that the algorithm is indeed $O(n^3)$ in complexity.

PROBLEM

10.1   Using the weighted matching algorithm as a guide, write out a procedure for max-min matching, parallel to that in Chapter 5, Section 7.

11

The Chinese Postman's Problem

Recall the statement of the Chinese Postman's Problem given in Section 2. The problem is to find a minimum length closed path, with repeated arcs as necessary, which contains each arc of a given undirected network.

We assume that the network is connected and that all arc lengths are nonnegative. If the degree of each node is even, then the network is Eulerian and the solution is simply an Euler path. (See Chapter 2, Section 9.) Such a path, which contains each arc exactly once, is certainly as short as any closed path which contains each arc at least once.

Now suppose that the network G is not Eulerian. Consider any feasible closed path, and use it to construct a network G^*, where G^* has the same nodes as G, and as many copies of an arc (i, j) as the arc (i, j) appears in the path. The graph G^* (or "multi-graph," since it has multiple arcs) is Eulerian. Also, if the path is optimal then no arc (i, j) appears in G^* no more than twice. (Why?) This means, of course, that it is unnecessary for the postman to traverse any street more than twice.

These observations enable us to reformulate the Postman's problem, as follows. Given a connected network G, where each arc is assigned a nonnegative length, find in the graph a set of arcs of minimum total length, such that when these arcs are duplicated, the degree of each node becomes even. That is, find a set of arcs such that an odd number of arcs in the set meets each odd-degree node and an even number in the set meets each even-degree node.

One possible solution method is to start with any given feasible solution, and then to make successive improvements in it through the modification of arc weights and the discovery of negative cycles, described as follows. This was the technique originally proposed by Mei-ko Kwan.

Consider, for example, the network shown in Figure 6.17a. It has four odd-nodes: 1, 2, 4, and 5. A feasible set of arcs for duplication is the set $\{(1, 3), (3, 4), (2, 3), (3, 5)\}$. Now a new network is constructed, exactly like the original, except that each of the arcs which we propose to duplicate is given the negative of its original length, as shown in Figure 6.17b. If this new network contains a negative cycle, such a cycle can be used to improve the solution. All we have to do is work our way around the cycle, duplicating each arc which was previously not duplicated, and unduplicating each edge which was. Without much difficulty, we can show that the converse is also true, and thereby establish an "augmenting path" theorem: The duplicated arcs have minimum length if and only if there is no negative cycle.

The only trouble with these observations, as Edmonds pointed out, is that it is not apparent how one should detect negative cycles in an

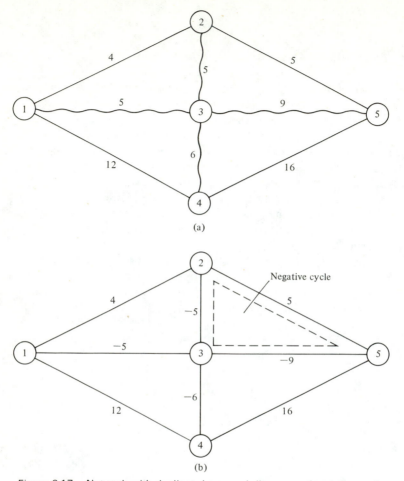

(a)

(b)

Figure 6.17   Network with duplicated arcs and discovery of negative cycle

undirected network. The ordinary shortest path computations do not apply to undirected networks in which some arcs have negative length. And any apparent process of enumeration involves a lengthy computation.

By contrast, Edmonds' solution of the Chinese Postman's Problem is $O(n^3)$. It employs both shortest path and weighted matching computations as subroutines, and proceeds as follows:

ALGORITHM FOR CHINESE POSTMAN'S PROBLEM

Step 1 (*Identification of Odd Nodes*)   Identify the nodes of odd degree in the graph G. If there are none, go to Step 4.

Step 2 (*Shortest Paths*)   Compute the shortest paths between all pairs of odd-nodes.

Step 3 (*Weighted Matching*)   Partition the odd-nodes into pairs, so that the sum of the lengths of the shortest paths joining the pairs is minimal. Do this by solving a weighted matching problem over the complete graph G^* whose nodes are the odd-nodes of the network, and in which w_{ij}, the weight of arc (i, j), is given by the relation

$$w_{ij} = M - a_{ij}$$

where a_{ij} is the length of a shortest path between i and j, and M is a large number. (Note that there is a complete matching in a complete graph with an even number of nodes.) The arcs of G in the paths identified with arcs of the matching are arcs which should be traversed twice. Duplicate these arcs in G.

Step 4 (*Construction of Tour*)   Use any efficient procedure to construct an Euler path in G. //

PROBLEMS

11.1   Apply Edmonds' algorithm to the network shown in Figure 6.17a.

11.2   Show that no arc can appear in more than one of the shortest paths picked out by an optimal solution to the matching problem in Step 3 of the algorithm.

11.3   Formulate the Postman's Problem for directed networks, and show that it can be solved by network flow techniques. What do you suppose can be done for the case of a "mixed" graph, ie., one in which some arcs are directed and some are undirected?

11.4   Suppose that the length of an arc is a function of the number of times it has been traversed. Does this change the formulation and solution of the problem? Does it change the directed version of the problem?

11.5   Devise a procedure to detect a negative cycle in an undirected, arc-weighted graph.

COMMENTS AND REFERENCES

SECTION 2

The two-processor scheduling problem was originally solved by

M. Fujii, T. Kasami, and K. Ninomiya, "Optimal Sequencing of Two Equivalent Processors," *SIAM J. Appl. Math.*, **17** (1969) 784–789.
"Erratum." *SIAM J. Appl. Math.*, **20** (1971), 141.

An $O(n^2)$ procedure for solving this special case of the matching problem is described in

E. G. Coffman, Jr. and R. L. Graham, "Optimal Scheduling for Two-Processor Systems," *Acta Informatica,* **1** (1972) 200–213.

The formulation of the undirected shortest path problem was pointed out to the author by Roger Tobin.

SECTION 3

The equivalence of nonbipartite matching and bidirected network flows was demonstrated in

J. Edmonds, "An Introduction to Matching," mimeographed notes, Engineering Summer Conference, The University of Michigan, Ann Arbor, 1967.

SECTION 4

The augmenting path theorem can be found in

C. Berge, "Two Theorems in Graph Theory," *Proc. Natl. Acad. Sci. U.S.,* **43** (1957) 842–844.
R. Z. Norman and M. O. Rabin, "An Algorithm for a Minimum Cover of a Graph," *Proc. Amer. Math. Soc.,* **10** (1959) 315–319.

The proof given here is due to Edmonds.

SECTION 5

This material was originally presented in

J. Edmonds, "Path, Trees, and Flowers," *Can. J. Math.,* **17** (1965) 449–467.

SECTION 6

The labeling procedure described herein is the author's. Other labeling procedures, which appear to be neither as efficient nor as useful in the case of weighted matching, are given in

C. Witzgall and C. T. Zahn, Jr., "Modification of Edmonds' Algorithm for Maximum Matching of Graphs," *J. Res. NBS,* **69B** (April-June 1965) 91–981.
M. L. Balinski, "Labelling to Obtain a Maximum Matching," mimeographed paper, 1967.

The Hopcroft-Karp algorithm for bipartite matching has been generalized to the nonbipartite case:

S. Even and O. Kariv, "An $O(n^{2.5})$ Algorithm for Maximum Matching in General Graphs," *Proc. 16th Annual Symp. on Foundations of Computer Science,* IEEE, New York, 1975, pp. 100–112.

SECTION 7

Theorem 7.1 is due to Edmonds. (See reference for Section 5.) Tutte's work on matchings can be found in

W. T. Tutte, "The Factorization of Linear Graphs," *J. London Math. Soc.,* **22** (1947) 107–111.

W. T. Tutte, "The Factors of Graphs," *Can. J. Math.,* **4** (1952) 314–328.

W. T. Tutte, "A Short Proof of the Factor Theorem for Finite Graphs," *Can. J. Math.,* **6** (1954) 347–352.

SECTIONS 8–10

The weighted matching problem was solved by Edmonds in

J. Edmonds, "Maximum Matching and a Polyhedron with 0, 1 Vertices," *J. Res. NBS,* **69B** (April–June 1965) 125–130.

Extensions, modifications, and various theoretical and computational results can be found in

E. L. Johnson, "Networks, Graphs, and Integer Programming," Ph.D. thesis, issued as Report ORC 65-1, Operations Research Center, The University of California, Berkeley, 1965.

R. J. Urquhart, "Degree Constrained Subgraphs of Linear Graphs," Ph.D. dissertation, The University of Michigan, Ann Arbor, 1967.

L. J. White, "A Parametric Study of Matchings and Coverings in Weighted Graphs," Ph.D. dissertation, The University of Michigan, Ann Arbor, 1967.

J. Edmonds and E. L. Johnson, "Matching: A Well-Solved Class of Integer Linear Programs," in *Combinatorial Structure and Their Applications,* R. Guy, editor, Gordon and Breach, New York, 1970, pp. 89–92.

Descriptions of computer programs are given in

J. Edmonds, E. L. Johnson, S. Lockhart, "Blossom I, A Code for Matching," unpublished report, IBM T. J. Watson Research Center, Yorktown Heights, New York, 1969.

S. Lockhart, "An Annotated Fortran Program for Matching," unpublished report, IBM T. J. Watson Research Center, Yorktown Heights, New York, 1969.

An $O(n^3)$ algorithm for weighted matching has also been developed by

H. Gabow, "An Efficient Implementation of Edmond's Maximum Matching Algorithm," Tech. Report 31, Stanford Univ. Comp. Science Dept., June 1972.

SECTION 11

Mei-ko Kwan, "Graphic Programming Using Odd and Even Points," *Chinese Math.,* **1** (1962) 273–277.

J. Edmonds, "The Chinese Postman Problem," *Operations Research,* **13**, Suppl. 1 (1965) 373.

J. Edmonds and E. L. Johnson, "Matching, Euler Tours and the Chinese Postman," *Math. Programming,* **5** (1973) 88–124.

SEVEN

Matroids and the Greedy Algorithm

1
Introduction

Matroid theory was founded by Hassler Whitney in 1935 as a product of his investigations of the algebraic theory of linear dependence. This theory has since been found to have ramifications in graph theory, lattice theory, projective geometry, electrical network theory, switching theory, and linear programming. In particular, Jack Edmonds has been responsible for pointing out the siginficance of matroid theory to combinatorial optimization and has provided many pioneering results.

Our objective in this book is simply to present those basic definitions and theorems of matroid theory which have most immediate application in the area of combinatorial optimization. Specifically, we shall try to show how matroid theory provides an interesting and potentially powerful generalization of network flow theory.

In this chapter we concentrate on matroid problems which can be solved by the simple and elegant approach known as the "greedy" algorithm. In the following chapter we present more elaborate, but computationally efficient, algorithms for more complex matroid problems. Included among these are the partitioning algorithm of Edmonds and the cardinality inter-section and weighted intersection algorithms of the present author.

2
Three Apparently Unrelated Optimization Problems

Let us consider three problems which at first glance seem to have very little in common except for their solution procedures.

A "SEMIMATCHING" PROBLEM

Let $W = (w_{ij})$ be an $m \times n$ nonnegative matrix. Suppose we wish to choose a maximum weight subset of elements, subject to the constraint that no two elements are from the same row of the matrix. Or, in other words, the problem is to

maximize

$$\sum_{i,j} w_{ij} x_{ij}$$

subject to

$$\sum_{j} x_{ij} \le 1 \qquad (i = 1, 2, \ldots, m)$$

$$x_{ij} \in \{0, 1\}.$$

This "semimatching" problem can be solved by choosing the largest element in each row of W. Or alternatively: *choose the elements one at a time in order of size, largest first, rejecting an element only if an element in the same row has already been chosen.* For example, let

$$W = \begin{bmatrix} 4 & ⑥ & 4 & 5 \\ 3 & ⑧ & 1 & 6 \\ 2 & 9 & 2 & ⑩ \\ 1 & 2 & 3 & ⑱ \end{bmatrix}$$

The elements chosen by the algorithm are encircled.

A SEQUENCING PROBLEM

A number of jobs are to be processed by a single machine. All jobs require the same processing time, e.g., one hour. Each job j has assigned to it a dead-line d_j, and a penalty w_j, which must be paid if the job is not completed by its deadline. What ordering of the jobs minimizes the total penalty costs?

It is easily seen that there exists an optimal sequence in which all jobs completed on time appear at the beginning of the sequence in order of deadlines, earliest deadline first. The late jobs follow, in arbitrary order. Thus, the problem is to choose an optimal set of jobs which can be completed on time. The following procedure can be shown to accomplish that objective.

Choose the jobs one at a time in order of penalties, largest first, rejecting a job only if its choice would mean that it, or one of the jobs already chosen, cannot be completed on time. (This requires checking to see that the total amount of processing to be completed by a particular deadline does not exceed the deadline in question.)

For example, consider the set of jobs below, where the processing time of each job is one hour, and deadlines are expressed in hours of elapsed time.

Job j	Deadline d_j	Penalty w_j
1	1	10
2	1	9
3	3	7
4	2	6
5	3	4
6	6	2

Job 1 is chosen, but job 2 is discarded, because the two together require two hours of processing time and the deadline for job 2 is at the end of the first hour. Jobs 3 and 4 are chosen, job 5 is discarded, and job 6 is chosen. An optimal sequence is jobs 1, 4, 3, and 6, followed by the late jobs 2 and 5.

THE MAXIMAL SPANNING TREE PROBLEM

A television network wishes to lease video links so that its stations in various cities can be formed into a connected network. Each link (i, j) has a different rental cost a_{ij}. How can the network be constructed with minimum total cost?

Clearly, what is wanted is a minimum cost spanning tree of video links. In order to turn this into a maximization problem, replace a_{ij} by a weight $w_{ij} = N - a_{ij}$, where N is a large number, and find a maximum weight spanning tree. Kruskal has proposed the following solution: *Choose the arcs one at a time in order of their weights, largest first, rejecting an arc only if it forms a cycle with arcs already chosen.*

For example, suppose the network is as shown in Figure 7.1. The arcs chosen by the algorithm are indicated by wavy lines.

Each of the algorithms described above can be characterized as "greedy," because at each step they attempt to add the choicest possible morsel to the solution. A curious aspect of this procedure is that the computation does not in any way depend upon the actual numerical values of the weights involved, but only on their *relative* magnitudes.

Our goal in the next several sections is to introduce enough mathematical machinery to enable us to justify all three of these greedy algorithms in one fell swoop, and to explain such facts as the unimportance of the actual numerical values of the weights.

PROBLEMS

2.1 Construct a simple example to show that the greedy algorithm is not valid for the weighted matching problem. That is, no two elements of W are to be chosen from the same row or the same column.

2.2 Find an optimal selection of jobs which can all be performed on time.

Job j	Deadline d_j	Penalty w_j
1	1	10
2	3	9
3	2	7
4	1	6
5	4	5
6	5	4

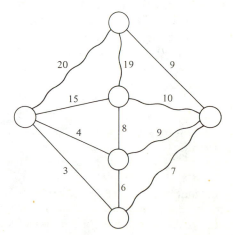

Figure 7.1   Network with maximal spanning tree

3

Matroid Definitions

Consider a matrix whose elements are from an arbitrary field. Any subset of the columns of the matrix is either linearly independent or linearly dependent; the subsets thus fall into two classes. As Whitney pointed out in his classic paper, "On the Abstract Properties of Linear Dependence," these classes are not at all arbitrary. For instance, any subset of an independent set is independent. Also, if I_p and I_{p+1} are independent sets of p and $p + 1$ columns respectively, then I_p together with some column of I_{p+1} forms an independent set of $p + 1$ columns.

On the other hand, there are systems that satisfy these two properties but do not correspond to subsets of columns of any matrix. Algebraic systems which generalize these properties of matrices are known as "matroids."

Definition   A *matroid* $M = (E, \mathscr{I})$ is a structure in which E is a finite set of *elements* and $\mathscr{I}$ is a family of subsets of E, such that

(3.1) $\varnothing \in \mathscr{I}$ and all proper subsets of a set I in $\mathscr{I}$ are in $\mathscr{I}$.

(3.2)   If I_p and I_{p+1} are sets in $\mathscr{I}$ containing p and $p + 1$ elements respectively, then there exists an element $e \in I_{p+1} - I_p$ such that $I_p + e \in \mathscr{I}$.

The system $M = (E, \mathscr{I})$ is said to be the *matroid of the matrix* A if E corresponds to the set of columns of A, and $\mathscr{I}$ contains all linearly independent subsets of columns. A matroid is said to be *matric* if it is the matroid of some matrix A.

Matroids also have a close connection with graphs, as we can see by considering the matroid of the node-arc incidence matrix of the graph G, where the 0, 1 elements of the matrix are taken to be elements of the field of integers modulo 2. In this case, a linearly independent subset of the columns corresponds to a subset of arcs which is cycle-free, i.e., a tree, or a forest of trees, in the graph. A matric matroid $M = (E, \mathscr{I})$ is said to be the *matroid of the graph* G if E is the set of arcs of G and a subset $I \subseteq E$ is in $\mathscr{I}$ if and only if I is a cycle-free subset of arcs. Such a matroid is said to be *graphic*.

Much of the terminology of matroid theory is drawn from linear algebra. For example, a subset I in $\mathscr{I}$ is said to be an *independent set* of the matroid $M = (E, \mathscr{I})$. ("Independence" is a property stemming from membership in $\mathscr{I}$, and not the other way around.) A maximal independent set is said to be a *base* of the matroid, and the *rank* $r(A)$ of a subset $A \subseteq E$

is the cardinality of a maximal independent subset of A. (All maximal independent subsets of A must have the same cardinality; see Problem 3.1.) A subset of E which is not independent is *dependent*.

Other terminology is drawn from graph theory. For example, a minimal dependent set is called a *circuit*. Still other terminology is common to both linear algebra and graph theory. Thus, the *span* of a set $A \subseteq E$, denoted sp(A), is the maximal superset of A having the same rank as A. Clearly, if B is a base, then sp(B) $= E$; i.e., "a base spans the matroid." A set A which is equal to its own span, i.e., $A = $ sp(A), is said to be a *closed set*.

Theorem 3.1   The span of a set is unique.

PROOF   Let A be given and assume A_1 and A_2 are distinct maximal supersets of A such that $r(A) = r(A_1) = r(A_2) = p$. Let $e_2 \in A_2 - A_1$. Then $r(A_1 + e_2) > r(A)$, else A_1 would not be maximal with respect to the property of having equal rank. Let $I_p \subseteq A$ and $I_{p+1} \subseteq A_1 + e_2$ be independent sets having p and $p + 1$ elements respectively. By (3.2), there must be an element $e \in I_{p+1} - I_p$ such that $I_p + e$ is independent. But the only such element can be e_2. Hence $I_p + e_2$ is independent. But $I_p + e_2 \subseteq A_2$, contrary to the assumption that $r(A_2) = p$. It follows that the assumption that there can be two distinct spans A_1 and A_2 is false. //

As an example, consider the matroid of the graph G shown in Figure 7.2. Arcs $(1, 2)$, $(1, 3)$, and $(4, 5)$ form an independent set. These arcs, plus any one of the arcs $(1, 4)$, $(2, 5)$, $(3, 4)$, $(3, 5)$ form a base. The arcs $(1, 2)$, $(1, 3)$, $(4, 5)$ plus both the arcs $(1, 4)$ and $(2, 5)$ form a dependent set, since it contains the cycle $(1, 2)$, $(2, 5)$, $(4, 5)$, $(1, 4)$. This cycle is a circuit of the matroid. Each cycle of a graph G is a circuit of its matroid. Since cycles

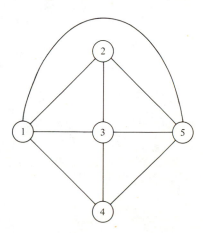

Figure 7.2   Example graph

may contain differing numbers of arcs, it follows that not all circuits have the same cardinality.

Consider the dependent set $A = \{(1, 2), (1, 3), (2, 3), (2, 5)\}$. Note that $r(A) = 3$ and that arcs $(1, 5)$ and $(3, 5)$, but no others, can be added to A without increasing its rank. Hence $\mathrm{sp}(A) = \{(1, 2), (1, 3), (1, 5), (2, 3), (2, 5), (3, 5)\}$. Another characterization of the span of a set is that $\mathrm{sp}(A)$ contains all elements in A plus all elements e such that $A' + e$ is a circuit, for some $A' \subseteq A$.

Another useful theorem that follows almost directly from the definitions is the following.

Theorem 3.2 If I is independent and $I + e$ is dependent, then $I + e$ contains exactly one circuit.

PROOF   Suppose there are two distinct circuits C_1 and C_2 in $I + e$. Obviously $e \in C_1 \cap C_2$ and $(C_1 \cup C_2) - e$ is independent. Choose $e' \in C_1 - C_2$. $C_1 - e'$ is independent and can be augmented with elements of $(C_1 \cup C_2) - e$ (by repeated application of (3.2), using subsets of $(C_1 \cup C_2) - e$) to obtain an independent set $I' \subseteq C_1 \cup C_2$ such that $|I'| = |(C_1 \cup C_2) - e|$. Thus there is only one element e'' of $C_1 \cup C_2$ not in I'. Either $e'' \in C_2 - C_1$ or $e'' = e'$. In the first case C_1 would be independent and in the second case C_2 would be. This contradiction rules out the existence of two circuits. //

PROBLEMS

3.1 Let E be an arbitrary subset of n elements. (a) For given p, $0 \le p \le n$, let $\mathscr{I}$ contain all subsets of E with p or fewer elements. Is $(E, \mathscr{I})$ a matroid? (b) For given e_1, e_2, let $\mathscr{I}$ contain all subsets of E which do not contain both e_1 and e_2. Is $(E, \mathscr{I})$ a matroid?

3.2 Let $M = (E, \mathscr{I})$ be a matroid and S be an arbitrary subset of E. Prove that $M \text{ del } S = (E - S, \mathscr{I}')$ is a matroid, where

$$\mathscr{I}' = \{I' | I' \in \mathscr{I}, I' \subseteq E - S\}.$$

($M \text{ del } S$ is the matroid obtained by "deleting" the elements of S.)

3.3 Let $E = 1, 2, ..., 7$, and let $\mathscr{I}$ contain as bases all subsets of three elements, except $\{1, 2, 4\}$, $\{1, 3, 5\}$, $\{1, 6, 7\}$, $\{2, 3, 6\}$, $\{2, 5, 7\}$, $\{3, 4, 7\}$, and $\{4, 5, 6\}$. Verify that $(E, \mathscr{I})$ is a matroid. Does this matroid have any circuits with two elements? (This is cited by Whitney as an example of a nonmatric matroid; it corresponds to a well-known example of a finite projective geometry. If you are ambitious, try to demonstrate that it is nonmatric.)

3.4 Construct a simple example to show that two nonisomorphic graphs can have the same matroid.

4

Matching, Transversal, and Partition Matroids

In the previous section two types of matroids were defined: matric matroids and graphic matroids. We now introduce three other types of matroids: matching, transversal, and partition matroids, in order of increasing specialization.

Theorem 4.1 (*Edmonds and Fulkerson*)   Let $G = (N, A)$ be a graph and E be any subset of N. Let $\mathscr{I}$ be the family of all subsets $I \subseteq E$ such that there exists a matching which covers all the nodes in I. Then $M = (E, \mathscr{I})$ is a matroid, called a *matching* matroid.

PROOF   Clearly axiom (3.1) is satisfied.

Now suppose I_p and I_{p+1} are sets in $\mathscr{I}$ containing p and $p + 1$ nodes, respectively. Let X_p and X_{p+1} be matchings covering I_p and I_{p+1}, respectively. Assume that for all $e \in I_{p+1} - I_p$, e is not covered by X_p, else X_p covers $I_p + e$, for some $e \in I_{p+1} - I_p$, and (3.2) is verified immediately. Consider the symmetric difference of the matchings X_p and X_{p+1}, which is composed of alternating cycles and alternating paths (as in the proof of Theorem 4.1 in Chapter 6). At least one of the alternating paths must extend between a node not in I_p and a node $e \in I_{p+1} - I_p$. The symmetric difference of this alternating path and X_p yields a matching which covers $I_p + e$. Hence axiom (3.2) is verified and M is a matroid. //

As a simple example, consider the graph pictured in Figure 7.3. The set I_3 is covered by the matching containing the two arcs drawn as wavy lines and I_4 by the matching containing the three arcs drawn as straight lines. The alternating path containing arcs $(3, 6)$, $(3, 4)$, and $(4, 7)$ enables us to obtain the matching $(1, 2)$, $(3, 6)$, $(4, 7)$, which covers nodes 1, 2, 3, 6, and 7. Thus, nodes 6 or 7 (or both) can be added to I_3.

Recall the definitions of partial transversals, transversals, and systems of distinct representations given in Section 1, Chapter 5. Let

$$Q = \{q_i | i = 1, 2, ..., m\}$$

be a family of (not necessarily distinct) subsets of a set

$$E = \{e_j | j = 1, 2, ..., n\}.$$

Let $G = (Q, E, A)$ be a bipartite graph where arc $(i, j) \in A$ if and only if $e_j \in q_i$. By applying Theorem 4.1 to the bipartite graph we obtain the following corollary.

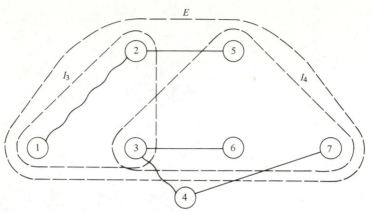

Figure 7.3   Example of matching matroid

Corollary 4.2   For any family Q of subsets of E, $M = (E, \mathscr{I})$ is a matroid, where $\mathscr{I}$ is the set of partial transversals of Q.

Let us say that a subfamily $Q' \subseteq Q$ is *assignable* if there is a matching in $G = (Q, E, A)$ which covers all the nodes in Q'. By letting Q now play the role of E in Theorem 4.1 and again applying that theorem to the bipartite graph G, we have:

Corollary 4.3   For any family Q of subsets of E, $M = (Q, \mathscr{I})$ is a matroid, where $\mathscr{I}$ is the set of assignable subfamilies of Q.

Any matroid whose structure is like that of the matroids of Corollaries 4.2 or 4.3, we call a *transversal* matroid.

Now let π be a partition which separates the finite set E into m disjoint blocks $B_1, B_2, \ldots, B_m$, and let d_i, $i = 1, 2, \ldots, m$ be m given non-negative integers.

Corollary 4.4   For any E, π, and d_i, $i = 1, 2, \ldots, m$, $M = (E, \mathscr{I})$ is a matroid, where

$$\mathscr{I} = \{I \,|\, I \subseteq E, \left|I \cap B_i\right| \leq d_i, i = 1, 2, \ldots, m\}.$$

PROOF   Let Q contain each block $B_i \subseteq E$ exactly d_i times and apply Corollary 4.2. //

Any matroid whose structure is like that of the matroids of Corollary 4.4 is called a *partition* matroid. Quite commonly, we assume that each of the numbers d_i, $i = 1, 2, \ldots, m$, is unity, and fail to mention this fact explicitly.

As an example, let $G = (N, A)$ be a directed garph. Then $M_1 = (A, \mathscr{I}_1)$ is a partition matroid, where $\mathscr{I}_1$ contains all subsets of arcs, no two of which are incident *to* the same node. $M_2 = (A, \mathscr{I}_2)$ is also a partition matroid, where $\mathscr{I}_2$ contains all subsets of arcs, no two of which are incident *from* the same node. Any set $I \in \mathscr{I}_1 \cap \mathscr{I}_2$ consists of a node-disjoint set of directed paths and cycles.

PROBLEMS

4.1 Formulate the "semimatching" problem of Section 2 as a problem involving a partition matroid.

4.2 Formulate the sequencing problem of Section 2 as a problem involving a transversal matroid. Show that this transversal matroid has a special "convex" structure, like that described in Section 6, Chapter 5.

5

Matroid Axiomatics

Some insight into matroid structures can be gained by examining alternative axiom systems.

Theorem 5.1   Let $\mathscr{I}$ be the family of independent sets of a matroid. Then:

(5.1)   For any $A \subseteq E$, if I and I' are maximal subsets of A in $\mathscr{I}$, then $|I| = |I'|$.

Conversely, if $M = (E, \mathscr{I})$ is a finite structure satisfying (3.1) and (5.1), then M is a matroid.

PROOF   Suppose (3.2) holds. Let A be given and suppose I and I' are maximal subsets of A in $\mathscr{I}$ such that $|I| < |I'|$. Let $I'' \subseteq I'$ be such that $|I| + 1 = |I''|$. By (3.2), there exists an $e \in I'' - I$ such that $I + e \in \mathscr{I}$, contrary to the assumption that I is maximal in A. This is a contradiction. Hence there can exist no such maximal sets I and I' with $|I| < |I'|$.

Conversely, suppose (5.1) holds. Let I_p, I_{p+1} be sets in $\mathscr{I}$ with p and $p + 1$ elements, respectively. Let $A = I_p \cup I_{p+1}$. It follows from (5.1) that I_p cannot be maximal in A. Hence there must exist an $e \in I_{p+1} - I_p$ such that $I_p + e \in \mathscr{I}$, and (3.2) is established. //

Theorem 5.1 asserts that for any $A \subseteq E$, all maximal independent sets in A have the same cardinality. The rank function $r(A)$ is thus well defined.

The specialization of Theorem 5.1 to graphic matroids yields the following corollary.

Corollary 5.2 All spanning trees of a connected graph contain the same number of arcs.

Theorem 5.1 shows that condition (5.1) is an alternative to axiom (3.2). There are other alternative characterizations of matroids, as indicated below.

Theorem 5.3 (*Whitney*) Let $\mathscr{B}$ be the set of bases of a matroid. Then:

(5.2) $\mathscr{B} \neq \varnothing$ and no set in $\mathscr{B}$ contains another properly.
(5.3)   If B_1 and B_2 are in $\mathscr{B}$ and e_1 is any element of B_1, then there exists an element e_2 in B_2 such that $B_1 - e_1 + e_2$ is in $\mathscr{B}$.

Conversely, if $(E, \mathscr{B})$ is a finite structure satisfying (5.2) and (5.3), then $M = (E, \mathscr{I})$ is a matroid, where

$$\mathscr{I} = \{I \mid I \subseteq B, \quad \text{for some } B \in \mathscr{B}\}.$$

PROOF   The proof is left as an exercise. //

The specialization of Theorem 5.3 to graphic matroids yields the following corollary.

Corollary 5.4 Let T_1 and T_2 be two spanning trees of a connected graph and let e_1 be any arc in T_1. Then there exists an arc e_2 in T_2 such that $T_1 - e_1 + e_2$ is also a spanning tree.

Theorem 5.5 (*Whitney*) Let r be the rank function of a matroid. Then:

(5.4) $r(\varnothing) = 0$
(5.5)   For any subset $A \subseteq E$, and any element e not in A, either

$$r(A + e) = r(A)$$

or

$$r(A + e) = r(A) + 1.$$

(5.6)   For any subset $A \subseteq E$ and elements e_1, e_2 not in A, if

$$r(A + e_1) = r(A + e_2) = r(A),$$

then

$$r(A + e_1 + e_2) = r(A).$$

Conversely, if r is a function over the finite set E satisfying (5.4) through (5.6), then $M = (E, \mathscr{I})$ is a matroid, where

$$\mathscr{I} = \{I \mid r(I) = |I|\}.$$

PROOF   It is not too difficult to verify that conditions (5.4) through (5.6) are satisfied by a matroid. The converse, however, is more difficult, and the reader is referred to Whitney's original paper. //

Theorem 5.6   (*Whitney*)   Let $\mathscr{C}$ be the family of circuits of a given matroid. Then:

(5.7) $\varnothing \notin \mathscr{C}$ and no set in $\mathscr{C}$ contains another properly.
(5.8)   If C_1 and C_2 are in $\mathscr{C}$, $C_1 \neq C_2$ and $e \in C_1 \cap C_2$, $e' \in C_1 - C_2$, then there is a set $C_3 \subseteq (C_1 \cup C_2) - e \in \mathscr{C}$ such that $e' \in C_3$.

Conversely, if $(E, \mathscr{C})$ is a finite structure satisfying (5.7) and (5.8), then $M = (E, \mathscr{I})$ is a matroid, where

$$\mathscr{I} = \{I \mid C \nsubseteq I, \quad \text{for all } C \in \mathscr{C}\}.$$

PROOF   The reader should be able to prove that (5.7) and (5.8) are satisfied by any matroid. However, proving the converse is more difficult. The reader is referred to Section 8 of Whitney's original paper, where Whitney defines the "rank" of a subset of E in terms of the sets C in which it contains, and then shows that this notion of rank satisfies (5.4) through (5.6). //

As an example of the application of Theorem 5.6, consider again the matroid of the graph G shown in Figure 7.2. Let $C_1 = \{(1, 3), (2, 3), (2, 5), (4, 5), (1, 4)\}$, $C_2 = \{(1, 2), (1, 3), (2, 3)\}$, and let e be $(1, 3)$. Then $C_3 = \{(1, 2), (2, 5), (4, 5), (1, 4)\}$.

PROBLEMS

5.1   Prove Theorem 5.3.
5.2   Prove that conditions (5.4) through (5.6) are satisfied by a matroid.
5.3   Prove that conditions (5.7) and (5.8) are satisfied by a matroid.
5.4   Devise an algorithm, based on conditions (5.7) and (5.8), to determine, for a given set E and a family of subsets $\mathscr{C}$, whether $\mathscr{C}$ is the set of circuits of a matroid. Estimate computational complexity as a function of $|E|$ and $|\mathscr{C}|$.

6
The Matroid Greedy Algorithm

Let $M = (E, \mathscr{I})$ be a matroid whose elements e_i have been given weights $w(e_i) \geq 0$. We wish to find an independent set for which the sum of the weights of the elements is maximal.

Any weighting of the elements induces a lexicographic ordering on the independent sets. Thus, suppose

$$I_1 = \{a_1, \ldots, a_m\} \quad \text{and} \quad I_2 = \{b_1, b_2, \ldots, b_n\}$$

are two independent sets, where the elements are listed in order of weight, i.e., $w(a_1) \geq w(a_2) \geq \ldots w(a_m)$ and $w(b_1) \geq w(b_2) \geq \ldots \geq w(b_n)$. Then we say that I_1 is *lexicographically greater* than I_2 if there is some k such that $w(a_i) = w(b_i)$, for $1 \leq i \leq k - 1$ and $w(a_k) > w(b_k)$ or else $w(a_i) = w(b_i)$, for $1 \leq i \leq n$ and $m > n$. A set which is not lexicographically less than any other set is said to be *lexicographically maximum*. Clearly, such a lexicographically maximum independent set must be a base, and if all element weights are distinct this base is unique.

Theorem 6.1 (*Rado, Edmonds*) Let $\mathscr{I}$ be the family of independent sets of a matroid. Then:

(6.1) For any nonnegative weighting of the elements in E, a lexicographically maximum set in $\mathscr{I}$ has maximum weight.

Conversely, if $M = (E, \mathscr{I})$ is a finite structure satisfying (3.1) and (6.1), then M is a matroid.

PROOF Let $\mathscr{I}$ be the family of independent sets of a weighted matroid. Let B be a lexicographically maximum base and let $I = \{a_1, a_2, \ldots, a_m\}$ be any other independent set, where the elements are indexed in order of weight, i.e., $w(b_1) \geq w(b_2) \geq \ldots \geq w(b_n)$ and $w(a_1) \geq w(a_2) \geq \ldots \geq w(a_m)$. It cannot be the case that $w(b_k) < w(a_k)$, for any k. For then consider the independent sets

$$B_{k-1} = \{b_1, b_2, \ldots, b_{k-1}\}$$
$$I_k = \{a_1, a_2, \ldots, a_k\}.$$

By (3.2), the set $\{b_1, b_2, \ldots, b_{k-1}, a_i\}$, for some i, $1 \leq i \leq k$, is an independent set, and is lexicographically greater than B. This contradicts the assumption that B is lexicographically maximum. It follows that $w(b_p) \geq w(a_p)$ for all p, and B is clearly a maximum weight independent set.

Conversely, suppose M is not a matroid. Then, by Theorem 5.1 there must be a subset $A \subseteq E$ and two maximal subsets I and I' of A in $\mathscr{I}$, where $|I| < |I'|$. Let each element in I have weight $1 + \varepsilon$, where $\varepsilon > 0$ is small, each element in $I' - I$ have weight 1, and each of the remaining elements in E have zero weight. Then I is contained in a lexicographically maximum set whose weight is less than that of I'. Hence (6.1) does not hold. //

The proof of Theorem 6.1 suggests that a lexicographically maximum base has an even more impressive property than that of simply having maximum weight. Such a base is element-by-element weightier than any other independent set. That is, if B is a lexicographically maximum base and I is any other independent set, then the weight of the kth largest element of B is at least as great as that of the kth largest element of I, for all k. We shall say that a set B in $\mathscr{I}$ is *Gale optimal in $\mathscr{I}$* if, for any other set I in $\mathscr{I}$ there exists a one-to-one mapping $h: I \to B$ such that $w(e) \le w(h(e))$, for all e in I. (Note that, by this definition, only bases can be Gale optimal.)

Theorem 6.2   (*Gale*)   Let $\mathscr{I}$ be the family of independent sets of a matroid. Then:

(6.2)   For any weighting of the elements in E, there exists a set B which is Gale optimal in $\mathscr{I}$.

Conversely, if $M = (E, \mathscr{I})$ is a finite structure satisfying (3.1) and (6.2), then M is a matroid.

PROOF   The proof uses essentially the same reasoning as that for Theorem 6.1. (Note that a Gale-optimal set must be lexicographically maximal.) //

Theorems 6.1 and 6.2 show that a lexicographically maximal base is of maximal weight (if weights are nonnegative), and is Gale optimal. A lexicographically maximal base can be found by the matroid greedy algorithm. Namely, *choose the elements of the matroid in order to size, weightiest element first, rejecting an element only if its selection would destroy independence of the set of chosen elements.* The problem of applying the greedy algorithm to any particular matroid thus reduces to the problem of being able to decide whether or not any given set is independent. This issue, and some applications, are dealt with in later sections.

In the case that some element weights are negative and one seeks a maximum-weight independent set, the greedy algorithm is applied to the point where only negative elements remain, and all of these are rejected. This is equivalent to applying the greedy algorithm to the matroid obtained by deleting negative elements.

There are several possible variations of the greedy algorithm. We postpone mentioning these until we have discussed matroid duality.

PROBLEM

6.1   Show that when the greedy algorithm has chosen k elements, these k elements are of maximum weight with respect to all independent sets of k or fewer elements.

7

Applications of the Greedy Algorithm

Recall the problems discussed in Section 2.

A "SEMIMATCHING" PROBLEM

The elements of the matrix W are elements of a partition matroid and their weights are equal to their numerical values. The independent sets of the matroid contain at most one element from each row of W.

A SEQUENCING PROBLEM

The jobs to be processed are elements of a transversal matroid and their weights are the penalty values. This transversal matroid has a simple structure, so that testing for independence is particularly easy (cf. Section 6, Chapter 5).

THE MAXIMAL SPANNING TREE PROBLEM

The video links are elements of a graphic matroid. The problem of testing for independence is equivalent to the problem of testing a subset of arcs for the existence of a cycle. In Section 10 we see that the naive greedy algorithm for this case can be improved upon.

In addition to these problems consider the following application of the greedy algorithm to a matric matroid.

EXPERIMENTAL DESIGN

An agronomist knows that n minerals are important for improving the production of a certain crop. He assumes that there is a linear relation between the amount of minerals added to the soil and the improvement in crop yield. Specifically, the added yield Y is given by the formula

$$Y = a_1 x_1 + a_2 x_2 + \ldots + a_n x_n,$$

where x_i is the amount of the ith mineral applied in the form of chemical fertilizers. His problem is to design a set of experiments to determine the coefficients $a_1, a_2, \ldots, a_n$.

Suppose that the agronomist can make a number of separate experiments, each with a different commercially available fertilizer. Fertilizer

j contains a_{ij} units of mineral i and its application to a standard test plot costs c_j dollars. What is the least costly choice of fertilizers that will enable the agronomist to determine the coefficients a_i?

The various fertilizers correspond to the columns of the matrix $A = (a_{ij})$. The agronomist must choose a subset of columns which has rank n. But if he chooses for his experiment a subset of the columns which is linearly dependent, he is doing more than is necessary to determine the desired information (assuming the accuracy of the model and disregarding experimental error); the production for at least one of the fertilizers could have been predicted from the production of the others. Thus, what he seeks is a linearly independent subset of n columns, for which the sum of the c_j's is as small as possible.

Let column j have "weight" $w_j = W - c_j$ where W is suitably large. Then the problem is to find a lexicographic maximum set of linearly independent columns. The testing of linear independence can be carried out quite systematically, using Gaussian elimination. The following procedure can be used.

GREEDY ALGORITHM FOR MATRIC MATROIDS

Step 0   (*Start*)   Order the columns of the matrix so that the largest is at the left and the smallest at the right, i.e., $w_1 \geq w_2 \geq \ldots \geq w_n$. Set $k = 1$.

Step 1   (*Elimination*)

(1.1)   If column k is zero, go to Step 1.2. Otherwise, choose any nonzero entry in the column, say a_{ik}, and use it to eliminate nonzero entries to the right, i.e., subtract a_{ij}/a_{ik} times column k from each column $j > k$.
(1.2)   If $k < n$, set $k = k + 1$ and return to Step 1.1. Otherwise, stop. The nonzero columns are identified with an optimal base, and the number of such nonzero columns is equal to the rank of the matrix. //

PROBLEMS

7.1   Find a maximum-weight linearly independent subset of columns for the real matrix below:

$$\begin{bmatrix} 1 & 0 & 2 & 0 & 1 \\ 0 & -1 & -1 & 1 & 1 \\ 3 & 2 & 8 & 1 & 4 \\ 2 & 1 & 5 & 0 & 2 \end{bmatrix}$$

Weights   10   9   8   4   1

7.2   Estimate the computational complexity of the greedy algorithm for matric matroids.

8
Matroid Duality

For any given matroid $M = (E, \mathscr{I})$, there is a *dual* matroid $M^D = (E, \mathscr{I}^D)$, in which each base of M^D is the complement of a base (a *cobase*) of M, and vice versa. The circuits of M^D are called *cocircuits* of M, and vice versa.

Theorem 8.1   If $M = (E, \mathscr{I})$ is a matroid, then $M^D = (E, \mathscr{I}^D)$ is a matroid.

PROOF   Axiom (3.1) is clearly satisfied by M^D. Moreover, $\mathscr{I}^D \neq \varnothing$ since $\varnothing \in \mathscr{I}^D$. Let I_p, I_{p+1} be two sets in $\mathscr{I}^D$ containing p, $p + 1$ elements, respectively. Let B_p, B_{p+1} be bases of M disjoint from I_p, I_{p+1}, respectively.

Case 1   Suppose $I_{p+1} - (I_p \cup B_p) \neq \varnothing$. Let $e \in I_{p+1} - (I_p \cup B_p)$. Then $I_p + e$ is disjoint from B_p, $I_p + e \in \mathscr{I}^D$ and axiom (3.2) holds.

Case 2   Suppose $I_{p+1} - (I_p \cup B_p) = \varnothing$. We first wish to show that $B_{p+1} - (B_p \cup I_p)$ is nonempty. Assume $B_{p+1} - (B_p \cup I_p) = \varnothing$, i.e., $B_{p+1} \subseteq B_p \cup I_p$. Then we have the relations

$$(B_{p+1} - I_p) \cup (I_{p+1} - I_p) \subseteq B_p,$$

$$(B_{p+1} \cap I_p) \cup (I_{p+1} \cap I_p) \subseteq I_p,$$

from which it follows that

$$B_{p+1} \cup I_{p+1} \subseteq B_p \cup I_p$$

and

$$|B_{p+1}| + p + 1 \leq |B_p| + p \leq |B_{p+1}| + p,$$

which is a contradiction. Hence $B_{p+1} - (B_p \cup I_p) \neq \varnothing$.

Now choose any element $e \in B_{p+1} - (B_p \cup I_p)$. $B_p + e$ contains a unique circuit in M. Let e' be any element of this circuit other than e. The set $B'_p = B_p + e - e'$ is a base of M disjoint from I_p. If $I_{p+1} - (I_p \cup B'_p) \neq \varnothing$, then Case 1 applies. If $I_{p+1} - (I_p \cup B'_p) = \varnothing$, then repeat the argument with B'_p in the role of B_p until a base B'_p is obtained such that $I_{p+1} - (I_p \cup B'_p) \neq \varnothing$. This must occur in a finite number of iterations or else we will run out of elements in $B_{p+1} - (B_p \cup U_p)$. //

Theorem 8.2   The rank functions of a matroid M and its dual M^D are in the relation

$$r^D(A) = |A| + r(E - A) - r(E) \qquad (8.1)$$

for all $A \subseteq E$.

PROOF   The rank of A in M^D is determined by a base of M with a minimum number of elements in A. The maximum cardinality of an independent set of M, disjoint from A, is $r(E - A)$. Such a set is contained in a base with $r(E)$ elements, of which $r(E) - r(E - A)$ are contained in A. The number of elements in A not contained in this base is $|A| + r(E - A) - r(E)$. //

In the special case of a graphic matroid M, the dual matroid M^D is said to be *cographic*. If the graph is connected, the spanning trees of the graph are bases of M, and the cotrees are bases of M^D. The cycles of the graph are circuits of M and the cocycles are circuits of M^D. (Note that it is not necessarily true that a cocycle is the complement of a cycle, nor is it necessarily true for a matroid that the complement of a circuit is a co-circuit.) If the graph has n nodes, m arcs, and p components, the number of elements in a base of M is $n - p$ and in a base of M^D is $m - n + p$. In terms of the two rank functions,

$$r(E) = n - p$$
$$r^D(E) = m - n + p$$
$$= |E| - r(E).$$

The more general relation (8.1) holds for an arbitrary set of arcs A.

Thus, there are two matroids associated with every graph G, a graphic matroid M and a cographic matroid M^D. If the graph G has a dual G^D, then the roles of M and M^D are reversed for G^D: M^D is the graphic matroid of G^D and M is the cographic matroid. This is consistent with our knowledge that each cycle of G is a cocycle of G^D, and vice versa.

What if G does not have a dual? Then the graphic matroid M is not the cographic matroid of any graph, and the cographic matroid M^D is not graphic. *A necessary and sufficient condition for a graph to be planar is that its graphic matroid be cographic or, equivalently, that its cographic matroid be graphic.* (Note that this statement is of no particular help in testing graphs for planarity; testing a graphic matroid for cographicness is essentially the same problem as testing for the existence of a dual graph.)

Now consider the relation between the operations of deletion and contraction when performed on a matroid and its dual. Given a subset of elements $S \subseteq E$, the *deletion* of the elements S from $M = (E, \mathscr{I})$ yields the matroid M del $S = (E - S, I')$, where $\mathscr{I}'$ contains all subsets $I' \subseteq E - S$ which belong to $\mathscr{I}$, i.e., all subsets $I' \subseteq E - S$ such that $r(I') = |I'|$. The *contraction* of the elements S yields the matroid M ctr $S = (E - S, \mathscr{I}'')$, where $\mathscr{I}''$ contains all subsets $I'' \subseteq E - S$ such that $r(I'' \cup S) = |I''| + r(S)$. The application of the deletion operation to a matroid corresponds to contraction operation on its dual, and vice versa.

Theorem 8.3 For any matroid $M = (E, \mathscr{I})$ and subset $S \subseteq E$

$$(M \text{ del } S)^D = M^D \text{ ctr } S,$$

$$(M \text{ ctr } S)^D = M^D \text{ del } S.$$

PROOF   Omitted. //

    This theorem is illustrated for a planar graph in Figure 7.4. We note that in this case $G \text{ del } \{a, b\}$ and $G^D \text{ ctr } \{a, b\}$ are indeed graphical duals.
    The following theorem illustrates still further relations between a matroid and its dual.

Theorem 8.4   (*Minty*) Let E be an arbitrary finite set of elements and $\mathscr{C}$ and $\mathscr{D}$ be two families of subsets of E. $\mathscr{C}$ and $\mathscr{D}$ contain circuits of a dual pair of matroids if and only if the following conditions are satisfied:

(1)   No set in $\mathscr{C}$ contains another properly; no set in $\mathscr{D}$ contains another properly.

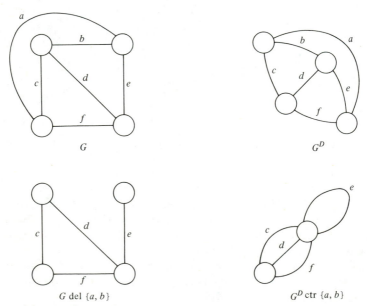

G

G^D

$G \text{ del } \{a, b\}$

$G^D \text{ ctr } \{a, b\}$

Figure 7.4   Example of contraction and deletion

(2)   For any $C \in \mathscr{C}$ and any $D \in \mathscr{D}$, their intersection does not contain exactly one element, i.e., $|C \cap D| = 0, 2, 3, \ldots$.

(3)   For any painting of the elements of E red, yellow, and green, with exactly one element painted yellow, precisely one of the following conditions holds:

(a) There is a set in $\mathscr{C}$ containing the yellow element, but no red ones (i.e., a yellow-green circuit) or

(b) There is a set in $\mathscr{D}$ containing the yellow element, but no green ones (i.e., a yellow-red cocircuit).

We shall not prove this theorem, but merely observe its relation to the more specialized painting theorem for undirected graphs. The matroid properties observed in the theorem have been used by Minty as the basis for a self-dual axion system for matroids. Systems $(E, \mathscr{C}, \mathscr{D})$ which satisfy the properties of the theorem he calls *graphoids*.

PROBLEMS

8.1 Prove that if C and D are a circuit and a cocircuit of the same matroid, then $|C \cap D| \neq 1$.

8.2 What type of matroid is the dual of a partition matroid? What is the effect of contraction on a partition matroid?

9

Variations of the Greedy Algorithm

Suppose, for some ordering of the elements of E, A is a lexicographic maximum base. Then $E-A$ is a lexicographic minimum cobase. It is clear that solving a maximization problem for the primal matroid also solves a minimization problem for the dual matroid; a greedy algorithm for the primal corresponds to an "abstentious" algorithm for the dual, and vice versa.

Each element which is discarded by the greedy algorithm is the smallest element of at least one circuit of the matroid. For suppose $A = e_1, e_2, \ldots, e_k$ have already been chosen by the greedy algorithm, but $A + e_{k+1}$ is found to be dependent, and e_{k+1} is therefore discarded. Since A is independent and $A + e_{k+1}$ is dependent, it follows that e_{k+1} forms a circuit with some subset of the elements of A, and all of these elements are known to be larger than e_{k+1}, because of the order of processing. Similarly, each element which is discarded by the abstentious algorithm applied to the dual matroid is known to be the largest element of at least one cocircuit of the primal matroid.

These duality relations have been noted by various authors, particularly Rosenstiehl, who made the following observation about spanning-tree computations. All algorithms for computing the maximum spanning tree of a graph are governed by two principles:

(9.1)   No arc of the maximum spanning tree is the smallest arc of any cycle of the graph.

(9.2)   Each arc of the maximum spanning tree is the largest arc of at least one cocycle of the graph.

For matroids in general, we can formulate a computational procedure which requires only the construction of circuits and/or cocircuits. For example, consider the following procedure.

VARIANT OF GREEDY ALGORITHM

Step 0   (Start)   Set $A = A' = \emptyset$, $B = E$. (A and A' are to contain elements of the optimal set and its complement; B is to contain elements about which no decision has been made.)

Step 1   (Selection of Elements)   Perform either one of the following steps in any order:

(1.1)   Try to find a circuit of elements in $A \cup B$. If a circuit C exists, move the smallest element of C from B to A'. Otherwise (if no circuit exists), move the remaining elements of B to A, and stop.

(1.2)   Try to find a cocircuit of elements in $A' \cup B$. If a cocircuit D exists, move the largest element of D from B to A. Otherwise (if no cocircuit exists), move the remaining elements of B to A', and stop. //

A further variation makes use of the deletion and contraction operations. For example, the following can be substituted for Steps 1.1 and 1.2 in the previous algorithm.

(1.1)   Try to find a circuit of elements of B. If a circuit C exists, move the smallest element of C from B to A' and delete the element from the matroid. Otherwise, move the remaining elements of B to A, and stop.

(1.2)   Try to find a cocircuit of elements of B. If a cocircuit D exists, move the largest element of D from B to A and contract the element in the matroid. Otherwise, move the remaining elements of B to A', and stop. //

Such questions as to whether it is easier to construct circuits and cocircuits, or to perform deletions and contractions, or to work with the matroid or its dual, must be determined for the particular problem at hand.

The properties of matroid greedy algorithms are useful for proving and interpreting various theorems of graph theory and other mathematical specialties. For example, consider the following theorem: Let B_1 and B_2 be minimal or maximal (in total number of arcs) basis systems of the vector cycles of a graph G. Then there exists a length-preserving mapping ψ of the set of cycles $C_1, \ldots, C_{v(G)}$ of B_1 onto the set of cycles $C'_1, \ldots, C'_{v(G)}$ of B_2. (Here $v(G)$ is the cyclomatic number of the graph.) This theorem was proved by Stepanets by finding a complete matching in a certain bipartite graph that he assigns to a pair of bases of vector cycles. However, the same result could have been obtained quite easily by noting that the extremal bases can be obtained by the greedy algorithm, and that the greedy algorithm has the property that the kth largest element selected always has the same size, regardless of how ties are resolved in the course of the algorithm.

PROBLEM

9.1   For a given graph G, to what matroid should the greedy algorithm be applied, in order to obtain an extremal basis of vector cycles?

10

Prim Spanning Tree Algorithm

Since every graphic matroid is matric, the matric greedy algorithm described in Section 7 can be used for maximal spanning tree computations, by operating on the node-arc incidence matrix of the graph. However, this would imply an $O(n^4)$ computation for the complete graph on n nodes, whereas an $O(n^2)$ computation is possible.

A procedure proposed by Prim constructs a larger and larger set of optimally connected nodes. This set of nodes we denote by the letter P, to correspond with the permanently labeled set of nodes in Dijkstra's related shortest path computation, described in Chapter 3. The complement of the set P is denoted T.

We begin with an arbitrary node in the set P, and find the heaviest arc between this node and any of the nodes in T. This node is added to the solution, and the node k at the other end of the arc is added to P. We then compare, for each node i in T, the weight of the arc (i, k) with the weight of the heaviest arc from i to any other node in P, as previously recorded, and then find the maximum weight of all arcs extending between T and P. This yields us the heaviest arc in the (T, P)-cutset, and this arc is brought into the solution. The T-node to which this arc is incident then becomes node k; it is added to the set P and the process is repeated.

The Prim algorithm is as follows.

MAXIMAL SPANNING TREE ALGORITHM (PRIM)

Step 0   (Start)   The connected graph $G = (N, A)$ is given, with a weight w_{ij} for each arc $(i, j) \in A$.
    Set $i(j) = 1$ and $u_j = w_{1j}$, for $j = 2, 3, \ldots, n$.
    Set $P = \{1\}$, $T = \{2, 3, \ldots, n\}$.
    Set $S = \varnothing$.

Step 1   (Addition of Arc to Tree)   Find $k \in T$, where $u_k = \max\limits_{j \in T} \{u_j\}$.
    Set $T = T - k$, $P = P + k$.
    Set $S = S + (i(k), k)$.
    If $T = \varnothing$, stop; the arcs in S form a maximal spanning tree.

Step 2   (Revision of Labels)   For all $j \in T$, if $w_{kj} > u_j$, set $u_j = w_{kj}$ and $i(j) = k$. Go to Step 1. //

PROBLEMS

10.1   Verify that the Prim algorithm is $O(n^2)$ in complexity for a complete graph. Estimate its complexity as a function of n and $m = |A|$.

10.2   Apply the Prim algorithm, step by step, to the network in Figure 7.1.

11

An Application: Flow Network Synthesis

An interesting application of maximal spanning tree computations has been found in flow network synthesis. Suppose we are given a symmetric $n \times n$ matrix $R = (r_{ij})$ of *flow requirements*. We shall call a network *feasible* if it is possible to induce a flow of value v_{ij} between nodes i and j, where $v_{ij} \geq r_{ij}$. A problem which suggests itself is that of constructing a feasible network which minimizes some prescribed function of the arc capacities c_{ij}, e.g.,

$$\sum_{i,j} a_{ij} c_{ij},$$

where a_{ij} may be thought of as the cost of providing one unit of capacity in an arc between i and j.

The above is a linear programming problem, and can be solved by applying the dual simplex method to a system of $2^n - 1$ linear inequalities of the form,

$$\sum_{\substack{i \in S \\ j \in T}} c_{ij} \geq \max_{\substack{i \in S \\ j \in T}} \{r_{ij}\},$$

one for each cutset (S, T) of the network. Gomory and Hu have suggested a computational procedure that does not require an explicit enumeration of these constraints. We shall not discuss this general synthesis problem here. Instead, we shall describe the simpler version of the problem which arises when all the a_{ij}'s are equal.

The Gomory-Hu procedure will be illustrated by reference to the following requirements matrix.

$$R = \begin{bmatrix} 0 & 4 & 9 & 1 & 3 \\ 4 & 0 & 6 & 5 & 3 \\ 9 & 6 & 0 & 1 & 2 \\ 1 & 5 & 1 & 0 & 7 \\ 3 & 3 & 2 & 7 & 0 \end{bmatrix} \qquad (11.1)$$

NETWORK SYNTHESIS ALGORITHM (GOMORY AND HU)

Step 1 (*Dominant Requirement Tree*)   Let r_{ij} represent the weight of the arc (i, j) in a graph on the n nodes and solve the maximal spanning-tree problem. The resulting tree is called the *dominant requirement tree*. (The dominant requirement tree for (11.1) is shown in Figure 7.5.)

Step 2 (*Decomposition of Dominant Requirement Tree*)   Decompose the dominant requirement tree into a "sum" of a "uniform" requirement tree plus a remainder, by subtracing the smallest in-tree requirements. Decompose each remaining nonuniform tree in the same way, until the tree is expressed as a sum of uniform requirement subtrees. (For the example, this results in the decomposition shown in Figure 7.6.)

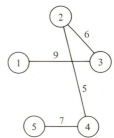

Figure 7.5   Dominant requirement tree

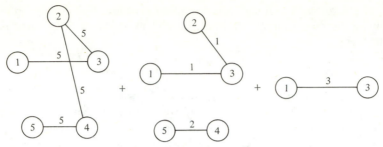

Figure 7.6   Decomposition of dominant requirement tree

Step 3   (*Cycle Synthesis*)   Synthesize each uniform tree of the decomposition as a cycle through its nodes, in any order. Each arc of a cycle has capacity equal to one half of the uniform requirement. (See Figure 7.7.) Superpose the resulting cycles to form the final network and add the corresponding arc capacities. (See Figure 7.8.) Each arc of the final network corresponds to an arc of the required capacity in each direction. (The final network for the example is shown in Figure 7.9.) //

To justify the algorithm, it is first necessary to prove that the final network is feasible, and then that it is optimal. To do the latter, note that for any feasible network,

$$\sum_{j} c_{ij} \geq \max_{j} \{r_{ij}\}, \quad i = 1, 2, \ldots, n.$$

That is, the sum of the capacities of arcs incident from any node i must be at least as great as the maximum of the flow requirements out from i.

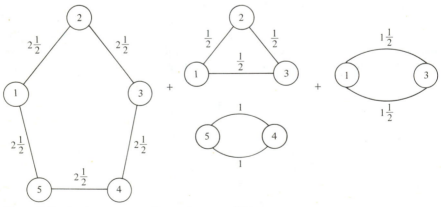

Figure 7.7   Cycles corresponding to decomposition

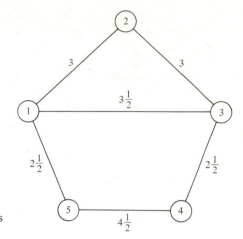

Figure 7.8 Superposition of cycles

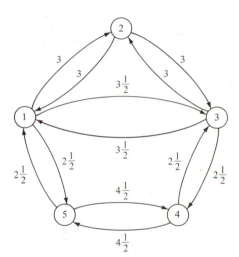

Figure 7.9 Final network

Yet this inequality is satisfied with equality for the network synthesized by the algorithm. Therefore, the network is optimal.

The final network is not unique, because of the different trees which may be obtained in Step 1, and the many different choices of cycles in Step 3. However, any one of the networks which results from the algorithm is optimal.

PROBLEMS

11.1 Prove that the final network is indeed feasible.

11.2 Of all the minimal capacity networks which can be obtained from the construction, there is one whose flow function dominates all others. That is, there is a network G^* such that

$$v_{ij}^* \geq v_{ij},$$

where v_{ij} is the flow function of any other feasible, minimal capacity network. Show that this dominant network can be obtained by applying the algorithm to a requirements matrix R^*, where

$$r_{ij}^* = \min \{\max_k r_{ik}, \max_k r_{kj}\}$$

$$\geq r_{ij}.$$

12
The Steiner Problem and Other Dilemmas

We have seen that the minimal spanning tree problem can be solved in $O(n^2)$ steps. However, a problem which appears to be closely related has resisted solution in a polynomial-bounded number of steps. The *Steiner Problem* is to find a minimum length tree which spans n given points in the Euclidean plane. Such a minimum tree, called a *Steiner tree*, may contain nodes other than the points which are to be spanned; these are called *Steiner points*. Consider the situation in Figure 7.10, in which the points to be connected (indicated by double circles) are at the corners of a unit square.

The Steiner Problem has been solved for three points. Let the three points to be spanned be denoted A, B, and C. A fourth point P is sought so that the sum $a + b + c$ is a minimum, where a, b, c denote the three distances from P to A, B, and C, respectively. If in the triangle ABC all angles are less than $120°$, then P is the point from which each of the three sides, AB, BC, CA subtends an angle of $120°$. If, however, an angle of ABC, e.g., the angle at C, is equal to or greater than $120°$, then the point P coincides with the node C.

The generalization of these ideas to more than three points appears to be difficult.

A problem which is easier (at least because it can be solved by enumeration) is the *Steiner network problem*. Here n specified nodes of an

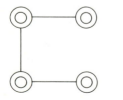
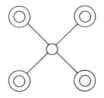

Figure 7.10   Steiner problem for unit square

$(n + s)$-node weighted graph are to be spanned by a tree of minimum weight. The tree may include any of the other s nodes as Steiner points.

The Steiner network problem (or semi-Steiner problem, as it is sometimes called) has an interesting matroid interpretation. Let T be a tree with $n - 1$ arcs spanning the n specified nodes. (If the network does not contain such a tree, add sufficient arcs to the network and give them very large weights.) The problem can now be formulated as follows. In the graphic matroid of the network, find a minimum-weight independent set I such that $\mathrm{sp}\,(I) \supseteq \mathrm{sp}\,(T)$.

Although no polynomial-bounded algorithm for the Steiner network problem is known, we are able to describe two algorithms, where one is polynomial in n, the number of nodes to be spanned, and the other is polynomial in s, the number of possible Steiner points. Thus, if one holds s constant and increases n, or vice-versa, the number of computational steps grows as a polynomial function.

We present first an algorithm which is polynomial in n and exponential in s. It is based on the idea that one can solve a minimal spanning tree problem for each of several possible choices of Steiner points.

Lemma 12.1 Suppose the arc lengths a_{ij} of a network satisfy the metric requirement, i.e., they are nonnegative and

$$a_{ij} \le a_{ik} + a_{kj},$$

for all i, j, k. Then, for any n points to be spanned, there exists a Steiner tree in the network which contains no more than $n - 2$ Steiner points.

PROOF Let p denote the number of Steiner points in a minimal tree. Let x denote the mean number of tree arcs incident to a Steiner point, and y denote the mean number of tree arcs incident to the n points to be spanned. The number of arcs in the tree is

$$n + p - 1 = \frac{px + ny}{2},$$

but, because of the metric condition, $x \ge 3$; and certainly $y \ge 1$. It follows that

$$n + p - 1 \ge \frac{3p + n}{2}$$

and

$$p \le n - 2.\,//$$

We now have a way (although not a very good one) to solve the Steiner network problem. We illustrate the algorithm by reference to the

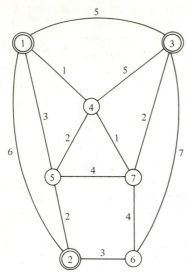

Figure 7.11   Example network

network in Figure 7.11. The nodes 1, 2, and 3 are to be connected; the remaining nodes are possible Steiner points.

STEINER NETWORK ALGORITHM

Step 1 (*Shortest Path Computation*)   If the arc weights do not satisfy the metric conditions, compute shortest paths between all pairs of nodes, and replace the arc weights with shortest path lengths, adding arcs to the network where necessary.

In the example, we have as the original arc lengths,

$$
\begin{array}{c c c c c c c c}
 & 1 & 2 & 3 & 4 & 5 & 6 & 7 \\
1 & \infty & 6 & 5 & 1 & 3 & \infty & \infty \\
2 & 6 & \infty & \infty & \infty & 2 & 3 & \infty \\
3 & 5 & \infty & \infty & 3 & \infty & 7 & 2 \\
4 & 1 & \infty & 3 & \infty & 2 & \infty & 1 \\
5 & 3 & 2 & \infty & 2 & \infty & \infty & 4 \\
6 & \infty & 3 & 7 & \infty & \infty & \infty & 4 \\
7 & \infty & \infty & 2 & 1 & 4 & 4 & \infty
\end{array}
$$

These distances do not satisfy the conditions of a metric, so we solve the shortest path problem for all pairs of nodes, which yields as arc lengths

$$
\begin{array}{c c}
 & \begin{array}{c c c c c c c} 1 & 2 & 3 & 4 & 5 & 6 & 7 \end{array} \\
\begin{array}{c} 1 \\ 2 \\ 3 \\ 4 \\ 5 \\ 6 \\ 7 \end{array} &
\begin{bmatrix}
1 & 5 & 4 & 1 & 3 & 6 & 2 \\
5 & 0 & 7 & 4 & 2 & 3 & 5 \\
4 & 7 & 0 & 3 & 5 & 6 & 2 \\
1 & 4 & 3 & 0 & 2 & 5 & 1 \\
3 & 2 & 5 & 2 & 0 & 5 & 3 \\
6 & 3 & 6 & 5 & 5 & 0 & 4 \\
2 & 5 & 2 & 1 & 3 & 4 & 0
\end{bmatrix}
\end{array}
$$

Step 2 (*Minimum Spanning Tree Computation*)   For each possible subset of $n - 2$ or fewer Steiner points, solve a minimal spanning tree problem.

In the case of the example, there are five spanning tree problems to solve, as follows:

Problem	Nodes to be Spanned	Weight of Minimum Spanning Tree
(1)	(1, 2, 3)	9
(2)	(1, 2, 3, 4)	8
(3)	(1, 2, 3, 5)	9
(4)	(1, 2, 3, 6)	12
(5)	(1, 2, 3, 7)	9

Step 3 (*Construction of Steiner Tree*)   Select the least costly spanning tree from among those computed in Step 2, and transform it into a tree of the original network, i.e., replace each arc of the spanning tree with the arcs of the shortest path between the nodes in question.

The least costly tree obtained in Step 2 is shown in Figure 7.12, and the Steiner tree is shown in Figure 7.13. //

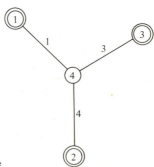

Figure 7.12   Minimum cost tree

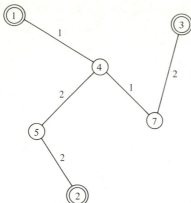

Figure 7.13   Final netowrk

The preceding algorithm requires the solution of a minimal spanning-tree problem on no more than $2n - 2$ nodes for each of σ choices of Steiner points, where

$$\sigma = \sum_{i=0}^{n-2} \binom{s}{i} \le 2^s.$$

It follows that the overall computational complexity is no worse than $O(n^2 2^s)$, which is polynomial in n, as claimed. (This does not count the shortest path computation of Step 1 which is $O(n + s)^3).)$

We now present a computational method due to Dreyfus and Wagner, where the number of computational steps is polynomial in s and exponential in n. This method employs a recursive relation between the length of an optimal Steiner tree for a given subset of nodes and the lengths of optimal Steiner trees for smaller subsets. Or, in other words, having obtained optimal Steiner trees for all subsets of $1, 2, \ldots, p - 1$ nodes, we shall be able to use these trees to construct optimal Steiner trees for subsets of p nodes. Finally, we shall be able to construct an optimal Steiner tree for the set N itself.

Let N be the set of nodes to be spanned and S be the set of possible Steiner points, where $|N| = n$, $|S| = s$. Let $K \subseteq N$ and $i \in N \cup S$. (Thus $K + i$ contains at most one node from S.) Let

$T(K + i) =$ the length of an optimal Steiner tree spanning the set $K + i$.

$T_i(K) =$ the length of an optimal Steiner tree spanning $K + i$, subject to the constraint that i is an interior node of the tree, i.e., the degree of node i is at least 2.

We first note a simple functional relationship for $T_i(K)$. Since node i is to be an interior node, an optimal Steiner tree spanning $K + i$ is the union of two subtrees, one of which is an optimal Steiner tree for $K' + i$ and another that is an optimal Steiner tree for $(K - K') + i$, where K' is a nonempty proper subset of K. (See Figure 7.14.) By minimizing over all possible choices of K', we have

$$T_i(K) = \min_{\varnothing \subset K' \subset K} \{T(K' + i) + T(K - K' + i)\}. \qquad (12.1)$$

Now let us obtain a functional relationship for $T(K + i)$. Assume Lemma 12.1 applies. There are three possible cases for an optimal Steiner tree spanning $K + i$:

Case 1   Node i is an interior node of the tree. In this case, $T(K + i) = T_i(K)$.

Case 2   Node i is a leaf of the tree, and the only arc incident to node i is (i, j), where $j \notin K$. Node j is a Steiner point in an optimal Steiner tree for $K + i$, and has degree at least three, by Lemma 12.1. The tree for $K + i$ is thus composed of the arc (i, j) plus an optimal Steiner tree for $K + j$, where it is known that j is an interior point. In this case, $T(K + i) = a_{ij} + T_j(K)$.

Case 3   Node i is a leaf of the tree and the only arc incident to node i is (i, j), where $j \in K$. In this case, $T(K + i) = a_{ij} + T(K)$.

Putting these observations together, and minimizing over all alternatives, we obtain

$$T(K + i) = \min \begin{Bmatrix} \min_{j \notin K} \{a_{ij} + T_j(K)\} \\ \min_{j \in K} \{a_{ij} + T(K)\} \end{Bmatrix}. \qquad (12.2)$$

(Note that Case 1 is accounted for by $j = i \notin K$, where $a_{ii} = 0$.)

Equations (12.1) and (12.2), together with appropriate initial conditions, e.g., $T(\varnothing) = 0$, imply a straightforward computation for $T(N)$,

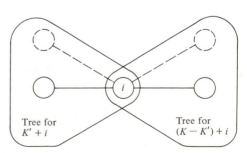

Figure 7.14   Steiner tree for $K + i$

with no implicit functional relationships. Let us consider how much work is involved. The number of additions and comparisons occasioned by equations (12.1) is of the same order as the number of possible choices of i, K, and K'. Each of the n nodes in N belongs to exactly one of the three sets K, K', or $N - K$. Hence the number of computational steps attributable to (12.1) is $O((n + s) \, 3^n)$.

There are $(n + s) \, 2^n$ equations of the form (12.2). Each equation involves minimization over at most $n + s$ alternatives. Hence the computation attributable to equations (12.2) is $O((n + s)^2 \, 2^n)$.

Thus, the overall computation is $O((n + s) \, 3^n + (n + s)^2 \, 2^n)$, which is polynomial in s, as claimed. (An initial shortest path computation which is $O((n + s)^3)$ may be required, so that Lemma 12.1 applies, and the final solution transformed into the original set of arcs, as in the previous algorithm.)

In addition to the Steiner problem, it is possible to cite a number of other unsolved problems concerning trees and forests of networks. Among these are the *degree-constrained spanning-tree* problem, about which we will have more to say in a later chapter. There are several versions of the *star-forest problem*. A *star tree* is a tree which contains at most one node of degree greater than unity. One may wish to find a forest of star trees which is minimal with respect to the sum of the arc weights of the trees, plus the sum of certain node weights assigned to their "centers."

PROBLEM

12.1 Show that, for fixed n, the first algorithm given in this section is also polynomial in s, by establishing a bound of $O(n^2 s^{n-2})$.

COMMENTS AND REFERENCES

SECTIONS 1, 3, 5
The original paper of Whitney

H. Whitney, "On the Abstract Properties of Linear Dependence," *Amer. J. Math.,* **57** (1935) 509–533.

is very much worth reading today and highly recommended.

Some books on matroid theory are

W. T. Tutte, *Introduction to the Theory of Matroids,* American Elsevier, New York, 1971.

H. H. Crapo and G.-C. Rota, *On the Foundations of Combinatorial Theory: Combinatorial Geometries,* (preliminary edition). The M.I.T. Press, Cambridge, Mass., 1970.

R. von Randow, *Introduction to the Theory of Matroids,* Lecture notes in Economics and Math. Systems, 109, Springer-Verlag, Berlin and New York, 1975.

D. J. A. Welsh, *Matroids and Their Applications,* in preparation.

> Crapo and Rota feel that the term "matroid" is "ineffably cacaphonic" and prefer the term "pregeometry." Essentially matroid-like structures have been studied under still other names, e.g., "geometric lattices." See

G. Birkhoff, *Lattice Theory,* Amer. Math. Soc. Colloq. Publ. 25, 1940, 1948, 1967.

> Several of the papers of a conference on matroid theory are published in a single issue of the *Journal of Research of the National Bureau of Standards.* For example,

W. T. Tutte, "Lectures on Matroids," *J. Res. NBS,* **69B** (1965) 1–48.

> Another conference proceedings is

C. P. Bruter, editor, *Théorie des Matroides,* Springer-Verlag, New York, 1971.

> Some matroid papers of interest include

W. T. Tutte, "Matroids and Graphs," *Trans. Amer. Math. Soc.,* **90** (1959) 527–552.

D. J. A. Welsh, "On Dependence in Matroids," *Can. Math. Bull.,* **10** (1967) 599–603.

F. Harary and D. J. A. Welsh, "Matroids Versus Graphs," *The Many Facets of Graph Theory,* G. Chartrand and S. F. Kapoor, editors, Springer-Verlag, New York, 1969, pp. 155–170.

C. A. Holzmann and F. Harary, "On the Tree Graph of a Matroid," *SIAM J. Appl. Math.,* **22** (1972) 187–193.

SECTION 4
Matching, transversal and partition matroids were introduced in

J. Edmonds and D. R. Fulkerson, "Transversals and Matroid Partition," *J. Res. NBS* **69B** (1965) 147–153.

SECTION 6
Edmonds applied the term "greedy algorithm" to Kruskal's procedure for constructing optimal spanning trees, and announced the extension of the procedure to arbitrary matroids at least as early as 1967 at the International Symposium on Mathematical Programming, Princeton, New Jersey. See

J. Edmonds, "Matroids and the Greedy Algorithm," *Mathematical Programming,* **1** (1971) 127–136.

> The matroid generalization of Kruskal's algorithm was made independently by Gale and by Welsh:

D. Gale, "Optimal Assignments in an Ordered Set: An Application of Matroid Theory," *J. Combinatorial Theory,* **4** (1968) 176–180.

D. J. Welsh, "Kruskal's Theorem for Matroids," *Proc. Cambridge Phil. Soc.,* **64** (1968) 3–4.

The greedy algorithm has been generalized to infinite matroids

V. Klee, "The Greedy Algorithm for Finitary and Cofinitary Matroids," *Combinatorics* (Proc. Sympos. Pure Math., Vol. XIX), Amer. Math. Soc., Providence, Rhode Island, pp. 137–152.

The theorem on vector cycles mentioned at the end of the section is due to

G. F. Stepanets and G. E. Vieduts, "A Method of Describing Algorithmically the Cyclic Structure of a Graph," *Zh. Vych. Mat. i Mat. Fiz.*, **3** (1963) 585–586; trans: *USSR Comp. Math.* **3** (1963) 781–786; Abstract: *Math. Reviews,* **27** (1963) 381.

G. F. Stepanets, "Basis Systems of Vector Cycles with Extremal Properties in Graphs," *Uspehi Mat. Nauk,* **19** (1964) 171–175; abstracts: Ref. *Z. L. Math,* No. 12A267 (1964), and *Math. Review,* **30** (1965) 484.

Stepanets work was cited in

J. Turner and W. H. Kautz, "A Survey of Progress in Graph Theory in the Soviet Union," *SIAM Rev.,* **12** (1970), suppl., iv + 68pp.

SECTION 8
An excellent discussion of matroid duality can be found in the intriguing paper

G. J. Minty, "On the Axiomatic Foundations of the Theories of Directed Linear Graphs, Electrical Networks, and Network Programming," *J. Math. and Mechanics,* **15** (1966) 485–520.

SECTION 9
An investigation of the role of graphic duality in variations of the spanning tree algorithm, on which this section is based, is

P. Rosenstiehl, "L'Arbre Minimum d'un Graphe," in *Theory of Graphs,* P. Rosenstiehl, editor, Gordon and Breach, New York, 1967

who cites

G. Choquet, "Etude de Certains Reseaux de Route," *C. R. Ac. Sc.,* **206** (1938), 310.

SECTION 10
The greedy algorithm for the spanning tree problem was presented in

J. B. Kruskal, Jr., "On the Shortest Spanning Subtree of a Graph and the Traveling Salesman Problem," *Proc. Amer. Math. Soc.,* **7** (1956) 48–50.

Kruskal cited the earlier work on the same problem by

O. Boruvka, "On a Minimal Problem," *Prace Moravske Predovedecke Spolecrosti,* **3** (1926).

Prim's procedure is given in

R. C. Prim, "Shortest Connection Networks and Some Generalizations," *Bell System Tech. J.*, **36** (1957) 1389–1401.

The same procedure was devised independently by Dijkstra:

E. W. Dijkstra, "A Note on Two Problems in Connexion with Graphs," *Numerische Mathematik*, **1** (1959) 269–271.

The running time for finding optimal spanning trees can be reduced to $O(m \log \log n)$, which is a substantial improvement in the case of sparse graphs. See

A. C.-C. Yao, "An $O(|E| \log \log |V|)$ Algorithm for Finding Minimum Spanning Trees," *Info. Processing Letters*, **4** (1975) 21–25.

D. Cheriton and R. E. Tarjan, "Finding Minimum Spanning Trees," to appear in *SIAM J. Comput.*

SECTION 11

The network synthesis procedure is due to

R. E. Gomory and T. C. Hu, "Multi-terminal Network Flows," *SIAM J. Appl. Math.*, **9** (1961) 551–570.

SECTION 12

For various results on the Steiner problem, and related topics, see

R. Courant and H. Robbins, *What is Mathematics?*, Oxford University Press, New York, 1941, pp. 354–361.

Z. A. Melzak, "On the Problem of Steiner," *Canad. Math. Bull.*, **4** (1961) 143–148.

F. P. Palermo, "A Network Minimization Problem," *IBM J. Res. Dev.*, **5**, (1961) 335–337.

E. N. Gilbert, "Random Minimal Trees," *SIAM J. Appl. Math.* **13** (1965) 376–387.

M. Hanan, "On Steiner's Problem with Rectilinear Distances," *SIAM J. Appl. Math.*, **14** (1966) 255–265.

E. N. Gilbert and H. O. Pollak, "Steiner Minimal Trees," *SIAM J. Appl. Math.*, **16** (1968) 1–29.

E. J. Cockayne, "On the Steiner Problem," *Can. Math. Bull.* **10** (1969) 431–450.

S. E. Dreyfus and R. A. Wagner, "The Steiner Problem in Graphs," *Networks*, **1** (1972) 195–207.

M. R. Garey, R. L. Graham, and D. S. Johnson, "Some NP-Complete Geometric Problems," *Proceedings Eighth Annual ACM Symposium on Theory of Computing*, Assoc. for Computing Mach., New York, 1976, pp. 10–22.

EIGHT

Matroid Intersections

1
Introduction

The greedy algorithm is an efficient method for computing a maximum weight independent set of a single given matroid. The comparable problem for two matroids is as follows. Given $M_1 = (E, \mathscr{I}_1)$ and $M_2 = (E, \mathscr{I}_2)$, two matroids over the same weighted set E, find a maximum weight *intersection* $I \in \mathscr{I}_1 \cap \mathscr{I}_2$. In this chapter we are concerned with the development of efficient computational procedures for solving such intersection problems.

It is a simple matter to show that the bipartite matching problem is a matroid intersection problem involving two partition matroids over the set of arcs of the given bipartite graph. Since network flow problems are reducible to bipartite matching problems, it follows that matroid intersection theory provides a generalization not only of bipartite matching theory but of network flow theory as well.

It is perhaps not surprising that the augmenting path methods of bipartite matching are suggestive of a similar procedure for matroid intersection problems. The notion of an "augmenting sequence" is introduced in Section 3 of this chapter, and an efficient procedure for solving the "cardinality" intersection problem is described in Section 4. This procedure yields a constructive proof of a duality theorem which generalizes the König-Egervary theorem of bipartite matching.

Interestingly, the cardinality intersection problem is equivalent to a matroid "partitioning" problem, as follows. Given k matroids, $M_1 = (E, \mathscr{I}_1), M_2 = (E, \mathscr{I}_2), \dots, M_k = (E, \mathscr{I}_k)$ over the same set E, does there exist a partitioning of E into k sets $I_1, I_2, \dots, I_k$, where $I_i \in \mathscr{I}_i$, for $i = 1, 2, \dots, k$? The relationship between the cardinality intersection problem and the partitioning problem is discussed in Section 7, and an efficient partitioning algorithm due to Edmonds is presented.

Two different methods for solving the weighted intersection problem are presented. A "primal" algorithm, based on the notion of weighted augmenting sequences, is described in Sections 9 and 10. This algorithm is analogous to the procedure of Busacker, Gowan and Jewell for finding minimum cost network flows. A "primal-dual" algorithm is described in Sections 13 and 14. This method is analogous to the Hungarian method for finding maximum weight matchings.

2

Problem Formulations

Let us consider some examples of matroid intersection problems.

BIPARTITE MATCHING

Let $G = (S, T, A)$ be a given bipartite graph. Let π_1 be a partition of A which places two arcs in the same block if and only if they are incident to the same S-node. Similarly, let π_2 be defined by the T-node incidence relationships. Let $M_1 = (A, \mathscr{I}_1)$ and $M_2 = (A, \mathscr{I}_2)$ be partition matroids determined by the partitions π_1 and π_2. A subset $I \subseteq A$ is a matching in G if and only if I is an intersection of M_1 and M_2.

The nonbipartite matching problem can be formulated as an intersection problem involving two partition matroids, but with additional constraints in the form of symmetry conditions. The construction parallels that used in Chapter 6 to show equivalence to the symmetric assignment problem. In the next chapter we shall show how the nonbipartite matching problem can be formulated as a matroid problem with "parity conditions."

MATRIC MATROID INTERSECTION

Let C be an $m \times n$ matrix. Suppose a horizontal line is drawn through C so that there are m_1 rows above the line and m_2 below. We can speak of a subset of the columns as being linearly independent both "above the line" and "below the line." In other words, the projections of those columns are independent in an "upper" m_1-dimensional space, and also in a "lower" m_2-dimensional space. Any such subset of columns is an intersection of two matric matroids.

COMMON TRANSVERSALS

A set of elements that is a transversal of each of two different families of subsets is known as a *common transversal* of those families. Clearly, the computation of a common transversal is a problem involving the intersection of two transversal matroids. Just as in the case of bipartite matching, specialized methods have been developed for this problem.

A NETWORK SYNTHESIS PROBLEM

Suppose $G_1 = (N_1, A)$ and $G_2 = (N_2, A)$ are two connected graphs constructed from the same set of arcs A. A subset $I \subseteq A$ is an intersection of the two cographic matroids if and only if the arcs in $A\text{-}I$ form connected subgraphs in both G_1 and G_2.

Suppose, as in Chapter 7, a broadcasting network wishes to rent video links to connect together various cities. Except now we shall complicate the situation (perhaps quite artificially). Each month there is a different set of cities to be connected, as broadcasting stations enter and leave the network. (These changes are known for some time in advance.) Moreover, each video link can be rented for a single month at one rate or for two consecutive months at a cost somewhat less than twice the single-month rate. The network wishes to plan the rental of video links for several months in advance so as to minimize the total rental charges.

The problem can be formulated in the following manner. For month t construct a multigraph $G(t) = (N(t), A(t))$ as follows. The nodes in $N(t)$ represent cities to be connected together that month. There may be as many as three arcs joining each pair of cities i and j in $N(t)$, depending upon whether or not i and j also appear in $N(t-1)$ and $N(t+1)$. One arc, which appears in $G(t)$ only, is assigned a cost equal to the single-month rental for that particular link. Another arc joins the same two cities in $N(t-1)$ and is assigned a cost equal to the two-month rental. Still another arc joins the same two cities in $N(t+1)$ and is also assigned a cost equal to the two-month rental.

Treat $N(1), N(2), \ldots$ as disjoint sets of nodes. Let G_1 be the graph obtained by taking the union of $G^{(1)}, G^{(3)}, \ldots, G^{(2k+1)}$ and let G_2 be obtained by taking the union of $G^{(2)}, G^{(4)}, \ldots, G^{(2k)}$. The network synthesis problem becomes a weighted intersection problem involving cographic matroids of G_1 and G_2. The reader should be able to fill in the details.

As a simple example, consider the two-period problem indicated in Figure 8.1. The number shown with each arc e_i, $i = 1, 2, \ldots, 14$, is its rental cost. If the arc appears in the network for both time periods, the rental cost is for two periods. If an arc appears in the network for the first time period, but not in the network for the second, it can be considered to be a self-loop in the second network, and vice versa. The problem of finding a minimum cost subset of arcs connecting all cities in both time periods can be solved by the algorithm given in Section 10.

PAINTING A GRAPH

We wish to paint each arc of a given graph G either red, white, or blue, subject to the constraint that not all the arcs of any cycle are painted the same color. Depending upon the graph, it may or may not be possible to paint the graph in this manner.

An equivalent formulation of this problem calls for a partitioning of the arcs into three forests. Create a graph G^* which is the union of three copies of G, i.e., a "red," a "white," and a "blue" copy. There are thus three copies of each of the m arcs of G, one in each copy of the graph. Let M_1 be the graphic matroid of G^* and let M_2 be a partition matroid over the $3m$ arcs. Each independent set of M_2 contains no more than one copy of each of the arcs of G. There exists a feasible painting of G if and only if there exists an m-element intersection of M_1 and M_2.

Assuming that a feasible painting exists, an optimization problem

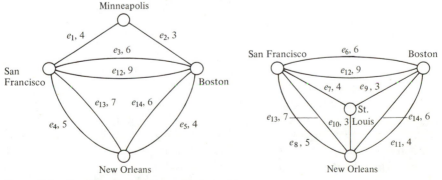

Figure 8.1   Example of network synthesis problem

can be defined as follows. For each arc (i, j) let there be three parameters r_{ij}, w_{ij}, b_{ij} indicating the number of quarts of red, white, and blue paint, respectively required to paint that arc. What painting requires the smallest total amount of paint? The reader should have no difficulty in formulating this as a weighted intersection problem.

DIRECTED SPANNING TREES

Let $G = (N, A)$ be an arc-weighted directed graph. Suppose we wish to find a maximum weight spanning tree directed from a prescribed root node with in-degree zero. Any subset of arcs I forming such a tree must satisfy two conditions. First, it must contain no cycle. Hence I must be an independent set of the graphic matroid of G (in which the directions of the arcs are ignored). Second, it must contain no more than one arc *into* any given node. Hence I must be an independent set of the partition matroid which is defined by a partition of the arcs which places all the arcs directed into a given node in the same block. A directed spanning tree exists if and only if there is an $(n - 1)$-element intersection of these two matroids. (Actually, testing for the existence of such a spanning tree is quite simple, see Problem 14.1.)

A weighted version of the directed spanning tree problem is the following: A military commander wishes to form a directed tree, rooted from himself, for the propagation of orders to all the men under his command. (Edmonds has called such an organization a "branchocracy.") There is a weight associated with each directed arc that indicates its desirability for use in such a tree. What directed tree is optimum?

It turns out that this particular matroid intersection problem permits an especially simple and elegant method of solution, which is described in Section 14.

THE TRAVELING SALESMAN PROBLEM

Supoose we wish to find a Hamiltonian cycle in a given graph G. Create an $(n + 1)$st node, and let each arc directed into node 1 be redirected into node $n + 1$. There exists a Hamiltonian circuit in G if and only if there exists a path from node 1 to node $n + 1$ which passes through each of the other nodes exactly once.

Let M_1 be the graphic matroid of the $(n + 1)$-node graph. Let M_2 be a partition matroid whose independent sets contain no more than one arc directed *into* any given node and M_3 be a partition matroid whose independent sets contain no more than one arc directed *out of* any given node. There exists a Hamiltonian cycle in the n-node graph G if and only if there exists an n-element intersection of M_1, M_2, and M_3.

The formulation of the traveling salesman problem as a problem calling for a maximum weight intersection of M_1, M_2, and M_3 should be evident.

Unfortunately, there is no known polynomial-bounded algorithm for computing optimal intersections of three or more matroids. The traveling salesman problem, the three-dimensional assignment problem, and others like them, are beyond the scope of the methods described in this chapter.

PROBLEMS

2.1 Formulate the three-dimensional assignment problem as a problem involving the intersection of three matroids.

2.2 A university department chairman must recommend the appointment of a departmental representative to each of m interdepartmental committees. For each faculty member, he has a list of the committees for which that person is qualified and interested. However, before solving the bipartite matching problem which is implied by these data, it occurs to the chairman that he should limit the number of committee appointments within each rank, i.e., no more than m_1 appointees should be assistant professors, no more than m_2 should be associate professors, and no more than m_3 should be full professors. Formulate the problem of obtaining a feasible assignment as a cardinality intersection problem (with two matroids).

2.3 Try to solve "by inspection" the network problem illustrated in Figure 8.1.

3

Augmenting Sequences and Border Graphs

Bipartite matching algorithms solve intersection problems involving two partition matroids. These algorithms can be generalized to solve intersection problems involving arbitrary pairs of matroids. Our first task in generalizing the bipartite matching algorithms is to find an appropriate generalization of the idea of an augmenting path.

Let I be any intersection of two matroids, M_1 and M_2. We can construct an "augmenting sequence" with respect to I as follows. The first element e_1 of such a sequence is such that $I + e_1$ is independent in M_1. If $I + e_1$ is independent in M_2 as well, the sequence is completed. Otherwise $I + e_1$ contains a unique circuit in M_2 and we choose e_2 to be an element other than e_1 in that circuit. $I + e_1 - e_2$ is clearly independent in both M_1 and M_2. Now we try to find an element e_3 such that $I + e_1 - e_2 + e_3$ is independent in M_1, whereas $I + e_3$ is not. Such an element e_3 is in $\text{sp}_1(I) - \text{sp}_1(I - e_2)$, where "$\text{sp}_1$" denotes span in M_1. If $I + e_1 - e_2 + e_3$ is independent in M_2, we are done. Otherwise $I + e_1 - e_2 + e_3$

contains a unique circuit in M_2 and we choose e_4 to be an element in that circuit, and so on.

In other words, the addition to I of the 1st, 3rd, 5th, ... elements preserves independence in M_1 but creates dependence in M_2, whereas the removal of the 2nd, 4th, 6th, ... elements restores independence in M_2. This manner of playing off independence in M_1 against independence in M_2 is quite analogous to the way that we played off incidence of arcs to nodes in one part of a bipartite graph against incidence of the same arcs to nodes in the other part in the construction of an augmenting path in the matching problem.

These ideas may become clearer by actually working out an example. Each of the multigraphs G_1 and G_2 shown in Figure 8.2 is constructed from the same arcs $E = \{e_1, e_2, ..., e_8\}$. We wish to find the largest possible subset of arcs which contains a cycle in neither G_1 nor G_2. In other words, we wish to solve the cardinality intersection problem for the graphic matroids of G_1 and G_2.

Note that $I = \{e_4, e_5\}$ is a *maximal* intersection, since the addition of any single arc to I creates a cycle in either G_1 or G_2. For example, $I = e_1$ contains the cycle $C_1 = \{e_1, e_4\}$ in G_1, $I + e_2$ contains the cycle $C_2 = \{e_2, e_4\}$ in G_2, and so on. However, I is not a *maximum-cardinality* intersection, as we shall see.

One can carry out a search for an "augmenting sequence" with respect to I, by growing "alternating trees," much as in the case of bipartite matching. Each node of these trees corresponds to a matroid element, i.e., one of the arcs of G_1, G_2. Each tree is rooted to an element e_i such that $e_i \in E - \mathrm{sp}_1(I)$, i.e., e_i can be added to I without forming a cycle in G_1. There are three trees, rooted to e_2, e_7, and e_8, respectively. Each tree will

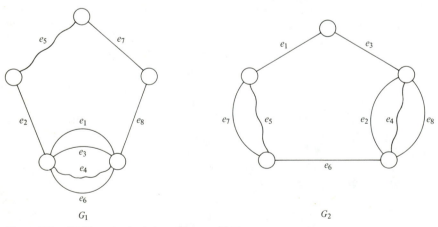

Figure 8.2   Multigraphs for intersection problem

be constructed in such a way that any path from the root will pass through an alternation of nodes, corresponding to elements in I and not in I.

Now consider how the trees can be extended from each of the roots e_2, e_7, e_8. The addition of arc e_2 forms a cycle in G_2, the cycle containing the arcs e_2 and e_4. Thus, if arc e_2 is added to I, arc e_4 must be removed. Accordingly, we extend the tree rooted to e_2 by adding an arc leading to e_4. The addition of arc e_7 forms a cycle containing arcs e_5 and e_7 in G_2, so if arc e_7 is added to I, e_5 must be removed. Accordingly, we extend the tree rooted to e_7 by adding an arc leading to e_5. The addition of arc e_8 forms a cycle containing arcs e_4 and e_8 in G_2. But e_4 is already in the tree rooted to e_2, so we do not extend the tree rooted to e_8.

Now consider the effect in G_1 of removing either one of the arcs e_4 or e_5 from I. Removing arc e_4 permits any one of the arcs e_1, e_3, or e_6 to be added to I without forming a cycle in G_1. Accordingly, we extend the tree by adding arcs leading from e_4 to e_1, e_3, e_6. On the other hand, removing arc e_5 does not permit any arc to be added to I without forming a cycle in G_1, other than arcs which already appear in the tree. Therefore, the tree is not extended beyond the arc e_5. The situation is now as shown in Figure 8.3.

We now consider the effect in G_2 of adding any one of the arcs e_1, e_3, e_6. The addition of any one of these arcs to I does not form a cycle in G_2. By tracing back to the root of the tree from e_1, e_3, e_6, we identify three distinct augmenting sequences (e_2, e_4, e_1), (e_2, e_4, e_3), and (e_2, e_4, e_6). Arbitrarily choosing the first of these, we augment I by adding arcs e_2 and e_1 and removing arc e_4 to obtain a new intersection $I = \{e_1, e_2, e_5\}$. This new intersection is indicated by wavy lines in Figure 8.4.

The repetition of the tree construction process for the new set

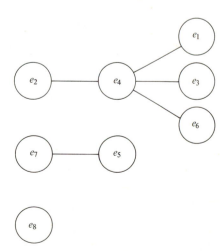

Figure 8.3   Alternating trees

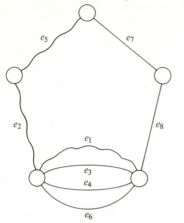

Figure 8.4   Augmented intersections

$I = \{e_1, e_2, e_5\}$ yields the alternating trees shown in Figure 8.5. No aug-menting sequences are discovered, and we assert that $I = \{e_1, e_2, e_5\}$ is a maximum-cardinality intersection.

We note that arcs e_2, e_5 of I are in the Hungarian trees in Figure 8.5, but arc e_1 is not. Now,

$$\mathrm{sp}_1(\{e_1\}) = \{e_1, e_3, e_4, e_6\}$$

and

$$\mathrm{sp}_2(\{e_2, e_5\}) = \{e_2, e_4, e_5, e_7, e_8\}$$

so that

$$\mathrm{sp}_1(\{e_1\} \cup \mathrm{sp}_2(\{e_2, e_5\})) = E.$$

We will show in Section 5 that these two spans constitute an optimal solution for a covering problem dual to the intersection problem for which $I = \{e_1, e_2, e_5\}$ is optimal.

We are now prepared to formalize some of these ideas. Let I be an intersection of two matroids $M_1 = (E, \mathscr{I}_1)$ and $M_2 = (E, \mathscr{I}_2)$. Let $S =$

Figure 8.5   Hungarian trees

$(e_1, e_2, \ldots, e_s)$ be a sequence of distinct elements, where $e_i \in E - I$, for i odd, and $e_i \in I$, for i even. Let $S_i = (e_1, e_2, \ldots, e_i)$, for $i \leq s$. We say that S is an *alternating sequence* with respect to I if

(3.1) $I + e_1 \in \mathscr{I}_1$.

(3.2) For all even i, $\mathrm{sp}_2(I \oplus S_i) = \mathrm{sp}_2(I)$. Hence $I \oplus S_i \in \mathscr{I}_2$.

(3.3) For all odd $i > 1$, $\mathrm{sp}_1(I \oplus S_i) = \mathrm{sp}_1(I + e_1)$. Hence $I \oplus S_i \in \mathscr{I}_1$.

If, in addition,

(3.4) $|S| = s$ is odd and $I \oplus S \in \mathscr{I}_2$, we say that S is an *augmenting sequence* with respect to I.

It is clear that if an intersection admits an augmenting sequence, then that intersection does not contain a maximum number of elements. The converse, however, is not so evident. In order to facilitate the study of this and other related questions, we introduce the notion of the "border graph" of an intersection.

For a given intersection I, the *border graph* $BG(I)$ is a directed bipartite graph constructed as follows. For each node $e_i \in E - I$ such that $e_i \in \mathrm{sp}_1(I)$, there is an arc (e_j, e_i) directed *from* each $e_j \in C_i^{(1)} - e_i$, where $C_i^{(1)}$ is the unique M_1-circuit in $I + e_i$. If $e_i \notin \mathrm{sp}_1(I)$, then e_i is a *source* in $BG(I)$ (in-degree zero). For each node $e_i \in E - I$ such that $e_i \in \mathrm{sp}_2(I)$, there is an arc (e_i, e_j) directed *to* each $e_j \in C_i^{(2)} - e_i$, where $C_i^{(2)}$ is the unique M_2-circuit in $I + e_i$. If $e_i \notin \mathrm{sp}_2(I)$, then e_i is a *sink* in $BG(I)$ (out-degree zero).

We shall have occasion to refer to two special subgraphs of $BG(I)$. The subgraph $BG_1(I)$ contains all arcs directed from I to $E - I$ and subgraph $BG_2(I)$ contains all arcs directed from $E - I$ to I. These subgraphs indicate incidences of elements in $E - I$ with M_1-circuits and M_2-circuits, respectively. We call $BG_1(I)$, $BG_2(I)$ *simple border graphs*.

The border graph for the intersection $I = \{e_4, e_5\}$ of the example is shown in Figure 8.6. Note that e_2, e_7, e_8 are sources, and e_1, e_3, e_6 are sinks. Each of the augmenting sequences (e_2, e_4, e_1), (e_2, e_4, e_3), (e_2, e_4, e_6) is identified with a directed path from a source to a sink. The reader should be able to pick out other source-sink paths which also yield augmenting sequences.

It is true that every augmenting sequence is identified with a source-sink path in $BG(I)$, However, the converse is not true. A source-sink path (without repetition of nodes) does not necessarily yield an augmenting sequence. One way to insure that a path does yield an augmenting sequence is to require that it admit no shortcuts.

Suppose that S is a source-sink path in $BG(I)$ and S passes through

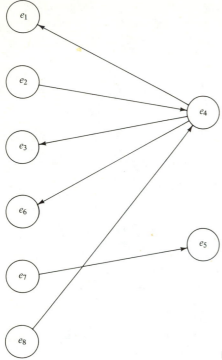

Figure 8.6   Border graph for example

nodes $e_1, e_2, \ldots, e_s$. The path is said to admit a *shortcut* if there exists an arc (e_k, e_j) in $BG(I)$, where $1 \leq k \leq j - 2 \leq s - 2$.

In the statement of the lemma which follows, and in other discussions concerning border graphs, we shall use the terms "element" and "node" interchangeably. We shall let a path be defined by the sequence of nodes through which it passes, e.g., $S = (e_1, e_2, \ldots, e_s)$ is the path from e_1 to e_s, passing through intermediate nodes $e_2, e_3, \ldots, e_{s-1}$. Thus, we may say that a source-sink path S "is" an augmenting sequence.

Lemma 3.1   (*Krogdahl*)   If S is a source-sink path in $BG(I)$ which admits no shortcut, then S is an augmenting sequence with respect to I.

PROOF   Without loss of generality, let $S = (e_1, e_2, \ldots, e_s)$. Since e_1 is a source, $I + e_1 \in \mathscr{I}_1$ and (3.1) holds.

Now let i be even. We wish to show that $\text{sp}_2(I \oplus S_i) = \text{sp}_2(I)$. We shall do this by dealing with pairs of elements in "reverse" order, i.e., first adding e_{i-1} to I and deleting e_i, then adding e_{i-3} and deleting e_{i-2}, and finally adding e_1 and deleting e_2. As an aid in visualizing the process, consider the subgraph of $BG_2(I)$ induced on $S_i = (e_1, e_2, \ldots, e_i)$. Because

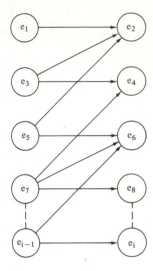

Figure 8.7   Subgraph of $BG_2(I)$ in proof of Lemma 3.1

S admits no shortcuts, when this subgraph is drawn as in Figure 8.7, there are no arcs directed downward. That is, $e_j \notin C_k^{(2)}$, for any odd $j, k, j < k$.

$I + e_{i-1}$ contains the unique M_2-circuit $C_{i-1}^{(2)}$, where $e_i \in C_{i-1}^{(2)}$. Hence $sp_2(I + e_{i-1} - e_i) = sp_2(I)$. By inductive hypothesis, assume $sp_2(I^{(k)}) = sp_2(I)$, where $I^{(k)} = I + e_k - e_{k+1} + e_{k+2} - \dots + e_{i-1} - e_i$. $I^{(k)} + e_{k-2}$ contains a unique M_2-circuit. Moreover, this circuit is $C_{k-2}^{(2)}$, because $C_{k-2}^{(2)} \subseteq I^{(k)} + e_{k-2}$. It follows that $sp_2(I^{(k-2)}) = sp_2(I)$. Hence $sp_2(I^{(1)}) = sp_2(I)$, where $I^{(1)} = I \oplus S_i$ and condition (3.2) holds.

The proof for condition (3.3) is, of course, similar. //

Lemma 3.2   (*Krogdahl*)   Let I, J be intersections such that $|I| + 1 = |J|$. There exists a source-sink path S in $BG(I)$, where $S \subseteq I \oplus J$.

PROOF   If J contains an element e_1 that is not in $sp_1(I) \cup sp_2(I)$, then e_1 is both a source and a sink in $BG(I)$ and $S = (e_1)$ is the desired path. So assume $J \subseteq sp_1(I) \cup sp_2(I)$.

Partition $J - I$ into three sets J_1, J_2, J_3, consisting of the sources, the sinks, and the other elements in $J - I$. Consider now the subgraph $H_1 \subseteq BG_1(I)$ induced on the nodes in $I \oplus J$. Each node in $J_2 \cup J_3$ has nonzero in-degree in H_1. Moreover, for any subset $J' \subseteq J_2 \cup J_3$, there are at least $|J'|$ nodes in $I - J$ with arcs directed to nodes in J', because J' cannot be spanned in M_1 by fewer than $|J'|$ elements in $I - J$. For the moment, ignore the directions on arcs in H_1 so as to consider H_1 to be an undirected graph. We have shown that the conditions of the well-known Philip Hall theorem (Theorem 7.2) have been satisfied in such a way as to guarantee the existence of a matching X_1 in H_1 which covers all the nodes in $J_2 \cup J_3$.

J–I   I–J

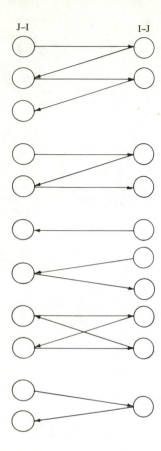

Figure 8.8   Typical components of H in proof of Lemma 3.2

Similarly, we can form the subgraph $H_2 \subseteq BG_2(I)$ induced on the nodes in $I \oplus J$ and show that there is a matching X_2 in H_2 covering all the nodes in $J_1 \cup J_3$.

Now consider the subgraph $H \subseteq BG(I)$ with node set $I \oplus J$ and arc set $X_1 \cup X_2$ (with the directions of the arcs restored). Each connected component of H is either a directed path or a directed cycle. (See Figure 8.8.) Since $|J - I| > |I - J|$, at least one component must contain one more node in $|J - I|$ than in $|I - J|$. Such a component is the desired source-sink path S in $BG(I)$. //

If S is a source-sink path in $BG(I)$, then there exists a source-sink path $S' \subseteq S$, where S' admits no shortcuts. The path S' is obtained from S by simply "shortcutting" S until no further shortcuts remain. This observation, together with Lemmas 3.1 and 3.2, enable us to establish the following theorems.

Theorem 3.3 Let I_p, I_{p+1} be intersections of M_1, M_2 with p, $p + 1$ elements, respectively. Then there exists an augmenting sequence $S \subseteq I_p \oplus I_{p+1}$ with respect to I_p.

Theorem 3.4 An intersection is of maximum cardinality if and only if it admits no augmenting sequence.

Theorem 3.5 For any intersection I there exists a maximum cardinality intersection I^*, such that $sp_1(I) \subseteq sp_1(I^*)$ and $sp_2(I) \subseteq sp_2(I^*)$.

PROOF The definition of augmenting sequences is such that $sp_1(I) \subseteq sp_1(I \oplus S)$, $sp_2(I) \subseteq sp_2(I \oplus S)$. Apply this result and Theorem 3.4 transitively. //

4
Cardinality Intersection Algorithm

The essential ideas of the cardinality intersection algorithm should now be clear. In fact, the attentive reader should be able to write down the steps of the algorithm for himself.

Any "breadth-first" labeling procedure that fans out from source nodes in $BG(I)$ will find a source-sink path without shortcuts, if such a path exists. The usual method for constructing alternating trees, as described informally in the previous section, is equivalent to such a procedure.

CARDINALITY INTERSECTION ALGORITHM

Step 0 (Start) Let I be any intersection of M_1, M_2, possibly the empty set. No elements are labeled.

Step 1 (Labeling)

(1.0) For each element $e_i \in E - I$, find $C_i^{(1)}$, $C_i^{(2)}$, if these circuits exist. Apply the label "$\varnothing^+$" to each element $e_i \in E - sp_1(I)$.

(1.1) If all labels have been scanned, go to Step 3. Otherwise, find the element e_i with the oldest unscanned label. If the label is a "$+$" label go to Step 1.2; if it is a "$-$" label, go to Step 1.3.

(1.2) Scan the "$+$" label on e_i as follows. If $I + e_i \in \mathscr{I}_2$, go to Step 2. Otherwise, give the label "i^-" to each unlabeled element in $C_i^{(2)}$. Return to Step 1.1.

(1.3) Scan the "$-$" label on e_i by giving the label "i^+" to each unlabeled element e_j such that $e_i \in C_j^{(1)}$. Return to Step 1.1.

Step 2 (*Augmentation*)   An augmenting sequence S has been discovered, of which e_i (found in Step 1.2) is the final element. Identify the elements in S by backtracing from the label on e_i. Augment I by adding to I all elements in the sequence with "$+$" labels and removing from I all elements with "$-$" labels. Remove all labels from elements and return to Step 1.0.

Step 3 (*Hungarian Labeling*)   No augmenting sequence exists and I is of maximum cardinality. The labeling is "Hungarian" and can be used to construct a minimum-rank covering dual to I. (See Section 5.) Halt. //

Let us now estimate the complexity of the algorithm. Suppose the ranks of the matroids M_1, M_2 are R_1, R_2, respectively, and let $R = \min \{R_1, R_2\}$. Thus, no intersection can contain more than R elements and there can be no more than R augmentations.

Assume there are subroutines available for independence testing in M_1, M_2. Suppose the running times of these subroutines are $c_1(m)$, $c_2(m)$, respectively, where $m = |E|$. Let $c(m) = \max \{c_1(m), c_2(m)\}$. For each augmentation, and each subsequent application of the labeling procedure, there is a computation of $C_i^{(1)}$, $C_i^{(2)}$ for each $e_i \in E - I$. The running time for this task is no greater than $O(mRc(m))$.

The labeling procedure, exclusive of circuit computation, is $O(m^2)$ and backtracing, if an augmenting sequence is found, is $O(m)$. Since there are $O(R)$ applications of the labeling procedure, the overall running time of the algorithm is no greater than $O(m^2R + mR^2c(m))$.

In the case of bipartite matching in a graph with n nodes and m arcs, where m is $O(n^2)$, R can be taken to be $m^{1/2}$. The computation of the circuits $C_i^{(1)}$, $C_i^{(2)}$ is trivial, and can be ignored. ($C_i^{(1)}$ contains all arcs of the matching incident to the same S-node as arc e_i^1, $C_i^{(2)}$ all arcs incident to the same T-node.) The overall running time is $O(m^{2.5})$ or $O(n^5)$. The difference between $O(n^5)$ and $O(n^3)$, the running time for the conventional matching algorithm, is attributable to the fact that labels are applied to arcs of the graph rather than to nodes. This observation serves as an example of the value of exploiting the special structure which may exist for a particular problem.

PROBLEMS

4.1   Show that for the case of bipartite matching in G the border graph $BG(I)$ is the line graph of G, with an appropriate orientation of arcs. How does the orientation change with each augmentation?

4.2   Specialize the cardinality intersection algorithm to bipartite matching, writing down an explicit statement of the steps to be performed, using only graphical, not matroid, terminology.

4.3   Repeat Problem 4.2 for the intersection of the graphic matroids of two graphs G_1 and G_2.

5
Duality Theory

The cardinality intersection computation provides a constructive proof of a duality theorem for matroid intersections. This theorem is of the max-min variety, similar to the max-flow min-cut theorem of network flows and the König-Egervary theorem, of which it represents a proper generalization.

We say that a pair of subsets E_1, E_2 of E is a *covering* of E if $E_1 \cup E_2 = E$. With respect to a given pair of matroids M_1, M_2, we define the *rank* of a covering $\mathscr{E} = (E_1, E_2)$ to be $r(\mathscr{E}) = r_1(E_1) + r_2(E_2)$.

Lemma 5.1   For any covering $\mathscr{E}$ and any intersection I, $r(\mathscr{E}) \geq |I|$.

PROOF   Let $I_1 = I \cap E_1$, and $I_2 = I \cap (E_2 - E_1)$. Clearly $|I_1| \leq r_1(E_1)$ and $|I_2| \leq r_2(E_2)$ which implies $|I| = |I_1| + |I_2| \leq r(\mathscr{E})$. //

Theorem 5.2   (*Matroid Intersection Duality*)   For any two matroids M_1, M_2, the maximum cardinality of an intersection is equal to the minimum rank of a covering.

PROOF   By the lemma, the rank of a covering cannot be less than the cardinality of an intersection. The intersection algorithm enables us to construct a covering whose rank is equal to the cardinality of an intersection, as follows.

At the conclusion of the algorithm (when the labeling has become "Hungarian"), let the set I_L contain the elements of I that are labeled and I_U contain those which are not. Let $E_1 = \mathrm{sp}_1(I_U)$, $E_2 = \mathrm{sp}_2(I_L)$. Suppose $e_i \in E - I$. If e_i is labeled, then $e_i \in \mathrm{sp}_2(I_L)$, by Step 1.2 of the algorithm. (The scanning of e_i labels all elements in $C_i^{(2)} - e_i$. Hence $e_i \in \mathrm{sp}_2(C_i^{(2)} - e_i) \subseteq \mathrm{sp}_2(I_L)$.) If e_i is unlabeled, then $e_i \in \mathrm{sp}_1(I)$, by Step 1.0 and hence $e_i \in \mathrm{sp}_1(I_U)$, by Step 1.3. (The scanning of any labeled element in $C_i^{(1)} - e_i$ would label e_i. Hence $C_i^{(1)} \cap I_L = \varnothing$, $C_i^{(1)} - e_i \subseteq I_U$.) It follows that $e_i \in E_1 \cup E_2$ and $\mathscr{E} = (E_1, E_2)$ is a covering, with $r(\mathscr{E}) = |I|$. //

A duality theorem for the max-min intersection problem follows from Theorem 5.2 in exactly the same way that the duality theorem for the max-min bipartite matching problem is derived from the König-Egervary theorem.

Theorem 5.3   Let $M_1 = (E, \mathscr{I}_1)$, $M_2 = (E, \mathscr{I}_2)$ be any two matroids and $w(e)$ be any weighting of the elements. Then, for any k,

$$\max_I \min \{w(e) | e \in I, I \in \mathscr{I}_1 \cap \mathscr{I}_2, |I| = k\}$$
$$= \min_{A_1, A_2} \max \{w(e) | e \in E - (A_1 \cup A_2), r_1(A_1) + r_2(A_2) = k - 1\}.$$

PROOF   Let I^*, $|I^*| = k$, be an intersection which is max-min optimal with respect to all intersections containing k elements. Let e^* be such that

$$w(e^*) = \min \{w(e) \,|\, e \in I^*\},$$

and let

$$A^* = \{e \in E \,|\, w(e) > w(e^*)\}.$$

Clearly a maximum cardinality intersection contained within A^* has at most $k - 1$ elements, for otherwise I^* would not be optimal. It follows from Theorem 5.2 that A^* can be partitioned into two sets, A_1^*, A_2^* such that $r_1(A_1^*) + r_2(A_2^*) \leq k - 1$. (Apply the theorem to the two matroids after deleting all elements not in A^*.) But e^* is the element with largest weight not in $A_1^* \cup A_2^*$. Hence we have established that

$$\max_I \min \{w(e)\} \geq \min_{A_1, A_2} \max \{w(e)\}.$$

Conversely, let A_1^*, A_2^*, $r_1(A_1^*) + r_2(A_2^*) = k - 1$, be a min-max optimal solution to the dual covering problem. Let e^* be such that

$$w(e^*) = \max \{w(e) \,|\, e \in I - (A_1^* \cup A_2^*)\}.$$

It follows from Theorem 5.2 that a maximum-cardinality intersection contained within A^* has at most $k - 1$ elements. Thus, any intersection with k elements must contain at least one element not in A^*. At best this is e^*. Hence we have established that

$$\max_I \min \{w(e)\} \leq \min_{A_1, A_2} \max \{w(e)\}.$$

This establishes inequality in both directions and the proof is complete. //

PROBLEMS

5.1   For a bipartite matching over a graph $G = (S, T, A)$, a covering consists of two subsets of arcs E_1 and E_2, such that every arc in A either meets one of the arcs in E_1 at an S-node or one of the arcs in E_2 at a T-node. Obtain similar characterizations of coverings for each of the following types of matroid intersection problems:
(a) M_1 and M_2 are graphic matroids.
(b) The directed spanning tree problem.
(c) The common transversal problem.

5.2   Write out the steps of a max-min matroid intersection algorithm and estimate its complexity.

6

Generalized Mendelsohn-Dulmage Theorem,
Matroid Sums and Matroid Partitions

The Mendelsohn-Dulmage Theorem (Theorem 4.1, Chapter 5), generalizes to the case of matroid intersections as follows.

Theorem 6.1 (*Kundu and Lawler*) Let M_1, M_2 be two matroids on E, and I_1, I_2 two intersections. Then there exists an intersection $I \subseteq I_1 \cup I_2$ such that $\text{sp}_1(I) \supseteq \text{sp}_1(I_1)$ and $\text{sp}_2(I) \supseteq \text{sp}_2(I_2)$.

PROOF If $\text{sp}_2(I_1) \supseteq I_2$ there is nothing to prove. Let $e \in I_2 - \text{sp}_2(I_1)$, where $I_1 + e$ is in $\mathscr{I}_2$. If $I_1 + e$ belongs to $\mathscr{I}_1$ let $I'_1 = I_1 + e$. Otherwise, there exists a M_1-circuit C such that $e \in C \subseteq I_1 + e$. Now $C - e \nsubseteq I_1 \cap I_2$ is in $\mathscr{I}_1$. Choose $e' \in C \cap (I_1 - I_2)$ and define

$$I'_1 = I_1 - e' + e.$$

We have $I'_1 \in \mathscr{I}_1$ and $\text{sp}_1(I'_1) = \text{sp}_1(I_1)$ and also I'_1 is trivially independent in M_2, However,

$$|I'_1 \cap I_2| > |I_1 \cap I_2|.$$

Thus we can apply the same procedure to define $I_1^{(k)}$, $k = 1, 2, \ldots$ such that

$$\text{sp}_1(I_1^{(k)}) \supseteq \text{sp}_1(I_1), \qquad I_1^{(k)} \in \mathscr{I}_1 \cap \mathscr{I}_2$$

until $\text{sp}_2(I_1^{(k)}) \supseteq I_2$. Then $I = I^{(k)}$. //

Suppose θ_1 and θ_2 are two different criteria of optimality, such that

$$\text{sp}_i(A) \supseteq \text{sp}_i(B)$$

implies

$$A \geq B \quad (\theta_i), \qquad i = 1, 2,$$

i.e., A is to be preferred to B with respect to criterion θ_i. Let I_1, I_2 be sets in the family $\mathscr{I}_1 \cap \mathscr{I}_2$, which are maximal with respect to θ_1, θ_2, respectively. Then by Theorem 6.1 there exists a set $I \in \mathscr{I}_1 \cap \mathscr{I}_2, I \subseteq I_1 \cup I_2$, which is maximal with respect to both θ_1 and θ_2.

Theorem 6.1 provides a relatively simple and direct proof of a theorem of Nash-Williams.

Theorem 6.2 (*Nash-Williams*) Let $M_1 = (E, \mathscr{I}_1)$ be a matroid and $h: E \to E_0$ be a mapping of E into E_0. Then $M_0 = (E_0, \mathscr{I}_0)$ is a matroid, where

$$\mathscr{I}_0 = \{I_0 \subseteq E_0 | \text{ for some } I_1 \in \mathscr{I}_1, h(I_1) = I_0\}.$$

PROOF   It is sufficient to show that if I_p, I_{p+1} are two sets in $\mathscr{I}_0$, respectively with p and $p+1$ elements, there exists a set $h(I) \in \mathscr{I}_0$ with $p+1$ or more elements such that $I_p \subseteq h(I) \subseteq I_p \cup I_{p+1}$. Let $M_2 = (E, \mathscr{I}_2)$ be a partition matroid where

$$\mathscr{I}_2 = \{I_2 \subseteq E \mid |I_2 \cap h^{-1}(e)| \leq 1, \text{ for all } e \in E_0\}.$$

Let I'_p, I'_{p+1} be sets in $\mathscr{I}_1$, respectively with p and $p+1$ elements, such that $h(I'_p) = I_p$ and $h(I'_{p+1}) = I_{p+1}$. The sets I'_p, I'_{p+1} are independent in M_2 as well as M_1, and we can apply Theorem 6.1. Thus there is a set $I \in \mathscr{I}_1 \cap \mathscr{I}_2$ such that

$$\text{sp}_1(I) \supseteq \text{sp}_1(I'_{p+1}).$$

Hence $|I| \geq p+1$, and

$$\text{sp}_2(I) \supseteq h(\text{sp}_2(I'_p)),$$

from which it follows that

$$h(I) \supseteq \text{sp}_2(I'_p),$$

and hence

$$h(I) \supseteq h(I'_p) = I_p.$$

Also h is one-to-one on I and $I \subseteq I'_p \cup I'_{p+1}$, which implies that $|h(I)| \geq p+1$ and $h(I) \subseteq I_p \cup I_{p+1}$. Thus $\mathscr{I}_0$ defines the independent sets of a matroid. //

The rank functions in M_1 and M_0 are in the relation:

$$r_0(E_0) = \min_{A \subseteq E_0} \{r_1(h^{-1}(A)) + |E_0 - A|\}. \tag{6.1}$$

We leave the proof of this relation for the reader.

Another important way to form a new matroid is to take the "sum" of two matroids.

Theorem 6.3 (*Nash-Williams*)   Let $M_1 = (E_1, \mathscr{I}_1)$, $M_2 = (E_2, \mathscr{I}_2)$ be matroids and $E = E_1 \cup E_2$,

$$\mathscr{I} = \{I \mid I = I_1 \cup I_2, I_1 \in \mathscr{I}_1, I_2 \in \mathscr{I}_2\}.$$

Then $M = (E, \mathscr{I})$, the *sum* of M_1 and M_2, is a matroid.

PROOF   Let E'_2 be a new set obtained by priming each element of E_2 and let $M'_2 = (E'_2, \mathscr{I}'_2)$ be defined in the obvious way. Because E_1 and E'_2 are disjoint, it follows almost immediately from definitions that $M' = (E', \mathscr{I}')$ is a matroid, where $E' = E_1 \cup E'_2$ and

$$\mathscr{I}' = \{I' \mid I' = I_1 \cup I'_2, I_1 \in \mathscr{I}_1, I'_2 \in \mathscr{I}'_2\}.$$

Now apply Theorem 6.2 to M' and M, with $h: E' \to E$ defined by the relation

$$h(e) = e, e \in E_1$$
$$h(e') = e, e' \in E'_2.$$

By Theorem 6.2, M is a matroid. //

From the fact that the sum of two matroids is a matroid, it follows that the sum of any finite collection of matroids $M_1, M_2, \ldots, M_k$ is also a matroid. A relation between the rank function r in the new matroid and the rank functions of the matroids entering into the sum is given by

$$r(E) = \min_{A \subseteq E} \left\{ \sum_{i=1}^{k} r_i(A) + |E - A| \right\}. \tag{6.2}$$

As in the case of relation (6.1), we leave the proof to the reader.

Now suppose $M = (E, \mathscr{I})$ is the sum of $M_i = (E_i, \mathscr{I}_i)$, $i = 1, 2, \ldots, k$. We have available subroutines for determining whether or not a given subset $A \subseteq E$ is independent in any one of the matroids $M_1, M_2, \ldots, M_k$. How can we determine whether or not a given subset $A \subseteq E$ is independent in M?

Clearly A is independent in M if and only if A can be partitioned into k blocks $I_1, I_2, \ldots, I_k$, where $I_i \in \mathscr{I}_i$. This is one variation of the *matroid partitioning* problem. A special case of the partitioning problem is: given a single matroid $M = (E, \mathscr{I})$ and a subset $A \subseteq E$, is it possible to partition A into k independent sets $I_1, I_2, \ldots, I_k$? (Consider taking the sum of M with itself $k - 1$ times.) Or, what is the *smallest number* k of independent sets into which A can be partitioned?

Partitioning problems can be reduced to cardinality intersection problems, as follows. If the sets $E_1, E_2, \ldots, E_k$ are not disjoint, make them so, by creating extra copies of the elements. Let $M^{(1)}$ be the matroid obtained by summing the k matroids over these disjoint sets. For a given set A which is to be partitioned, let $M^{(2)}$ be a partition matroid in which each independent set contains at most one copy of each element in A and no element from $E - A$. Now solve the cardinality intersection problem for $M^{(1)}$ and $M^{(2)}$. The maximum cardinality of an intersection is equal to the cardinality of A if and only if partitioning is possible. If partitioning is possible, a feasible partition can be determined directly from such a maximum-cardinality intersection.

Now let us consider the reduction of the intersection problem to the partitioning problem. Let $M_1 = (E, \mathscr{I}_1)$ and $M_2 = (E, \mathscr{I}_2)$ be the two matroids for which a maximum-cardinality intersection is to be found. Suppose we partition E into three blocks, I_1, I_2, I_3, where I_1 is a base in

M_1^D, the dual of M_1, I_2 is independent in M_2, and I_3 is arbitrary (independent in the trivial matroid for which every subset of E is independent). Then I_2 is an intersection of M_1 and M_2. As it turns out, it is easy to arrange for Edmonds' partitioning algorithm (described in the next section) to yield a maximum-cardinality block I_2, subject to the condition that I_1 is a base of M_1^D.

PROBLEMS

6.1 Show explicitly that the Mendelsohn-Dulmage theorem is a corollary of Theorem 6.1.

6.2 Let G be an acyclic but otherwise arbitrary directed graph. Let the nodes of G with in-degree zero be identified with the elements of a matroid $M_1 = (E, \mathscr{I})$. Let E_0 be the subset of nodes with out-degree zero, and $\mathscr{I}_0$ be a family of subsets such that $I_0 \subseteq E_0$ is in $\mathscr{I}_0$ if and only if there exists a set of node-disjoint paths from an independent set I in $\mathscr{I}$ to the nodes in I_0. Use Theorem 6.2 to show that $M_0 = (E_0, \mathscr{I}_0)$ is a matroid.

6.3 Prove that a matroid is a transversal matroid if and only if it is the sum of matroids of rank one. (A matroid $M = (E, \mathscr{I})$ is of rank one if $r(E) = 1$.)

6.4 Prove relations (6.1) and (6.2).

6.5 Let G be an arbitrary directed graph. Let us say that a subset of arcs S *covers* a given subset of nodes I if for each node j in I there is an arc (i, j) in S directed into j. Use Theorem 6.2 to show that the family of subsets of nodes which are covered by forests constitutes the family of independent sets of a matroid. Show that the problem of determining whether or not there exists a forest covering a given subset of nodes is a matroid intersection problem. (*Note:* A forest is a subset of arcs which contains no *undirected* cycle.)

7

Matroid Partitioning Algorithm

Let $M_i = (E, \mathscr{I}_i)$, $i = 1, 2, \ldots, k$, be k given matroids. The algorithm of Edmonds given below constructs a partition of E into k blocks I_i, $i = 1, 2, \ldots, k$, where $I_i \in \mathscr{I}_i$, if such a partition exists. Moreover, the partition constructed is lexicographically maximum, in that $|I_1|$ is maximum, $|I_2|$ is as large as possible subject to $|I_1|$ being maximum, and so on.

MATROID PARTITIONING ALGORITHM (EDMONDS)

Step 0   (Start)   Set $I_i = \varnothing$, for $i = 1, 2, \ldots, k$. Set $U = E$. (U is the subset of elements which have not been assigned to blocks I_i.)

Step 1   (Computation of Sequence $S_0, S_1, \ldots$)

(1.0)   Set $S_0 = E$ and $j = 1$.
(1.1)   Find the smallest index i such that $|I_i \cap S_{j-1}| < r_i(S_{j-1})$. If there is no such block I_i, halt; E is not partitionable. (See the text following.)
(1.2)   Set $S_j = S_{j-1} \cap \mathrm{sp}_i(I_i \cap S_{j-1})$. Set $l(j) = i$.
(1.3)   If $U \subseteq S_j$, set $j = j + 1$ and go to Step 1.1; otherwise choose e to be any element in $U - S_j$ and go to Step 2.

Step 2   (Augmentation of Partition)

(2.0)   Remove e from U.
(2.1)   Add e to $I_{l(j)}$. If $I_{l(j)}$ is independent in $M_{l(j)}$, go to Step 2.3.
(2.2)   Find the unique circuit $C \subseteq I_{l(j)}$ and choose e' to be any element in $C - S_{j-1}$. (Such an element e' must exist; see the following text.) Remove e' from $I_{l(j)}$, set $e = e'$, set $j = j - 1$, and go to Step 2.1.
(2.3)   If U is nonempty, go to Step 1. If U is empty, all elements of E have been assigned to blocks of the partition, and the computation is completed. //

The reader will readily see that $l(j)$ acts as a "labeling function," which serves to direct a form of backtracing in Step 2. Note that this backtracing may involve the same block more than once; i.e., it can be that $l(i) = l(j)$, for $i \neq j$.

In Step 1.1, if it is not possible to find a block I_i such that $|I_i \cap S_{j-1}| < r_i(S_{j-1})$, it follows that

$$|I_i \cap S_{j-1}| \geq r_i(S_{j-1}) \geq r_i(A),$$

for all i and all $A \subseteq S_{j-1}$. If we choose e to be any element in $U \cap S_{j-1}$, and let

$$A = \{e\} \cup \left(S_{j-1} \cap \bigcup_{i=1}^{k} I_i \right),$$

then it follows that

$$|A| > \sum_{i=1}^{k} |I_i \cap S_j| \geq \sum_{i=1}^{k} r_i(A). \tag{7.1}$$

This inequality will be used in the proof of Theorem 7.1.

In Step 2.2 the circuit C in $I_{l(j)}$ must of course be unique because $I_{l(j)}$ was independent before e was added to $I_{l(j)}$. Moreover not all elements of C can be in S_{j-1}. If they were, then they would all be in S_j as well, by the construction of S_j in Step 1.2. But the element e was chosen (either in Step 1.3 or in the previous execution of Step 2.2) not to be a member of S_j.

It is not possible for $I_{l(1)}$ to be dependent in Step 2.1. If $I_{l(1)}$ were dependent, it would contain a circuit C, and by the observation above, at least one element of C would not be contained in S_0. But $S_0 = E$, and clearly this is an absurdity; thus, the decrementing of j in Step 2.2 never proceeds below $j = 1$.

We can evaluate the complexity of the algorithm as follows. Each subset S_j is a proper subset of its predecessor, because of the condition in Step 1.1, subject to which I_i is chosen. Hence, the inner loop, Steps 1.1 through 1.3, is performed at most m times for each execution of Step 1. Likewise, the inner loop, Steps 2.1 and 2.2 of Step 2, is performed at most m times for each execution of Step 2. Steps 1 and 2 are themselves executed at most m times, once for each element in E. Hence, the overall computation grows as $m^3 c(m)$, where $c(m)$ is the maximum number of steps required to test for independence in any one of the k matroids $M_1, M_2, \ldots, M_k$.

Both the cardinality intersection algorithm and the matroid partitioning algorithm have been seen to be $O(m^3 c(m))$ in complexity. However, this does not mean that the algorithms have the same complexity when applied to the opposite type of problem. For example, consider the application of the partitioning algorithm to the intersection problem. Recall that it is necessary to determine whether or not a set A is independent in M_2^D. But $A \in \mathscr{I}_2^D$ if and only if $r_2(E - A) = r_2(E)$, and testing for this condition requires $O(mc(m))$ steps, where $c(m)$ steps are required for independence testing in M_2. Thus, the complexity of the intersection computation actually becomes $O(m^4 c(m))$ when performed by the partitioning algorithm.

Conversely, suppose the cardinality intersection algorithm is applied to the problem of partitioning a set A into k independent sets, where k is of order m. Then independence testing in the matroid $M^{(1)}$ (recall the notation from the previous section) becomes $O(mc(m))$ in complexity, where $c(m)$ is the number of steps required for independence testing in a single matroid $M_1, M_2, \ldots, M_k$. Thus, the complexity of the partitioning computation becomes $O(m^4 c(m))$ when performed by the intersection algorithm.

The partitioning algorithm provides a constructive proof of the following theorem.

Theorem 7.1 (*Edmonds and Fulkerson*) Let $M_i = (E, \mathscr{I}_i)$, $i = 1, 2, \ldots, k$, be k given matroids. A set $I \subseteq E$ can be partitioned into k subsets I_i, $i = 1, 2, \ldots, k$, where $I_i \in \mathscr{I}_i$, if and only if for all $A \subseteq I$,

$$|A| \leq \sum_{i=1}^{k} r_i(A). \tag{7.2}$$

PROOF Suppose I is partitionable into subsets I_i, $i = 1, 2, \ldots, k$. Clearly, for all $A \subseteq I$,

$$|A| = \sum_{i=1}^{k} |I_i \cap A|,$$

and, for each I_i,

$$|I_i \cap A| \leq r_i(A),$$

from which (7.2) follows immediately.

Conversely, suppose (7.2) is satisfied for all $A \subseteq E$. Then the partitioning algorithm will construct a partition of E, since an appropriate subset I_i can always be found in Step 1.1. (If this were not the case (7.1) would be satisfied in contradiction to (7.2).) The result for arbitrary $I \subseteq E$ is obtained by applying the algorithm to the matroids M_i, $i = 1, 2, \ldots, k$, restricted to the elements I (i.e., delete $E - I$.) //

The celebrated Philip Hall Theorem of transversal theory follows as a corollary of Theorem 7.1.

Theorem 7.2 (*Philip Hall Theorem*) There exists a transversal (SDR) of the family $Q = \{q_j; j = 1, 2, \ldots, m\}$ if and only if for $r = 1, 2, \ldots, m$, the union of any r of the sets q_i contains at least r distinct elements.

PROOF For each element e_i, let $M_i = (Q, \mathcal{I}_i)$ be such that

$$\mathcal{I}_i = \{\varnothing\} \cup \{\{q_j\} | e_i \in q_j\}.$$

There exists an SDR of Q if and only if Q can be partitioned into sets $I_i \in \mathcal{I}_i$.

For any $A \subseteq Q$,

$$
\begin{aligned}
r_i(A) &= 1, && \text{if } e_i \text{ is contained in the} \\
       &   && \text{union of the subsets } q_j \\
       &   && \text{in } A, \\
       &= 0, && \text{otherwise.}
\end{aligned}
$$

Hence $\sum r_i(A)$ counts the number of distinct elements in the union of the sets q_i in A. The desired result follows immediately from Theorem 7.1. //

PROBLEMS

7.1 Formulate the cardinality intersection problem solved in Section 3 as a matroid partitioning problem, and solve by Edmonds' algorithm.

7.2 Carry out a detailed analysis of the partitioning algorithm when it is applied to the problem of computing a transversal of a given family Q. Show that in this case the labeling function is such that $i \neq j$ implies $l(i) \neq l(j)$.

8

The Shannon Switching Game

The Shannon Switching Game is played on the arcs of a graph. Two distinct nodes of an arbitrary graph G are designated as *terminal nodes*. There are two players in the game, called *short* and *cut*. The players alternately tag arcs of the graph not already tagged by either player. The short player wins if he tags all the arcs in some path connecting the terminal nodes. The cut player wins if he prevents the short player from obtaining such a path. Each player has complete information about the other's moves. The game continues until one player wins.

It is clear that any such game must have a winner. When all the arcs have been tagged, either the short player has succeeded in connecting the terminal nodes, or he has not. Moreover, any given instance of the game can be characterized as *cut*, *short*, or *neutral*, depending upon the nature of the graph G. A cut (short) game is one that can always be won by the cut (short) player, playing second. (If a cut (short) player can win by playing second, he can certainly win by playing first.) A neutral game is one that always can be won by the first player, whether cut or short.

Let us indicate the terminal nodes of the graph by connecting them with a special arc e, which is not to be tagged by either player. Using this convention, very simple examples of cut, short, and neutral games are shown in Figure 8.9.

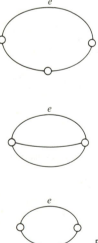

Figure 8.9   Examples of cut, short, neutral games

Lehman applied matroid theory to the analysis of the Shannon Switching Game, suggested the classification into cut, short, and neutral games, and characterized a winning strategy for the short player. Edmonds improved this analysis and provided a good characterization of a winning strategy for the short player. The statement of Theorem 8.1 is a further refinement due to Bruno and Weinberg.

We say that two subsets $A, A' \subseteq E$ are *cospanning* in a matroid $M = (E, \mathscr{I})$ if they have the same spans, i.e., $\mathrm{sp}(A) = \mathrm{sp}(A')$.

Theorem 8.1 Let G be the graph of a Shannon Switching Game in which e is the nonplayable edge. Then exactly one of the following statements holds:

(8.1) G contains two disjoint cospanning trees spanning but not containing e. The spans are taken with respect to the graphic matroid of G. Equivalently, the game is a short game.

(8.2) G contains two disjoint cospanning cotrees spanning but not containing e. The spans are taken with respect to the cographic matroid of G. Equivalently, the game is a cut game.

(8.3) G contains two disjoint cospanning trees, and e is a member of one of the trees. The spans are taken with respect to the graphic matroid of G. G also contains two disjoint cospanning cotrees and e is a member of one of the cotrees. The spans are taken with respect to the cographic matroid of G. Equivalently, the game is a neutral game.

We shall not prove this theorem, but we should comment on some of its implications. First, it seems evident that a variation of the matroid partitioning algorithm can be used to determine whether any given game is cut, short, or neutral. Bruno and Weinberg make use of a procedure due to Kishi and Kajitani which can be viewed as a variant of the matroid partitioning algorithm.

Second, the disjoint cospanning trees and cotrees mentioned in (8.1) and (8.2) of the theorem provide clues to the winning strategies for the short and cut players in short and cut games. For example, in the case of a short game, each time the cut player tags an arc in one of the cospanning trees, the short player tags an arc e' in the other tree, so that when e' is contracted in G, the arcs of the two trees untagged by the cut player are again cospanning. If the cut player tags an arc that is not in either cospanning tree, the short player's move is arbitrary.

It is not hard to devise variations of the switching game which are effectively unsolved. For example, suppose that neither player is allowed to have more than k arcs tagged at any time. One can imagine that there are a fixed number of markers, and at each move a player is allowed to move one marker.

Also, very little is known about the game of Hex, which is played on a square tesselation of hexagons, similar to the tiles in the floor of a public washroom (where the game allegedly originated at M.I.T.). The players alternately tag hexagons, with one player attempting to form a chain from one side of the tesselation to the other, and the other player attempting to block him.

9

Weighted Augmenting Sequences

We now return to the weighted matroid intersection problem. The "primal" procedure we shall propose is analogous to the algorithm of Busacker, Gowan, and Jewell for computing minimum cost network flows. The matroid algorithm proceeds by computing maximum weight intersections containing successively larger numbers of elements. Having obtained I_p, a maximum weight intersection with p elements, I_{p+1} is obtained from I_p by constructing a "maximum weight augmenting sequence," in exactly the same way that the corresponding network flow algorithm proceeds from a minimum cost flow of value v to one of value $v + \delta$ by means of a minimum-cost flow augmenting path.

The algorithm is characterized as "primal" because it does not involve dual variables or the calculation of a dual solution, as is the case with the "primal-dual" method described in Sections 12 and 13. The primal method is certainly conceptually much simpler, and possibly more efficient than the primal-dual method.

For any subset $A \subseteq E$ we let $w(A)$ denote the sum of the weights of the elements in A. That is,

$$w(A) = \sum_{e_j \in A} w_j.$$

Given an intersection I, and a set $S \subseteq E$, we define the *incremental weight of S* to be

$$\Delta(S) = w(S - I) - w(S \cap I).$$

Clearly,

$$w(I \oplus S) = w(I) + \Delta(S).$$

In order to establish the validity of the primal algorithm, we must introduce some additional definitions and terminology. A *border path* is either (1) a directed cycle in $BG(I)$ or (2) a directed path (without repetition of nodes) in $BG(I)$ from a node that is either in I or a source in $E - I$ to a node that is either in I or a sink in $E - I$. A border path is said to be either "positive," "neutral," or "negative," according to the following classification:

(9.1) A source-sink path S is *positive*. $|I \oplus S| = |I| + 1$.

(9.2) A directed cycle is *neutral*, as is a path from a source to a node in I, or path from a node in I to a sink. If S is a neutral path, then $|I \oplus S| = |I|$.

(9.3) A path S between two nodes in I is *negative*. $|I \oplus S| = |I| - 1$.

The reader should refer to Figure 8.8 and identify each path in the figure as positive, neutral, or negative.

Let S be a border path in $BG(I)$. A *simple border cycle* with respect to S is an undirected cycle in either $BG_1(I)$ or $BG_2(I)$ which uses arcs in S alternately. An example of a simple border cycle is shown in Figure 8.10. Arcs not in S are dashed in the figure.

Lemma 9.1 (*Krogdahl*) Let S be a border path in $BG(I)$. If S admits no simple border cycle, then $I \oplus S$ is an intersection. In particular, if S is a source-sink path which admits no simple border cycle, then S is an augmenting sequence with respect to I.

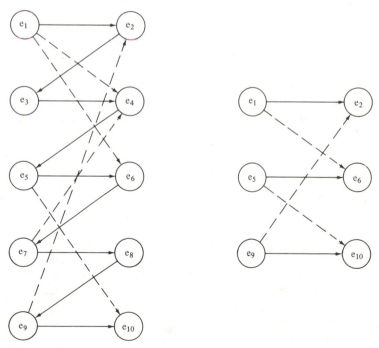

Figure 8.10   A border path with simple border cycle in $BG_2(I)$

PROOF   Without loss of generality, let $S = (e_1, e_2, \ldots, e_s)$. (If S is a directed cycle, choose an arbitrary node e_1 and let e_s be the last node reached before returning to e_1.) If S admits no simple border cycle in $BG_2(I)$, then it is possible to induce a partial ordering "$\leq$" on node pairs, where for $e_1, e_j \in E - I$, $(e_i, e_{i+1}) \leq (e_j, e_{j+1})$ if there is an arc (e_i, e_{j+1}) in $BG_2(I)$. One can then use this partial ordering to redraw the subgraph of $BG_2(I)$ induced on the nodes of S so that there are no "downward" arcs, as in the proof of Lemma 3.1. The proof that $I \oplus S$ is independent in M_2 then follows by a construction similar to that used in Lemma 3.1. The proof of independence in M_1 is, of course, similar. //

The reader should be able to verify that if a border path S admits no shortcuts, then S admits no simple border cycle. (If S is a directed cycle, any chord is a shortcut.) Thus Lemma 9.1 is a strict generalization of Lemma 3.1.

We say that an intersection I is *p-maximal* if $|I| = p$ and I is of maximum weight with respect to all intersections containing p elements.

Lemma 9.2   (*Krogdahl*)   Let I be p-maximal and S be a border path in $BG(I)$. If any shortcut of S yields a path with strictly less incremental weight, then $I \oplus S$ is an intersection.

PROOF   We wish to show that S does not admit a simple border cycle, so that Lemma 9.1 applies. So we shall assume that S admits a simple border cycle and show that this assumption leads to a contradiction.

Again without loss of generality, suppose $S = (e_1, e_2, \ldots, e_s)$. Any simple border cycle must contain at least one shortcut of S and at least one "cutback," an arc directed in the sense opposite to S. A shortcut yields a border path with strictly less incremental weight. Hence if (e_i, e_j) is a shortcut,

$$\Delta(\{e_{i+1}, e_{i+2}, \ldots, e_{j-1}\}) > 0. \tag{9.4}$$

A cutback (e_j, e_i) forms a directed cycle in $BG(I)$ with the subpath of S which lies between e_i and e_j. If this directed cycle admits no simple border cycle, then

$$\Delta(\{e_i, e_{i+1}, \ldots, e_j\}) \leq 0, \tag{9.5}$$

because I is p-maximal. (Otherwise $I \oplus \{e_i, e_{i+1}, \ldots, e_j\}$ would be an intersection with p elements, but with strictly greater weight than I.)

It is not difficult to show that inequalities (9.4) and (9.5) yield a contradiction for any simple border cycle. For example, in the case of the simple border cycle in Figure 8.10,

$$w(e_3) + w(e_5) > w(e_2) + w(e_4),$$
$$w(e_7) + w(e_9) > w(e_6) + w(e_8),$$

by (9.4), whereas

$$w(e_3) + w(e_5) + w(e_7) + w(e_9) \leq w(e_2) + w(e_4) + w(e_6) + w(e_8),$$

by (9.5).

It only remains to show that if S admits a simple border cycle, S must admit a simple border cycle for which inequality (9.5) is valid for each cutback in the cycle. This is a bit tricky.

Suppose a simple border cycle C contains nodes $e_{i(1)}, e_{i(2)}, \ldots, e_{i(k)}$ in $E - I$, where $i(1) < i(2) < \ldots < i(k)$. Define the "extension" of C to be the subpath of S between $e_{i(1)}$ and $e_{i(k)}$. (Recall $S = (e_1, e_2, \ldots, e_s)$.) Since S is assumed to admit a simple border cycle, there must be a simple border cycle C such that the extension of C is minimal and C contains a maximum number of arcs with respect to all other simple border cycles with the same extension. That is, if C' is any other simple border cycle, then the extension of C' is not a proper subpath of the extension of C, and if C' has the same extension as C, then C' contains no more arcs than C.

Now consider any cutback arc in C. Suppose the directed cycle S' formed by this cutback were to admit a simple border cycle C'. The alternate arcs of S' which appear in C' cannot be a subset of the alternate arcs of S which appear in C. Otherwise C' would also be a simple border cycle of S, with smaller extension than C. Hence the alternate arcs of S' in C' must include the cutback itself plus arcs of S "in between" the alternate arcs of S in C. But if this were the case, it would be possible to construct a simple border cycle of S, either with smaller extension than C, or with a larger number of arcs than C. We leave details to the reader.

It follows that if S admits a simple border cycle, it admits a simple border cycle for which inequality (9.5) holds for each cutback in the cycle. But this is a contradiction. Therefore, S admits no simple border cycle. //

If I is p-maximal, it follows immediately from Lemma 9.2 that a maximum (incremental) weight source-sink path S in $BG(I)$ is an augmenting sequence. We now wish to show that $I \oplus S$ is $(p + 1)$-maximal.

In proving the following key lemma we make use of two observations. First, if S_1 and S_2 are node-disjoint border paths, where S_1 is positive and S_2 is negative, then $S_1 \cup S_2$ can be treated as a single neutral border path. Second, if S is a border path, then repeated shortcutting of S (with weight nondecreasing shortcuts) yields a path $S' \subseteq S$ such that $\Delta(S') \geq \Delta(S)$ and $I \oplus S'$ is an intersection.

Lemma 9.3 (*Krogdahl*) Let I be a p-maximal intersection and J be any intersection with $|J| = |I| + 1$. Then there exists a source-sink path $S \subseteq I \oplus J$ in $BG(I)$ such that S is an augmenting sequence and $w(I \oplus S) \geq w(J)$.

PROOF   If J contains an element that is not in $\mathrm{sp}_1(I) \cup \mathrm{sp}_2(I)$, then e_1 is both a source and a sink in $BG(I)$ and $S = (e_1)$ is a source-sink path. Since $J - e_1$ is an intersection with p elements, $w(J - e_1) \leq w(I)$, which implies that $w(I + e_1) \geq w(J)$, as required. So assume $J \subseteq \mathrm{sp}_1(I) \cup \mathrm{sp}_2(I)$.

Now carry out exactly the same construction used in the proof of Lemma 3.2. That is, form the subgraph $H \subseteq BG(I)$ with node set $I \oplus J$ and arc set $X_1 \cup X_2$, where X_1, X_2 are matchings found as in the proof of the lemma. Each connected component of H is a border path. Since $|J - I| = |I - J| + 1$, the number of positive border paths is one greater than the number of negative border paths. Choose any one of the positive (source-sink) paths S and pair the remaining positive and negative paths to obtain neutral border paths. For any neutral path S', $\Delta(S') \leq 0$, because I is p-maximal. The sum of the incremental weights of all border paths is equal to $w(J - I) - w(I - J)$. It follows that $w(I \oplus S) \geq w(J)$. //

The key theorem below follows almost immediately from the lemma.

Theorem 9.4   Let I be a p-maximal intersection and S be a maximum incremental weight source-sink path in $BG(I)$. Then S is a maximum weight augmenting sequence and $I \oplus S$ is $(p + 1)$-maximal.

In the next section we shall show that maximum weight augmenting sequences can be computed by a procedure that is essentially a shortest path algorithm. Thus, it is clearly possible to start with the empty set and find maximum weight augmenting sequences to obtain $I_1, I_2, I_3, \ldots$, maximum weight intersections with $1, 2, 3, \ldots$ elements, respectively, stopping when no further augmentation is possible. One can then compare the weights of these various intersections so as to determine an intersection which has maximum weight without restriction on the number of elements.

However, "the maximum weight of intersections is concave in the number of elements," just as "the minimum cost of flows is convex in the value of the flow." This means that if one seeks to compute a maximum weight intersection without restriction on the number of elements, such a set is given by I_p, where p is the smallest number of elements such that $w(I_p) \geq w(I_{p+1})$.

In order to establish this concavity result, we need two additional lemmas.

Lemma 9.5   (*Krogdahl*)   Let I be a p-maximal intersection with $p \geq 1$ and J be any intersection with $|J| = |I| - 1$. Then there exists a negative border path $S \subseteq I \oplus J$ in $BG(I)$ such that $I \oplus S$ is an intersection and $w(I \oplus S) \geq w(J)$.

PROOF   The proof is essentially similar to that of Lemma 9.3, except that after pairing positive and negative border paths, there is one negative path left over. The other important difference is that we must provide for the case $J \nsubseteq \mathrm{sp}_1(I) \cup \mathrm{sp}_2(I)$ by using $(J - I) \cap (\mathrm{sp}_1(I) \cup \mathrm{sp}_2(I))$ instead of $J - I$ when the partition into sets J_1, J_2, J_3 is made. This means that there may be degenerate positive border paths consisting of single elements which are neither sources nor sinks, but this makes no difference. //

Lemma 9.6   (*Krogdahl*)   Let I be a p-maximal intersection with $p \geq 1$. Let S be a positive border path and S' be a negative border path in $BG(I)$. Then $\Delta(S) + \Delta(S') \leq 0$.

PROOF   If the two paths are disjoint, then $S \cup S'$ acts as a neutral path and the lemma follows immediately. So assume S and S' have at least one node in common. Take the subpath of S before this node and the subpath of S' after this node to obtain a neutral path R. Lkewise, take the subpath of S' before this node and the subpath of S after this node to obtain a second neutral path R'. (There may be repeated nodes in R and R', but this is of no consequence.) Now $\Delta(R) \leq 0$ and $\Delta(R') \leq 0$, because I is p-maximal. But

$$\Delta(R) + \Delta(R') = \Delta(S) + \Delta(S'),$$

so the lemma follows. //

Theorem 9.7   Let I_{p-1}, I_p, I_{p+1} be intersections which are $(p - 1)$-, p-, and $(p + 1)$-maximal, respectively. Then

$$w(I_p) - w(I_{p-1}) \geq w(I_{p+1}) - w(I_p).$$

PROOF   By Lemma 9.3, there is a positive border path S in $BG(I_p)$ such that $w(I_p) + \Delta(S) = w(I_{p+1})$. By Lemma 9.5, there is a negative border path S' in $BG(I_p)$ such that $w(I_p) + \Delta(S') = w(I_{p-1})$. Hence,

$$w(I_{p+1}) - w(I_p) = \Delta(S),$$
$$w(I_p) - w(I_{p-1}) = -\Delta(S').$$

But by Lemma 9.6, $\Delta(S) + \Delta(S') \leq 0$, which yields the desired result. //

As a final note, we might mention that Theorem 9.7 also follows immediately from the linear programming formulation of the weighted intersection problem, discussed in Sections 11 through 13. That is, I_{p-1}, I_p, I_{p+1} can be shown to be feasible solutions of a certain linear programming problem. The convex combination $\frac{1}{2}I_{p-1} + \frac{1}{2}I_{p+1}$ is also a feasible solution and is dominated by an optimal solution at an extreme point of the polyhedron identified with a p-maximal intersection. This line of reasoning parallels that used in Chapter 4 to show that the minimum cost of flows is convex in the value of the flow.

10
Primal Weighted Intersection Algorithm

A maximum incremental weight source-sink path in a border graph can be found by a procedure that is similar to a shortest path computation. Each node $e_j \in E - I_p$ in $BG(I_p)$ is given weight w_j and each node $e_j \in I_p$ is given weight $-w_j$. One then wishes to find a source-sink path of maximum total node weight. Since I_p is assumed to be p-maximal, there are no directed cycles in $BG(I_p)$ with positive node weight.

   Let

$\Delta(e_j) = $ the weight of a maximum weight alternating sequence, with e_j as the last element.

We propose to compute $\Delta(e_j)$ by successive approximations, as in the Bellman-Ford shortest path algorithm. In effect, at successive iterations we compute $\Delta^{(1)}(e_j), \Delta^{(2)}(e_j), ..., \Delta^{(m)}(e_j)$, where

$\Delta^{(k)}(e_j) = $ the weight of a maximum weight alternating sequence containing no more than k elements, with e_j as the last element.

Since no alternating sequence contains more than m elements, where $|E| = m$, it is clear that a maximum weight augmenting sequence has weight $\Delta(S)$, where

$$\Delta(S) = \max_{e_j \notin I} \{\Delta^{(m)}(e_j) | I_p + e_j \in \mathscr{I}_2\}.$$

   A labeling procedure for computing these successive approximations to $\Delta(e_j)$ can be implemented as follows. (Superscripts on $\Delta(e_j)$ are eliminated for conciseness.)

   Initially, apply the label "$\varnothing^+$" to each element $e_j \in E - \text{sp}_1(I_p)$ and set $\Delta(e_j) = w_j$. For all other elements e_j, set $\Delta(e_j) = -\infty$.

   Thereafter, find an element e_i with an unscanned label and scan it as follows. If the label is a "$+$" label and $I + e_i$ is dependent in M_2, apply the (unscanned) label "i^-" to each element $e_j \in C_i^{(2)} - e_i$ for which $\Delta(e_i) - w_j > \Delta(e_j)$, and set

$$\Delta(e_j) = \Delta(e_i) - w_j.$$

If the label is a "$-$" label, apply the (unscanned) label "i^+" to each element e_j such that $e_i \in C_j^{(1)}$ and $\Delta(e_i) + w_j > \Delta(e_j)$, and set

$$\Delta(e_j) = \Delta(e_i) + w_j.$$

   Continue scanning and labeling until all labels are scanned. We assert that at that point $\Delta(e_j)$ has attained the correct value for all e_j. (Labels may be scanned in any order. However, in order to achieve a bound of $O(m^3)$ on the labeling procedure, it is necessary that labels be scanned in the order in which they are applied.)

We now summarize the primal algorithm.

PRIMAL WEIGHTED INTERSECTION ALGORITHM

Step 0   (Start)   Let $I = \varnothing$. No elements are labeled.

Step 1   (Labeling)

(1.0)   For each element $e_i \in E - I$, find $C_i^{(1)}$, $C_i^{(2)}$, if these circuits exist. Set $\Delta(S) = -\infty$, $\Delta(e_i) = -\infty$, for all $e_i \in \mathrm{sp}_1(I)$. Apply the label "$\varnothing^+$" to each element $e_i \in E - \mathrm{sp}_1(I)$ and set $\Delta(e_i) = w_i$.

(1.1)   If there are no unscanned labels and $\Delta(S) > -\infty$, go to Step 2. If there are no unscanned labels and $\Delta(S) = -\infty$, go to Step 3. Otherwise, from among the elements whose labels are unscanned, find that element e_i whose label was first to be applied. If the label is a "$+$" label, go to Step 1.2; if it is a "$-$" label, go to Step 1.3.

(1.2)   Scan the "$+$" label on e_i as follows. If $I + e_i$ is independent in M_2 and $\Delta(e_i) > \Delta(S)$, set $\Delta(S) = \Delta(e_i)$ and $s = i$. Otherwise, apply the (unscanned) label "i^-" (replacing any existing label) to each element $e_j \in C_i^{(2)} - e_i$ for which $\Delta(e_j) < \Delta(e_i) - w_j$ and set $\Delta(e_j) = \Delta(e_i) - w_j$. Return to Step 1.1.

(1.3)   Scan the "$-$" label on e_i as follows. Apply the (unscanned) label "i^+" (replacing any existing label) to each element e_j such that $e_i \in C_j^{(1)}$ and $\Delta(e_i) + w_j > \Delta(e_j)$, and set $\Delta(e_j) = \Delta(e_i) + w_j$. Return to Step 1.1.

Step 2   (Augmentation)   A maximum weight augmenting sequence S can be identified by backtracing from e_s. If $\Delta(S) \le 0$, stop; the existing intersection I is of maximum weight. Otherwise, augment I, remove all labels from elements, and return to Step 1.0.

Step 3   (Hungarian Labeling)   No augmenting sequence exists. I is not only of maximum weight but of maximum cardinality. The labeling is "Hungarian" and can be used to construct a minimum-rank covering dual to I. Halt. //

It is quite easy to estmiate the complexity of the primal algorithm. Let $R = \min\{r_1(E), r_2(E)\}$. Consider the running time for each of R possible applications of the labeling procedure. The computation of $C_i^{(1)}$, $C_i^{(2)}$, for all $e_i \in E - I$ requires $O(mRc(m))$ running time. Each of the m

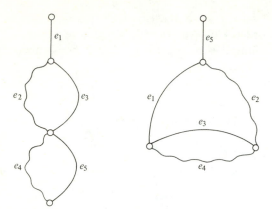

Figure 8.11   Multigraphs for Problem 10.1

elements may receive $O(R)$ labels (corresponding to $\Delta^{(1)}(e_j), \Delta^{(2)}(e_j), \dots$) and the scanning of each label requires $O(m)$ running time. Hence the labeling procedure consumes $O(m^2R)$ running time per augmentation. Backtracing and other operations are dominated by those already mentioned. It follows that the overall running time is $O(m^2R^2 + mR^2c(m))$.

PROBLEM

10.1   Let M_1, M_2 be the graphic matroids of the multigraphs G_1, G_2 shown in Figure 8.11. Let the arcs of these multigraphs be given weights $w_1 = 3$, $w_2 = 5$, $w_3 = 6$, $w_4 = 10$, $w_5 = 8$. Find a maximum weight intersection, starting with the 2-maximal intersection $I_2 = \{e_2, e_4\}$, indicated by wavy lines in the figure.

11

Matroid Polyhedra

In order to formulate the weighted intersection problem as a linear programming problem, we first formulate a system of linear inequalities which are satisfied by an independent set of a single matroid $M = (E, \mathscr{I})$. Clearly, if I is an independent set, then

$$|I \cap S| \le r(S), \qquad (11.1)$$

for any subset $S \subseteq E$, and in particular for any closed set S.

Equivalently, let A be an incidence matrix of closed sets and elements of E. In other words, each row i of A corresponds to a closed set of the matroid (the indexing of these sets being arbitrary) and each column j corresponds to an element e_j. We set

$$a_{ij} = 1, \quad \text{if } e_j \text{ belongs to closed set } i,$$
$$= 0, \quad \text{otherwise.}$$

Let $r = (r_1, r_2, \ldots, r_n)$ be a vector, where r_i is the rank of closed set i. We shall show that the vertices of the convex polyhedron defined by the inequalities

$$Ax \leq r$$

$$x \geq 0$$

are in one-to-one correspondence with the independent sets of M. That is to say, if x is a vertex, then each component x_j is either 0 or 1, where $x_j = 1$ if element e_j is a member of the independent set identified with the vertex, and $x_j = 0$, if it is not.

As a simple example, consider the graphic matroid of the graph shown in Figure 8.12. There are nine nontrivial closed sets of this matroid (i.e., closed sets other than the empty set) and the incidence matrix A and rank vector r are the following:

$$
\begin{array}{c}
\{e_1\} \\
\{e_2\} \\
\{e_3\} \\
\{e_4\} \\
\{e_1, e_4\} \\
\{e_2, e_4\} \\
\{e_3, e_4\} \\
\{e_1, e_2, e_3\} \\
\{e_1, e_2, e_3, e_4\}
\end{array}
\quad A =
\begin{bmatrix}
1 & 0 & 0 & 0 \\
0 & 1 & 0 & 0 \\
0 & 0 & 1 & 0 \\
0 & 0 & 0 & 1 \\
1 & 0 & 0 & 1 \\
0 & 1 & 0 & 1 \\
0 & 0 & 1 & 1 \\
1 & 1 & 1 & 0 \\
1 & 1 & 1 & 1
\end{bmatrix}
\quad r =
\begin{bmatrix}
1 \\
1 \\
1 \\
1 \\
2 \\
2 \\
2 \\
2 \\
3
\end{bmatrix}
$$

$$e_1 \; e_2 \; e_3 \; e_4$$

It is not difficult to show that the only feasible solutions to the system

$$Ax \leq r$$

$$x_j = 0 \text{ or } 1$$

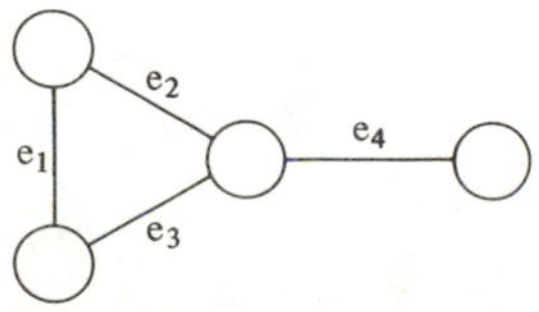

Figure 8.12   Example graph

are those which correspond to independent sets, and vice versa. What is more surprising is that when these constraints are used to define a linear programming problem, the (0, 1) restriction on the variables can be dropped, and the existence of an optimal integer solution is guaranteed.

Theorem 11.1 (*Edmonds*) For any matroid M, all vertices of the convex polyhedron defined by the system of inequalities

$$Ax \leq r,$$

$$x \geq 0,$$

have integer components. Moreover, the vertices and the independent sets of the matroid are in one-to-one correspondence.

PROOF It is sufficient to show that for any set of element weights, $w = (w_1, w_2, \ldots, w_m)$, the linear programming problem

maximize wx
subject to

$$Ax \leq r$$

$$x \geq 0$$

has an integer optimal solution.

It is known that for any given set of weights, one can find a maximum weight independent set by applying the greedy algorithm. In other words, from among the elements whose weights are strictly positive, choose the element of greatest weight, then second greatest weight, and so on, unless the selection of an element would cause the set of chosen elements to be dependent. If we can show that such a maximum weight independent set chosen by the greedy algorithm yields an optimal solution to the linear programming problem, the theorem will have been proved.

The dual linear programming problem is

minimize ru
subject to

$$A^T u \geq w$$

$$u \geq 0.$$

The orthogonality conditions which guarantee optimality of feasible primal and dual solutions are:

$$x_j > 0 \Rightarrow (A^T u)_j = w_j,$$

$$u_i > 0 \Rightarrow (Ax)_i = r_i.$$

Suppose, without loss of generality, the elements chosen by the greedy algorithm are $e_1, e_2, \ldots, e_k$, where $w_1 \geq w_2 \geq \ldots \geq w_k$, and that $u_1, u_2, \ldots, u_k$ are the dual variables corresponding to the closed sets

$$S_1 = \mathrm{sp}(\{e_1\}),$$
$$S_2 = \mathrm{sp}(\{e_1, e_2\}),$$
$$S_k = \mathrm{sp}(\{e_1, e_2, \ldots, e_k\}),$$

respectively. We shall show that

$$x_j = 1 \qquad (j = 1, 2, \ldots, k)$$
$$= 0 \qquad (j = k + 1, \ldots, n)$$

is an optimal primal solution.

From the nature of the greedy algorithm, it is clear that

$$r(S_i) = i$$
$$= (Ax)_i$$
$$= r_i,$$

so it is permissible for $u_i > 0$, $i = 1, 2, \ldots, k$. If we set

$$u_k = w_k,$$

$$u_{k-1} = w_{k-1} - u_k,$$

$$\vdots$$

$$u_i = w_i - \sum_{l=i+1}^{k} u_l,$$

$$\vdots$$

$$u_1 = w_1 - \sum_{l=2}^{k} u_l,$$

we find that

$$(A^T u)_j = w_j \qquad (j = 1, 2, \ldots, k).$$

Furthermore,

$$A^T u \geq w,$$

because of the "greedy" nature of the algorithm.

This establishes that each vertex of the polyhedron corresponds to an independent set. Conversely, each independent set is a unique maximum weight set for some weighting of the elements, and therefore corresponds to a vertex of the polyhedron. //

Let M_1, M_2 be two matroids over the same set of elements E and let A and B be the closed set incidence matrices of M_1 and M_2, respectively. Let r and s be the rank vectors associated with these two matrices. We propose to solve the weighted intersection problem by solving the linear programming problem

maximize wx
subject to

$$Ax \leq r$$

$$Bx \leq s$$

$$x \geq 0.$$

If this linear programming problem has an integer optimal solution, then this is a valid approach. At this point it is by no means clear that the integrality property holds. However, the primal-dual weighted intersection algorithm will provide a constructive proof of the integrality property, just as the greedy algorithm provided a constructive proof of Theorem 11.1.

Theorem 11.2 (*Matroid Polyhedral Intersection Theorem—Edmonds*) For any two matroids M_1 and M_2, all vertices of the convex polyhedron defined by the system of linear inequalities

$$Ax \leq r$$

$$Bx \leq s$$

$$x \geq 0$$

have integer components. Moreover, the vertices and the intersections of the two matroids are in one-to-one correspondence.

An equivalent statement of the theorem is that *the intersection of two matroid polyhedra is a polyhedron whose vertices are vertices of each of the two intersected polyhedra*. Note, however, that the intersection polyhedron is not necessarily a matroid polyhedron, so the theorem, unhappily, does not extend to three or more polyhedra.

PROBLEMS

11.1   Determine the exact nature of the closed set incidence matrices and the closed set-rank inequalities for each of the following types of matroids. Which inequalities, if any, are redundant in each case?
(a) Partition matroid
(b) Transversal matroid
(c) Graphic matroid
(d) Cographic matroid

11.2   Suppose, in addition to the inequality constraints,

$$Ax \leq r$$

$$x \geq 0$$

we add the constraint

$$\sum x_j \geq r(E).$$

Show that the resulting system defines a polyhedron whose vertices correspond to the bases of the matroid.

12

Explanation of Primal-Dual Method

The primal-dual algorithm described below provides a constructive proof of the polyhedral intersection theorem of Edmonds. That is, it is shown that, regardless of what element weights $w = (w_1, w_2, \ldots, w_m)$ are chosen, the linear programming problem

maximize wx

subject to

$$Ax \leq r$$

$$Bx \leq s \tag{12.1}$$

$$x \geq 0$$

has an optimal solution in zeros and ones.

The primal problem is as indicated in (12.1). The dual problem is

minimize $ru + sv$

subject to

$$A^T u + B^T v \geq w \tag{12.2}$$

$$u, v \geq 0,$$

where each dual variable u_i is identified with a closed set of M_1 and v_k with a closed set of M_2.

Orthogonality conditions necessary and sufficient for optimality of a pair of feasible primal and dual solutions are

$$x_j > 0 \Rightarrow (A^T u + B^T v)_j = w_j \tag{12.3}$$

$$u_i > 0 \Rightarrow (Ax)_i = r_i \tag{12.4}$$

$$v_k > 0 \Rightarrow (Bx)_k = s_k. \tag{12.5}$$

The algorithm begins with the feasible primal solution $x_j = 0$, for $j = 1, 2, ..., m$ (i.e., $I = \varnothing$), and with the feasible dual solution in which each dual variable u_i or v_k is zero, except u_E, the dual variable identified with the closed set E. We set $u_E = \max \{w_j\}$. Thus, at the beginning of the computation the only orthogonality condition which is violated is

$$u_E > 0 \Rightarrow |I| = r_1(E). \tag{12.6}$$

The algorithm proceeds in stages. At each stage either the primal solution is revised by augmenting the existing intersection, or the values of the dual variables are revised. At all times, both primal and dual feasibility are maintained. Moreover, at each stage the only orthogonality condition which is not satisfied is (12.6). After a finite number of stages (in fact, a number bounded by a polynomial function in the number of elements in E), the condition (12.6) is also satisfied, and the primal and dual solutions existing at that point are optimal.

For a given pair of primal and dual solutions, a variant of the labeling routine of the cardinality intersection algorithm is applied, in an attempt to augment the primal solution. Clearly, the use of any augmenting sequence will result in a new feasible primal solution. However, the labeling routine must be modified in such a way that the only augmenting sequences which can be discovered are those for which all the orthogonality conditions except (12.6) continue to be satisfied.

If the application of the labeling routine, as restricted, does not result in the discovery of an augmenting sequence, then the dual solution is modified. The change in the dual solution must be such as to maintain dual feasibility, maintain satisfaction of all orthogonality conditions except (12.6), and also provide some progress toward the termination of the algorithm with optimal primal and dual solutions.

As a consequence of the fact that (12.6) is the only unsatisfied orthogonality conditions, *the intersection I existing at any intermediate stage of the computation is of maximum weight, relative to all intersections containing* $|I|$ *or fewer elements.* For suppose there were an additional constraint of the form

$$\sum_j x_j \le k,$$

and we were to incorporate this constraint with the objective function via a Lagrange multiplier λ. Then an intermediate solution is easily shown to be optimal for $\lambda = u_E$ and therefore for a value of k equal to $|I|$.

At each stage of the computation, no more than $2m$ dual variables are permitted to be nonzero. These nonzero variables, except u_E, are identical with spans of subsets of I in two different families $\mathscr{U}$ and $\mathscr{V}$. Notationally, we let

$$\mathscr{U} = \{U_0, U_1, ..., U_p\}$$

and

$$\mathscr{V} = \{V_0, V_1, \ldots, V_q\},$$

where

$$U_0 = \varnothing, \quad U_i \subset U_{i+1}, \quad U_p = I,$$

$$V_0 = \varnothing, \quad V_k \subset V_{k+1}, \quad V_q = I.$$

Associated with subsets U_i and V_k are dual variables u_i and v_k, where u_i is identified with the closed set $\text{sp}_1(U_i)$ and v_k with $\text{sp}_2(V_k)$.

Suppose the primal solution I is augmented by the application of an augmenting sequence $S = (e_1, e_2, \ldots, e_s)$. We propose to revise the families $\mathscr{U}$ and $\mathscr{V}$ as follows. For $j = 3, 5, \ldots, s$ replace e_{j-1} by e_j in each of the subsets U_i in which e_{j-1} is contained. For $j = 1, 3, \ldots, s - 2$, replace e_{j+1} by e_j in each of the subsets V_k in which e_{j+1} is contained. If $u_p = 0$, set $U_p = I \oplus S$. Otherwise, (if $u_p > 0$), set $p = p + 1$ and then set $U_p = I \oplus S$. Finally, if $v_q = 0$, set $V_q = I \oplus S$. And if $v_q > 0$, set $q = q + 1$ and set $V_q = I \oplus S$.

Of course, this revision of the families $\mathscr{U}$, $\mathscr{V}$ does not affect the dual solution, in the sense that the values of no dual variables u_i, v_k are affected. However, unless the augmenting sequence S is of a restricted type, a proper relation will not be maintained between the sets U_i, V_k and the dual variables u_i, v_k. Specifically, it is necessary that the spans $\text{sp}_1(U_i)$, $\text{sp}_2(V_k)$ be unaffected by the changes in membership of U_i and V_k. This objective is attained by a modification of the labeling procedure.

The labeling procedure is modified in two ways. First, no element is given a label, unless it belongs to the set

$$E^* = \{e_j \,|\, (A^T u + B^T v)_j = w_j\}.$$

This insures that any augmenting sequence discovered by the labeling procedure will maintain satisfaction of the orthogonality conditions (12.3).

Second, the rules for scanning are modified so as to maintain invariance of the spans of the sets in $\mathscr{U}$, $\mathscr{V}$ after augmentation. When a "$-$" label on $e_j \in I$ is scanned, find the smallest set U_i in which e_j is contained. Denote the index of this set by $u(j)$. Then apply the label "$j+$" to each unlabeled element $e_i \in E^*$ such that $e_j \in C_i^{(1)}$ and $C_i^{(1)} - e_i \subseteq U_{u(j)}$.

When a "$+$" label on $e_j \in E^* - I$ is scanned, determine if $I + e_j$ is independent in M_2. If so, an augmenting sequence has been found. Otherwise, find the smallest set V_k such that $C_j^{(2)} - e_j \subseteq V_k$. Then apply the label "$j-$" to each unlabeled element in $C_j^{(2)} - V_{k-1}$.

We assert that this system of labeling, in conjunction with the previously mentioned system of replacement of elements in $\mathscr{U}$, $\mathscr{V}$, does indeed maintain invariance of spans after augmentation.

Alternating sequences constructed by this modified labeling procedure are valid alternating sequences. For example, suppose we seek a maximum weight intersection of the graphic matroids M_1, M_2 of the multi-graphs G_1, G_2 shown in Figure 8.11, with element weights $w_1 = 3$, $w_2 = 5$, $w_3 = 6$, $w_4 = 10$, $w_5 = 8$. Assume that the computation has progressed to the point that $I = \{e_2, e_4\}$, with the following dual solution:

$$u_E = 2,$$

$$U_1 = \{e_4\}, \qquad u_1 = 4,$$

$$U_2 = \{e_2, e_4\}, \qquad u_2 = 2,$$

$$V_1 = \{e_4\}, \qquad v_1 = 1,$$

$$V_2 = \{e_2, e_4\}, \qquad V_2 = 1.$$

The reader can easily verify that the dual solution is feasible. In fact, $E^* = E = \{e_1, e_2, \ldots, e_5\}$. Moreover, it satisfies all orthogonality conditions except (12.6).

Now if the unmodified labeling procedure of the cardinality intersection algorithm is applied, the only augmenting sequence constructed is $S = (e_1, e_4, e_5)$, yielding the three-element intersection $I \oplus S = \{e_1, e_2, e_5\}$, with weight 16. However, when the modified labeling procedure is applied, the only augmenting sequence constructed is $S' = (e_1, e_2, e_3, e_4, e_5)$, which yields the three-element intersection $I \oplus S' = \{e_1, e_3, e_5\}$ with weight 17.

The reader should be able to verify that the existing dual solution fails to satisfy orthogonality condition (12.5) for $I \oplus S$. However, the dual solution does satisfy all orthogonality conditions, except (12.6), for $I \oplus S'$. Hence $I \oplus S'$ is a maximum weight intersection of three elements.

If the labeling procedure, as modified above, terminates without the discovery of an augmenting sequence, then the dual solution is revised. This is done as follows.

First, we create additional sets in the families $\mathcal{U}$, $\mathcal{V}$, in such a way that each set $U_i - U_{i-1}$ or $V_k - V_{k-1}$ will contain only labeled elements or only unlabeled elements. Let I be partitioned into subsets I_L, I_U of labeled elements and unlabeled elements. For each set U_i, such that $U_i - U_{i-1}$ contains both labeled and unlabeled elements, add one to the indices of the sets $U_i, U_{i+1}, \ldots, U_p$, and then create a new set

$$U_i = U_{i-1} \cup (U_{i+1} \cap I_U),$$

and set $u_i = 0$. (In the expression for the new set U_i, U_{i+1} is the old U_i, with incremental index.) For each set V_k, such that $V_k - V_{k-1}$ contains both labeled and unlabeled elements, add one to the indices of the sets $V_k, V_{k+1}, \ldots, V_q$, and then create a new set

$$V_k = V_{k-1} \cup (V_{k+1} \cap I_L),$$

and set $v_k = 0$.

Let δ be a positive number yet to be determined. The dual variables are changed as follows. Variable u_E is decreased by δ. If the elements of $U_p - U_{p-1}$ are unlabeled, u_p is increased by δ. If, for $i = 1, 2, ..., p - 1$, the elements of $U_i - U_{i-1}$ are labeled (unlabeled) and those of $U_{i+1} - U_i$ are unlabeled (labeled), then U_i is decreased (increased) by δ. If the elements of $V_q - V_{q-1}$ are labeled, v_q is increased by δ. If for $k = 1, 2, ..., q - 1$, the elements of $V_k - V_{k-1}$ are labeled (unlabeled) and those of $V_{k+1} - V_k$ are unlabeled (labeled), then V_k is increased (decreased) by δ. No other dual variables are changed in value.

The reader should convince himself that if the elements in $U_i - U_{i-1}$ are labeled, then the effect of the changes in the dual variables is to decrease $(A^T u)_i$ by δ, for each $e_j \in \text{sp}_1(U_i) - \text{sp}_1(U_{i-1})$. However, if the elements in $U_i - U_{i-1}$ are unlabeled, there is no change in $(A^T u)_i$. Similarly, if the elements in $V_k - V_{k-1}$ are labeled, the effect of the changes in the dual variables is to increase $(B^T v)_k$ by δ, for each $e_j \in \text{sp}_2(V_k) - \text{sp}_2(V_{k-1})$. And if the elements in $V_k - V_{k-1}$ are unlabeled, there is no change in $(B^T v)_j$.

Quite clearly, then, for each element $e_j \in I$ (for which $x_j = 1$) there is no change in $(A^T u + B^T v)_j$ caused by the revision of the dual solution. Hence conditions (12.3) continue to be satisfied.

The only dual variables u_i and v_k whose values are increased are those which are associated with sets U_i, V_k. For all such sets U_i and V_k, it is the case that $(Ax_i) = r_i$ and $(Bx)_k = s_k$. Hence conditions (12.4) and (12.5) continue to be satisfied by the revision of the dual solution.

We next need to show that there is a strictly positive value of δ, such that dual feasibility is maintained. First, we confirm that the only dual variables u_i, v_k which are decreased by δ are those which are associated with sets U_i, V_k existing before the creation of new sets in $\mathscr{U}$, $\mathscr{V}$. The dual variables identified with these sets had strictly positive values before the revision of the dual solution. Hence there exists a $\delta > 0$ such that the non-negativity of u, v is maintained.

Now let us consider inequalities of the form $(A^T u + B^T v) \geq w$. We have already disposed of the case that $e_j \in I$. Suppose $e_j \in E - \text{sp}_1(I)$. There is no set U_i such that $e_j \in \text{sp}_1(U_i)$, hence the only change in $(A^T u)_j$ is that occasioned by the change in u_E by $-\delta$. The element e_j is labeled if and only if $(A^T u + B^T v)_j = w_j$. If e_j is labeled, then there is some smallest set V_k such that $e_j \in \text{sp}_2(V_k)$, and all the elements in $V_k - V_{k-1}$ are labeled. (There must be such a set V_k, else $S = (e_j)$ would be an augmenting sequence.) In this case the net effect on $B^T v$ is $+\delta$, and the net change in $(A^T u + B^T v)_j$ is zero. If e_j is unlabeled, the net change in $(A^T u + B^T v)_j$ may be either zero or $-\delta$. (The reader should verify that the change is zero if and only if the labeling and scanning of e_j would not result in the labeling of any previously unlabeled elements.) In any case, if e_j is unlabeled then $(A^T u + B^T v)_j > w_j$, so there is some strictly positive value of δ which will not cause the dual inequality for e_j to be violated.

Now suppose $e_j \notin I$, but $e_j \in \mathrm{sp}_1(I)$, from which it follows that there is a smallest set U_i such that $e_j \in \mathrm{sp}_1(U_i)$. If e_j is labeled, the labeling resulted from the scanning of a labeled element $e_{j-1} \in I$ contained in U_i but not in U_{i-1}. Hence, the elements in $U_i - U_{i-1}$ are labeled and the net change in $(A^T u)_j$ is $-\delta$. There must be a smallest V_k such that $e_j \in \mathrm{sp}_2(V_k)$, else e_j would be the final element of an augmenting sequence. The elements in $V_k - V_{k-1}$ are labeled, hence the net change in $(B^T v)_j$ is $+\delta$ and that in $(A^T u + B^T v)_j$ is zero. This is appropriate since the fact that e_j is labeled implies $(A^T u + B^T v)_j = w_j$.

Finally, suppose $e_j \notin I$, $e_j \in \mathrm{sp}_1(I)$, and e_j is not labeled. Let U_i be the smallest set in $\mathcal{U}$ such that $e_j \in \mathrm{sp}_1(U_i)$. It is the case that either the elements in $U_i - U_{i-1}$ are unlabeled or the elements in $U_i - U_{i-1}$ are labeled and $(A^T u + B^T v)_j > w_j$. In the first case, $(A^T u)_j$ is unchanged, and in the second $(A^T u)_j$ is decreased by δ. Without analyzing the effects of the changes in the dual variables on $(B^T v)_j$, we observe that $(A^T u - B^T v)_j$ is decreased only if $(A^T u + B^T v)_j > w_j$.

We now conclude that there does exist a strictly positive value of δ which can be chosen, such that dual feasibility is maintained. Let I^- denote the indices of dual variables u_i, other than u_E, which are to be decreased by δ, K^- the indices of dual variables u_k which are to be decreased by δ, and J^- the indices of elements e_j for which $(A^T u + B^T v)_j$ is to be decreased by δ. Then we may choose

$$\delta = \min \{u_E, \delta_u, \delta_v, \delta_w\} > 0,$$

where

$$\delta_u = \min \{u_i \,|\, i \in I^-\},$$

$$\delta_v = \min \{v_k \,|\, k \in K^-\},$$

$$\delta_w = \min \{(A^T u + B^T v)_j - w_j \,|\, j \in J^-\}.$$

If $\delta = u_E$, then condition (12.6) is satisfied, the primal solution and the new dual solution are orthogonal and optimal, and the computation is completed. If $\delta < u_E$, but $\delta = \delta_u$ or δ_v, one or more of the dual variables u_i, v_k are reduced to zero and the corresponding sets U_i, V_k (except U_p, V_q) are removed from the families $\mathcal{U}$, $\mathcal{V}$ before the labeling procedure is resumed. This may enable additional elements to be labeled. If $\delta = \delta_w$. then at least one more element e_i enters E^* and is eligible for labeling.

If all the element weights e_j are integers, all arithmetic is integer, and each revision of the dual solution reduces u_E by an integer amount. This observation is sufficient to establish finite termination for the algorithm. However, a more sophisticated argument is given in the next section.

PROBLEM

12.1 Show that the spans of sets in $\mathcal{U}$, $\mathcal{V}$ remain unchanged by augmentation of the intersection.

13
Primal-Dual Weighted Intersection Algorithm

The labeling scheme described in the previous section can be interpreted in terms of the border graph $BG(I)$, as follows. The graph is constructed exactly as for the cardinality intersection problem, except that only nodes for elements in E^* are provided. In effect, two numbers $u(j)$, $v(j)$ are assigned to each node $e_j \in I$. These indicate the indices of the smallest sets U_i, V_k in which e_j is contained.

The labeling procedure amounts to a search for a source-sink path according to the following scheme. Each source node in $E^* - I$ is given the label "$\varnothing^+$." In effect, when the label on a node $e_i \in E^* - I$ is scanned, the maximum value of $v(j)$ is found, for all arcs (e_i, e_j), directed from e_i, and the label "$i-$" is applied to all unlabeled e_j with this maximum value. When the label on a node $e_i \in I$ is scanned, the label "$i+$" is applied to an unlabeled node e_j, provided $u(i)$ is maximum for all arcs directed into e_j.

We now specify the steps of the primal-dual algorithm in detail. In the statement of the algorithm we let $\bar{w}_j = (A^T u + B^T v)_j - w_j$.

PRIMAL-DUAL ALGORITHM FOR
WEIGHTED MATROID INTERSECTIONS

Step 0   (*Start*)   Set

$$I = \varnothing,$$

$$u_E = \max_j \{w_j\},$$

$$\mathcal{U} = \{U_0\} = \{\varnothing\},$$

$$\mathcal{V} = \{V_0\} = \{\varnothing\},$$

$$u_0 = v_0 = 0, \quad p = q = 0,$$

$$\bar{w}_j = u_E - w_j, \qquad j = 1, 2, \dots, m.$$

$$E^* = \{e_j | \bar{w}_j = 0\}.$$

No elements are labeled.

Step 1   (*Labeling*)

(1.0)   Compute $C_j^{(1)}$, $C_j^{(2)}$, for all $e_j \in E^* - I$. Give each element in $E^* -$ $\mathrm{sp}_1(I)$ the label "$\varnothing^+$."

(1.1)   If there are no unscanned labels, go to Step 3. Otherwise, find an element e_j with an unscanned label. If the label is a "$+$" label go to Step 1.2; if it is a "$-$" label go to Step 1.3.

(1.2)   Scan the "$+$" label on e_j as follows. If $I + e_j$ is independent in M_2, go to Step 2. Otherwise, find the smallest set V_k such that $C_j^{(2)} - e_j \subseteq V_k$ and give each unlabeled element in $C_j^{(2)} - V_{k-1}$ the label "$j-$." Return to Step 1.1.

(1.3)   Scan the "$-$" label on e_j as follows. Find the smallest set $U_{u(j)}$ in which e_j is contained. Apply the label "$j+$" to each unlabeled element $e_i \in E^*$ such that $e_j \in C_i^{(1)}$ and $C_i^{(1)} - e_i \subseteq U_{u(j)}$. Return to Step 1.1.

Step 2 (*Augmentation of Primal Solution*)   An augmenting sequence S has been discovered, of which e_j (found in Step 1.2) is the last element. The elements in S are identified by backtracing. Augment I by adding to I all elements in the sequence with "$+$" labels and removing from I all elements with "$-$" labels.

Suppose, without loss of generality, the augmenting sequence $S = (e_1, e_2, \ldots, e_s)$. Revise the families $\mathcal{U}, \mathcal{V}$ as follows. For $j = 3, 5, \ldots, s$ replace e_{j-1} by e_j in each of the subsets U_i in which e_{j-1} is contained. For $j = 1, 3, \ldots, s - 2$, replace e_{j+1} by e_j in each of the subsets V_k in which e_{j+1} is contained. If $u_p = 0$, set $U_p = I$. Otherwise (if $u_p > 0$), set $p = p + 1$ and then set $U_p = I$. If $v_q = 0$, set $V_q = I$. Otherwise, set $q = q + 1$ and set $V_q = I$.

Remove all labels from elements and return to Step 1.0.

Step 3   (*Revision of Dual Solution*)   Let I_L, I_U denote the subsets of labeled and unlabeled elements of I. for each set $U_i \in \mathcal{U}$ such that $U_i - U_{i-1}$ contains both labeled and unlabeled elements, add one to the indices of the sets $U_i, U_{i+1}, \ldots, U_p$, and then create a new set

$$U_i = U_{i-1} \cup (U_{i+1} \cap I_U),$$

and set $u_i = 0$. For each set V_k such that $V_k - V_{k-1}$ contains both labeled and unlabeled elements, add one to the indices of the set $V_k, V_{k+1}, \ldots, V_q$, and then create a new set

$$V_k = V_{k-1} \cup (V_{k+1} \cap I_L),$$

and set $v_k = 0$.

Form sets I^+, I^-, K^+, K^-, as follows:

$$I^+ = \{i | i = p, U_p - U_{p-1} \subseteq I_U, \text{ or } i < p, U_{i+1} - U_i \subseteq I_L, U_i - U_{i-1} \subseteq I_U\},$$

$$I^- = \{i | i < p, U_{i+1} - U_i \subseteq I_U, U_i - U_{i-1} \subseteq I_L\},$$

$$K^+ = \{k | k = q, V_q - V_{q-1} \subseteq I_L, \text{ or } k < q, V_{k+1} - V_k \subseteq I_U, V_k - V_{k-1} \subseteq I_L\},$$

$$K^- = \{k | k < q, V_{k+1} - V_k \subseteq I_L, V_k - V_{k-1} \subseteq I_U\}.$$

Form sets J^+, J^- as follows. For each element e_j, let $U_{u(j)}$, $V_{v(j)}$ denote the smallest sets, if any, in $\mathcal{U}$, $\mathcal{V}$ such that $e_j \in \mathrm{sp}_1(U_{u(j)})$, $e_j \in \mathrm{sp}_2(V_{v(j)})$. If these sets do not exist (because $e_j \in E - \mathrm{sp}_1(I)$, $e_j \in E - \mathrm{sp}_2(I)$, respectively), let $U_{u(j)} - U_{u(j)-1} = I_L$, $V_{v(j)} - V_{v(j)-1} = I_U$.

Set

$$J^+ = \{j \mid U_{u(j)} - U_{u(j)-1} \subseteq I_U, V_{v(j)} - V_{v(j)-1} \subseteq I_L\},$$

$$J^- = \{j \mid U_{u(j)} - U_{v(j)-1} \subseteq I_L, V_{v(j)} - V_{v(j)-1} \subseteq I_U\}.$$

Set

$$\delta = \min \{u_E, \delta_u, \delta_v, \delta_w\},$$

where

$$\delta_u = \min \{u_i \mid i \in I^-\},$$

$$\delta_v = \min \{v_k \mid k \in K^-\},$$

$$\delta_w = \min \{\overline{w}_j \mid j \in J^-\}.$$

Set

$$u_E = u_E - \delta$$

$$u_i = u_i + \delta, \text{ for } i \in I^+$$

$$u_i = u_i - \delta, \text{ for } i \in I^-$$

$$v_k = v_k + \delta, \text{ for } k \in K^+$$

$$v_k = v_k - \delta, \text{ for } k \in K^-$$

$$\overline{w}_j = \overline{w}_j + \delta, \text{ for } j \in J^+$$

$$\overline{w}_j = \overline{w}_j - \delta, \text{ for } j \in J^-.$$

If $u_E = 0$, stop; the primal and dual solutions are optimal. Otherwise, remove from $\mathcal{U}$, $\mathcal{V}$ all sets U_i, V_k, other than U_p, V_q for which $u_i = 0$, $v_k = 0$ and renumber the sets in $\mathcal{U}$, $\mathcal{V}$ accordingly. Set $E^* = \{e_j \mid \overline{w}_j = 0\}$. Remove all labels and return to Step 1.0. //

Let us now estimate the complexity of the algorithm. We make the same assumptions about R and $c(m)$ as in Section 4. For each augmentation, the computation of circuits $C_i^{(1)}$, $C_i^{(2)}$ requires $O(mRc(m))$ running time, as before.

There may be many revisions of the dual variables, each revision requiring $O(m)$ steps for the revision itself, plus a reapplication of the labeling procedure, which is $O(m^2)$. If all element weights w_i are integer, then the maximum number of revisions of the dual variables is $W = \max \{w_i\}$, where W is the initial value of u_E. There is also an application of the labeling procedure for each of the R possible augmentations. Thus, we conclude that the overall running time is no greater than $O(m^2(R + W) + mR^2c(m))$.

Even if the element weights are not integral, or even rational, a bound that is polynomial in m and $c(m)$ can be obtained. Each time a revision is made in the dual solution, at least one of the dual variables u_i, v_k or one of the $\bar{w}_j$ is reduced to zero. With this observation and a careful analysis of the algorithm, we can conclude that at most $O(R^2)$ revisions of the dual solution are possible between successive augmentations. This yields a bound of $O(m^2R^2 + mR^2c(m))$, the same as the bound for the primal algorithm.

PROBLEMS

13.1   Carry out a detailed analysis to show that at most $O(m^2)$ revisions of the dual solution are possible between augmentations.

13.2   Show that labels which have been applied prior to a revision of the dual solution remain valid after revision.

14
A Special Case: Directed Spanning Trees

Recall the formulation of the directed spanning tree problem from Section 2. An arc-weighted directed graph $G = (N, A)$ is given, and it is desired to find a maximum weight spanning tree directed from a specified root node with in-degree zero. Any subset of arcs I forming such a tree must be independent in the graphic matroid of G, and must also be independent in the partition matroid which has as its independent sets all subsets of arcs, no two of which are directed into the same node.

A particularly simple and elegant procedure has been devised for solving this special case of a weighted matroid intersection problem. The procedure is illustrated with reference to the network in Figure 8.13.

First apply the greedy algorithm to find a maximum weight solution with respect to the partition matroid only. That is, for each node choose the heaviest arc directed into that node. In the case of the graph in Figure 8.13, these arcs are indicated by wavy lines. If the arcs chosen in this way do not contain a cycle, then the problem is solved.

However, it is seen in the example that arcs e_5, e_7, and e_8 form a cycle passing through nodes 3, 4, and 5. (Note that any such cycle must be a directed cycle.) The next step is to contract the arcs of such a cycle, so that nodes 3, 4, and 5 are replaced by a single pseudonode. All self-loops created by this contraction are discarded. The weights of the arcs in the contracted

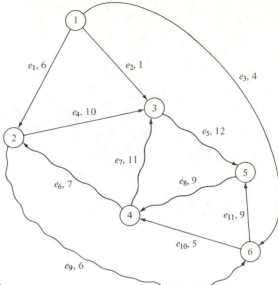

Figure 8.13   Example network

network are the same as in the original network, except for the weights of arcs directed into the pseudonode. These weights are modified as follows.

Suppose (i, j) is an arc of the original network, where j is contained in the cycle C, but i is not. Then arc (i, j) is represented in the contracted network by an arc (i, k) directed into the pseudonode k resulting from the contraction of C. In the contracted network set $w_{ik} = w_{ij} - (w_{i(j),j} - \delta)$, where $(i,(j), j)$ is the unique arc of C directed into node j and

$$\delta = \min_{p \in C} \{w_{i(p),p}\}.$$

In the example, the minimum of the arc weights in the cycle is 9. Hence in the contracted network the weight of arc e_2 becomes $1 - (11 - 9) = -1$, the weight of arc e_4 becomes $10 - (11 - 9) = 8$, the weight of arc e_{10} becomes $5 - (9 - 9) = 5$, and the weight of arc e_{11} becomes $9 - (12 - 9) = 6$. The complete contracted network is shown in the upper part of Figure 8.14.

The procedure is now repeated for the contracted network. That is, for each node (or pseudonode) the heaviest arc directed into that node is chosen. If this solution contains one or more cycles, these cycles are contracted and weights are modified. In the example, this results in the network shown in the lower part of Figure 8.14.

The process is repeated until finally a contracted network is obtained for which the arcs chosen do not contain a cycle. An optimal directed

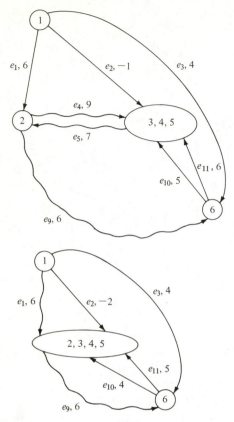

Figure 8.14   Contracted networks

spanning tree is then constructed by expanding the pseudonodes in the opposite order from that in which they were formed. The arcs chosen in the final network are entered into the solution. Thereafter, as each pseudonode is expanded, all but one of the arcs in the cycle identified with the pseudonode are entered into the solution. We discard the unique arc of the cycle whose entry into the solution would cause two arcs to be directed into the same node.

The expansion of the example network is illustrated in Figure 8.15. Arcs e_1 and e_9 are entered into the solution from the final contracted network in Figure 8.14. The pseudonode $(2, 3, 4, 5)$ is expanded to obtain pseudonodes (2) and $(3, 4, 5)$, Arc e_4 is entered into the solution and arc e_5 is discarded, because arc e_1 of the solution is directed into node 2. Pseudonode $(3, 4, 5)$ is expanded to obtain nodes $(3, 4)$ and (5) and arcs e_4 and e_8 are entered into the solution, and e_7 is discarded because arc e_7 is directed into node 3. Arcs e_1, e_4, e_5, e_8, and e_9 form an optimal directed spanning tree with a weight of 43.

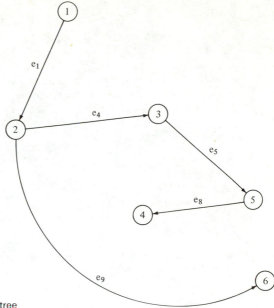

Figure 8.15   Optimal directed tree

The algorithm as we have described it yields a maximum weight spanning tree, which is not necessarily a maximum weight matroid intersection. That is, for a given network there may be a forest of directed trees which has greater total weight than any single spanning tree. If a maximum weight forest is desired, the procedure is modified to ignore any arcs whose weights become negative as a result of network contractions. This means that for a given pseudonode in one of the contracted networks, no arc directed into that pseudonode may be chosen for the solution because all such arcs have negative weights. When such a pseudonode is expanded, the lightest arc in the cycle identified with that pseudonode is discarded.

The reader should also be able to solve the problem in which there is no prescribed root node for the directed spanning tree. The first set of arcs chosen must necessarily contain a cycle, because there will be n such arcs and a tree can contain only $n - 1$. The network must be contracted until a pseudonode is created with in-degree zero in the solution.

The procedure is quite elegant and relatively easy to implement. However, a proof of its validity is another matter. A proof by Edmonds, based on linear programming duality, is rather tortuous. Even a "simple" proof due to Karp is fairly involved. The interested reader should refer to the original papers for these proofs.

PROBLEMS

14.1 Resolve the example problem in Figure 8.13, with arcs $e_1, \ldots, e_{11}$ given weights 1, 2, 3, 12, 20, 18, 2, 16, 1, 3, 2.

14.2 Solve the example problem by the primal matroid intersection algorithm.

14.3 Formulate the dual to the directed spanning tree problem. (Note that a maximum weight intersection is not necessarily a spanning tree; another constraint is necessary.) Find a dual solution for the example network.

14.4 The following simple procedure determines whether or not there exists a directed spanning tree from node 1:

> *Step 0*   Apply the label "$\emptyset$" to node 1.

> *Step 1*   If all nodes are labeled, halt; there exists a directed spanning tree. If all labels are scanned, but some nodes are unlabeled, halt; there is no directed spanning tree. Otherwise, find a node i with an unscanned label and go to Step 2.

> *Step 2*   Scan the label on node i as follows. For each arc (i, j) incident to node i, apply the label "i" to node j, unless node j already has a label. Return to Step 1.1.

> (a)   Estimate the complexity of this algorithm as a function of m and n, the number of arcs and nodes.
> (b)   Generalize this algorithm to solve the max-min directed spanning tree problem. Estimate the complexity of the algorithm.
> (c)   Generalize the algorithm still further to solve the max-min version of the "directed" Steiner network problem. Estimate the complexity of the algorithm.

COMMENTS AND REFERENCES

The bulk of the material in this chapter, including the cardinality intersection algorithm, the primal algorithm, and the primal-dual algorithm, are from

E. L. Lawler, "Optimal Matroid Intersection," *Combinatorial Structures and Their Applications, Proceedings of the Calgary International Conference*, R. Guy, editor, Gordon and Breach, New York, 1970, abstract only, p. 233.

E. L. Lawler, "Matroid Intersection Algorithms," *Mathematical Programming*, **9** (1975) 31–56.

SECTION 3

The lemmas in this section, and those in Section 9, are from

S. Krogdahl, "A Combinatorial Proof of Lawler's Matroid Intersection Algorithm," unpublished manuscript, 1975.

SECTION 4

An algorithm for the cardinality intersection problem can also be found in

M. Aigner and T. A. Dowling, "Matching Theory for Combinatorial Geometries," *Trans. American Math. Society,* **158** (1971) 231–245.

SECTION 5

The matroid intersection duality theorem is due to Edmonds. An alternate proof can be found in

D. J. A. Welsh, "On Matroid Theorems of Edmonds and Rado," *J. London Math. Soc.,* **45** (1970) 251–256.

SECTION 6

S. Kundu and E. L. Lawler, "A Matroid Generalization of a Theorem of Mendelsohn and Dulmage," *Discrete Mathematics,* **4** (1973) 159–163.

C. St. J. A. Nash-Williams, "An Application of Matroids to Graph Theory," in *Theory of Graphs,* P. Rosenstiehl, editor, Gordon and Breach, New York, 1967.

SECTION 7

Theorem 7.1 is from

J. Edmonds and D. R. Fulkerson, "Transversals and Matroid Partition," *J. Res. NBS,* **69B** (1965) 147–153.

The Philip Hall Theorem dates from

P. Hall, "On Representations of Subsets," *J. London Math. Soc.,* **10** (1935) 26–30.

Edmonds' partitioning algorithm is from

J. Edmonds, "Minimum Partition of a Matroid into Independent Subsets," *J. Res. NBS,* **69B** (1965) 67–72.

Earlier work on partitioning, for the special case of graphs, can be found in

W. T. Tutte, "On the Problem of Decomposing a Graph into *n* Connected Factors," *J. London Math Soc.,* **36** (1961) 221–230.

C. St. J. A. Nash-Williams, "Edge-Disjoint Spanning Trees of Finite Graphs," *J. London Math. Soc.,* **36** (1961) 445–450.

C. St. J. A. Nash-Williams, "Decomposition of Finite Graphs into Forests," *J. London Math. Soc.,* **39** (1964) 12.

Another type of partitioning problem, and an efficient algorithm, similar to Edmonds', has been developed by

G. Kishi and V. Kajitani, "On Maximally Distinct Trees," *Proc. Fifth Annual Allerton Conference on Circuit and System Theory,* University of Illinois, Urbana, 1967.

In this paper, the authors show that the edges of any graph can be decomposed into a certain three-block partition they call the "principal partition" of the graph. This yields a determination of the number of topological degrees of freedom of the graph, or equivalently, the "minimum hybrid rank" of the graph. The minimum hybrid rank is equal to the number of equations needed to solve an electrical network problem, and this number is less than or equal to the minimum of the rank and the nullity of the graph.

SECTION 8

C. E. Shannon, "Game Playing Machines," *J. Franklin Inst.,* **206** (1955) 447–453.

A. Lehman, "A Solution to the Shannon Switching Game," *SIAM J. Appl. Math.,* **12** (1964) 687–725.

J. Edmonds, "Lehman's Switching Game and a Theorem of Tutte and Nash-Williams," *J. Res. NBS,* **69B** (1965) 73–771.

L. J. White, "Minimum Partitions and the Shannon Switching Game," unpublished technical report, Systems Engineering Laboratory, The University of Michigan, July 1967.

J. Bruno, "Matroids, Graphs, and Resistance Networks," Ph.D. dissertation in Electrical Engineering, City College of the City University of New York, 1968.

J. Bruno and L. Weinberg, "A Constructural Graph-Theoretic Solution of the Shannon Switching Game," *Proc. Sixth Annual Allerton Conference on Circuit and System Theory,* Univ. of Illinois, Urbana, 1968.

Bruno and Weinberg provide a characterization of the switching game in terms of the principal partition of the graph, and apply Kishi and Kajitani's algorithm, cited previously, to the analysis of the game.

The game of Hex has been shown to be "polynomial space complete," which means that it is very difficult, indeed, to analyze. See

S. Even and R. E. Tarjan, "A Combinatorial Problem Which is Complete in Polynomial Space," *Proc. ACM Symposium on Theory of Computing,* May 1975.

SECTION 10

An algorithm for the weighted intersection problem has also been developed by

M. Iri and N. Tomigawa, "An Algorithm for Finding an Optimal 'Independent Assignment'," University of Tokyo, unpublished manuscript, 1975.

An algorithm for finding a maximum weight intersection of two transversal matroids is given in

B. J. Lageweg, "An Algorithm for a Maximum Weighted Common Partial Transversal," Report BW 25/73, Mathematisch Centrum, Amsterdam, 1973.

SECTION 11

The properties of matroid polyhedra and the matroid polyhedron intersection theorem were announced by Edmonds at least as long ago as 1964. See also

J. Edmonds, "Submodular Functions, Matroids and Certain Polyhedra," *Combinatorial Structures and Their Applications, Proceedings of the Calgary International Conference,* R. Guy, editor, Gordon and Breach, New York, 1970, pp. 69–87.

SECTION 14
The solution to the directed spanning tree problem is generally credited to Edmonds. See

J. Edmonds, "Optimum Branchings", *J. Res. NBS,* **71B** (1967) 233–240, and also *Mathematics and the Decision Sciences,* Part 1, G. B. Dantzig and A. F. Veinott, Jr., editors, *Amer. Math. Soc. Lectures Appl. Math.,* **11** (1968) 335–345.

However, it appears that priority should be given to

Chu Yoeng-jin and Liu Tseng-hong, "On the Shortest Arborescence of a Directed Graph," *Scientia Sinica* [Peking], **4** (1965) 1396–1400, *Math. Rev.* 33 # 1245 (D. W. Walkup).

Essentially the same algorithm was rediscovered by

Bock, F. C., "An Algorithm to Construct a Minimum Directed Spanning Tree in a Directed Network," *Developments in Operations Research,* B. Avi-Itzak, editor, Gordon and Breach, New York, 1971, pp. 29–44.

The proof of Chu and Liu is graphical, whereas those of Edmonds and of Bock rely on linear programming theory. A graphical proof has also been offered by Karp in

Karp, R. M., "A Simple Derivation of Edmonds' Algorithm for Optimum Branching," *Networks,* **1** (1971) 265–272.

See also

J. D. Murchland, "Historical Note on Optimum Spanning Arborescences," *Networks,* **3** (1973) 287–288.

R. E. Tarjan, "Finding Optimum Branchings," to appear in *Networks.*

R. E. Tarjan, "Arbitrary Subsets of Branchings, *Info. Proc. Letters,* **3** (1974).

NINE

The Matroid Parity Problem

1
Introduction

Let $M = (E, \mathscr{I})$ be a matroid whose elements are arranged in pairs. That is, every element $e \in E$ has a uniquely specified *mate* $\bar{e} \in E$. A *parity set* $A \subseteq E$ is a set such that, for each element e, $e \in A$ if and only if $\bar{e} \in A$. The object of the *matroid parity problem* is to find an optimal (maximum cardinality or maximum weight) independent parity set in M.

The matroid parity problem is a generalization of both the matroid intersection problem and the nonbipartite matching problem, as we show in the next section. Thus, matroid parity theory embraces virtually all of the problem types we have studied so far, as shown in Figure 9.1. We have included the "semimatching" problem in that figure because it appears to be a greatest common specialization of the other problem types.

It appears that matroid parity problems should be amenable to solution by augmentation methods employing the methodology of the matroid intersection algorithms and the nonbipartite matching algorithms.

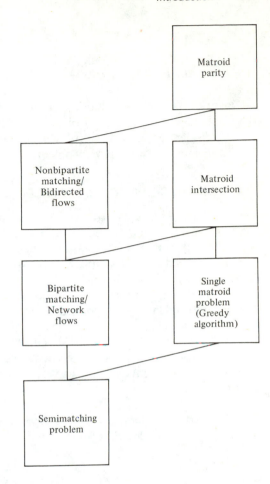

Figure 9.1   Relationships between problem types

However, there are a number of technical problems which must be overcome in the development of an algorithm with polynomial-bounded running
time. Although we conjecture that such an algorithm exists, we present
here only limited evidence.

    We conclude this chapter and book with a discussion of generaliza-
tions of the matroid parity problem. One such generalization is obtained
by arranging the elements of the matroid into triples, rather than pairs.
A polynomial-bounded solution procedure for this problem would imply
a solution to all of the hard problems listed in Chapter 1. But that is very
unlikely to occur, to say the least. Hence we conclude that the matroid
parity problem, as we have defined it, is probably about as far as we can
go with the type of theory presented in this book.

2

Problem Formulations

Let us first consider the reduction of the matroid intersection problem and the nonbipartite matching problem to the matroid parity problem. Then let us consider an equivalent problem we call the "matroid matching problem," and some representative problem formulations.

MATROID INTERSECTION PROBLEM

Let $M_1 = (E, \mathscr{I}_1)$ and $M_2 = (E, \mathscr{I}_2)$ be two matroids for which an optimal intersection is sought. Create a matroid $\overline{M}_2$, isomorphic to M_2, over a set $\overline{E}$ disjoint from E, with a natural one-one correspondence between elements e in E and $\bar{e}$ in $\overline{E}$. It is apparent that there is a one-one correspondence between intersections of M_1, M_2 and parity sets of $M_1 + \overline{M}_2 = (E \cup \overline{E}, \mathscr{I})$. (Cf. Theorem 6.3 of Chapter 7.) It follows that any algorithm for solving the parity problem can be applied to solve the intersection problem.

We can characterize those parity problems which can be reduced to intersection problems as follows. Let $M = (E, \mathscr{I})$ be a matroid with its elements arranged in pairs. M is said to be *separable* with respect to the pairing of the elements, if it is possible to partition E into two sets E_1 and E_2 such that:

(2.1)   For each element $e \in E$, $e \in E_1$ if and only if $\bar{e} \in E_2$.

(2.2)   For each circuit C of the matroid, either $C \subseteq E_1$ or $C \subseteq E_2$.

Clearly, if M is separable, then $M = M_1 + M_2$, where $M_1 = M$ del $E_2 = M$ ctr E_2 and $M_2 = M$ del $E_1 = M$ ctr E_1. It is clear that under these conditions the parity problem reduces to an intersection problem for M_1, M_2, after the elements of one of these two matroids are renamed to correspond to elements of the other.

NONBIPARTITE MATCHING PROBLEM

Let $G = (N, A)$ be a graph in which an optimal matching is desired. Subdivide the graph to obtain a graph $G^* = (N^*, A^*)$, in which each arc of G is replaced by a pair of arcs e and $\bar{e}$. Let $M = (A^*, \mathscr{I})$ be a partition matroid induced by incidences of arcs in G^* on the (original) set of nodes $N \subseteq N^*$. It is clear that there is a one-one correspondence between independent parity sets of M and matchings in G. Thus, an algorithm for solving the parity problem can be applied to solve the matching problem.

A matroid parity problem reduces to a matching problem if and only if the matroid is a partition matroid. If the partition matroid is separable, then the matching problems is bipartite.

MATROID MATCHING PROBLEM

We define the *matroid matching problem* as follows. Let $G = (N, A)$ be a graph and $M = (N, \mathscr{I})$ be a matroid over the nodes of the graph. For any matching $X \subseteq A$ in G, let $I(X) \subseteq N$ denote the set of nodes covered by the matching. The object of the problem is to find an optimal (maximum cardinality or maximum weight) matching X, subject to the condition that $I(X)$ is independent in M.

Clearly, if M is the trivial matroid of rank $m = |E|$, (M has no circuits) then the matroid matching problem is nothing more than an ordinary graphic matching problem.

The matroid matching problem reduces to the matroid parity problem with the following construction. If G is a graph in which each node has degree one, then the matroid matching problem is already equivalent to a matroid parity problem. Otherwise, replace the graph G by a graph G^* in which each node of degree d is replaced by d copies of the node, with exactly one arc incident to each of these new nodes. Replace the matroid M by a matroid M^*, in which each element of M is represented by d "parallel" copies in M^*. Then the matroid matching problem for G, M, becomes a parity problem for M^*.

CREW SELECTION PROBLEM

A spaceship is being made ready for a long voyage and the process of crew selection is underway. Each space voyager must be assigned a job for which he or she is qualified and every job aboard ship must be filled.

Ordinarily we could choose a crew from among the set of applicants by simply solving an assignment problem. But there is a complication. Some of the applicants are married and it is agreed that a husband will be chosen if and only if his wife is chosen as well. Also, since it is to be a long voyage, each unmarried crew member should be provided with a suitable conjugal partner in the crew.

The solution is to construct a graph $G = (N, A)$ whose nodes are applicants and whose arcs extend between feasible conjugal partners. (This graph can be arbitrary, and not even bipartite.) We seek an optimal matching in G, subject to the constraint that the matched applicants can be assigned jobs aboard ship. In other words, the set of nodes covered by the matching must be independent in the transversal matroid induced by the relation between applicants and jobs for which they are qualified.

GENERALIZATION OF SEQUENCING PROBLEM

Recall the statement of the sequencing problem given in Chapter 7, Section 2. Let all of the specifications of the problem be the same, except that jobs have processing times of one hour or two hours. A two-hour job can be interrupted and processed in two nonconsecutive one-hour periods.

The reader should be able to reformulate this generalized form of the sequencing problem as one calling for a maximum weight independent parity set in a transversal matroid. (Note that one-hour jobs should be paired with dummy jobs to obtain a proper problem formulation.)

RADIALLY SYMMETRIC SPANNING TREE

Suppose the $2n + 1$ nodes of a graph G are arranged in radially symmetric pairs, i, $\bar{i}$, around a central node 0. We seek to find a maximum weight spanning tree in this graph, subject to the constraint that an arc is chosen if and only if the arc between the symmetric pair of nodes is chosen.

This problem is quite clearly a matroid parity problem for the graphic matroid of G. A typical radially symmetric tree that results from a solution to such a problem is indicated by wavy lines in Figure 9.2.

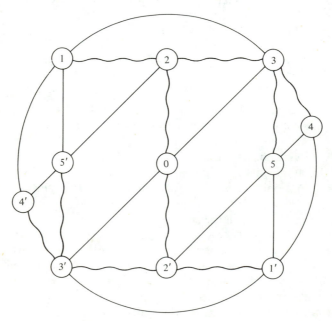

Figure 9.2   Radially symmetric spanning tree

GENERALIZATION OF NETWORK SYNTHESIS PROBLEM

Recall the statement of the network synthesis problem given in Chapter 8, Section 2. This problem called for an optimal intersection of two cographic matroids. One of these matroids was induced by the graph of cities to be connected during odd time periods and the other during even time periods.

Now suppose the reduced two-period rental can be obtained by renting a video link for any two time periods, consecutive or not. The reader should easily be able to reformulate the problem to one calling for a maximum weight independent parity set in a single cographic matroid.

MINIMAL CONNECTED HYPERGRAPH

A *hypergraph* $H = (N, A)$ is like an ordinary graph, except that its arcs may be incident to arbitrary subsets of nodes, instead of to exactly two nodes. Many of the conventional definitions of graph theory carry over to hypergraphs. For example, a *path* from i to j is a sequence of arcs $a_k \in A$, $k = 1, 2, ..., p$, such that $i \in a_1$, $j \in a_p$ and $a_k \cap a_{k+1} \neq \emptyset$, for $k = 1, 2, ...,$ $p - 1$. A hypergraph is said to be *connected* if there is a path between each pair of nodes.

Let H be a given arc-weighted connected hypergraph in which each arc is incident to exactly three nodes. Suppose we wish to find a minimum weight subhypergraph of H which connects all the nodes of H.

Let us form a (multi)graph G from H in which each arc $a = (i, j, k)$ of H is represented by a mated pair of arcs $e = (i, j)$, $\bar{e} = (j, k)$. (Or $e =$

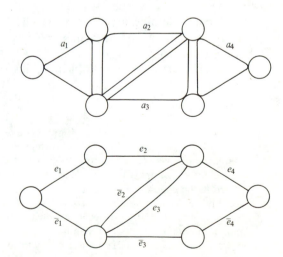

Figure 9.3   Example of hypergraph problem. (a) Hypergraph H. (b) Graph G

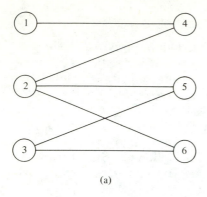

(a)

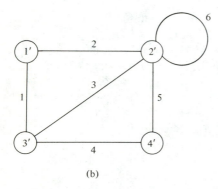

(b)   Figure 9.4

(i, k), $\bar{e} = (k, j)$ or $e = (i, j)$, $\bar{e} = (i, k)$; we are indifferent as to which pair is chosen.) Let arcs e, $\bar{e}$ be assigned weights so that $w(e) + w(\bar{e}) = w(a)$. The problem of finding a minimum weight connecting subhypergraph is equivalent to that of finding a maximum weight independent parity set in the cographic matroid of G.

An example of such a problem is illustrated in Figure 9.3.

PROBLEMS

2.1 Let $G = (N, A)$ be as shown in Figure 9.4a and $M = (N, \mathcal{I})$ be the graphic matroid of the graph $G' = (N', N)$ shown in Figure 9.4b. Show that the matroid matching problem for G, M reduces to a matroid intersection problem. (*Note*: G is clearly nonbipartite. Is there a node that can be deleted from G without affecting the problem?)

2.2 Recall the "semimatching" problem formulated in Chapter 7, Section 2. Suppose it is desired to solve the problem subject to the additional constraint that elements are chosen in symmetric pairs, i.e., w_{ij} is chosen if and only if w_{ji} is chosen as well. Formulate as a matroid matching problem. (Be sure to provide for diagonal elements w_{ii}.) Is there any straightforward way to solve this problem?

2.3   Let $M = (E, \mathscr{I})$ be a matroid and π be a partition on E. Suppose we wish to find an optimal independent set I of M, subject to the constraint that I contains an *even* number of elements from each block of π. Reduce this problem to a matroid parity problem.

3

Augmenting Sequences

The notion of augmenting sequences seems to generalize to matroid parity problems in a straightforward way. The only real difference would seem to be that mated element pairs, e_i, $\bar{e}_i$ replace single elements in the definition for matroid intersections.

Let $M = (E, \mathscr{I})$ be a matroid with paired elements, and let I be an independent parity set. Let $S = (e_1, \bar{e}_1, e_2, \bar{e}_2, \ldots, e_s, \bar{e}_s)$ be a sequence of distinct elements, where $e_i, \bar{e}_i \in E - I$ for i odd, and $e_i, \bar{e}_i \in I$ for i even. Let $S_i = (e_1, \bar{e}_1, e_2, \bar{e}_2, \ldots, e_{i-1}, \bar{e}_{i-1}, e_i)$, for $i \leq s$. S is said to be an *alternating sequence* with respect to I if

(3.1) $I + e_1 \in \mathscr{I}$.

(3.2)   For all $i \leq s$, $\mathrm{sp}(I \oplus S_i) = \mathrm{sp}(I + e_1)$. Note that $|I \oplus S_i| = |I| + 1$, and hence $I \oplus S_i \in \mathscr{I}$ for all $i \leq s$. It follows that for odd $i < s$, $I \oplus (S_i + \bar{e}_i) \notin \mathscr{I}$.

If, in addition to (3.1) and (3.2), it is the case that

(3.3) s is odd and $I \oplus S \in \mathscr{I}$, S is said to an *augmenting sequence* with respect to I. In this case, $|I \oplus S| = |I| + 2$ and $\mathrm{sp}(I \oplus S) \supset \mathrm{sp}(I)$.

Unfortunately, however, this definition is defective. If I is an independent parity set with less than a maximum number of elements, then it is *not true* that an augmenting sequence must exist, as can be shown by counterexample.

Virtually the only result we are able to state is the following theorem.

Theorem 3.1   Let I be any independent parity set. Then there exists an independent parity set I^* of maximum cardinality such that $I \subseteq \mathrm{sp}(I^*)$.

PROOF   Let J be a maximum cardinality independent parity set such that $|J| > |I|$. If $I \subseteq \mathrm{sp}(J)$, there is nothing to prove. Otherwise, choose any element $e \in I - \mathrm{sp}(J)$. It must be the case that $\bar{e} \in \mathrm{sp}(J)$, else J would not be of maximum cardinality. Find any element $f \in C - I$ where C is the unique circuit in $J + \bar{e}$. (There must be such an element f, else I would be dependent.) Then $J' = (J - \{f, \bar{f}\}) \cup \{e, \bar{e}\}$ is also a maximum cardinality parity set, and $|I - J'| < |I - J|$. Iterate until a set J' is found, with $I \subseteq sp(J')$ and let $I^* = J'. //$

4

Generalizations

The matroid parity problem generalizes all of the polynomial-bounded problems studied in this book, and it is conjectured to be polynomial bounded as well. What further generalizations might also be polynomial bounded?

The fondest wish of workers in the area of combinatorial optimization is to find a polynomial-bounded algorithm for one, and therefore, all of the problems on the "hard" list given in Chapter 1. A suitably efficient algorithm for the three-dimensional assignment problem would do the job. Yet we can show, by the constructions given below, that a polynomial-bounded algorithm for the three-dimensional assignment problem would imply a similar algorithm for the n-dimensional assignment problem, for arbitrarily large n. This reinforces our opinion that such an algorithm will not be forthcoming (and perhaps also suggests something about the mystical power of "twoness").

The three-dimensional assignment problem is equivalent to a problem involving the intersection of three partition matroids. The three-matroid intersection problem is a special case of a matroid parity problem in which each element e has not one but two mates $\bar{e}$ and $\bar{\bar{e}}$. That is, an independent set is to be found, subject to the constraint that e is a member if and only if $\bar{e}$ and $\bar{\bar{e}}$ are members.

Let us refer to a matroid parity problem in which each element may have as many as $k - 1$ mates as a k-parity problem. We shall now indicate the reduction of the problem of finding a maximum cardinality k-parity set to the problem of finding a maximum cardinality three-parity set in a different matroid.

First consider the reduction of the four-parity problem to the three-parity problem. Let the given matroid be $M = (E, \mathscr{I})$, with $|E| = 4m$, and suppose e_1, e_2, e_3, e_4 are mates. Define a partition matroid M' over the set of elements $A = \{a_1, \ldots, a_5\}$, disjoint from E, where no more than three of the elements $a_1, \ldots, a_5$ are in an independent set. Replace M by $M + M'$ and reassign mates so that a_1, e_1, e_2 are mates, a_2, e_3, e_4 are mates and a_3, a_4, a_5 are mates. By similar transformations, replace all sets of four mates with sets of three mates.

Now notice that a maximum cardinality independent parity set I in the new matroid with $9m$ elements cannot contain all three of the parity sets $A_1 = \{a_1, e_1, e_2\}$, $A_2 = \{a_2, e_3, e_4\}$, and $A_3 = \{a_3, a_4, a_5\}$. If I contains both A_1 and A_2 it does not contain A_3. If I contains A_3, it does not contain either A_1 or A_2. If I contains A_1 but not A_2 or A_3, then $I' = (I \cup A_3) - A_1$, with $|I'| = |I|$, is also an independent parity set. Similarly, if I contains A_2 but not A_1 or A_3. We conclude that a solution to the three-parity problem for the new matroid yields a solution to the original four-parity problem.

Now consider the reduction of the $2k$-parity problem to the $(k + 1)$-parity problem. Suppose $e_1, e_2, \ldots, e_{2k}$ are mates. Define a partition matroid over the set of elements $A = \{a_1, a_2, \ldots, a_{k+3}\}$, where no more than $k + 1$ of the elements $a_1, \ldots, a_{k+3}$ are in an independent set. An analysis similar to that given above with respect to the parity sets

$$A_1 = \{a_1, e_1, \ldots, e_k\},$$
$$A_2 = \{a_2, e_{k+1}, \ldots, e_{2k}\},$$
$$A_3 = \{a_3, a_4, \ldots, a_{k+3}\}$$

shows that a solution to the $(k + 1)$-parity problem for the new matroid yields a solution to the original $2k$-parity problem.

Repeated application of the above procedure yields a reduction of the k-parity problem to the three-parity problem. Moreover, if the given k-parity problem is one for a matroid with km elements (m parity sets of k elements each), the three-parity problem will be one for approximately $k^{1.6}m$ elements. We have thus proved the following theorem.

Theorem 4.1 A maximum cardinality k-parity problem on km elements reduces to a maximum cardinality three-parity problem on approximately $k^{1.6}m$ elements.

Notice that the construction is such that if one begins with a partition matroid for the k-parity problem, one obtains a partition matroid for the three-parity problem. Hence the previous comment about the reduction of the n-dimensional assignment problem to the three-dimensional assignment problem.

The construction we have given does not lend itself well to the weighted case. But for this case there is a much simpler and more efficient construction.

Suppose we seek a maximum weighted independent parity set for the matroid $M = (E, \mathscr{I})$, where $e_1, e_2, \ldots, e_k$ are mates. Let M' be a rank k matroid over the set $A = \{a_1, a_2, \ldots, a_k\}$, disjoint from E, for which all subsets of A are independent. Let $M_1 = M + M' = (E \cup A, \mathscr{I}_1)$. Let

$M_2 = (E \cup A, \mathscr{I}_2)$ be a partition matroid, where $I_2 \in \mathscr{I}_2$ if and only if not both e_i, a_i belong to I_2, for $i = 1, 2, \ldots, k$. Let $M_3 = (E \cup A, \mathscr{I}_3)$ be a partition matroid, where $I_3 \in \mathscr{I}_3$ if and only if not both e_i and a_{i+1}, $i = 1, 2, \ldots,$ $k - 1$, or e_k and a_1, belong to I_3. By similar transformations deal with all other sets of k mates, and thus obtain three matroids over a set of $2m$ elements, $e_1, e_2, \ldots, e_m, a_1, a_2, \ldots, a_m$.

As a consequence of this construction, a maximum cardinality intersection of M_1, M_2, and M_3 contains exactly m elements. Moreover, there is a one-one correspondence between these m-element intersections and independent parity sets in the original matroid M.

If the weight of e_i in the original parity problem was $w(e_i)$, let its weight in the three-matroid intersection problem be $w(e_i) + K$. Let the weight of each of the elements a_i be K. If K is suitably large, a maximum weight intersection in the intersection problem is necessarily a maximum cardinality intersection. We thus have the following theorem.

Theorem 4.2   A weighted k-parity problem on m elements reduces to a weighted three-matroid intersection problem on $2m$ elements, where two of the matroids are partition matroids.

It follows immediately from the theorem, and the construction in Section 2, that a weighted k-parity problem on m elements reduces to a weighted three-parity problem on $6m$ elements.

We have shown that k-parity problems and k-matroid intersection problems are equally difficult for all k, with respect to the criterion of polynomial boundedness. We can reasonably conjecture that these problems are nonpolynomial and we know that they are no worse than exponential. (There are only 2^m possible solutions for an m element problem and these can be inspected exhaustively.) It appears that methods of partial enumeration may be the best approach to these problems.

PROBLEM

4.1   The statement is made that the construction for Theorem 4.1 produces a three-parity problem with $k^{1.6}m$ elements. Justify.

COMMENTS AND REFERENCES

E. L. Lawler, "Polynomial Bounded and (Apparently) Non-Polynomial Bounded Matroid Computations," in *Combinatorial Algorithms,* R. Rustin, editor, Algorithmics Press, New York, 1972.

E. L. Lawler, "Matroids with Parity Conditions: A New Class of Combinatorial Optimization Problems," Memorandum No. ERL-M334, Electronics Research Laboratory, University of California, Berkeley, November 1971.

In the above papers the author asserted the existence of a polynomial-bounded algorithm for the parity problem. Unfortunately, this assertion was premature, at best.

A method of partial enumeration for the k-parity problem has been proposed by

P. M. Camerini and F. Maffioli, "Heuristically Guided Algorithm for K-Parity Matroid Problems," Politecnico di Milano, Italy, to be published.

P. M. Camerini and F. Maffioli, "Bounds for 3-Matroid Intersection Problems," *Information Processing Letters*, **3** (1975) 81–83.

Author Index

Page numbers in *italic* refer to references at the end of chapters.

Subject Index